# Chain
# Reaction

ALSO BY THOMAS BYRNE EDSALL

*The New Politics of Inequality*
*Power and Money: Writing About Politics, 1971–1987*

# Chain Reaction

## The Impact of
## Race, Rights, and Taxes
## on American Politics

THOMAS BYRNE EDSALL

with MARY D. EDSALL

W·W·NORTON & COMPANY

New York    London

Printed in the United States of America.

The text of this book is composed in Janson Alternate,
with the display set in Baker Danmark.
Composition and manufacturing by the Haddon Craftsmen, Inc.
Book design by Jack Meserole.

Library of Congress Cataloging-in-Publication Data
Edsall, Thomas Byrne.
Chain reaction / Thomas Byrne Edsall with Mary D. Edsall.
p. cm.
Includes index.
1. Presidents—United States—Election—History—20th century.
2. Republican Party (U.S.: 1854–    )—History—20th century.
3. Electioneering—United States—History—20th century. 4. United
States—Race relations—History—20th century. 5. Taxation—United
States—History—20th century. I. Title.
JK524.E28 1991
324.973′092—dc20                    90–27632

ISBN 0-393-02983-2

W.W. Norton & Company, Inc., 500 Fifth Avenue, New York, N.Y. 10110
W.W. Norton & Company, Ltd., 10 Coptic Street, London WC1A 1PU

1 2 3 4 5 6 7 8 9 0

*To Our Daughter, Alexandra*

# Contents

# Preface and Acknowledgments

The disintegration of the liberal coalition is a subject I have explored since first coming to Washington in 1974. This project represents a substantial change, however, in method and conclusion. In the past, I have focused on those forces and trends that have functioned to weaken liberal politics at an elite level: campaign finance; the manipulation of television by specialized consultants; the emergence of a technology-driven politics; the funding by corporate interests of conservative foundations, journals, and university research; and the emerging schism between the national media and the working and lower-middle class.

The shortcomings of this approach became apparent to me throughout the 1980s. A series of opportunities presented themselves to proponents of a liberal state wishing to challenge conservatism—opportunities such as the recession of 1981–82, the Iran-Contra scandal, and the increasing regressivity of income distribution—but each development failed to revive the political coalition of those falling in the bottom half of the income distribution. Clearly, obstacles to the revival of an effective liberalism had emerged, obstacles greater than those constructed by the manipulative tactics and strategies of elites.

Most important in expanding my own views was the experience of reporting on national politics for the *Washington Post:* covering voter registration drives across the country in 1984; the 1986 gubernatorial race in Tennessee; mayoral elections in Chicago in 1987 and 1989 and in Philadelphia in 1987; affirmative action litigation by firefighters in Birmingham, Alabama, in 1989; and extensive traveling during the 1988 presidential election. These assignments illuminated for me political realities invisible at the elite level. At various times in the 1980s in pursuit of these assignments,

I followed the advice of my colleague David Broder and spent a substantial amount of time walking through neighborhoods, going door to door. I did this in areas where support for Democratic candidates, especially at the presidential level, but often at the local level as well, had dropped precipitously: the working-class suburbs of Detroit, especially Dearborn and Macomb county; southwest and northwest Chicago, and the adjoining suburbs; Parma and Lorraine, Ohio; Peoria, Illinois; East Birmingham and adjoining Bessemer and Hueytown; Jefferson Parrish, Louisiana; and Charleston, South Carolina.

The views of many of the people I met on these walks were not easily digestible, all too often marked by direct expressions of racism towards blacks and intolerance toward a host of other individuals and groups. At the same time, I came to understand that the decline of liberalism was not simply the result of well-financed conservative elites dominating the political process. A set of genuine barriers had grown up over the years between key members of the liberal coalition. The post–1965 liberal agenda had engendered fundamental conflicts over values, rights, and taxes, and race was driving the process in many complex ways. Conservatism, in turn, has capitalized on these conflicts with growing sophistication.

Elites on both sides fanned the flames, but the source of the heat was deeply imbedded in the American electorate. This book focuses on the political—not the moral—consequences of the conflation of race with a host of other issues for key segments of the electorate, especially the swing white voters whose ballots have been critical to the outcome of presidential elections over the past generation; it is an attempt to understand the interaction of real conflict and tension at the grassroots level with elites determined to use those forces to their advantage.

The book covers the two and a half decades in American politics following the passage of the Civil Rights Act and the Voting Rights Act: 1964 to 1990. The first chapter is a synopsis of the argument developed throughout the book. Subsequent chapters pursue the influence on presidential politics of race, rights, values, and taxes. Although the chapters are generally in chronological order, the book is neither a history of the civil rights movement nor a description of the evolution of black political power; instead, it is an attempt to explore race-laden and race-driven conflicts that now structure much of the nation's politics.

---

There are a host of people to whom I am deeply indebted. These include my editors and colleagues at work; fellow reporters on the campaign trail; the network of consultants and pollsters; numerous academics, congressional staffers, elected officials, political operatives—a long list of people, some of whom have become friends. I would like to thank by name those who were particularly helpful in the development of this book.

First on this list is my uncle, John Edsall, who at the age of 88 read the manuscript with a critical and generous eye, and whose comments were consistently on target. My father-in-law, Karl W. Deutsch, has set a standard for the development of a larger perspective that I have tried to emulate over the twenty-seven years I have known him.

I would also like to thank Bob Kaiser at the *Washington Post* who made possible not only an initially generous leave of absence, but who extended that leave many times. I would in addition like to extend special thanks to Lee Atwater, Harrison Hickman, Sidney Blumenthal, Haynes Johnson, Fred Siegel, Juan Williams, Paul Hancock, Jim Wetzler, Gary Orfield, and Peter Silberman.

During the writing of this book, those to whom I owe a substantial debt fall into three general groups, 1) journalists and writers, 2) politicians, public officials, and political operatives, and 3) academics.

The journalists and writers include Dan Balz, Jack Bass, Jack Beatty, Pete Behr, Ken Bode, Dave Broder, Lou Cannon, E. J. Dionne, Bob Dowling, Kathleen Francovic, Curtis Gans, Todd Gitlin, John Judis, Bob Kuttner, Lars Erik Nelson, Steve Pearlstein, Bill Peterson, Maralee Schwartz, Steve Stark, Frank Swoboda, Paul Taylor, Stuart Taylor, and Ed Walsh.

The politicians, public officials, and political operatives include Howard Berman, Jackie Blumenthal, John Buckley, Kent Cooper, Tom Donilon, Stanley Greenberg, Marcia Hale, Jim Jaffe, Jim Jordan, David Lyles, Bob McIntyre, John Morgan, Abner Mikva, Frank Parker, Wendell Primus, Ed Rollins, Jim Shannon, Frederick Steeper, Robert Teeter, and Richard Viguerie.

The academics include Earl Black, Merle Black, Alfred Blumstein, John Bound, David Brady, Alan Brinkley, Ted Carmines, Jacqueline Cohen, Natalie Davis, Nick Edsall, Randall Kennedy, Steve Erie, Richard Freeman, Gary Gerstle, Christopher Jencks, Martin Kilson, Mark Kleiman, Donald Kinder, Frank Levy, Allen Matusow, Arthur Miller, Kevin Murphy, John Petrocik, Gerald Pomper, Peter Reuter, Derek Shearer, Paul Sniderman, James Stimson, Martin Wattenberg, Alexandra Wigdor, and Roger Wilkins.

My wife Mary was central to the writing of this book, from the formulation of the general approach, to the gathering and sorting of detailed information, to the enlargement of the scope of the project to include such subjects as values and rights. Her ideas, her analysis, her research, her editing, and her careful watchfulness over the coherence of the entire project made this book possible, and her own creativity is present in every chapter. Over six years, she took over whatever needed to be done, assuming responsibilities that made it possible for my own imagination to roam. Since serving in VISTA together in 1966 and 1967, we have been intimate observers of the political process. This book, then, is a testament to the generativity of our relationship.

THOMAS B. EDSALL

# Chain
# Reaction

# 1

# Building a Top-Down Coalition

THE RISE of the presidential wing of the Republican party over the past generation has been driven by the overlapping issues of race and taxes. The Republican party has been able to capitalize on these two issues, capturing the White House in five of the last six elections, and shaping a new polarization of the electorate—a polarization which has replaced the traditional New Deal cleavages that sustained the Democratic party from 1932 to 1964.

The overlapping issues of race and taxes have permitted the Republican party to adapt the principles of conservatism to break the underlying class basis of the Roosevelt-Democratic coalition and to build a reconfigured voting majority in presidential elections. Together, the twin issues of race and taxes have created a new, ideologically coherent coalition by pitting taxpayers against tax recipients, by pitting the advocates of meritocracy against proponents of special preference, by pitting the private sector against the public sector, by pitting those in the labor force against the jobless, and by pitting those who bear many of the costs of federal intervention against those whose struggle for equality has been advanced by interventionist government policies.

In a steady evolutionary process, race and taxes have come to intersect with an entire range of domestic issues, from welfare policy to civil-service testing, from drug enforcement to housing regulation, from minority set-aside programs to the decline in urban manufacturing jobs, from prison construction to the globalization of economic competition, from college admissions standards to suburban zoning practices, from highway con-

3

struction to Federal Communications Commission licensing procedures. In the struggle for government and private-sector resources, race has become a powerful wedge, breaking up what had been the majoritarian economic interests of the poor, working, and lower-middle classes in the traditional liberal coalition. Taxes, in turn, have been used to drive home the cost to whites of federal programs that redistribute social and economic benefits to blacks and to other minorities.

Race and taxes, on their own, have changed the votes of millions of once-Democratic men and women. But it was the collision of race and taxes with two additional forces over the past twenty-five years that created a *chain reaction*, a reaction forcing a realignment of the presidential electorate. These two additional forces were, first, the rights revolution, a revolution demanding statutory and constitutional protections for, among others, criminal defendants, women, the poor, non-European ethnic minorities, students, homosexuals, prisoners, the handicapped, and the mentally ill; and, second, the rights-related reform movement focusing on the right to guaranteed political representation that took root within the Democratic party in the late 1960s and throughout the 1970s.

This chain reaction—a point of political combustion reached as a linked series of highly charged issues collide—acted most powerfully on two key swing voter groups, the white, European ethnic, often Catholic, voters in the North, and lower-income southern white populists. For as long as these voters cast Democratic ballots, the liberal coalition thrived; when they did not, the liberal coalition collapsed. Throughout the 1970s and 1980s, these two key groups of voters, once the mainstay of the New Deal alliance, determined the viability of the conservative presidential majority. The collapse of the political left and the ascendance of a hybrid conservative populism dominated by the affluent have had enormous policy consequences. The holders of power under the new conservative regime encouraged and endorsed, through tax, debt, and budgetary policy, a substantial redistribution of income from the bottom to the top.

The shift in political power has, in turn, helped to erode the belief among working-class whites that the condition of the poor and, more generally, of those in the bottom third of the income distribution is the result of an economic system that needed to be challenged through the Democratic party and through the union movement. Instead, the pitting of whites and blacks at the low end of the income distribution against each other has intensified the view among many whites that the condition of life for the disadvantaged—particularly for disadvantaged blacks—is the responsibility of those afflicted, and not the responsibility of the larger society.

As the civil rights movement became national, as it became clearly associated with the Democratic party, and as it began to impinge on local neighborhoods and schools, it served to crack the Democratic loyalties of key white voters. Crucial numbers of voters—in the white, urban and suburban neighborhoods of the North, and across the South—were, in addition, deeply angered and distressed by aspects of the expanding rights revolution. It has been among the white working and lower-middle classes that many of the social changes stemming from the introduction of new rights—civil rights for minorities, reproductive and workplace rights for women, constitutional protections for the criminally accused, immigration opportunities for those from developing countries, free-speech rights to pornographers, and the surfacing of highly visible homosexual communities—have been most deeply resisted. Resentment of the civil rights movement among key white voters was reinforced and enlarged by cultural and economic conflicts resulting from the rights revolution.

These two forces—race and rights—were, in turn, further charged—that is, were injected with catalytic potential—by the procedural reform movement within the Democratic party. This intraparty reform drive, erupting in the wake of the 1968 convention in Chicago, tapped for Democratic party leadership the ranks of the civil rights, anti-war, women's, and student movements, and became a vehicle for the ascendency of an upper-middle-class, college-educated culturally liberal elite within the Democratic party. This Democratic reform elite, in turn, served as the perfect foil for conservatives seeking to portray the Democratic party as a new establishment intent on imposing an alien—elitist and liberal—racial and cultural agenda on the mass of American voters.

Of the four issues—race, rights, reform, and taxes—race has been the most critical, and the most powerful, in effecting political change. Race has crystalized and provided a focus for values conflicts, for cultural conflicts, and for interest conflicts—conflicts over subjects as diverse as social welfare spending, neighborhood schooling, the distribution of the tax burden, criminal violence, sexual conduct, family structure, political competition, and union membership. Race has provided a mechanism to simultaneously divide voters over values, and to isolate one disproportionately poor segment of the population from the rest of the electorate.

Just as race was used, between 1880 and 1964, by the planter-textile-banking elite of the South to rupture class solidarity at the bottom of the income ladder, and to maintain control of the region's economic and political systems, race as a national issue over the past twenty-five years has broken the Democratic New Deal "bottom-up" coalition—a coalition dependent on substantial support from all voters, white and black, at or below the median income. The fracturing of the Democrats' "bottom-up" coalition permitted, in turn, those at the top of the "top-down" conservative coalition to encourage and to nurture, in the 1980s, what may well have been the most accelerated upwards redistribution of income in the nation's history—a redistribution fed by the tax, spending, and regulatory policies of the Reagan and Bush administrations.

The traditional ideological partisan divide—between Democratic liberalism supportive both of domestic-spending initiatives and of an activist federal regulatory apparatus, on the one hand, and Republican conservatism generally opposed to government regulation and in favor of reduced domestic spending, on the other hand—has been infused, over the past two-and-a-half decades, with racial and race-coded meanings.

For traditional Democratic liberalism, the convictions and resentments of many of its own core voters have become deeply problematic, defying incorporation into party ideology, and precluding, a priori, a functioning biracial political coalition.

In an interview at the campaign headquarters of a GOP state senator in 1988, Dan Donahue, a Chicago carpenter, explained:

> You could classify me as a working-class Democrat, a card-carrying union member. I'm not a card-carrying Republican, yet. . . . We have four or five generations of welfare mothers. And they [Democrats] say the answer to that is we need more programs. Come on. . . . It's well and good we should have compassion for these people, but your compassion goes only so far. I don't mind helping, but somebody has got to help themselves, you've got to pull. When you try to pick somebody up, they have to help. . . . Unfortunately, most of the people who need help in this situation are black and most of the people who are doing the helping are white. . . . We [white, Cook County voters] are tired of paying for the Chicago Housing Authority, and for public housing and public transportation that we don't use. . . . They hate it [the school board levy] because they are paying for black schools that aren't even educating kids, and the money is just going into the Board of Education and the teachers union.[1]

Dan Donahue's remarks are echoed by significant numbers of working and lower-middle-class white voters across the country—in focus groups, in door to door interviews, in streetcorner and living room conversations.[2]

For the Democratic party, the party that has taken the lead over the past twenty-five years in the struggle for racial equality, the consequences of such divisions in the electorate have been devastating. Democratic leaders take comfort in poll findings that the electorate remains liberal in its policy commitments, supportive of government spending to rebuild the infrastructure of roads and bridges and to provide improved education, day care, recreation facilities, public transit, and housing for the homeless.

But these leaders neglect underlying information suggesting that a majority of the electorate is unwilling to grant the Democratic party executive-branch authority to set and fund a traditionally liberal agenda—in part out of fear that a Democratic president will raise taxes from the largely white lower-middle and middle classes in order to direct benefits towards the disproportionately black and Hispanic poor—benefits often seen as wastefully spent.

––––––––––

The polarization of the two parties on issues of race had its inception over twenty-five years ago in the most ideological confrontation in twentieth-century American politics, the 1964 presidential election between Lyndon Johnson and Barry Goldwater. Goldwater, the leader of the conservative insurgency that broke the hammerlock of the Eastern Establishment on the presidential wing of the Republican party, publicly defined the Republican party as anti–civil rights with his opposition to the Civil Rights Act of 1964—by far the most salient issue before the nation that year. Johnson, conversely, firmly established the commitment of the Democratic party to civil rights, repeatedly crushing the Southern segregationist wing of the party that had once dominated the Senate.

These partisan divisions were reinforced by a change in the civil rights agenda itself. That agenda shifted away from an initial, pre-1964 focus on government guarantees of fundamental citizenship rights for blacks (such as the right to vote and the right to equal opportunity), and shifted toward a post-1964 focus on broader goals emphasizing equal outcomes or results for blacks, often achieved through racial preferences. These broader objectives were strenuously opposed by conservatives and by the Republican party. Opposition from the right intensified insofar as such objectives required government action to forcibly redistribute private and public goods—goods ranging, on the one hand, from jobs to education to housing, and extending, on the other, to valued intangibles such as cultural authority, prestige, and social space.

The growing saliency of busing throughout the 1970s—when the presidential platforms of each party took sharply opposing stands on perhaps the nation's most divisive question—established one of the most distinct cleavages between the two parties. Affirmative action—and a generally widening system of compensatory preferences favoring blacks over whites—followed on the heels of busing, again splitting the two parties and their presidential platforms, a split that endures to this day.

The contrasting stands of the two national parties on such broad issues as affirmative action and busing have had powerful reverberations into presidential voting patterns, as race has become a pervasive factor in the allocation of limited resources by city, state, and federal governments. Zoning regulations on Long Island, municipal employment residency requirements in black Detroit and in its white suburbs, the location and course offerings of "magnet" schools in Birmingham, the content of promotion exams for New York City police and firemen, the choice of basketball or tennis courts in Los Angeles parks—all of these are racially loaded issues placing black, white, and Hispanic citizens in a distributional competition on an almost daily basis in communities across the country.

These controversies, in turn, affect an extraordinarily broad range of outcomes, from the nature and quality of recreational facilities, to housing, to the caliber of schools, to property values, to the kinds of jobs available, to the sense of security, safety, and even ease enjoyed by ordinary citizens. Central to almost all of these issues are such basic questions as how much taxes are to be raised, for whose benefit; and whose interest will be served in the governmental spending, rule-making, and regulatory processes. At the state and local level, race-freighted issues have not yet been translated into hard and fast, racially-spurred partisan divisions, although that kind of split began to emerge in the 1980s in cities as diverse as Chicago, Birmingham, Philadelphia, and Columbia, South Carolina. But just as the federal government has been the main advocate of racial equality, so it has been primarily at the federal level that racial cleavages between the two parties have become most apparent: in congressional voting patterns, in the ideological differences between the convention delegates of the two parties, in the two national party platforms, in the thrust and focus of presidential campaigns, and in presidential election-day results.

———

The commitment of the Democratic party in 1964 to the cause of civil rights, and the opposition of Republican presidential nominee Barry Goldwater to the 1964 Civil Rights Act, set in motion a larger political process. That process altered the core meanings of both liberalism and conservatism, and changed as well the public perceptions of the Democratic and Republican parties. Instead of being seen as advancing the economic well-being of all voters, including white mainstream working and middle-class voters, liberalism and the Democratic party came to be perceived, in key sectors of the electorate, as promoting the establishment of new rights and government guarantees for previously marginalized, stigmatized, or historically disenfranchised groups, often at the expense of traditional constituencies.

In the view of crucial numbers of voters, the Democratic party became the political home of the beneficiaries and advocates of new legal and social rights, from the right to privacy (including the right to sexual privacy) to the rights of blacks, Hispanics, and Asians, to the rights of non-Christian religious minorities. In some respects, the Democratic party became the advocate and champion of a liberal agenda institutionalized by the Warren Court—and for a time by the Burger Court. During the Warren and early Burger years, the Supreme Court expanded far beyond congressional expectation the remedies for discrimination and for racial segregation, and granted legal rights and procedural guarantees to previously unprotected, sometimes unpopular and often controversial groups of once outcast or invisible Americans.

Insofar as the granting of rights to some groups required others to sacrifice tax dollars and authority, to compromise longstanding values, to jeopardize status, power, or the habitual patterns of daily life, this new liberalism became, to a degree, a disruptive force in American life, and particularly so within the Democratic party. At the extreme, liberalism inflamed resentment when it required some citizens—particularly lower-income whites—to put homes, jobs, neighborhoods, and children at perceived risk in the service of bitterly contested remedies for racial discrimination and segregation.

The remedies were established, in the eyes of key voters, not by elected representatives, but by a coercive federal judiciary and by an intrusive federal bureaucracy. The fundamental coalitional structure of the Democratic party, which in the New Deal era had produced an alliance of interests seeking to develop policies and programs benefitting the voting majority, became, in part, a forum for a zero-sum competition. The Democratic party learned only in retrospect to assess the political impact of a mandated redistribution of rights. Only in defeat have Democrats attempted to "read" the political ramifications of an ideology that—no matter how morally coherent or morally justifiable—nonetheless entailed the imposition of substantial costs on voters who had access to election-day retaliation.

The association of the national Democratic party with the newly empowered, frequently controversial groups it sought in the 1960s and 1970s to enfranchise and protect created a backlash among some of the Democrats' traditional constituencies. This backlash was, in turn, fostered and driven for partisan advantage by the Republican opposition. The linkage of the presidential wing of the Democratic party to newly protected groups—often labeled by the GOP as "special interests"—became a gold mine for the Republican party. The GOP set out to reinforce that linkage as part of a strategy first developed in the 1960s and early 1970s—a strategy designed to exploit the unpopularity of Democratic elites and of their protégés, and to publicly isolate the national Democratic party from the country's voting mainstream.

To an extraordinary degree, the presidential campaigns of Barry Goldwater, George Wallace, and Richard Nixon in the 1960s and 1970s shaped the rhetoric, themes, and tactics of the Reagan and Bush campaigns of the 1980s. Wallace and Nixon added a new, pejorative meaning to the word "liberal." Under the influence of their rhetoric, liberalism came to connote, for key voters, the favoring of blacks over whites and permissiveness towards drug abuse, illegitimacy, welfare fraud, street crime, homosexuality, anti-Americanism, as well as moral anarchy among the young.

Wallace and Nixon, together with Goldwater—profiting initially from the massive resistence to court-ordered desegregation—established a beachhead in the South for a rapidly evolving presidential Republicanism. Each candidate, including the nominally Democratic Wallace, went on to contribute to a spreading Republican populism, a right-populism attractive to working and lower-middle-class voters seeking to defend themselves from the strictures of a liberal Democratic establishment.

Wallace, of all the candidates seeking to build a right coalition in American politics, provided a sense of moral legitimacy to those whites who felt themselves under seige in the civil rights revolution. Wallace began the process of deflecting attention from blacks, whose own moral claim to equality was indisputable, and instead focused the anger of displaced whites onto a newly conceptualized, liberal establishment—the judges, lawyers, senators, newspaper editors, churchmen, and well-to-do do-gooders who were the champions of the government-led drive to end segregation. Wallace performed for the Republican party a critically important function, pioneering the specter of a new, hated liberal establishment to compete with the reviled corporate upper-class conservative establishment traditionally targeted by American populist politics.

Wallace, in effect, painted the national Democratic party, its elitist cadres, and its government bureaucracies as bastions of entrenched, arrogant privilege; a counterweight to the New Deal left-populist picture of the rich battening on the underpaid labor of the exploited working poor.

--------

In many respects, Ronald Reagan in his quest for the presidency consolidated, updated, and refined the right-populist, race-coded strategies of Wallace and Nixon. The 1980s were marked less by Republican political innovation than by the drive to adjust, renovate, and strengthen messages established in the previous two decades. This drive, in turn, was made possible by the party's well-funded development of powerful new tools of political technology: computerized direct mail, tracking polls, focus groups, marketing techniques, and the manipulation of voter lists, of paid and unpaid television, as well as of demographic, psychological, and geographic data.

In the 1980s, Republicans became master craftsmen, expert at the modernization of political skills introduced into campaigns a generation earlier. What stands out today even more strikingly, however, is the unintentionally cooperative role of the national Democratic party in shaping presidential politics to the advantage of the GOP, as Democrats, over the course of two-and-a-half decades, increased inexorably, their own vulnerability in a political debate structured around the issues of race and taxes.

———

The race and tax agenda was crucial to the realization of a fundamental goal of the civil rights era Republican party: the "embourgeoisement" of a decisive sector of previously Democratic voters. The issues of race and taxes fostered the creation of a middle-class, anti-government, property-holding, conservative identification among key white voters who had previously seen their interests as aligned with a downwardly-redistributive federal government. This re-identification in the years following 1964—an identification with the importuned rather than with the importuning— was all the more remarkable because it was not accompanied, in many cases, by any genuine movement on the part of such voters into, or even toward, the top half of the income distribution. The "embourgeoisement" of working and lower-middle-class white voters was critical, nonetheless, to the enactment during the Reagan administration of redistributive tax and spending legislation that shifted the rewards of government upwards, from the bottom to the top of the income distribution.

Race and taxes—with their "values," "rights," and redistributive dimensions—functioned to force the attention of the public on the costs of federal policies and programs. Those costs were often first experienced in terms of loss—the loss of control over school selection, union apprenticeship programs, hiring, promotions, neighborhoods, public safety, and even over sexual morals and a stable social order. Those losses or "costs" were then driven home by rising tax burdens to pay for such services as busing, Medicaid, subsidized public housing, law enforcement, prisons, welfare, and new lawyers of civil rights enforcement at every level of government.

The race and tax agenda effectively focused majority public attention onto what government takes, rather than onto what it gives. For millions of white voters, whose loyalty to the Democratic party had been locked into place by such programs as Social Security, unemployment compensation, the G.I. Bill, and federal mortgage assistance, the post–1964 policy agenda abruptly and negatively transformed their relationship to government.

The costs and burdens of Democratic-endorsed policies seeking to distribute economic and citizenship rights more equitably to blacks and to other minorities fell primarily on working and lower-middle-class whites who frequently competed with blacks for jobs and status, who lived in neighborhoods adjoining black ghettos, and whose children attended schools most likely to fall under busing orders.

The class-tilt of the costs of integration and of racial equality—a disproportionate share of which was borne by low and lower-middle-income whites—turned the resentment of those white working-class voters into a powerful mobilizing force. That resentment was increasingly amplified and channeled by the Republican party, in the wake of the civil rights movement, not just toward blacks, but toward Wallace's original target: the affluent, largely white, universe of liberal "experts" who were pressing the legal claims of blacks and other minorities—experts often sheltered, in their private lives, and largely immune to the costs of implementing minority claims.

The vulnerability of the least-privileged whites to the full impact of the rights-enforcement process provided an ongoing opportunity for the Republican party to reshape public opinion, as Wallace and Nixon had demonstrated, in subtle but critically important ways. In the Wallace tradition, the Republican party was increasingly able to define the Democratic party, its intellectual allies, and the bureaucracy that enforced redistributive laws, as a new left elite—an effective alternative target, as Wallace had shown, to the "fat cat" business class which, between 1929 and 1964, had reliably attracted the lion's share of popular resentment.

The adoption by the post–civil rights GOP of Wallace's demonized "liberal Democratic establishment" facilitated the development of a full-blown Republican-conservative populism. A central pillar of Reagan's success was the skill of his political entourage in manipulating the new Republican agenda of race and taxes in order to portray the Reagan administration as protecting the working man against "big government." Big government was painted, in turn, as fueled by Democrats seeking ever larger infusions of revenue, not only to raise welfare payments and government salaries, but to impose racial preferences on government contracts, on college admissions, and on employment and promotion in the public and private sectors. At the core of Republican-populist strategy was a commitment to resist the forcing of racial, cultural and social liberalism on recalcitrant white, working and middle-class constituencies. Republican-populist strategies and themes were expertly wielded as recently as the 1988 campaign to repackage—and even to reconstitute—George Bush, making possible the "popularization" of his patrician class background, and wiping out the 17-point lead held by the Democratic nominee as late as July of that year.

---

The development of a Republican populism has been reinforced both by the strategy the party has adopted to stake out the conservative side of racial issues, and by the changing nature of the racial issues themselves. The GOP has positioned itself just where the overwhelming majority of white Americans stand on racial policy: in favor of the principle of equality, but opposed to the enforcement mechanisms developed by the courts and the federal regulatory system. Over the past twenty-five years, poll data reveal that American voters, at least on the record, have moved beyond passive acquiescence in the principles of racial equality, to actual endorsement of those principles.[3] For politicians in virtually every region of the country, a direct appeal to racism would be fatal.

The parties have sharply diverged, however, on such issues as busing and "quotas"—race-based preferential hiring or promotion and affirmative action programs in government spending and in college admissions. The Republican party has firmly established itself as the adversary of these enforcement remedies. This stand places the GOP in support of the position of the majority of the white electorate, and in populist opposition to a powerful federal judiciary and to the civil rights enforcement bureaucracy: the new "establishment."

At the same time, Republican opposition to racial preferences in hiring or promotion or in school admissions is based on the ostensibly egalitarian principle that merit, not special favor, should determine job advancement and access to college—an inherently populist argument.

The Republican party, in developing a populist stance around the issues of race and taxes, has partially resolved one of the central problems facing a political party seeking to build a conservative majority: how to persuade working and lower-middle-class voters to join in an alliance with business interests and the affluent. Opposition to busing, to affirmative action, to quotas, and to housing integration have given a segment of the traditionally Democratic white electorate ideological common ground with business and the affluent in shared opposition to the federal regulatory apparatus. Shared opposition to taxes provides affluent and working-class voters—adversaries in the pre–civil rights era—with a common ground in the fight to restrict the growth of the coercive, redistributive state. Under the banner of a conservative "egalitarianism," the political right can maintain the loyalty of its low-income supporters by calling for an end to "reverse discrimination," while simultaneously maintaining the loyalty of the richest citizens by shaping to their advantage government policies that provide them with the greatest economic benefits.

———

As the costs of political initiatives designed to promote racial equality have grown, the national Democratic party has in a number of ways insulated itself from learning about these costs. The party has consequently lost an opportunity to gain better control of the debate and an opportunity to clearly understand the logistics of a modern national majority coalition. The presidential wing of the Democratic party in the late 1960s and early 1970s—the party's reform wing—enacted new rules governing the nomination process. These rules, which seemingly attempted to increase access to the nomination process, in fact functioned to reduce the role of white working and lower-middle-class voters—just the voters who would become pivotal to the outcome of general elections. The presidential selection process was changed, in other words, in a way that cut off feedback and information vital, in terms of successful general election competition, to the party's candidates and to their managers.

The post-1968 Democratic party rules shifted power to constituencies that with rare exception endorsed an agenda of racial, cultural, and social liberalism, while the influence of more conservative interests, particularly of ethnic, working-class leaders, over the selection of the Democratic nominee was substantially reduced.

These leaders represented white voters who were on the frontlines of urban housing integration, who were the subjects of busing orders, who were competitors for jobs as policemen, firemen, and union craftsmen governed by affirmative action consent decrees, and who found the liberal Supreme Court rules on criminal rights, abortion, school prayer, busing, and obscenity incomprehensible. These voters and their political representatives were, and still are, relegated to a largely peripheral status in the Democratic presidential primary competition. And in the absence of these voters from the early stages of the nomination process, Democratic presidential candidates have negotiated that process in the context of an artificially liberal and unrepresentative primary electorate which provides virtually no training for the candidates in the kinds of accommodation and bargaining essential to general election victory.

The political isolation created by the changes in the Democratic nominating rules has coincided over the past two decades with a degree of self-imposed intellectual isolation and intolerance on the part of much of the Democratic party elite—particularly the highly educated, "new class" elite. This isolation and intolerance began to surface in the second half of the 1960s, as many Democratic activists found themselves unable to acknowledge the political and social costs of the liberal agenda. To some degree, events overtook the ability of the new-class, activist, reform wing of the party to respond to the forces accompanying and unleashed by the tide of rising expectations. The outbreak of urban rioting in the 1960s challenged the nonviolent civil rights movement and accelerated the conservative reaction that became known as "white backlash." The enactment of civil rights legislation and of a barrage of measures directed primarily toward helping the black poor coincided with a sharp increase in crime rates, particularly violent crime, in the 1960s.[4] In the same decade, evidence of the deterioration of black family life began to accumulate, as illegitimate birthrates climbed dramatically, as single parenthood became the norm in black communities, and as the number of households on welfare nearly tripled.[5] Social dysfunction among those at the bottom of the income ladder served to blot out—or at the very least, to diminish—public recognition of the extraordinary advances of many working and middle-class blacks in the wake of the civil rights revolution.

Black and white liberals were unable to account for the mounting evidence of violence and social decay, evidence used by conservatives to challenge the legitimacy both of the civil rights movement and of such federal initiatives as the war on poverty, subsidized housing, food stamps, Medicaid, and more generous welfare regulations. Under siege, Democratic liberalism became unreceptive, if not hostile, to new, contradictory, and sometimes frightening information. The public repudiation of racism and the stigmatization of overtly racist expression was a groundbreaking achievement of the 1960s and 1970s. The repudiation of racist expression had an unintended consequence, however, for liberalism and for much of the Democratic party: an almost censorious set of prohibitions against discussion of family structure among the black poor, absent fathers, crime, lack of labor-force participation, welfare dependency, illegitimacy, and other contentious race-freighted issues.

This refusal to address conflicting evidence—of policy failure as well as of policy success—permitted the political right to capture the debate. By the early 1980s, domestic policy making had become dominated by the conservative argument that rising illegitimate birth rates, joblessness, and welfare dependency grew out of—or were reinforced by—economic incentives to bear out-of-wedlock children and the disincentives to work created by the Great Society.

Declining liberal influence over the domestic policy debate meant, in turn, that inadequate recognition was given not only to issues of structural unemployment, low wage scales, and the global transformations that were reshaping American industry, but that inadequate recognition was also given to the successful role of the federal government in expanding the black middle and upper-middle classes. These classes together grew from just 20 percent of black households in 1940, to better than 55 percent in 1980.[6]

While the black middle class grew substantially, conditions in the predominately black and Hispanic underclass grew worse. From prisons to welfare, the government agencies most closely tied to the problems of poverty and of the underclass are now serving constituencies that have a plurality of blacks. In a nation that is 12 percent black and 84 percent white, there were more black prison inmates than white in 1986[7] and, in 1988, more black welfare recipients than white[8]; in 1986, 55.6 percent of all black families with children were one-parent families headed by women[9]; and in 1988, 63.5 percent of all black children were born out of wedlock.[10] According to figures compiled by the Department of Justice in its 1987 criminal victimization survey of 46,000 households—the survey considered by law enforcement professionals to contain the most reliable data on race—30.7 percent of violent crimes in which the race of the offender was identified by the victim were committed by blacks, and a decisive majority of robberies, 59.9 percent, were committed by blacks.[11]

For those committed to racial equality, the trends in crime, welfare dependency, illegitimacy, drug abuse, and joblessness among the worst-off within the black community—in the aftermath of strong anti-discrimination legislation and of expanded social-service entitlements—represent a complex and seemingly intractable set of problems. If the Democratic party does not become a forum for a tough-minded exploration of issues of individual conduct, family structure, patterns of socialization, and other so-called moral/cultural matters—as well as a forum for exploring how such issues interact with larger structural questions of labor markets, wage ladders, deindustrialization, discrimination, etc.—the Democrats will remain vulnerable to challenge—both moral and economic—from the right.

The symptoms of social disorder, which the Democratic left to a large extent has excluded from public debate for most of the past twenty-five years,[12] and which black leaders have resisted talking about in morally unambiguous terms, have become so severe in the nation's cities—and, most difficult of all, so closely associated with race and with liberalism—that continued Democratic avoidance of these issues risks the national party's already-eroded credibility with the voting majority.

———

The pattern of liberal Democratic neglect of powerful and volatile issues involving race was repeated around a second set of explosive issues, as the party failed during the 1970s to recognize the pressure building towards a full-scale tax revolt. Throughout that decade, inflation and real rising incomes were combining to rapidly push Democratic voters, including many who considered themselves members of the working class, up the bracket system of the federal tax code, forcing them to pay higher and higher marginal rates. Many of these voters, furthermore, saw their rising tax burdens going to finance programs disproportionately serving black and Hispanic constituencies, programs such as low-income health care, public and subsidized housing, the Job Corps, women and infant nutrition programs, Head Start, food stamps, teenage pregnancy counseling, drug rehabilitation, prison construction, and Aid to Families with Dependent Children (AFDC).

In the years just preceding the full-scale outbreak of the tax revolt, when Democrats had the opportunity to adjust the tax structure to take into account the effects of inflation, Democratic attention was diverted by another issue altogether: Watergate. The scandals of the Nixon administration were a short-lived political bonanza for the Democratic party, handing party activists a temporary reprieve—and a set of blinders. Those blinders blocked from view what should have been alarming signs of tax discontent. From 1974 to 1977, major gains in the Senate (five seats) and in the House (a total of fifty seats in the 1974 and 1976 elections)—along with a razor-thin presidential victory in 1976—gave the Democrats false comfort, allowing the party to continue to turn its attention away from the issues of race, values, and taxes.

The party operated on the premise that the public response to Watergate constituted de facto assent to a liberal Democratic agenda, and that the pursuit of such an agenda would lead the Democratic party once again to majority status.

The pitfalls of this strategy became apparent in 1978, and even more so in 1980, when support for the Democrats nose-dived under pressure from a precipitously unraveling economy: unemployment by 1980 had risen to 7.1 percent; inflation had climbed as high as 13.5 percent; regular gasoline, in the midst of spiraling energy costs and a second OPEC oil shock, had reached $1.19 a gallon up from .35 a gallon in 1970 and interest rates had reached an extraordinary 21.5 percent. In the elections of 1978 and 1980, Democrats lost a combined total of fifteen Senate seats, fifty House seats, and the presidency.

The tax revolt, foreshadowing at the state level what would soon become a national issue, forced its way onto the public agenda with the passage in June 1978 of Proposition 13 in California, a referendum measure fixing property taxes at one percent of actual value, barring any new tax hikes, and rolling back real estate assessments to 1976 levels.

Proposition 13 provided, in miniature, an ideal polarizing mechanism for the conservative movement: the only opponents of the tax roll-back measure among all major demographic groups in California were blacks and public employees. At the same time citizen hostility toward government was focused on welfare and public housing, two programs closely associated in the public mind with blacks.

The Republican party moved swiftly to capitalize on Proposition 13, taking the unusual step of making an official party endorsement in the off-year elections of the Kemp-Roth 30 percent across-the-board federal income-tax cut proposed by Republican Representative Jack Kemp of New York and Republican Senator William Roth of Delaware. With the endorsement of Kemp-Roth as a major new Republican policy initiative calling for significant reductions in the levels of individual taxation, the high-profile, anti-tax and anti-government stand of the GOP was firmly established.

———

Republican ideological positions in favor of reduced taxes and curtailed government spending place the GOP in a directly adversarial position to the black community. Just as blacks have traditionally been far more supportive of an expansive, interventionist government than whites, they have had strong economic grounds for this position. Not only have a much higher percentage of blacks than of whites received direct government support through welfare, food stamps, Medicaid, and other programs targeted to the poor, over the past three decades, but fully half of all blacks holding professional and managerial-level jobs are employed by local, state, or federal government agencies, compared to just over a quarter of whites.[13] Most of the expansion of black employment in the private sector over the past twenty-five years has, furthermore, been in firms and companies falling under the jurisdiction of the Equal Employment Opportunity Commission (EEOC).[14] For blacks, then, the attack by the GOP on government, on the taxes that support government, and on the governmental regulatory apparatus amounted to a direct assault on the economic underpinnings of the black community.

The relationship of blacks to the federal government, and the dependence of blacks on all levels of government for direct employment, for benefits, and for protection in the courts and in the workplace, reflect the pervasive and mutually reinforcing power of a political agenda based on race and taxes. Race and taxes have been essential, at another level as well, to a key expansion of the Republican coalition: to the initial Republican mobilization in the 1970s of the white fundamentalist Christian community. This mobilization was based, in part, on the willingness of the GOP to vigorously oppose Internal Revenue Service policies prohibiting tax-exempt status for the network of segregated Christian academies that have flourished in the South in the aftermath of stringent federal integration standards for public schools.

Race and taxes, linked together at crucial junctures throughout the political system, have drawn into a coherent framework seemingly disparate issues and values. The forced focus by the Bush 1988 campaign of public attention on Michael Dukakis as a "liberal" and as a "card carrying member of the ACLU," (echoing in "card carrying" the preoccupation of the GOP in the 1950s with Communist party membership) aimed to create a public perception of Dukakis as the exemplar of an elite, rights-oriented, "Harvard Yard boutique" establishment—soft on taxes, soft on "alternate life styles," soft on criminals, soft on defense, and, by implication, soft on social doctrines of forced equality.

The focusing of public attention by the Bush campaign on the prison furlough of Willie Horton tapped not only voter resentment over the prisoners' rights, prison reform, and criminal defendents' rights movements, but tapped these concerns through a particularly threatening and dangerous archetype: of the black man as the rapist of a white woman.

---

The presence of race and taxes as factors touching upon almost every domestic issue has permitted the Republican party to capitalize on legitimate public concerns in order to conceptualize and construct a majority conservative coalition. For an electorate worried about crime, drugs, rising taxes, and the escalating costs of social-service spending, the Republican issues of strict law enforcement, tightened welfare eligibility, and a reduced poverty-oriented entitlement sector provided ostensibly race-neutral mechanisms to appeal to racially polarized sectors of the electorate.

The power of the joined themes of race and taxes, in concert with the suburban populism of the Republican party, and with the links of the Democratic party to tax-consuming special-interest groups, has resulted in a Republican credibility advantage over the national Democratic party in a number of critical areas. The party standing firm against an array of liberal interests seeking new sources of revenue, and standing firm against a redistributive federal government, is more likely to put its weight behind tough national anti-drug, anti-crime policies than behind civil liberties or criminal rights. The party advocating free-market rather than centralized-government solutions to the problems of racial inequality, is more likely, in this view, to be vigilant in conserving American wealth and autonomy in the face of redistributive claims from a developing world—as vigilant as it is in curtailing domestic social spending.

The public image of the national Democratic party as more permissive on a wide range of domestic issues, including crime, sex, pornography, and drugs, has coincided with a parallel image of the Democratic party as more acquiescent to Third World and other threatening foreign interests. The mutually reinforcing images of domestic and international permissiveness have limited the ability of the Democratic party to capitalize on the dissolution of the Soviet Bloc and on the potential support for redirected—and in the long run possibly reduced—military spending.

Just as a significant segment of the white electorate mistrusts the ability of the national Democratic party to administer improvements in medical care, education, and other domestic programs—goals supported by the public—without distributing benefits most heavily to blacks and to the very poor, the electorate has not been prepared to trust a Democratic president to cut back military spending while simultaneously making sure U.S. global concerns are fully protected.

The vulnerability of the Democratic party on this score was powerfully reinforced by the January 1991 House and Senate votes granting President Bush authority to wage war against Iraq in the Persian Gulf. With the near-unanimous backing of the GOP, Bush won the congressional vote, but 45 out of 55 Democratic senators, and 179 out of 265 House Democrats, voted against the war resolution. In the aftermath of Iraq's defeat by the United States, the congressional vote emerged as documentary evidence of Democratic unwillingness to forcibly confront a Third World dictator, and was seen by large numbers of voters as emblematic of Democratic weakness in foreign and military affairs. By March 1991, these developments had functioned to strengthen popular support for the Republican party, and to weaken backing for the Democratic party. When voters were asked in a Washington Post-ABC poll on March 3 and 4, 1991, which party they better trusted to handle the most pressing issues facing the nation, the GOP held a decisive 13 percentage point advantage.

———

As race and taxes have become organizing issues, the Republican party has achieved a substantial restructuring of the electorate in presidential elections. The Republican presidential coalition, which first emerged in full force in 1972, represents an economic inversion of the New Deal coalition: as Republican presidential candidates have won the support of traditional white Democratic voters at or below the center of the income distribution, the GOP has been able to fashion a presidential voting majority with the strongest levels of backing found among the affluent, smaller majorities in the center, and the weakest margins of support among those at the bottom of the ladder. This is the mirror image of the New Deal coalition, in which a majority was built from the bottom of the income distribution upward.

By constructing a "top-down" coalition around the issues of race and taxes, the Republican party has altered the balance of power in the traditional "have" versus "have-not" political confrontation, so that the segment of the electorate aligning and identifying with the "haves" outnumbers those aligned with the "have-nots." Insofar as the battle for power in American elections is fought out at the margins—in the eight elections since 1960, the winner's margin of victory has averaged 5.1 percent—the race-and-tax agenda, reinforced by culturally potent "rights" and "values" issues, has empowered the Republican party to convert what had been a minority coalition in presidential elections into a majority coalition.

The new Republican presidential majority does not result from the wholesale conversion of a major segment of the American electorate, but results instead from the piece-by-piece addition of smaller voting blocks, from the shifting of small fractions of the total vote. There has been, for example, what amounts to a realignment of presidential voting in Michigan, a state that voted Democratic in 1960, 1964, and 1968, but voted Republican in 1972, and in every election since then. The presidential realignment of Michigan was driven by the switched allegiance of a relatively small slice of suburban Detroit voters, a switch resulting in large part from an intensely bitter fight over a 1972 court-ordered plan (ultimately rejected by the Supreme Court) to require school busing between Detroit and its surrounding suburbs. While Detroit remained firmly Democratic, the busing fight provoked a realignment in the working-class Detroit suburbs that has transformed the presidential politics of the entire state for at least the past five elections.

Similarly, in the South, the realignment of white fundamentalist Christians between the elections of 1976 and 1980 transformed the presidential election outcome in 1980 in at least seven states. Carter carried Alabama, Arkansas, Kentucky, Mississippi, North Carolina, South Carolina, and Tennessee in 1976, but then lost each of these states to Reagan by a margin of one percent or less—and therefore all of their electoral votes—four years later.

In the winner-take-all system of American politics, changing the outcome of national elections does not require huge percentage shifts within any single voting group. Republican presidential victories have not been dependent on the wholesale conversion, for example, of white working-class voters to the GOP. Republican victories have instead relied on reducing or eliminating Democratic margins among white voters to the degree necessary to convert what was a minority Republican coalition into an election-day majority. The political manipulation of the themes of race and taxes—and of rights and values—is designed to produce relatively modest shifts in a political system where small movements in the electorate determine victory or defeat. Conservative political strategy has been aimed at, in effect, the marginal voter. The target voter is the white, working and lower-middle-class northern or southern populist, and the fundamental strategy is to break him or her loose from traditional Democratic moorings.

Relatively small shifts in voter allegiance can have major consequences. As recently as the Eisenhower and Nixon administrations, the continued presence of a majority in the electorate still committed to the Democratic party, if not to all of its candidates, acted as a brake on conservatism, severely restricting the range of conservative policy initiatives that could be successfully undertaken by the Republican party. Republican gains among voters over the past decade-and-a-half have severely weakened this liberal brake, and the piece-by-piece formation of a presidential majority of "haves" has produced major policy consequences.

The resulting shift to the right has been strengthened, in turn, by the determination of the conservative wing of the Republican party to build the right-leaning coalition in traditional political fashion: by rewarding the loyal and by penalizing the opposition. For the affluent, who form the most loyal members of the new coalition, the Republican party has pressed for enactment of tax cuts skewed in favor of those at the top of the income distribution—from Reagan's $749 billion 1981 tax cut, to Bush's efforts to win approval of a capital-gains tax reduction. For business, particularly business heavily regulated by such adversarial federal agencies as the Environmental Protection Agency (EPA), the Occupational Health and Safety Administration (OSHA), the Federal Trade Commission (FTC), and the anti-trust division of the Justice Department, the Republican party has sought to lessen not only the tax burden, but also to substantially lessen the regulatory burden.

The overlapping areas of domestic spending and civil rights policy have, at the same time, provided Republican strategists with the opportunity to reinforce the loyalty of those voters angered by social-service spending and by what they see as unfair competitive advantages for blacks, and to simultaneously impose penalties on the nation's most Democratic constituencies, the poor and the black.

On this front, the success of the GOP in transforming spending and other race-relevant policies of the federal government has been politically impressive. From 1980 to 1988, for example, discretionary domestic spending as a share of the gross national product was cut by 33.9 percent.[15] The Reagan Justice Department during this period committed itself to dismantling much of the federal civil rights regulatory structure and became the systematic adversary of busing and of affirmative action. The steady stream of conservative Republican appointments to the Supreme Court—Rehnquist, O'Connor, Scalia, and Kennedy—bore fruit in 1989 with a series of five rulings that weakened the legal position of minority and women plaintiffs bringing job discrimination suits, strengthened the leverage of white employees in negotiations over affirmative action consent decrees, and threatened the future of minority contracting "set-aside" programs developed by state and local governments.[16]

In terms of straightforward economic rewards, the Republican-dominated decade of the 1980s produced one of the most dramatic redistributions of income in the nation's history. While overall family *after-tax* income rose by 15.7 percent, the income of families in the bottom decile fell by 10.4 percent, from $4,791 to $4,295 (in constant 1990 dollars) while the income of those in the top one percent rose by 87.1 percent, from $213,675 to $399,697.[17]

The configuration of elections into majority "top-down" versus minority "bottom-up" confrontations, in effect, permits the GOP to perform the basic function of a political party far more effectively than its Democratic opponents. From 1968 to 1988—the twenty years since the race, tax, and rights agenda superseded an agenda of traditional economic liberalism—the Democratic party has been unable, with the exception of the Carter victory of 1976, to develop a strategy that mobilizes a majority of the electorate in behalf of its presidential candidate.

The building of a majority top-down coalition (incorporating whites from the lower-middle through the upper classes), versus a minority alliance of blacks, Hispanics, the poor, the discriminated-against, and diminishing numbers of whites (excepting a block of well-educated liberals) has proven to be a gold mine for GOP media specialists. Television commercials developed by the Reagan and Bush campaigns, and the institutional television advertising produced by the Republican National Committee throughout the 1980s, crafted powerful campaign messages out of seemingly innocent images of pastoral middle-class life—as in the "It's Morning Again in America" advertisements of the 1984 Reagan campaign. Such a marketing strategy works on the assumption that, buried in the heart of the majority electorate, lies a conviction, sometimes explicit, sometimes implicit, about the values of the Republican party: that the GOP and its presidential candidates are aligned with the fundamental values of the American middle class, and that the Democratic party and its presidential candidates are not.

———

The 1980 election, unlike previous Republican victories—Eisenhower in 1952 or Nixon in 1968—presented the first successful substantive ideological challenge to New Deal liberalism since its beginnings in 1932. In the struggle of the Republican party to achieve majority status, all of the factors favoring partisan realignment coalesced. The tax revolt had by 1980 spread far beyond California's borders; inflation, high interest rates, and unemployment had seriously eroded public trust in the Democratic party to produce prosperity; and the capture of fifty-three American hostages in Iran, the second OPEC oil shock, and the Soviet invasion of Afghanistan, suggested that American international interests were not secure in the hands of a Democratic administration. The 1980 election—in which the GOP took control of the Senate, picked up 35 House seats to gain defacto control of the House, and won 302 state senate and state house seats— represented a repudiation of the national Democratic party that offered the GOP the opportunity to secure a solid majority base in the electorate.

The Republican party won a mandate in 1980 to redirect the course of public policy, and the Reagan administration immediately capitalized on that mandate to win enactment both of the 1981 Conable-Hance tax cut and of the Gramm-Latta budget cuts—major legislation that undermined the liberal principles of progressive taxation and substantially eroded the Great Society programs of the 1960s.

———

It is one of the ironies of modern politics that it took monetary policies set in motion in 1979 by Paul Volcker, Carter's chairman of the Federal Reserve Board, to stall the newly ascendant GOP and to decisively set back the conservative Republican realignment—monetary policies designed by a Democratic administration to wring rampant inflation out of the economy; policies that led to the brutal recession of 1981–82, with its factory closings, farm bankruptcies, and unemployment rates of 10.5 percent in the month before the 1982 midterm elections.

The loss of conservative momentum during the 1981–82 recession gave the Democratic party the opportunity to regroup. Throughout the 1980s, Democrats learned to use the power of incumbency aggressively, in order to insulate the party from unfavorable trends in public opinion. Incumbency not only gave Democrats access to campaign contributions to tighten control on elective office—access which they learned surprisingly late to take full advantage of—but incumbency also gave them the power to draw U.S. House and state legislative districts favorable to the election of Democrats.

Democratic strategists now privately acknowledge that their control of a majority of legislatures and governorships in 1981 produced post-census congressional redistricting that gave the party control of twenty to twenty-five House seats, most of which would have gone to Republicans had lines been neutrally drawn.

Democratic regrouping in the early 1980s did not, however, involve a serious reassessment of the role of race, rights, or taxes in the collapse of the liberal presidential coalition. Nor did the Democrats make a serious attempt to develop the kinds of policies and political strategies that maintain the allegiance of the poor and of the working class, while muting cultural and values conflicts, racial conflict, and distributional competition. Instead, Democratic party reorganization during the 1980s in many respects involved an intensification of dependence on special interests.

House Democrats, recognizing the threat to their power represented by the 1980 election, sought in the wake of that defeat to enlarge and expand the protective fortress around each Democratic incumbent. Wielding the power of incumbency, House Democrats used implied threats of reprisal, along with numerous concessions to big business, to break the allegiance of the corporate political action committee (PAC) community to the GOP. By 1988, House Democratic incumbents had become, for the first time, more dependent on PACs for financial support than on individual donors.

In securing their hold on Congress, House Democrats, in the course of the 1980s, increasingly became prisoners of the Washington power structure, a dangerous dependence as the public became more and more distrustful of a national policy driven by negotiations between Washington-based interests. The combination of gerrymandered districts with the reliance of House Democrats on PACs and on the perquisites of office meant that the bastion of Democratic strength in Washington was in danger of losing its credibility as a legitimate representative of majority will. Once the party of reform, the national Democrats became by the late 1980s vulnerable to a Republican reform assault, reflected in part by GOP ethics challenges to a number of elected Democrats, including former House Speaker Jim Wright of Texas, Representative Barney Frank of Massachusetts, and former House majority whip Tony Coelho of California.

As Democratic hegemony eroded, and as conflicts over race, rights, and values fractured the once deeply felt loyalty of a plurality of voters to the national Democratic party, Democratic members of the House were forced to rely excessively on an essentially corrupt system of campaign finance, on gerrymandering, on pork-barrel spending, on weak Republican challengers, and on assorted manipulations of the elective process in order to thwart continuing ideological and demographic shifts favoring their opponents.

Democratic dependence on special interests has seriously inhibited the ability of the party to implement innovatively its commitment to America's wage earners, both white and black. The disproportiate influence of special interests has affected not only the economic policy positions but the overall image presented to the public by the national Democratic establishment.

Finally, the dependence on special interests has significantly restricted the range of Democratic responses to a political force of vastly increasing importance over the past fifteen years: the globalization of the economy.

The growth of international competition has directly assaulted a traditional province of the Democratic Party: protective measures designed to insulate vulnerable constituencies from the most destructive elements of unrestrained competition. These measures had amounted over time to a strategy for directing rising wages and steadily improving living conditions toward working-class voters. Democrats had been relatively successful since the New Deal in protecting unions from unbridled competition through a network of regulations and laws, including the National Labor Relations Act and the Davis-Bacon Act.[18] The Democratic party had, furthermore, supported affirmative action, itself a form of protectionist intervention into employment and job promotion markets. In an expanding economy, as long as competition had been largely confined to the territorial United States, these strategies were politically defensible.

As competition became international, however—as factories and production facilities moved to Mexico or overseas, and as corporations and capital traveled at a keystroke from one hemisphere to another—many of the protectionist policies of the Democratic party became futile, and in some cases dangerous to core constituencies.

The failure of Democratic economic policies, and the accompanying political liabilities, became most acute during the Carter years, when the overseas challenge to the domestic auto and steel industries erupted. The economic devastation to Detroit, Cleveland, Buffalo, Pittsburgh, Wheeling (West Virginia), and Birmingham—devastation stretching across the rust and steel belts—was catastrophic to the legitimacy of the national Democratic party. The collapse of heavily unionized industries and the recession of 1980 marked the first substantial Democratic party failure to protect its own voters at the most important level—that of jobs and wages—since the origin of the New Deal coalition.

As House Democrats became dependent on the universe of Washington-based special interests—a universe of interests, epitomized by PACs, generally seeking to preserve existing power arrangements and to prevent innovation—the ability of the Democratic party to respond imaginatively and effectively to the challenge of globalization was limited. In a period of retrenchment, the best organized interests are just those seeking to preserve the status quo; the best organized interests in this case were those dominating the Washington PAC community, a community that had begun, in the early 1980s, to channel more cash to the Democrats. In the process, the Democratic party compounded the loss it had incurred during the Carter years, the loss of perhaps its most precious commodity: the trust of the public in the ability of Democrats to handle the nation's economy. Throughout the later half of the 1980s, the public in poll after poll was more willing to entrust Republicans with responsibility to provide economic security than the Democrats, and the public saw the GOP as better equipped to represent the interests of the middle classes.[19] The Republican party only began to lose this advantage in 1990 when Bush abandoned his "read my lips—no new taxes" pledge and signed legislation aimed at reducing the federal defecit—legislation to cut spending and raise a broad range of federal taxes.

———

In many respects, the political consequences of a globalized economy provide a case study of how race interacts catalytically with seemingly race-neutral developments to produce a powerful reaction. Consider, for example, the Detroit metropolitan area, a heavily black city surrounded by largely white, working-class, once-firmly Democratic suburbs. From the time of the Detroit riots of 1967, through years when a deeply controversial busing proposal appeared likely to force cross-county student transfers, Democratic voting among the white working class steadily eroded. It was when the domestic automobile industry began to collapse in the late 1970s, however, in large part as a result of international competition, that an economic element was added to the persistent racial tension. Studies of the white voters of Macomb County and other suburbs, neighborhoods often dominated by United Auto Workers and auto-industry retirees, found an explosive anger at blacks and at Democratic regimes perceived by such white voters as favoring blacks and as redistributing declining resources to blacks.[20]

Not only in Detroit, but in every beleaguered industrial center, political messages began to be read through a "racial filter." Democratic rhetoric focusing on "fairness" was interpreted by key white voters as meaning "fairness to blacks"—fairness financed with tax dollars extracted from the stagnating and inflation-pinched paychecks of working whites. Already torn loose from their Democratic moorings by the racial, cultural, and values conflicts of the 1960s and 1970s, these key voters—soon to be known as "Reagan Democrats"—were further propelled into the arms of the GOP by international economic change; such voters, perceiving themselves as buffeted by economic threat, would come to embrace the GOP at the presidential level, and would periodically abandon their Democratic roots in contests for lower office.

———

The conflation of rising tax burdens, racial conflict, cultural change, and resource competition has been intensified by the growing public attention paid to the emergence of a heavily black underclass. At a time when the expansion of both the stable black working class and of the black middle class is functioning to cement black-white cooperation and to break up racial stereotypes, the underclass is serving at the other extreme, in the eyes of key voters, to counteract black success and to reinforce the most negative racial stereotypes.

As politics increasingly reflect a struggle over hotly contested cultural and moral values, and at a time when just under 50 percent of the nation's population live in the twenty largest metropolitan areas,[21] the urban underclass has become a driving force, giving much of the "values" debate a racial cast. The underclass, and the desperate tide of black illegitimacy, joblessness, poverty, crime, and welfare dependency in most of the nation's major cities, represent, for many Americans, the most significant and seemingly intractable challenge to traditional majoritarian values. These values, in turn, touch directly on voters' emotionally charged convictions about community, duty, the law, work, the family, sexual conduct, and social responsibility.

Insofar as the national Democratic party, in order to avoid divisive conflict, ignores or neglects majoritarian values issues, Democrats become increasingly vulnerable to accusations of elitism on the one hand, and to charges of moral indifference, on the other—and, finally, to allegations that Democrats are potentially dangerous to America's hard-won competitive leadership position in the world.

———

As politics are now structured, the pressures for the aggravation of racial conflict are in many respects intensifying. The main force behind the perpetuation of such conflict is the continuing growth of the predominately white suburbs, and the declining political importance of increasingly black and Hispanic central cities. The election of 1992 will be the first in the nation's history in which the suburban vote will constitute an absolute majority. The consequences of this development cannot be overestimated.

At the most critical level, the emergence of a suburban voting majority, often encircling center cities, means that the jurisdictional border between city and county—a boundary with an increasingly minority-dominated, Democratic urban electorate on one side, and a largely white, Republican-leaning suburban electorate on the other—will play a larger and larger role in determining the outcome of national elections.

Just as America's suburbs are becoming functionally independent of center cities, and newly rich in commercial services—with suburban lawyers, doctors, accountants, industrial parks, suppliers, shopping malls, office complexes, hospitals, tennis courts, swimming pools, movie theaters, book stores, and restaurants supplying local consumer needs—suburban voters are also increasingly able to provide for their civic needs through locally based taxes. These locally raised and locally spent taxes will not flow through what are seen by many suburbanites as wasteful Washington bureaucracies and their voracious clienteles.

In the past, public concern over issues such as education, recreation, and the quality of municipal services could be taken advantage of, in political terms, to build a national consensus in support of an activist federal government. Now, the growth of suburbia and of suburban government provides a means to address public concerns, while confining services and benefits to local residents. Affluent counties such as Fairfax (Virginia), Dupage (Illinois), Cobb (Georgia), Montgomery (Maryland), and Orange (California), are the new power centers of American politics. These counties provide avenues for their affluent and middle-class citizens to fulfill civic, social, and communitarian goals through what are often, in effect, racially exclusionary local policies and initiatives.

———

Partisan competition for the votes of black America has been absent for over a generation, and its absence has corrupted both parties. For the Democratic party, a secure base of support among black voters has stifled innovation, and has eliminated pressure to develop policies that productively reinforce the loyalty of the party's most reliable electorate. The GOP, in turn, has built its success for the past twenty-five years on the basis of racial and cultural flight from the Democratic party, becoming in the process a *de facto* white party.

Partisan competition is perhaps the most effective mechanism with which to force an assault on the problems of poverty, of the underclass, of the working poor, and on such long-range issues as the globalization of the economy. The political marketplace can be a profoundly generative arena and the importance of a healthy partisan competition cannot be overestimated. The failure of the political system to function as a generative force is reflected in part in the deterioration of conditions—of economic security, family, and employment—for those in the bottom third of the income distribution for nearly two decades.

The source of this failure is complex. From the 1930s to the mid-1960s, a period during which the beneficiaries of liberalism were in fact primarily white and constituted a majority of working men and women, the drive to empower those on the margins invigorated liberal Democratic politics. By the 1960s, however, liberalism had begun to press an agenda that increasingly targeted benefits to minorities and provoked often divisive reactions—including cultural and racial antagonisms, anger over reverse discrimination as well as over threatened white hegemony, fear of crime, and distress at continued family dissolution. The struggle to expand and enforce citizenship and constitutional rights became, by the late 1960s, a source of bitter, often subterranean, conflict, dividing rather than strengthening the once-powerful political coalition dominated by those at the bottom.

With liberal constituencies divided, conservatism—committed to protecting the affluent and to dismantling the political alliances of the "havenots"—is under pressure to mine for profit both racial conflict and the social dysfunction of the very poor, as well as to aggressively adopt positions that capitalize on liberal conflict.

The cold reality is that the presidential realignment of the electorate that began after the election of 1964 has created a politics in which neither national party effectively represents the shared economic interests of the poor and of the working and lower-middle classes. The Democratic party, and many of the voters who traditionally support liberal ideologies and institutions, have been badly wounded by the politics of race, rights, and taxes—and by the dynamic way that these issues have interacted to create a powerful nexus of liabilities for a center-left coalition.

Over the past twenty-five years, liberalism has evaded taking on, and learning from, the experience of voter rejection, as institutional power and a sequence of extraneous events—ranging from Watergate to the 1981–82 recession—have worked to prop up the national Democratic party. For the current cycle to reach completion, and for there to be a breakthrough in stagnant partisan competition, it may be that the Democratic party must go through the kind of nadir—intra-party conflict, challenge to ideological orthodoxy, in short, a form of civil war—experienced by the GOP and the right in the 1960s; that recapturing the ability to build a winning alliance requires learning the full meaning of defeat, developing a conscious awareness of precisely what the electorate will politically support, what it will not, and when—if ever—something more important is at stake.

# 2

# A Pivotal Year

THE HISTORY of American politics for the past twenty-five years has been defined in part by the political costs of a morally ambitious undertaking. For a century after the Civil War, blacks fought in the courts, the streets, the churches, the unions, at Democratic and Republican conventions, in back-country schoolhouses, in the halls of Congress, on the assembly line, in army barracks, and on the shop floor to force the nation's political and legal system to take up the issue of institutionalized racial inequality.

The civil rights struggle, building momentum with increasingly significant victories, acquired sufficient force by the start of the 1960s to dominate the public agenda, and in the process became the single most important factor determining the future of the Democratic and Republican parties. The struggle leading up to this critical turning point in American politics was the longest, most difficult, and most dangerous peacetime effort in the nation's history to force a substantial expansion of the commitment to egalitarian principle. In the legal arena, the NAACP and the NAACP Legal Defense Fund brought case after case to court on behalf of southern black plaintiffs—men and women willing to submit themselves to the gravest personal danger in order to discredit the system of legal segregation. In a strategy carefully implemented over the course of twenty-one years—from 1933 to 1954—the NAACP brought to the Supreme Court a series of cases to lay the groundwork for a direct assault on the legal foundation of segregation, the "separate but equal" principle set out by the Supreme Court in the 1896 decision, *Plessy v. Ferguson*.

The NAACP, in effect, progressively forced the Supreme Court to acknowledge that segregation inevitably produced inequality, that the *Plessy* doctrine of "separate but equal" was a contradiction in terms. The sustained legal challenge culminated in the presentation to the Supreme Court of five cases—carefully selected and crafted over six years of preparation, trial, and appeal—to demonstrate the inherent injustice to blacks of the system of formal segregation labeled Jim Crow. In the five cases—collectively known as *Brown v. Board of Education of Topeka, Kansas* (1954)—Chief Justice Earl Warren wrote in a 9–0 opinion: "We conclude that in the field of public education the doctrine of 'separate but equal' has no place. Separate educational facilities are inherently unequal."[1]

The legal challenges to the contradictions of segregation in a country founded on egalitarian ideals were reinforced by mounting political pressures. As blacks migrated from southern farms to northern cities—driven by the mechanization of southern agriculture and drawn by an expanding northern manufacturing sector (480,000 blacks migrated north in the 1930s, 1.58 million in the 1940s, and 1.6 million in the 1950s)[2]—newly mobilized blacks acquired the vote, amassed a degree of political power, and established their allegiance to the northern Democratic party.

It was the Democratic party of Franklin D. Roosevelt and the New Deal that, in the 1930s and 1940s, promised clout to those at the bottom of the economic and social ladder; it was the Democratic party that sought to shift power, wealth, and the protection of the state towards the working classes; and it was a Democratic president who signed the 1941 order prohibiting discrimination in hiring by federal contractors. By 1948, black political muscle, growing opposition to segregation among white liberals, and the increased dependence of northern city political bosses on black votes produced the first Democratic convention platform to include a strong civil rights plank. That same year, Democrat Harry S. Truman issued Executive Order Number 9980, which—even while lacking enforcement authority—prohibited discrimination in all federal employment.

The deepening alliance between the northern wing of the Democratic party and the black civil rights movement was driven by a rapidly evolving social and political order. The network of laws supporting legal segregation in the South—a system of legal discrimination and exclusion—stood in sharp contrast not only to the commitment to equality and citizenship rights embodied in the country's origins, but to the violent repudiation, in the wake of the Second World War, of doctrines of racial inferiority and of German eugenic ideologies. Racial segregation stood in contradiction to an evolving global awareness of human rights and to a burgeoning climate of national liberation and self-determination, a climate favoring successful decolonization movements, by the late 1940s, across Africa and Asia.

By the end of the 1940s, global trends coincided with internal pressures building within the Democratic party, pressures leading inevitably toward a rupture of the post–Civil War tie between the national Democratic party and the segregationist South. In the aftermath of the platform vote at the 1948 Democratic convention—a platform declaring: "The Democratic Party commits itself to continuing efforts to eradicate all racial, religious and economic discrimination,"[3]—Strom Thurmond, then governor of South Carolina, stalked out, taking with him his own state delegation, the entire Mississippi delegation, and half of the Alabama delegation.

Within two weeks of the Democratic convention, the States' Rights Democratic party (the "Dixiecrats") was formed at a gathering in Birmingham, Alabama. Thurmond and Fielding Wright, the governor of Mississippi, were chosen as the new party's presidential and vice-presidential nominees. Thurmond, running on a segregationist platform, won only 1,169,021 votes, a twentieth of the 24 million votes received by Truman. But Thurmond carried Mississippi, Louisiana, South Carolina, and Alabama—the heart of the deep South, establishing what sixteen years later would become the southern beachhead of the GOP.

The 1948 Thurmond campaign was of profound importance. It demonstrated the power of the issue of race to break the lock of the national Democratic party on the South, a step of critical consequence in a thirty-two-year long process that would produce a regional realignment in presidential elections by 1980.

By 1964, the political and moral pressure generated by the nonviolent black protest movement and by the violent white southern reaction to it compelled the national Democratic party to sever ties to its southern segregationist wing. A succession of events transformed the political landscape and ultimately forced a racially driven realignment of the two parties, events that began with the 1955 black-led boycott of the segregated bus system in Montgomery, Alabama, and included over the next decade the lynching in Mississippi of Emmett Till, a black 14-year-old; the integration under federal military protection of Central High School in Little Rock, Arkansas; lunch counter sit-ins from Greensboro to Nashville to Atlanta; the 1961 Freedom Rides; the 1963 non-violent Birmingham civil rights demonstrations where "Bull" Connor turned firehoses and police dogs on women and children; the assassination of Mississippi civil rights leader Medgar Evers; the 1963 March on Washington where Martin Luther King, Jr. gave his "I have a dream" speech; and the 1964 murder in Philadelphia, Mississippi, of three civil rights workers, whose disappearance on June 20 preceded by a week the first breaking of a Senate filibuster against federal civil rights legislation.

The tumultuous, moving, and often violent events of the decade led to congressional passage of the Civil Rights Act of 1964 and the Voting Rights Act of 1965—the two strongest pieces of civil rights legislation ever enacted—and set the stage for the Democratic and Republican parties to diverge sharply on the issues of civil rights. 1964 marked the beginning of a fundamentally new partisan configuration, based in large part on the politics of race.

The national Democratic party under the administrations of John F. Kennedy and Lyndon B. Johnson snapped the bond between the presidential wing of the Democratic party and the segregationist Democratic electorate, joining forces with the civil rights revolution to form a permanent Democratic party alignment with black America. The simultaneous toppling of the pro-civil rights, eastern-establishment wing of the Republican party (known in 1964 as the Rockefeller wing) by a conservative intraparty insurrection, drawing most heavily on the South for the core of its support, put the Democratic and Republican parties on a collision course over the issue of race for the first time since the Civil War.

The presidential contest of 1964 between Johnson, an outspoken proponent of the Civil Rights Act, and Barry Goldwater, an aggressively conservative opponent, marked the beginnings of what amounted to a racial realignment of the two parties. The 1964 Civil Rights Act was the most comprehensive measure of its kind ever passed, and it dominated news coverage of Washington for over a year—from June 19, 1963, when Kennedy sent the measure to Congress, through the breaking of the Senate filibuster on June 10, 1964, to final passage on July 2, 1964. The measure effectively declared illegal the structure of entrenched segregation in the South. It empowered the U.S. attorney general to file suit against segregated school systems, prohibited segregation in public facilities and accommodations, barred job discrimination by employers and unions, and provided for the termination of federal funds to schools, hospitals, and other institutions that discriminated. By the time of the 1964 election, poll data showed that an exceptionally high percentage of respondents, 75 percent, were aware of the fact that Congress had passed the Civil Rights bill; and of those familiar with the congressional action, a striking 96 percent knew that Johnson supported the bill, while 84 percent knew that Goldwater opposed it.[4]

As the 1964 Civil Rights bill worked its way from proposal to passage, and as the presidential campaign took its course, the public perception not only of Johnson and Goldwater, but also of the racial stands of the Democratic and Republican parties, changed radically. The biennial polls conducted for the National Election Studies (NES) reveal that the public before 1964 saw virtually no difference between the parties on issues of race. As recently as 1962, when respondents were asked which party "is more likely to see to it that Negroes get fair treatment in jobs and housing?" 22.7 percent said Democrats, 21.3 percent said Republicans, and 55.9 percent said there was no difference between the two parties.

By late 1964, however, the public saw clear differences between the two parties. When asked which party was more likely to support fair treatment in jobs for blacks, 60 percent of the respondents said the Democratic party, 33 percent said there was no difference between the parties, and only 7 percent said the Republican party. Similarly, when asked in 1964 which party was more likely to support blacks and whites going to the same school, 56 percent said the Democratic party, 37 percent said there was no difference, and 7 percent identified the Republican party.[5]

The events of 1964 gave rise to a process in which, over time, the partisan differences on race seen by the public would extend beyond presidential candidates to members of Congress, to the stands taken by the two party platforms, and to the attitudes of presidential convention delegates, party activists, and the much larger universe of voters who identify with the Republican and Democratic parties. By 1964, the Democratic party was on its way to becoming the home of racial liberalism, and the Republican party was on its way to becoming the home of racial conservatism.

———

In the immediate aftermath of the 1964 Johnson landslide, every indication was that the Republican party had fatally misjudged the American mood in choosing a racial conservative as its presidential nominee, and that the Democratic party had captured the spirit of the country. Not only did Johnson swamp Goldwater by 15.9 million votes, 43.1 million to 27.2 million, but Johnson secured a solid liberal majority in Congress, raising the Democratic margin to 68–32 in the Senate, the largest since 1943, and to 295–140 in the House, the largest since 1939.

In addition, the non-southern white electorate in the early and mid-1960s strongly endorsed the nonviolent civil rights movement. In both February 1964 and March 1965, the Gallup poll found the same percentage, 72 percent, of whites outside the South who thought Johnson was pushing civil rights "about right" or "not fast enough," and only 28 percent who thought he was moving "too fast."[6] Few elected officials and Democratic party strategists anticipated the political costs involved in *translating* the principle of equality into a powerful enforcement structure in the courts and in the federal bureaucracy.

The popularity of the civil rights cause foundered on a lack of broad-based support in the electorate for *implementing* far-reaching remedies, remedies that over the next decade and a half would be established by the courts and by the federal civil rights regulatory bureaucracy in support of the goals of racial equality. Johnson's commitment to the civil rights movement meant, in fact, much more than a political alliance with black leaders and voters.

Johnson and a Democratic Congress put the full force of the federal government behind the principle of racial equality, triggering a confrontation between black and white America, and setting off an ultimately distributional struggle that soon went substantially beyond the goal of eliminating legal segregation in the South. The Civil Rights Act of 1964, seeking and achieving new equality for vast numbers of American blacks through the power of the federal government, set the stage for the pervasive involvement of the federal judiciary, of a powerful centralized government bureaucracy, and of ranks of federal employees—in the nation's schools, military services, union halls, businesses, factories, employment offices, hospitals, neighborhoods, and civil-service systems.

To an extent, Johnson recognized the immediate political consequences of the 1964 Civil Rights Act—confiding to an aide that he believed he had "delivered the South to the Republican Party for a long time to come."[7] But both he and the Democratic leadership in Congress failed to foresee the full degree to which they had committed the federal government to what would soon encompass substantially more than a struggle for equal opportunity.

Johnson and the Democratic Congress unleashed the power of the federal government in behalf of American blacks who had previously been unrepresented in the battle for public- and private-sector resources, and who were now suddenly engaged in a racial struggle over the control of jobs, schools, housing, communities, and tax dollars. This battle, in turn, pitted the federal government not only against openly segregationist leaders, voters, and institutions—the target of the early, nonviolent civil rights movement—but against an angry and resistant segment of the working and lower-middle-class white electorate in the North.

Johnson and Congress set in motion a process in which the central issues of the civil rights struggle came to be defined in terms far more controversial than the simple granting of "equal rights" to minorities. The battleground of a deeply political conflict moved from the halls of Congress to the far less politically vulnerable—and far less politically responsive—federal court system, and to a vast network of civil-service employees mandated to enforce federal law.

In time, the national consensus behind the drive for black equality began to fray. The federal judiciary and the federal regulatory apparatus adopted remedies that sharply increased the political, economic, and social costs of the civil rights movement, including busing, affirmative action, strict legislative redistricting requirements, and a widening system of racial preferences. Traditionally Democratic whites—whites who felt themselves to be increasingly pressed economically, who felt that they bore the largest share of the burden of the civil rights revolution, and who chafed at what they perceived to be diminishing authority, autonomy, and prestige—decided at the ballot box that they were unable to voice their resentment and anger through Democratic party channels.

---

In 1964, neither Johnson nor the Democratic Congress anticipated that the church-led, nonviolent southern civil rights movement of the fifties and early sixties would soon be superseded in the public eye by a violent contagion of race riots in northern slums; nor that leadership of the civil rights movement would be seized by a highly visible new generation of activists committed to the rise of "black power"; nor that, just as the Supreme Court began to broaden the rights of criminal defendants, the crime rate would begin to skyrocket; nor that welfare expenditures and illegitimacy rates for blacks would start to soar; nor that a Democratic administration would become embroiled in a protracted war in Vietnam, critically constricting the ability of the federal government to finance a war on poverty; nor that black urban violence would be followed by a political and social revolution among white youths—protesting the draft, challenging the escalation of the Vietnam war, initiating a new liberalization in sexual mores and in drug use, threatening the most entrenched traditions of the middle class—and breaking, by 1968, Johnson's control of the Democratic party; nor that by the early 1970s the national economy would abruptly cease to follow its post-war course of steadily increasing prosperity.

None of this could be foreseen in 1964, and the election that year was widely read as a decisive endorsement by the voting public of the commitment of the Democratic Party to racial liberalism. The election had placed Johnson, the driving force behind the Civil Rights Act, against Goldwater, the arch-conservative, free-market avatar of an ascendant right-wing movement that had taken over control of the GOP presidential nomination process.

Just as Johnson had firmly aligned the Democratic party with the cause of civil rights, Goldwater represented a geographical and ideological shift for the Republican party. This shift was not only toward a new brand of sun-belt conservatism, but also toward an abandonment of the party's historical commitment to equality for blacks, a commitment dating back to the GOP of Abraham Lincoln, abolitionism, and the Civil War, and a commitment that had produced 30 percent black support for Eisenhower nationally as recently as 1956.

Goldwater, one of only eight Republican senators to cast his vote against the 1964 Civil Rights Act and representing a new strand of racial conservatism within the GOP, was crushed by Johnson. For Johnson, the November landslide signaled that the country was prepared to support a momentous expansion of the liberal welfare and regulatory state—in the form of a package of legislation known collectively as the "War on Poverty" and the "Great Society." With the Civil Rights Act and the Economic Opportunity Act already on the books in 1964, Johnson pushed through Congress a legislative agenda tilted toward the poor and toward blacks: the 1965 Voting Rights Act, Medicaid, model cities, rent supplements, and the Elementary and Secondary Education Act—legislation with significant redistributive impact, in economic as well as in broader social terms.

————

In the liberal, pro–civil rights atmosphere of 1964, the right-wing strategy of the Goldwater campaign was a short-term disaster. The conservative movement behind the Goldwater campaign, however, had in fact, succeeded at a level not immediately apparent to the public—by seizing control of the presidential nominating wing of the Republican Party in a revolution which placed the GOP in an optimal position to capitalize on the abrupt shift in public opinion that overtook the nation during the next four years.

The Draft Goldwater Committee used "concepts and language so harsh that they were unfit for the day-to-day operations or dialogue of American politics," wrote columnist Robert Novak (who later became a leading advocate of conservatism,) in 1964.[8] In fact, within just four years, the concepts and language of the failed 1964 Republican campaign became publicly accepted GOP strategy. The essential tactics devised by conservatives in the early plans to win in 1964 were, according to Novak:

> Policy A: Soft-pedal civil rights. While stopping short of actually endorsing racial segregation, forget all the sentimental tradition of the party of Lincoln. Because the Negro and Jewish votes are irrevocably tied to the Democrats anyway, this agnostic racial policy won't lose votes among the groups most sensitive to Negro rights. But it might work wonders in attracting white

southerners into the Republican Party, joining white Protestants in other sections of the country as hard-core Republicans. Policy B: Assume a vigorously strong anti-Communist line. . . . This wouldn't lose many votes among white Protestants and might snatch enough Catholic voters away from the Democratic Party to cut down Democratic margins in the big cities. Policy C: Except for the civil rights question, stick to orthodox Republicanism on domestic issues.[9]

The Goldwater movement irretrievably changed the structure of the Republican presidential nomination process, and in doing so, permanently changed the party. The campaign demonstrated 1) that conservatism provided an ideological mechanism for the Republican party to appeal to whites opposed to racial integration, without the liability of being labeled racist; and 2) that race could be used to break the economic class base of the New Deal Coalition among white voters, forcing an ideological shift to the right among a group once deeply committed to the redistributive and progressive economic agenda of the New Deal.

Perhaps most important, the Goldwater campaign served as the vehicle for an ideological revolution within the Republican party. This intraparty revolution ended the domination of the pro–civil rights, northeastern wing over the presidential selection process, and thus placed the GOP in position to capitalize on the white reaction that, in the second half of the 1960s, materialized in the North as well as the South. In 1964, however, evidence of these achievements was still concentrated in the Deep South, where its larger significance went largely unrecognized.

Goldwater ran in 1964 as an ideologically doctrinaire conservative, calling for the sale of the Tennessee Valley Authority, the evisceration of the Rural Electrification Administration, a voluntary system of Social Security, and the elimination of farm subsidies. None of these principled stands on the ideological right won him any states. In fact, in those states he did carry, each one of the government programs Goldwater sought to overturn had substantial, if not overwhelming, majority support.

There was, in reality, only one issue that permitted Goldwater to carry five states in addition to his home state of Arizona: civil rights. Goldwater declared himself personally opposed to segregation, but even more deeply opposed on principle to federal intervention to end segregation. "[I]t is wise and just for Negro children to attend the same schools as whites," Goldwater wrote in 1960, but, he added, "the federal Constitution does *not* require the States to maintain racially mixed schools. Despite the recent holding of the Supreme Court, I am firmly convinced—not only that integrated schools are not required—but that the Constitution does not permit any interference whatsoever by the federal government in the field of education."[10] In 1964, Goldwater cast his Senate vote against the Civil Rights Act.

For the white voters of the deep South, Goldwater's personal opposition to segregation was far less important than the public policies on race that grew out of his conservatism. Those southern voters responded by making Goldwater the first Republican since Reconstruction to carry the states most deeply opposed to integration: Mississippi, 87.1 percent; Alabama, 69.5 percent, South Carolina, 58.9 percent; Louisiana, 56.8 percent; and Georgia, 54.1 percent.[11]

Goldwater's success demonstrated that conservative ideology provided a new avenue for the Republican party into the South, an avenue that permitted the GOP to carry the most anti-black electorate in the nation without facing public condemnation. For a substantial segment of the white South, conservatism became a cloak with which to protect racial segregation.

At the same time, in a development that would soon have national relevance, Goldwater demonstrated that the socioeconomic class structure of the New Deal alignment in the deep South could be fractured by the issue of race. In the poorest white neighborhoods of Birmingham, the Republican vote shot up from 49 to 76 percent between 1960 and 1964; in Macon, Georgia, from 36 to 71 percent; in Atlanta, from 36 to 58 percent; in Montgomery, from 45 to 73 percent; in Charleston, South Carolina, from 57 to 82 percent. In these cities, the vote among the lowest income whites, which had been 22 percentage points more Democratic than in the most affluent white precincts in 1960, became virtually indistinguishable from the vote in upscale white neighborhoods in 1964.[12]

Detailed surveys conducted by the University of Michigan's Survey Research Center (SRC) suggest that these changes in class voting patterns were significant and of lasting ideological importance. The SRC data suggest that the issue of race actually produced an *ideological* conversion of poor southern whites from a deeply held economic liberalism to economic conservatism.

Although hostile to blacks, poor southern whites in the pre–civil rights period were among the nation's most liberal constituencies on non-racial economic issues, supportive of government intervention in behalf of full employment, improved education, and low-cost medical care. On these non-racial issues, the liberalism of poor white southerners in the 1950s was exceeded only by the nation's two most left-leaning constituencies, blacks and Jews, while such groups as Catholics, upper-status southern whites, rich and poor northern white Protestants, and border state whites were all more conservative.[13]

By the early 1970s, poor southern whites had moved decisively to the right on these economic issues, becoming more conservative than Catholics, border state whites, and middle and lower-status white northern Protestants. On the basic issue of government intervention to protect the less well-off, poor southern whites by the 1970s had become as conservative as upscale northern white Protestants, a key Republican constituency.[14] Those surveyed were native white southerners; the ideological shift did not result from an infusion of conservatism through migration from the Republican North. Southern whites had begun to link federal economic intervention with federal intervention in behalf of blacks. For native white southerners, economic liberalism became racial liberalism.

Without the underlying issue of race, the Goldwater movement would have been unable to alter fundamentally the structure of the Republican presidential nomination process, and in doing so, to transform the Republican party. The growing commitment of the Democratic party to civil rights under Kennedy and Johnson produced white defections to the GOP throughout the South, defections that were critical to the conservative take-over of the moribund Republican party structure in that region. Even more important, without race, the Goldwater campaign would have won at best only Arizona (which Goldwater took by a meager 4,782 votes out of 480,770 cast), and the conservative revolution would have been irretrievably discredited.

For the architects of the conservative revolution within the GOP, the southern reaction to the civil rights movement was a fortuitous and unplanned development. Like Goldwater himself, the men who organized the takeover of the GOP were conservative ideologues. Determined believers in free enterprise, enemies of big government, opponents of organized labor, fervent anti-communists, critics of domestic spending, and advocates of a strong military, these men had not entered politics because of racial issues. The thirty-two prosperous businessmen, lawyers, small-town newspaper publishers, oilmen, and bankers who met in 1961 to form a right-wing cadre—working under the direction of New York political consultant F. Clifton White—were determined to purge the Republican party of liberal influence. "[I]t was nothing less than a revolution that White and his colleagues were planning—the seizure of control of the Republican party by brand-new forces, based in the Midwest, the South, and the West rather than in the East and dedicated to the fast-growing cause of conservatism rather than to either liberalism or that pusillanimous cop-out called moderation," wrote William Rusher, publisher of the *National Review,* member of the inner core of Goldwater strategists, and one of the founding members of the emerging right-wing cadre.[15]

It was the civil rights movement, however, that gave the conservative insurgency a wider focus, a broader target, and an enlarged constituency. On a number of complementary fronts, the civil rights revolution interacted with the conservative movement to strengthen the right-wing drive within the GOP. The first was to provide the manpower for the takeover of the weak southern Republican party organizations of the early 1960s. As the ties of the national Democratic party to the drive for black equality grew stronger, members of the southern Bourbon elite, once dominant in the local, segregationist, Democratic party, began to leave in droves to create what amounted to a white Republican party.8

Evidence that the Goldwater drive was mobilizing a new breed of Republican began to surface at party gatherings. At the 1963 Republican National Committee meeting in Denver, northern Republican leaders, proud of their party's ties to Abraham Lincoln and the emancipation of the slaves midway through the Civil War, were stunned to hear southern chairman carrying on "boisterous conversation about "niggers" and "nigger lovers," " wrote columnist Novak in his book, *The Agony of the GOP 1964*. At the decisively pro-Goldwater 1963 convention of Young Republicans in San Francisco, there was, according to Novak, "no doubt [the] unabashed hostility toward the Negro rights movement was fully shared by the overwhelming majority of the convention delegates. In the cocktail lounges at the Sheraton-Palace, delegates from North and South talked with a single voice on the race question. . . . For the Young Republicans at San Francisco, their party was now a White Man's Party."[16]

In Memphis, Tennessee, at the same time, conservative forces wrested control of the GOP party structure from George Washington Lee, a local black leader who ran the Lincoln League, a virtually all-black local Republican party. "In about the early '60s [we] started what was called the Republican Association. Actually it was a white Republican party," recounted Jack Craddock, a conservative activist who later became Shelby County, Tennessee, GOP chairman. When the Goldwater movement was under full steam, in 1963 and 1964, "there was a real groundswell. People began to come in. We got ready to re-organize the party in late '63 or early '64. We literally had precinct caucuses in all the white precincts." Outnumbered when the Memphis party caucused, Lee took the fight all the way to the convention in San Francisco where he was voted down. "We loved it because it was all on TV. They seated our delegates. Lee sort of went fishing after that," Craddock said. "That's when the party came around."[17]

The leader of the southern drive to nominate Goldwater, Wirt A. Yerger, Jr., chairman of the Mississippi Republican party, was explicit in his goals for the creation of a competitive, two-party system in the South. The "overwhelming majority of Negroes are Democrats and could promise a bloc vote to Democratic candidates in Democratic primaries much more easily than they could make such an arrangement in a bi-partisan election," Yerger wrote in 1964 in *The Rebel Magazine,* the weekly publication of the Mississippi GOP.[18] Yerger, in a March 11, 1964, memorandum to key Republican leaders, warned that "various civil rights [leaders], leftists and minority groups are registering several hundred voters daily in Mississippi while white conservatives stand by." To counter this threat, Yerger announced that "your Mississippi Republican party is planning a white conservative voter registration campaign.... If we want responsible conservative government in Mississippi, unregistered white conservatives must register and vote."[19]

The infusion of conservative white support into the southern Republican party organization functioned, in turn, to make the national party receptive to the white reaction to civil rights that began to emerge in force outside of the South within a year of the 1964 election. In contrast to the 1960 Republican convention, which approved a strong civil rights plank, the 1964 GOP convention decisively rejected, by a vote of 897 to 409, an attempt to include in the party platform a strong stand in favor of civil rights.

Although Goldwater suffered one of the worst defeats in the nation's history, not all of his backers were downcast in the aftermath of the election. In South Carolina, where conservatives had demonstrated that they could break the Democratic lock on the deep South, "great rejoicing went on in the Thurmond ranks that election night," recalled Senator Strom Thurmond's political advisor, Harry S. Dent, the man who would go on to become a principal architect of Richard Nixon's southern strategy. "In the next two years, the seeds of the Republican Southern Strategy began to sprout and grow," Dent wrote. "The tree was bearing fruit. We South Carolina Republicans were now getting ready for the big coup—the White House—with this new Southern Strategy."[20]

William Rusher, in a retrospective examination of the developments that followed upon the 1964 election, wrote:

> It may seem perverse, and perhaps it is, to speak of a 'new majority' stirring in the immediate wake of a defeat as disastrous as Goldwater's was in 1964. And yet there seems no other way to describe what was happening on the American right in the years 1965–68.[21]

---

The civil rights movement created, and was created by, a broader civil rights revolution that, over the four post-World War II decades, introduced into every aspect of American life racial, ethnic, cultural, and religious minorities that had once been relegated to the margins of American society. The expansion by the federal courts of the civil rights agenda—an agenda for which political credit, as well as responsibility, fell heavily on the Democratic party—was only one aspect of the much *broader* agenda-setting role of the federal government. The Supreme Court of the 1960s and early 1970s, responding in part to the liberal and human rights–oriented climate of opinion emerging in the industrialized Western nations, effectively recast liberalism to include an even larger rights revolution. This revolution went beyond questions of race or ethnicity or faith; it was a revolution that sought new civil and citizenship rights for a range of previously stigmatized groups, groups often with few *political* supporters: criminal defendants, atheists, prisoners, homosexuals, the mentally ill, illegal aliens, publishers of pornography, and others. This revolution forced into the political arena such issues as school prayer, sexual liberation, criminal rights, abortion, deinstitutionalization, drug use, and prison reform.

Civil rights for blacks were won concomitantly with civil and human rights for other previously outcast and unprotected groups. In a series of decisions from 1957 to 1966, the Supreme Court found criminal defendants, many of them poor and black—and some clearly guilty—entitled to a new range of fundamental constitutional protections and rights. These included protections against illegally obtained evidence *(Mapp v. Ohio)* and against self-incrimination *(Malloy v. Hogan, Miranda v. Arizona);* and granted defendants the right to counsel *(Gideon v. Wainwright, Escobedo v. Illinois),* to silence *(Miranda),* to due process *(Pointer v. Texas),* and to a speedy trial *(Mallory v. United States).*

At the same time, as the Supreme Court was pioneering a spectrum of new rights, it was removing itself—and the state—as the bulwark and guardian of what would come to be called "traditional values." In 1962, in *Engel v. Vitale,* the Court barred prayer from the public schools. In 1962, in *Manual Enterprises v. Day,* the Court made prosecution of obscenity increasingly difficult, requiring that such material violate "community standards of decency"; in 1964, in *Jacobellis v. Ohio,* the Court made obscenity prosecution still more difficult, requiring proof that such material be "utterly without redeeming social importance." In 1965, in *Griswold v. Connecticut,* the Court handed down a decision recognizing a right to sexual privacy, legalizing the sale of contraceptive devices, and clearing the way for the widespread distribution of the recently invented birth control pill.

Just as the Supreme Court was issuing opinions provocative to socially and culturally conservative voters, and destabilizing to traditional power relations, it was also handing down decisions that dramatically weakened the political power of rural counties, a bastion of social conservatism. In *Baker v. Carr* (1962), and in a series of subsequent decisions, the Court instituted a major expansion of judicial authority over what had been legislative prerogative, ruling that the previously independent authority of state legislatures to draw their own districts was subject to strict "one-man, one-vote" standards.

While altering the balance of power between urban and rural constituencies, the Supreme Court granted new license to newspapers and television to adopt adversarial journalistic stands toward public officials and towards local power structures. The media, which during the years of civil rights protest came to be seen increasingly as siding with the forces of insurgency, gained new authority to scrutinize and criticize public officials, as the Court, in *The New York Times Co. v. Sullivan* in 1964, established the standard of so-called "actual malice"—independent of truth or falsehood—in cases seeking to collect damages for the libel of public figures.

The Court as a driving force in the promulgation of an expanded rights-oriented liberalism reached the culmination of its political influence in two cases of the early 1970s: asserting, in 1972, the preeminence of the federal government by overturning in *Furman v. Georgia* state capital-punishment laws; and ruling illegal, in *Roe v. Wade* in 1973, all state prohibitions against abortion. It was the decision in *Roe* that led over the next fifteen years to the mobilization behind the Republican party of millions of fundamentalist and evangelical Christians voters.

The Supreme Court of the 1960s and 1970s became, in effect, a dynamic force, thrusting a network of highly controversial issues to the forefront of the political agenda. In doing so, the Court placed the Democratic party in an increasingly ambiguous position. Largely through its commitment to civil rights—of which the rights of blacks were the primary focus—the Democratic party became the defender of an expanded network of broader rights established in a sequence of far-reaching decisions by the federal bench.

Unlike the original civil rights movement, which resulted in the full-scale conversion of blacks to the Democratic party, the rulings of the Supreme Court in behalf of defendants' rights and abortion rights—and against school prayer and the death penalty—functioned to mobilize many more citizen activists on the conservative than on the liberal side of these divisive issues. The Court-led agenda in the long run, while providing overdue rights to large numbers of disfranchised citizens, contained significant costs for the national Democratic party, and became a major mobilizing tool for an ascendant Republican party.

# 3
## After 1964:
### The Fraying Consensus

IN the immediate aftermath of the 1964 election, a majority of American voters had appeared ready to repudiate the ideology of the Goldwater wing of the Republican party, and to proceed to the second stage of a liberal revolution: to move government beyond what had been achieved by the New Deal, toward genuine equal opportunity for blacks, Hispanics, and other minorities by conducting a major assault on poverty in behalf of a more equitable, color-blind system of economic distribution.

The civil rights movement, under the leadership of Martin Luther King, Jr., picked up momentum, riveting public attention throughout the first half of 1965 as television news broadcasts showed Alabama state troopers beating nonviolent demonstrators who sought the right to vote, culminating in the "Bloody Sunday" police clubbing of blacks at the Edmund Pettus bridge in Selma. Lyndon Johnson, backed by the strongest Democratic majorities in Congress in twenty-five years, won approval of the most substantial expansion of the federal government for the poor and the black in the nation's history. The 1964 election was widely read as a decisive repudiation by the voting majority of the conservative opposition to civil rights—and, to a considerable degree, as a repudiation of the whole conservative agenda.

Throughout 1965, the public responded with overwhelming support for the Democratic party and for Johnson's Great Society. Pollster Lou Harris found that voters approved of every major element of the Johnson program by overwhelming margins, including voting rights for blacks, federal aid to education, and medical care for the aged. The lowest ap-

47

proval level was given to the antipoverty program, which was still backed by an impressive margin: 73–27. The Harris and Gallup polls found Johnson in late 1965 with approval ratings of 66 and 67 percent respectively.[1]

To most outward appearances, the civil rights movement had injected new life into liberalism and into the Democratic party, providing additional justification for the forceful use of the federal government to address both racial injustice and poverty.

An ascendent liberalism reached its postwar zenith on August 5, 1965, when Johr.son signed into law the Voting Rights Act. The legislation barred literacy tests in the deep South, provided for the appointment of federal examiners to force registration of qualified voters in recalcitrant communities, required preclearance of all voting-law changes in most of the South, and established penalties of up to five years in jail for violators. Within a year, exclusive white control of elections was broken. "[The slaves] came in darkness and they came in chains," Johnson declared at the signing ceremony. "Today we strike away the last major shackle of those fierce and ancient bonds."[2]

Six days later, on August 11, rioting broke out in the Watts section of Los Angeles, ignited when a crowd gathered to protest the arrest of a drunken driver. Five days of violent, televised, disorder opened the first major fissure in the consensus behind Democratic racial liberalism. Watts provided unmistakable evidence that the drive to achieve black equality would have tremendous costs as well as tremendous rewards. Watts forced acknowledgment of a new reality: that passage of civil rights legislation was not adequate to either assuage black anger, nor to produce the relatively trouble-free integration of the races that had been anticipated by many liberals.

While providing an impetus for increased federal spending targeted at poor blacks—in the hope of restoring social order—Watts was the first of a chain of events that would push a substantial segment of the American electorate to the right, producing nearly a decade of intense ideological, social, and racial conflict. This chain of events included:

- ghetto riots;
- the emergence of a separatist black power movement;
- the abrupt rise in rates of black crime and illegitimacy;
- the shift of civil rights protests to the North, where traditionally Democratic voters became polarized on issues of busing and open housing;
- an uprising among the nation's college-educated youth that challenged the Vietnam War, conventions of academic discipline, and traditional restrictions surrounding sex and drugs;

• the emerging women's movement and the broader rights revolution;
• the surfacing of white backlash as a powerful political force;
• the fostering of conflict by the War on Poverty between white elected officials and black protest leaders;
• an unprecedented surge in the number of applicants for welfare;
• intensified demands by blacks for jobs in two besieged institutions under the control of white Democrats—the labor unions and City Hall.

Liberalism had unleashed forces that its leaders could neither control nor keep within the confines of traditional political negotiation, and the once-dominant, left-center coalition began to crack. The Republican party, seen by many as verging on extinction after the 1964 election, was positioned to capitalize on the sudden divisions in the opposition party and among its supporters.

Goldwater had demonstrated, in the case of poor southern whites, how it was possible to use race to win the loyalty of a once-firmly Democratic, economically liberal constituency. With moderation, the same strategy would prove to have national applicability, and would serve to establish one of the pillars of Republican advantage in presidential elections, an advantage that would last for at least two decades.

———

Evidence that the alliance of the Democratic party with the civil rights movement carried serious political liabilities had begun to emerge before the outbreak of the Watts riot. White hostility in the North to the race revolution was already making itself felt. Alabama Governor George Wallace, who would become a major force in the presidential elections of 1968 and 1972, ran in 1964 as a segregationist in three northern and border state Democratic primaries, winning 34 percent of the vote in Wisconsin, 30 percent in Indiana, and 45 percent in Maryland. California voters in the same year decisively rejected a fair housing referendum that had been passed by the state legislature. At the same time, evidence that moderate black leaders could not contain the civil rights revolution—that it would breach the confines of the original peaceful, nonviolent movement—had already begun to accumulate. During the summer of 1964, violent rioting broke out in a number of northern cities, including Harlem and Bedford-Stuyvesant in New York City, Rochester, Philadelphia, and Patterson and Elizabeth in New Jersey.[3]

It was the violence in Watts, however, that was the most threatening. Blacks, throwing rocks and bottles at police, shouted "Burn, Baby, Burn!" for four days, as television viewers across the nation watched film clips of men, women, and children walking through broken plate-glass windows in department, grocery, and liquor stores, carrying out all they could handle. By August 16, after the National Guard had been called in and order slowly restored, there were 34 dead—some at the hands of the police and National Guard—1,072 injured, 977 buildings damaged or destroyed, and 4,000 arrests. Even Martin Luther King, Jr., who had been leading black protests since the Montgomery bus boycott in 1955, was unprepared for Watts. Stunned by the scope of anger among rioters, and by their perception that the civil rights movement had been largely irrelevant to improving conditions in the ghetto, King "was absolutely undone" after visiting Watts, his close associate, Bayard Rustin, recalled.[4]

Watts undermined the liberal premise behind civil rights legislation and behind the relatively modest redirection of federal resources toward the nation's poorest communities. Rather than producing the peaceful incorporation and assimilation of blacks into white-dominated society, Watts suggested that the civil rights movement had functioned, in the nation's ghettos, to bring to the surface grievances so intense that they found expression only in violence.

"The riot experience seems to have been associated with increased pride in the minds of many of the participants," the Kerner Commission, appointed in 1968 by President Johnson to investigate the riots, concluded on the basis of later surveys of rioters in Detroit and Newark. A participant in the Detroit riot told Kerner Commission interviewers, "I was feeling proud, man, at the fact that I was a Negro. I felt I was a first-class citizen. I didn't feel ashamed of my race because of what they did." Seventy-two percent of the riot participants surveyed by the commission said they agreed with the statement, "Sometimes I hate white people."[5]

Liberal reformers, white and black, had envisaged the liberation of black America through the enactment of legislation placing the full force of the federal government behind the principle of equal opportunity. These reformers had envisioned rapid progress out of poverty for blacks through the creation of well-intentioned programs providing job counseling, summer employment, and preschool training—programs combined with a modest degree of community control to encourage political empowerment. Watts demonstrated that the concentration of blacks into ghettos with astronomical rates of poverty, that the subjugation of an entire race in a country claiming to be founded on democratic principle, that the difficulties facing blacks in labor market competition, and that the build-up of deep hostility between white police and black citizens, had produced a combustible mixture. Upon the official—but for many blacks, cruelly irrelevant—renunciation of legal segregation, that mixture was as likely to ignite into an explosion as it was to give rise to a burst of middle-class achievement.

Watts was followed by a succession of violent outbursts over the next three years. "The events of 1966 made it appear that domestic turmoil had become part of the American scene," wrote the authors of the Kerner Report. That year, by official count, there were forty-three disorders and riots, including three days of burning, shooting, and looting in Chicago that left three blacks dead, and four nights of violence in the Hough section of Cleveland that left four blacks dead.[6] The next year, urban rioting intensified. In 1967, there were 164 disorders, eight of them ranked as "major" by the Kerner Commission on the grounds that they involved "multiple fires, intensive looting, and reports of sniping; violence lasting more than two days; sizeable crowds; and use of National Guard or federal forces as well as other control forces."[7] Over 83 people were killed, 90 percent of them blacks, 10 percent police, fire, and other public officials. More than half of the deaths were in two cities, Detroit (43) and Newark (23).[8] For the four-year period from 1964 to 1968, there was an estimated total of 329 significant outbreaks of violence in 257 cities.[9]

For proponents of the civil rights movement, the riots were devastating. Gary Orfield, a liberal political scientist at the University of Chicago wrote:

> Advocates of an integrated society found themselves without a convincing program and trapped between growing racial polarization, both within the left of the civil rights movement and within moderate to conservative white leadership. The political problem was severe. No administration since Lincoln's had so invested its political capital in black progress, and none had made more progress. . . . Yet, though there had been no serious black riots since World War II, a series of huge upheavals was beginning in the cities. Social scientists could offer theories about the way increasing opportunities and belief in the possibility of change triggered protests, but the political advantage went to conservatives, who could attack black leaders and denounce social programs as unsuccessful and counterproductive. Liberals could not outbid the conservatives in promising stronger police action, and they had no way to explain the need for basic changes in the ghetto system.[10]

For the Republican party, the riots provided the opportunity to change the direction of the national debate by initiating a full-scale assault on liberal social policies. "How long are we going to abdicate law and order—the backbone of any civilization—in favor of a soft social theory that the man who heaves a brick through your window or tosses a firebomb into your car is simply the misunderstood and underprivileged product of a broken home?" House Republican Leader—and future president—Gerald Ford of Michigan asked on September 20, 1966, at the Illinois State Fair.[11]

"The image of the Negro in 1966 was no longer that of the praying, long-suffering nonviolent victim of southern sheriffs; it was a defiant young hoodlum shouting 'black power' and hurling 'Molotov cocktails' in an urban slum," wrote James L. Sundquist, a liberal political scientist who worked for both presidents Kennedy and Johnson.[12]

---

The Democratic party was caught in a vise, a vise that would tighten around the party and around liberalism as the decade wore on. From 1960 to 1966, when the population grew by less than 10 percent, the number of crimes grew by more than 60 percent; from 1966 to 1971, the number of crimes grew by 83 percent.[13] According to data from the Uniform Crime Reports released by the Department of Justice and analyzed by the National Academy of Sciences, a disproportionate share of the increase in crime was committed by blacks, particularly crimes of violence. At the extreme, the black arrest rate on homicide charges increased by over 130 percent from 1960 to 1970, with the gap between black and white arrest rates steadily widening through the decade.[14] In the same period, the percentages of births to unmarried women began to rapidly escalate in the black community, going from 21.6 percent in 1960 to 34.9 percent in 1970, while for whites the percentages grew from 2.3 to 5.7.[15]

The crime and illegitimacy figures were clear warnings, not only that the process of incorporating blacks into mainstream society would be far more difficult and costly than anticipated by black leaders and white liberals, but also that the successful entry of significant numbers of blacks into the middle class was being accompanied by the growth of a predominately black underclass, where the problems associated with poverty were worsening, rather than improving. For the Democratic party, the underclass would prove to be a major political liability, providing critics of liberalism with highly visible and seemingly concrete evidence of the failure of federal intervention. At the same time, the left wing of the Democratic party, white and black, was reluctant to address the issues of crime, illegitimacy, drug use, joblessness, and welfare dependency, and effectively ceded these issues to the political right.

As liberalism came under siege in the second half of the 1960s, many on the left developed a dangerous intellectual intolerance. This intolerance grew out of number of factors. Strategically, a shift in the debate to consideration of such issues as illegitimacy and welfare dependency posed the danger to the left of shifting attention from white responsibility for the history and consequences of discrimination and slavery, to placing blame and responsibility on the black community itself, blame focused on the so-called "culture of poverty." The intellectual defensiveness of the left was spurred by a fear of information damaging to liberal goals, by a reluctance to further stigmatize blacks who were just emerging from centuries of legal oppression, by an unwillingness to raise issues straining the fragile liberal coalition, by a sympathy for those blacks who had endured segregation and who had prevailed, and by the confusion growing out of the upheaval in moral values among the white middle and upper-middle class.

The refusal to confront all the complex origins of social disorder amounted to a refusal to take into account, and to make political adjustments for, the liabilities as well as the rewards of liberal, rights-oriented legislative and regulatory initiatives. The Democratic party was seriously damaged by its own timidity, not only in the party's struggle to effect racial integration, but in a host of other competitive arenas. Few examples demonstrate the long-range destructiveness of ignorance better than the response of liberals and the Democratic party to warnings of the economic and social consequences of weakening family structure among poor blacks.

In mid-summer 1965, as the Voting Rights Act moved toward congressional approval, the Johnson administration was exploring ways to expand the scope of its role in implementing the civil rights agenda. In a June 4 speech at Howard University, Lyndon Johnson declared: "You do not take a person who, for years, has been hobbled by chains and liberate him, bring him to the starting line of a race and then say, 'you are free to compete with all the others,' and still justly believe that you have been completely fair." Central to the administration strategy was the development of proposals to help strengthen the black family structure: "Perhaps most important—its influence radiating to every part of life—is the breakdown of the Negro family structure. . . . It flows from the long years of degradation and discrimination, which have attacked [the Negro's] dignity and assaulted his ability to provide for his family," Johnson told the Howard graduating class of 1965.[16]

The principal architect of the Howard speech was future senator Daniel Patrick Moynihan of New York, then an assistant secretary in the Department of Labor. Moynihan had developed the analysis underlying the Howard speech in "The Negro Family: The Case for National Action"—a paper that would become known as "The Moynihan Report." The report not only echoed the reasoning of a long line of black historical sociologists, from W.E.B. Du Bois to E. Franklin Frazier,[17] but presaged many of the findings of William Julius Wilson's major 1987 study, *The Truly Disadvantaged*,[18] and anticipated much of the contemporary debate on the underclass.

When the Moynihan Report was released to the public in August 1965, however, it provoked a hostile outcry from black leaders, intellectuals, and from white liberals. The focus of their anger was on Moynihan's contention that, "At the heart of the deterioration of the fabric of Negro society is the deterioration of the Negro family. It is the fundamental source of the weakness of the Negro community at the present time approaching complete breakdown." Moynihan saw black male unemployment rates, which had been at "disaster levels for 35 years," as the central cause of the breakdown of black families. His goal was to initiate a massive federal drive to expand job opportunities as the next step in the civil rights struggle, so that "the distribution of success and failure within one group [would be] roughly comparable to that within other groups. . . . This is what ethnic politics are all about in America, and in the main the Negro American demands are being put forward in this now traditional and established framework."[19]

It was Moynihan's suggestion that many poor black families were caught in a "tangle of pathology", however, that brought intense pressure from blacks and from the white left to halt further debate on the black family structure. James Farmer, head of the Congress of Racial Equality (CORE), charged that the Moynihan Report "provides the fuel for a new racism. It succeeds in taking the real tragedy of black poverty and serving it up as an essentially salacious 'discovery' suggesting that Negro mental health should be the first order of business in a civil rights revolution."[20]

William Ryan, a white psychologist writing in *The Nation*, denounced the Moynihan Report in scathing terms as a form of intellectual "savage discovery": "The implicit point is that Negroes tolerate promiscuity, illegitimacy, one-parent families, welfare dependency, and everything else that is supposed to follow. . . . The all-time favorite 'savage' is the promiscuous mother who produces a litter of illegitimate brats in order to profit from AFDC."[21]

Writing twenty-two years after the initial publication of the Moynihan Report, William Julius Wilson, a black sociologist at the University of Chicago, pointed out in *The Truly Disadvantaged* that in the early and mid-1960s, some of the nation's best students of poverty, black and white, were beginning to "show the connection between the economic and social environment into which many blacks are born and the creation of patterns of behavior that, in [black sociologist Kenneth B.] Clark's words, frequently amounted to 'self-perpetuating pathology.' Why have scholars [since then] tended to shy away from this line of research? One reason has to do with the vitriolic attack by many blacks and liberals against Moynihan. . . . The harsh reception accorded 'The Negro Family' undoubtedly dissuaded many social scientists from following in Moynihan's footsteps." If liberal scholars were frightened away from examination of the interrelationships between race, class, family structure, and poverty "conservative thinkers were not so inhibited," Wilson noted.[22]

In the absence of a vital liberal debate on, and an analysis of, the relevance of evolving black family structures, conservative social strategies, by the early 1980s, came to dominate the formation of domestic public policy. Unchallenged by the Democratic party or by liberalism in the debate on crime, illegitimacy, narcotics abuse, lack of labor force participation, and rising welfare rates, the dominant conservative wing of the Republican party was free to adopt relatively clear-cut, politically appealing stands on a wide range of divisive issues, and to propel the public debate in a distinctly conservative direction.

———

The reluctance of liberalism and of the Democratic party to forthrightly acknowledge and address the interaction of crime, welfare dependency, joblessness, drug use, and illegitimacy with the larger questions of race and poverty reflected not only an aversion to grappling with deeply disturbing information, but compounded the political penalties the party would pay for its commitment to racial liberalism. Those penalties, in turn, would become more severe as the civil rights movement moved North.

By 1966, the civil rights revolution had expanded the scope of its goals beyond the borders of the South, and far beyond the issues of legal segregation and discrimination. The movement began to impinge not just on the segregationist and racist practices of southern whites, but on northern city dwellers and, to a lesser extent, on northern suburbanites.

For the Democratic party, the nationalization of the civil rights movement, together with rising public concern over violent crime, riots, drug trafficking, and the splintering of family life in the ghetto, was of critical importance. First, race was becoming fused in varying degrees with almost every social and economic issue on the domestic agenda. Secondly, race was becoming an integral element of partisanship. Before 1964, opinion polls show virtually no difference between the public perception of the Democratic party and the perception of the Republican party on race-related issues. Before 1964 the Democratic party was not seen as the home of racial liberalism nor was the Republican party seen as the home of racial conservatism. After 1964, all of this changed rapidly.

Comparing 1956 to 1968 poll data, Rutgers political scientist Gerald Pomper found:

The most striking change has occurred on racial issues. In 1956, there was no consensus on the parties' stands on the issues of school integration and fair employment. . . . and the Republicans were thought to favor civil rights as strongly as did the Democrats. By 1968, there was a startling reversal in this judgement. All partisan groups recognized the existence of different party positions on this issue, and all were convinced that the Democrats favor greater government action on civil rights than do Republicans.[23]

The meshing of race with partisanship was initially stronger for the Democratic party, which established its liberal racial identity as the party in power from 1960 to 1968. Through the campaign of 1968, and through administration policies once in office, Richard Nixon and his strategists accelerated public identification of the Republican party as the party of racial conservatism. John Petrocik of U.C.L.A. has charted changes in the public perception of the Democratic and Republican parties in the 1950s, in the mid-1960s, and in the 1970s. In the 1950s, Petrocik's analysis of the data shows that the public identified each party as close to the center on civil rights, with no noticeable difference on racial issues; by the mid-1960s, the Democrats had moved far over to the left on race, while the GOP remained close to the center; by the 1970s, the public placed each party at opposite extremes, with the Democrats on the left and the GOP well to the right.[24]

"[T]he American party system during the 1950s was organized around the [non-racial] economic welfare cleavage," Petrocik wrote. By the 1970s, "race conflict is the major new element in the party system agenda. . . . The most visible difference between the party coalitions that entered the turbulent 1960s and that exited in the middle of the 1970s is to be found in their new-found distinctiveness on race-related matters."[25]

———

The growing link between race and partisan allegiance tied the future of each party to the shifting contours of the civil rights movement; by 1966, every northern city with a substantial black population became a center in the evolving struggle for civil rights. In Massachusetts, on August 16, 1965, an alliance of blacks and suburban liberals won passage of legislation barring racial imbalance in state school systems, a measure that would pit white East and South Boston against black Roxbury in a battle over school busing which would last for more than a decade. A year later, in August 1966, a group of black public-housing tenants filed a suit charging that the Chicago Housing Authority assigned tenants and chose new building sites in a calculated effort to maintain residential segregation.[26]

At the federal level, there were early signs that pressure for school and housing integration would go far beyond the movement to repeal the legal apparatus of southern segregation. By 1967, prompted in part by southern charges of northern hypocrisy—as well as by influential southern members seeking to dilute federal interference—Congress directed the Department of Health, Education and Welfare (HEW) to assign half of its civil rights enforcement staff to the North. In February of the same year, the U.S. Commission on Civil Rights issued a report charging that racial isolation in public schools was increasing in large northern cities, and that this isolation was damaging the educational development of black children.[27]

By the end of 1967, it was clear that busing would soon become a weapon in the arsenal of the civil rights movement, and that busing was to be used in behalf of urban school integration—just as in the past busing had been used to implement segregation throughout much of the South. The courts and the powerful regulatory bureaucracies at HEW and at the Department of Justice were examining practices in northern school systems where residential housing patterns had created deeply rooted patterns of de facto segregation; those practices revealed the vulnerability of such systems to legal challenge. In 1968, the Supreme Court in *Green v. County School Board of New Kent County, Va.* effectively put an end to "freedom of choice" as the legal remedy to combat segregated school systems—a remedy that had put the burden of integration on students and their parents, who in theory were free to send white children to black schools and black children to white schools. "The [freedom of choice] plan has operated simply to burden children and their parents with a responsibility which [a prior court ruling] places squarely on the School Board," the Court wrote. School boards, the Court found, would henceforth "have the affirmative duty to take whatever steps might be necessary to convert to a unitary system in which racial discrimination would be eliminated root and branch." "Affirmative duty" frequently translated, over time, into busing.

In mid-1968, the Justice Department for the first time brought suits against northern cities, including suits against South Holland, a Chicago suburb, and Pasadena, California; by the end of the year, suits had been filed against Indianapolis, Tulsa, and East St. Louis.[28]

Northern opposition formed almost immediately as the drive towards school and residential integration in every section of the country picked up steam. In California, voters in 1964 had overwhelmingly rejected in a referendum fair housing legislation that had been passed by the legislature. In 1966, Martin Luther King shifted his attention from the South to the North, choosing Chicago as the target of a "freedom movement" to open up housing in the white ethnic communities on the northwest and southwest sides of the city, and in the all-white, working-class suburb of Cicero. "If we can break the system in Chicago, it can be broken anywhere in the country," King declared at an October 6, 1965, news conference. Nine months later, on August 5, 1966, King was hit in the head by a rock as he sought to lead 600 marchers through Chicago's Marquette Park where 4,000 whites chanted "We Want Martin Luther Coon" as they waved Confederate flags. "I think people from Mississippi ought to come to Chicago to learn how to hate," King declared. King suffered the worst defeat of his career in Chicago, where white resistance was far more effective than in the South.[29]

King's adversaries in Chicago were the generally Democratic, white, ethnic, working-class voters whose neighborhoods surrounded the city's expanding black ghetto. Throughout the 1960s, the national Democratic party was seen by key numbers of such voters as moving steadily towards an increasingly strong commitment to a liberal racial agenda, according to survey data collected by the University of Michigan's Survey Research Center (SRC).[30] The commitment of the Democratic party to racial liberalism was not shared by these white lower-income voters, a constituency in fact registering a growing opposition to civil rights.[31]

Just as the Goldwater campaign had revealed that the drive to achieve racial equality could break the class base of the New Deal alignment in the South, the civil rights movement in the North drove a wedge into the national Democratic coalition. As the movement shifted North, it began to undermine working-class support for the Democratic party in cities like Chicago, Boston, Detroit, and New York—just as it had in 1964 in the deep South.

———

Caught between conflicting pressures from traditional white Democrats, on the one hand, and from growing numbers of increasingly loyal and reliable black voters, on the other, the commitment of the national Democratic party to liberal racial policies came under attack from a different source altogether: the emergence of a radical left flank within the black leadership. This extremist wing of an emerging black leadership class sharply intensified white fears of organized violence and provided justification to those whites who opposed integration, allowing them to point out that their views were shared by certain prominent blacks.

In June 1966, Stokely Carmichael, newly elected president of the Student Nonviolent Coordinating Committee (SNCC), captured national attention when, during a demonstration in Greenwood, Mississippi, he led the chant "We want black power." It was the first time the phrase had been used at a civil rights demonstration. Young marchers shouted back, "Black Power," eclipsing the call for "Freedom Now" associated with Martin Luther King and the Southern Christian Leadership Conference (SCLC). Three months later, Carmichael wrote in *The New York Review of Books:* "Integration is a subterfuge for the maintenance of white supremacy. . . . [It] reinforces, among both black and white, the idea that 'white' is automatically better and 'black' is by definition inferior."[32]

In rapid succession, Huey Newton and Bobby Seale in October 1966, formed the Black Panthers in Oakland, California, organizing "black self-defense groups," armed with rifles and shotguns, "dedicated to defending our black community from racist police oppression and brutality," to patrol ghetto streets. A delegation of armed Panthers stalked onto the floor of the California State Assembly to protest pending gun control legislation, and their photographs made the front pages of newspapers across the country.[33]

---

As rioting broke out in desolate all-black ghettos in the summers of 1965 and 1966, as housing integration became a central legislative goal of the civil rights movement, and as the black power movement simultaneously gained prominence, northern white support for the civil rights movement began to erode. From 1962 through April 1965, decisive majorities of northern whites had endorsed the efforts of the Kennedy and Johnson administrations to press the cause of racial integration. In April 1965, 71 percent of those surveyed said the Johnson administration was "pushing racial integration" either "not fast enough" or "about right." Only 28 percent said "too fast." In August 1965, the month of the Watts riot, the "about right" and "not fast enough" responses fell to 64 percent, and those saying "too fast" rose to 36 percent. By September 1966, after riots and race-related disorders in Chicago, Cleveland, and forty-one other communities, the percentage of favorable responses had fallen to a minority of those surveyed, 48 percent, while those who said the administration was pushing too hard on civil rights had jumped to 52 percent.[34]

These poll findings were a modest warning of what the voters would do on election day. In the elections of 1966, "white backlash" became a central factor in northern as well as in southern politics, as the electorate made known its views. The results were devastating to the Democratic party. In the House of Representatives, the Republican party gained forty-seven seats, nullifying President Johnson's liberal majority. Twenty-four of the thirty-eight seats that the Democratic party had picked up in 1964 went back to the Republican party.

In the South, the GOP picked up thirteen House seats, six of them open seats, seven from Democratic incumbents. The distinguishing characteristic of all seven defeated southern Democratic incumbents was that each was a supporter of the Johnson administration's Great Society.[35] Eight governorships switched to the Republican party. In California, an outpouring of suburban white support for Ronald Reagan—who two years earlier had backed the referendum which killed the state's fair housing law—gave the former actor a margin of almost one million votes in his defeat of incumbent Governor Edmund G. Brown. In Florida, conservative Claude R. Kirk, Jr., became the first Republican governor since 1872.

The most revealing figures from the 1966 election, however, can be found by comparing 1960 and 1966 voting patterns in the Illinois U.S. Senate contest in the white wards of south and southwest Chicago—the hostile trenches of the civil rights battlefield. It was into these working-class Polish and Irish neighborhoods on the southern end of Chicago's bungalow belt that Martin Luther King had taken his drive for residential integration and had run into a stone wall of opposition. In 1960, before the civil rights movement reached Chicago, Senator Paul L. Douglas, a liberal Democrat and outspoken supporter of racial equality, had swept the state by a margin of 437,097 votes, carried by his massive 525,013 margin in Chicago, where he won forty-three of forty-five wards, including every white ward on the south side of the city.

In November 1966, after the King-led protests and a riot that left three dead, Douglas's support among white Chicago voters collapsed, as he lost to Republican Charles Percy by 422,302 votes statewide. Just over 80 percent of Douglas's margin of defeat can be attributed to the white voters of Chicago, where his margin fell by 339,303 votes. Douglas in 1966 lost nineteen Chicago wards, and won the overwhelmingly Democratic city by a paltry 185,710 votes. Douglas held his own in Chicago's heavily black wards, with his percentage rising in seven, falling in seven, and staying even in the other two. In the eight white ethnic wards in southwest and southeast Chicago—wards targeted by King's open-housing drive and abutting south Chicago's black ghetto—support for Douglas nosedived. In 1960, each one of these wards had voted Democratic, and together they had given Douglas a combined total of 87,151 more votes than his Republican opponent. In 1966, six of the eight wards voted Republican, giving Percy a cumulative 21,159 vote edge over Douglas. In other words, in just eight white wards of Chicago, Douglas lost a total of 108,310 votes between 1960 and 1966.[36]

The election figures in Chicago demonstrated that in communities experiencing severe racial tensions, for a candidate to be identified with the dominant liberal wing of the Democratic party had become a grave liability among white voters. Just as the poor southern whites who had been deeply loyal to the economic commitments of the New Deal Democratic party had voted for Goldwater when race became the central issue in 1964, substantial numbers of white working-class voters in Chicago abandoned their Democratic tradition under similar circumstances. Two years later, in 1968, the same six wards where Douglas's support had collapsed cast the highest percentages in the city for third-party candidate George C. Wallace. Insofar as these wards remained white into the 1980s, they provided Ronald Reagan with some of his strongest margins in the city. The Douglas-Percy election marked the emergence of what would become known in the 1980s as the "Reagan Democrat."

———

The Douglas-Percy Senate election was a contest between a liberal Democrat and a moderate Republican, a struggle in no way as polarized as the Johnson-Goldwater presidential fight. By 1966, however, voters had begun to make distinctions not just on the basis of individual candidates' records on racial issues, but on the basis of their party's records. In Congress, partisan voting patterns started to change radically in the mid-1960s, reinforcing the image of the national Democratic party as the home of racial liberalism and of the GOP as the home of racial conservatism, images that had first been partially established in 1964 at the presidential level.

The new congressional voting patterns represented a major shift for both parties. In votes on anti-lynching bills and other racial issues in the 1940s and 1950s, the GOP had been consistently more liberal than the Democratic party, and even through passage of the major civil rights bills—the Civil Rights Act of 1964 and the Voting Rights Act of 1965—the Republican party had provided stronger congressional margins of support than the Democratic party, which still had a strong southern segregationist wing. In the House vote on the 1964 bill, the GOP lined up 138 to 34, with 80 percent in favor and 20 percent opposed, while the Democrats were divided 156 to 96, a split of 62 percent to 38 percent. In the key Senate vote to cut off a filibuster, Democrats were split 44–23 in favor of the bill, or 66 to 34 percent, while the Republicans voted 27–6 to end the filibuster, an 82 percent to 18 percent split. Similarly, in votes on the Voting Rights Act, House Democrats were split 221–61 in favor, or 78 to 22 percent, and the GOP voted 112–24 in favor, or 82 to 18 percent; in the Senate, the Democrats voted 47–17 in favor, or 73 to 27 percent, and the GOP split 30–2 in favor, or 94 to 6 percent.

These votes, however, marked the end of two traditions: Republican allegiance to racial liberalism and the centrality of southern Democrats in fighting legislation seen as beneficial to blacks, a role that would be assumed by the GOP. The substantive content of racially significant legislation began, in addition, to change from a focus on civil rights to a focus on government-led redistributive efforts in behalf of blacks; in the process, Republican support for civil rights measures began to decline. The restructuring of the two parties around race-related issues became apparent in their votes on legislation that reached Congress in 1965 and 1966, measures as diverse as rent supplements, open housing, creation of the model cities program, a proposal to establish a rat eradication program, and approval of a new cabinet-level Department of Housing and Urban Development (HUD).

Rent supplements were among the most intensely debated initiatives of the Johnson administration. The program was seen in some quarters as a backdoor mechanism for promoting integration—giving blacks rent subsidies that could be used in any neighborhood.[37] In the key 208–202 House vote on the program, Republicans overwhelmingly opposed the subsidies, 130–4, as Democrats carried the measure, 204–72. In the Senate, almost exactly the same pattern emerged: Democrats voted 42–16 in favor of rent supplements, Republicans were opposed, 24–5. As would so often prove to be the case over the next twenty-five years, Republican free-market principles performed double duty: opposing government intervention in private markets and, consequently, opposing programs that had the effect of distributing benefits disproportionately to blacks.

A similar pattern of partisan voting emerged during congressional consideration of legislation creating the Model Cities program. Instead of southern Democrats taking the lead in opposing the legislation, Republican Representative Paul A. Fino of New York argued that the measure was a disguise to promote forced integration in the North. "If you vote for this measure," Fino said, "you are voting for forced busing, school pairing and [school] redistricting." House Republicans lined up 81–16 against the bill, Democrats 162–60 in favor. In the Senate, Democrats backed the measure, 43–10, while Republicans voted 17–10 against it.[38] In the next major battle over civil rights legislation, the 1966 drive to win approval of open housing legislation, House Republicans voted decisively against the measure, 86–50, while Democrats lined up in support by a margin of 172–104.

These trends in congressional voting were reinforced by the election results of 1964 and 1966, which had the effect of pushing the Republican party further to the right and pushing the Democratic party further to the left. The net result of both elections was, for the Republicans, to deplete the party's liberal ranks while strengthening its right, and, for the Democrats, to weaken the party's conservative faction while adding new members to its liberal wing. For the GOP, the movement toward the right both reflected and made the party more receptive to the conservative shift in public attitudes towards civil rights and the Great Society.

In 1964, the Republican party lost a total of forty-eight House seats and picked up ten, for a net loss of thirty-eight. The overwhelming majority of losses were seats held by Republicans who had voted for civil rights, so that most of the losses were absorbed by the moderate-liberal wing of the party. In contrast, seven of the ten seats the GOP gained were in the South, and all seven southern Republican freshmen were staunch conservative opponents of civil rights.

In the Senate, the GOP's moderate-to-liberal flank lost two votes in 1964 with the defeat of Senators J. Glenn Beall of Maryland and Kenneth Keating of New York, while ascendant Republican conservatives added two new members to their ranks with the election of former actor George Murphy as senator from California, and with the conversion of South Carolina Senator Strom Thurmond—the 1948 presidential nominee of the segregationist Dixiecrat party—from the Democratic to the Republican party.

The ideological-racial split between the two parties grew even wider after the 1966 election, when the GOP gained forty-seven seats in the House, many of them conservative, including ten new seats in the South, while the center-to-conservative base of the Democratic party was weakened.

These shifts in partisan and ideological strength in the House and Senate translated into increasingly polarized voting patterns on racial issues. Political scientists Edward Carmines and James Stimson, who analyzed roll call votes of both branches of Congress from 1945 to 1980, found that Republicans in the Senate were overwhelmingly more liberal on race issues than Democrats until 1958, when a sharp recession during the Eisenhower administration produced the defeat of ten generally pro–civil rights Republican senators, and their replacement by ten liberal Democrats. For the next six years, until 1964, the voting patterns of Democratic and Republican senators remained similar on race issues. After 1964, Democratic senators became steadily more liberal on matters of race, as southern Democrats were forced to accommodate black constituents enfranchised by the 1965 Voting Rights Act; Republican senators, in turn, moved to the right on race issues as moderates were replaced by conservatives.[39]

In the House, which experienced larger and more abrupt shifts in membership—the thirty-eight-seat Democratic pick-up in 1964, and the forty-seven-seat move back to the GOP in 1966—there was a sharper and more distinct change in the racial policies of the two parties. From the end of World War II to 1964, House Republicans were decisively to the left of House Democrats on issues of race. From 1964 to 1967, the two parties were roughly equal, but after 1967, the Republicans became decisively conservative and the Democrats decisively liberal.[40]

––––––

In the aftermath of the 1966 elections, racial conflict intensified as the conservative alliance between Republicans and southern Democrats on Capitol Hill gained strength and as black extremists gained prominence in the ghettos and in the media. With violence worsening on the streets, the liberal wing of the Democratic party, a majority within the party but no longer dominant in Congress, was caught between two adversaries, each of which had discovered that there was political capital to be made in challenge and confrontation. This situation is perhaps best captured by looking at a series of developments during the summer of 1967.

Through the spring and early summer of 1967, SNCC leaders Stokely Carmichael and H. Rap Brown adopted increasingly confrontational tactics in highly volatile circumstances. On June 15, Brown arrived in Cincinnati, where there had been four days of firebombings of stores and stoning of cars, with a list of twenty "demands," including one declaring that "at any meeting to settle grievances . . . any white proposal or white representative objected to by black representatives must be rejected automatically." Five days later, Carmichael appeared at a meeting in Atlanta where black and white leaders were struggling to prevent a confrontation between police and black youths from turning into a riot. To thunderous applause, Carmichael told those attending the meeting to "take to the streets and force the police department to work until they fall in their tracks. . . . We are not concerned with peace. We are concerned with the liberation of black people. We have to build a revolution." Carmichael's SNCC warned that black youths in Atlanta who volunteered for a special peacekeeping patrol would be treated as "Black Traitors" to be dealt with in the "manner we see fit."[41] The city barely avoided a violent outbreak.

A month later, on July 19, the House of Representatives voted overwhelmingly 347–70 for a Republican-sponsored anti-riot bill making it a crime to cross state lines to incite a riot, a measure Democratic Representative Frank Thompson of New Jersey described as a "bill of attainder aimed at one man—Stokely Carmichael." The bill was "aimed at those professional agitators," said Representative William C. Cramer (R-Fla.), the sponsor, who roam from city to city to "inflame the people . . . to violence and then leave the jurisdiction before the riot begins."[42]

The next day, July 20, the House killed by a vote of 207–176 a relatively modest Johnson administration proposal to spend $40 million over two years on rat eradication in the nation's slums. Southern Democrats and Republicans joked on the floor that the measure was a "civil rats bill," that would produce "rat patronage," a "rat bureaucracy," and "a high commissioner of rats." Virginia Republican Joel T. Broyhill told his colleagues: "I think the rat smart thing for us to do is vote down this rat bill rat now."[43] The full force of white backlash had reached the House of Representatives.

The House vote on the rat eradication bill reflected once again the partisan split on racially-loaded issues, as the GOP voted 148–24 to kill the measure, and Democrats voted 154–59 in favor of the bill.

The House vote set in motion new angry black protests, protests in which blacks vented their fury more at Democrats who had failed to muster a majority in support of the rat eradication bill than at Republicans who had become the adversaries of racial liberalism. First, on August 7, seventy-five black protesters from New York broke into the House chambers just after it had adjourned, chanting "Rats cause riots." As shoving matches broke out between demonstrators and Capitol police, one woman forced her way back into the House gallery to shout "You son of a bitch, you ought to bring that damn Johnson here." Beraneece Sims, assistant director of Harlem's Community Council for Housing, declared: "We no longer want to belong to this country. We shall declare our independence."

A week later, Harlem rent-strike leader Jesse Gray and roughly eighty other protestors met in Washington with a contingent of liberal Democratic members of the House. "We are not holding you responsible," Gray told the Democrats, "but I hold your party responsible." When Representative John Conyers, Jr., a black whose Detroit district in late July had experienced some of the most violent rioting in the nation's history, suggested that the group vent its anger at the polls, the protestors dismissed his strategy as a form of worn-out liberalism. An angry Conyers countered: "If you think burning down America is right, why come here. Just go get your [Molotov] cocktails and go to work and don't waste my time." The demonstrators marched out of the meeting, and, in front of reporters and television cameras, turned over to Capitol police a small brown rat. "His name is Lyndon," Sims, who participated in both protests, told police. "You can have him. We have a lot more where we came from."[44]

The demonstrations at the Capitol were part of a much larger trend. By 1967, the Democratic party was under siege from a black Left led by such figures as Carmichael, Rap Brown, Jesse Gray, and Huey Newton, as well as from a white Right within Democratic ranks, led by George Wallace, whose message was gaining strength throughout the nation. Each side had discovered the political power of polarizing messages—and that confrontation and rejection of accommodation were themselves mobilizing strategies.

At a local level, the centerpiece of the War on Poverty, the Community Action Program, was encouraging the development of parallel mobilizing strategies, strategies that divided rather than united Democratic constituencies. The Community Action Program was originally designed to provide the poor with the opportunity to develop innovative approaches to education, job training, and, in the long run, to acquire political and economic power. Local governments were required to set up governing boards for their anti-poverty programs in which there was to be "maximum feasible participation" of the poor. In theory, these boards would not only devise new programs, but would also reorganize the entire structure of services and agencies—welfare, public housing, emergency aid, etc.—to more effectively attack poverty.

In practice, many of the local community action programs became forums for sustained political warfare between white-controlled city halls and black-dominated organizations of the poor, leading to a series of confrontations that eroded political support for the anti-poverty program in Congress and among mayors, and also disillusioned black expectations.

The most controversial Community Action–generated conflicts generally took one of two forms. In the first group of conflicts, white mayors gained firm control of the local boards and community action agencies, infuriating ghetto activists and organizers, as in the case of Chicago, Philadelphia, and Atlanta. In Chicago, Mayor Richard J. Daley's grasp of the community action agency provoked an angry response from community leaders. The Rev. Lynwood Stevenson, of The Woodlawn Organization, denounced the program, declaring "there is no war on poverty, there is only more of the ancient galling war against the poor." Professional community organizer Saul Alinsky dismissed the poverty program in Chicago as "a prize piece of political pornography."[45]

In the second category of controversial programs, local boards gained power independent of the mayor, and became power bases for adversarial challenges to city hall. In Syracuse, poverty workers put together a voter registration drive clearly aimed at ousting Mayor William Welsh who warned federal Office of Economic Opportunity (OEO) staffers: "I'm not going to take this lying down." The head of the city's housing authority complained, "We are experiencing a class struggle in the traditional Karl Marx style in Syracuse, and I do not like it."[46]

In many respects, these conflicts were inevitable in communities where blacks were gaining enough strength to acquire power, and where the anti-poverty program provided a political base that accelerated the election of blacks to public office: in cities like Newark and Detroit, the election of a first black mayor; or in Baltimore, the election of Parren J. Mitchell, the former executive director of the city's community action agency, to the House of Representatives. The problem for the national Democratic party, however, was that Congress and the Johnson administration, in enacting the anti-poverty program, did not anticipate the political consequences. In city after city·experiencing intraparty, black-white competition for control of city council seats and city hall, the creation of the anti-poverty programs appeared to local political establishments to place the federal government on the side of black insurgents challenging white Democrats.

For a party facing intensified racial tension between core urban constituencies, the anti-poverty program not only signaled national Democratic support of programs empowering one faction in the struggle for power, but also represented the expenditure of tax dollars to weaken the political power of whites. Whites who for generations had supported the New Deal expansion of the federal government, and who had benefitted from it, resented deeply the use of the federal government to provide jobs, infrastructure, and a public forum for their political adversaries.

---

The promotion of conflict within the Democratic party became, among some leaders of the political Left, a conscious strategy designed to lead to the enactment of more progressive programs. In 1967, the National Welfare Rights Organization (NWRO) was formed with the express goal of creating a welfare-induced fiscal crisis in the nation's cities. The organization emerged from a strategy developed by Frances Fox Piven and Richard Cloward, white activist-theoreticians, aimed at vastly expanding the number of people on welfare rolls.

Piven and Cloward described in an article in *The Nation* the long-range goals of a welfare rights organization:

> Widespread campaigns to register the eligible poor for welfare aid, and to help existing recipients obtain their full benefits, would produce bureaucratic disruption in welfare agencies and fiscal disruption in local and state govern-

ments. . . . These disruptions would generate severe political strains, and deepen existing divisions among elements in the big-city Democratic coalition: the remaining white middle class, the white working class ethnic groups and the growing minority poor.

Piven and Cloward argued that in order "to avoid a further weakening of that historic coalition, a national Democratic administration would be constrained to advance a federal solution to poverty that would override local welfare failures, local class and racial conflict and local revenue dilemmas. . . . The ultimate goal of this strategy—to wipe out poverty by establishing a guaranteed annual income. . . . The ultimate aim of this strategy is a new program for direct income redistribution."[47]

Initially, the NWRO, under the direction of former associate national director of the Congress of Racial Equality (CORE) George Wiley, experienced tremendous success. In New York, a center of NWRO activity, the welfare caseload doubled to one million from 1966 to 1968.[48] A drive to force New York caseworkers to give recipients legally required but rarely authorized "special grants" for minimum levels of furniture, clothing, and housing equipment forced the city to increase special grants from $20 million in 1965 to $90 million in 1968.[49] Confrontations between social workers and welfare recipients became increasingly hostile. "NWRO's tactics grew tougher and [the leadership] lost control. Angry recipients destroyed case records and made a shambles of welfare offices; demonstrations turned into [small] riots," wrote Nick and Mary Lynn Kotz, two sympathetic biographers of Wiley.[50]

In terms of battling the welfare bureaucracy, the NWRO achieved significant national gains by successfully forcing welfare workers across the country to treat recipients with courtesy, ending, for example, midnight raids to see if men were staying overnight with recipients in violation of eligibility rules. In terms of federal legal protection, in 1970 the Supreme Court in *Goldberg v. Kelly* ruled that "welfare guards against the societal malaise that may flow from a widespread sense of unjustified frustration and insecurity," and held that welfare recipients had a constitutional right to an evidentiary hearing before their benefits could be terminated.[51]

In terms of overall political reaction to the welfare rights movement, however, the response was swift and hostile. By late 1968, two of the nation's most liberal states, Massachusetts and New York, both of which had been NWRO targets, placed sharp restrictions on the special grant program. In 1971, nineteen states cut welfare benefits, and nearly every state in the nation considered taking such action.[52]

Although the welfare system is clearly centrally involved in the structure of poverty, a confrontational attack demanding expanded and increased payments was guaranteed to provoke political retaliation. In the long run, the NWRO attack may have brought less attention to the inadequacies of welfare than to the dependency on tax dollars of the recipients. According to public opinion surveys, of all domestic federal programs, welfare has been by far the most unpopular.[53] There has been no popular consensus in support of welfare. In addition, there were deep, inherent contradictions in a campaign, such as the one led by the NWRO, to empower the poor by increasing welfare dependency.

After New York restricted the special grants program, Piven and Cloward wrote that welfare activists would "mount a 'spend the rent' campaign. . . . [The resulting] evictions will provoke street confrontations with the police and marshals and may constitute an even greater threat to placidity in the ghettos."[54] Instead of building momentum in support of a guaranteed annual income, however, benefits were cut and white hostility to black demands intensified. By 1975, the National Welfare Rights Organization was defunct.

———

As racial issues and racial conflict had begun to cause increasingly severe strains for the Democratic party, the underlying tenets of liberalism were changing. Just as the alignment of the Democratic party with the civil rights movement had added racial policy as a central issue dividing liberals from conservatives, other developments worked to move liberalism beyond its New Deal economic roots. The Supreme Court was forcing to the forefront the whole set of highly controversial issues which would become the topic of the intensely politicized social/moral "values" debate—sexual privacy, birth control, criminal defendants' rights, school prayer, obscenity—and, eventually, abortion and the death penalty.[55] Second, from 1965 to 1968, a powerful anti-war movement had emerged—largely within the Democratic party and among voters inclined to cast Democratic ballots—in opposition to the military draft and to President Johnson's steady escalation of the Vietnam War. Third, the anti-war movement dovetailed in many respects with the rising assertion throughout the 1960s and 1970s of expanded rights by blacks and women (groups with relatively wide backing)—and also by groups with far less public support—gays, lesbians, prisoners, pornographers, sexual liberationists, the mentally ill, atheists, undocumented workers, and so on.

The Democratic party did not initiate these developments, but if either party served as a defender of the new liberalism and of a broadened rights agenda, it was the national Democratic party—just as the Republican party had adopted an increasingly adversarial stance towards a broad rights agenda, northern Democrats, a majority in their own party but a minority in Congress as a whole, became, in effect, a bastion of the new social liberalism.

When, for example, Republican Senate Minority Leader Everett Dirksen of Illinois proposed a constitutional amendment on September 21, 1966, providing for the restoration of school prayer, the measure won a majority, 49–37, but fell nine votes short of the two-thirds required for a change in the Constitution. Republicans lined up solidly behind the prayer amendment, 27–3, while Democrats cast a majority of their votes, 34–22, against the legislation. Northern Democrats were overwhelmingly against the school prayer amendment, 29–7, while southern Democrats were in favor, 15–5.[56]

During the second half of the 1960s, very similar patterns of partisan division began to emerge around a host of sharply polarizing issues, including defendants' rights, advanced weapons systems, and the militant student campus rebellions. In 1968, the Senate decisively rejected an amendment to strike funds for the Sentinel antiballistic missile (ABM) system 46–27; of the 27 negative votes, 20 were cast by northern Democrats.[57] As the anti-war Left became increasingly active on the nation's campuses, the House enacted changes to the Higher Education Act barring federal aid to students who participated in campus "disorders" by a vote of 260–146. Again, the only strong dissent was among northern Democrats who voted against the provisions by a margin of 98–50, while Republicans backed the restrictions by a 134–43 margin, and southern Democrats were even more decisively behind the cutoff, 76–5.[58] In May 1968, a series of votes were called on proposals to take away from the Supreme Court the power to overturn criminal convictions in situations in which illegally obtained confessions or evidence had been used to obtain convictions. Again, northern Democrats stood nearly alone as the defenders of controversial high court decisions.

These congressional votes marked another profound shift in the ideological content of political partisanship. In the second half of the 1960s the Democratic party became identified not only with racial liberalism, but also with opposition to spending on the military, with valuing civil liberties over criminal punishment, with the departure of women from traditional roles, with a general climate of sexual and cultural permissiveness, and with rising tax burdens. To a certain extent, the Republican party in turn became identified with more traditional and more conservative position on each of these issues.

In the years following 1964, there was a substantial basis in fact for the evolving images of the two parties. The presidential candidates, the party platforms, patterns of voting on Capitol Hill, the attitudes of party functionaries and professionals, the makeup of each party's primary and caucus electorates, the differing structures of the Republican and Democratic national committees—all these, in varying ways and to varying degrees, contributed to what might be called a realignment of the public understanding of the bias or tilt within the Democratic and Republican parties.

The years between 1964 and 1968 shaped the politics of the next two decades; looking backwards at developments in those years, the failures of the Democratic party to attain the presidency is less surprising than the fact that the Democratic party survived as a vital force, continuing throughout the civil rights era and into at least the early 1990s to control Congress and a majority of state legislatures—surprising when the list of political troublespots of the 1960s is reviewed: The Democratic party became the home of liberal racial policies, and of most black voters, just when urban rioting dominated headlines and newscasts for three summers in a row. The Johnson administration in 1968 was forced by the cost of the Great Society and the Vietnam War to press for a 10 percent income tax surcharge, leading to the subsequent identification of the Democratic party with the costs of big government, as well as with the costs of racial liberalism. The Supreme Court issued controversail and unpopular rulings on crime, prayer, and obscenity, and northern Democrats became the principal defenders of those rulings. Fairly or unfairly, rioting and black radicalism were seen as fusing with a white student Left, a Left that had adopted Ho Chi Minh and Ché Guevera as revolutionary heros, and which championed lifestyles and rhetoric calculated to drive its most sought-after ally, the working class, into the arms of conservative Republicanism.

"Law and order was a *separable* issue from race, but it was not always a *separated* issue. Law and order was not completely separated from Vietnam either, for disrespect of the law also took the form of direct action against the war," James Sundquist wrote in 1983 in *Dynamics of the Party System*. "In the public perception, all these things merged. Ghetto riots, campus riots, street crime, anti-Vietnam marches, poor people's marches, drugs, pornography, welfarism, rising taxes, all had a common thread: the breakdown of family and social discipline, of order, of concepts of duty, of respect for law, of public and private morality."[59] While taxes at the state, local, and federal levels were rising, payments for the basic welfare program, Aid to Families with Dependent Children (AFDC), (in an initial response to the drive spearheaded by the National Welfare Rights Organization), were going up sharply: 10 percent in 1965, 13 percent in 1966, 22 percent in 1967, and 26 percent in 1968.[60] By 1968, 81 percent of those responding to the Gallup Poll agreed with the statement that "law and order has broken down in this country."[61]

The riots, the welfare rights movement, the black power movement, student disorders, the sexual revolution, radical feminism, recreational use of drugs such as marijuana and LSD, pornographic magazines and movies, and higher taxes merged in varying degrees in the minds of many voters with liberalism and with the Left. And that identification with liberalism, constituted a modest, but significant, link to the Democratic party. At the 1968 Democratic Convention in Chicago, the anti-war delegates supporting Eugene McCarthy inside the convention hall formed part of an ideological continuum that extended to the demonstrators outside the hall—a continuum extending at the extreme to the increasingly radical members of Students for a Democratic Society (SDS) and to such devoutly—and flagrantly—anti-establishment figures as Abbie Hoffman and Jerry Rubin. At the Republican convention in Miami, there was no such linkage between delegates and protestors. The Republican party and the anti-war movement were separated both by police lines and by an unbridgeable ideological chasm.

————

The liberal consensus behind the Democratic coalition was severely weakened by the events and developments of 1965–1968. Vietnam and the anti-war protests were essential to the decline of support for the then-dominant wing of the Democratic party, a wing controlled in large part by the old guard of organized labor, the last of the urban machine leaders, and by such political figures as Vice President Hubert H. Humphrey and the Democratic Senator Henry Jackson of Washington. It was, however, the *fusion* of race with an expanding rights revolution and with the new liberal agenda, and the fusion, in turn, of race and rights with the public perception of the Democratic party, and the fusion of the Democratic party with the issues of high taxes and a coercive, redistributive government, that created the central force splintering the presidential coalition behind the Democratic party throughout the next two decades, long after Vietnam and the counterculture had faded into the background.

"Go into any home, any bar, any barber shop and you will find people are not talking about Vietnam or rising prices or prosperity," said Democratic Representative Roman Puchinski, whose heavily Polish district dominated northwest Chicago. "They are talking about Martin Luther King and how they are moving in on us and what's happening to our neighborhoods." Initially a firm supporter of civil rights, including the failed attempt to win passage of open housing legislation in 1966, Puchinski by 1968 had become an opponent of open housing.[62]

The voters in Puchinski's district were not alone. In an ominous development for the Democratic party, an ugly disenchantment with the black revolution had spread not only to the bungalow wards of Chicago, but to prominent public intellectuals as well, including best-selling novelist and essayist Norman Mailer. On August 5, 1968, Mailer attended the Republican Presidential Convention in Miami, where, by his own account, waiting at a press conference for Ralph Abernathy, successor to Martin Luther King, Jr., at the Southern Christian Leadership Conference (SCLC), Mailer became aware "of a curious emotion in himself, for he had not ever felt it consciously before—it was a simple emotion and very unpleasant to him—he was getting tired of Negroes and their rights." Mailer wrote:

> He was so heartily sick of listening to the tyranny of soul music, so bored with Negroes triumphantly late for appointments, so depressed with Black inhumanity to Black in Biafra, so weary of being sounded in the subway by Black eyes, so despairing of the smell of booze and pot and used-up hope in blood-shot eyes of Negroes bombed at noon, so envious finally of that liberty to abdicate from the long year-end decade-drowning yokes of work and responsibility, that he must have become in some secret part of his flesh a closet Republican—how else could he account for his inner, 'Yeah man, yeah, go!' when fat and flatulent old Republicans got up in Convention Hall to deliver platitudes on the need to return to individual human effort.[63]

In a matter of four years, from Roman Puchinski to Norman Mailer, the consensus behind the black civil rights movement had disintegrated, and the center of gravity—the implicit ground rules as to what constituted the acceptable boundaries of public discourse—had swung far to the right.

# 4

# The Nixon Years

THE CONSERVATIVE MAJORITY that went on to determine five of the six following presidential elections was forged in 1968 in a three-way competition between Richard M. Nixon, Hubert H. Humphrey, and George C. Wallace, with Wallace running as the nominee of the American Independent Party. That election in many respects defined the structure of American politics for the next twenty years.

Race, the Vietnam War, student protests, the rights revolution, and what was seen by many as a rapid disintegration of the traditional social order, had produced deep fissures in the Democratic coalition, making the party vulnerable to challenge from the right. The 1968 election produced for the Republican party the basic strategies, not only for capitalizing on new schisms within the Democratic party, but, equally important, strategies for forging into a conservative alliance groups and interests that before 1968 had found little or no common ground.

Nixon and Wallace, who together collected 57 percent of the vote in 1968, established the framework for the success of Republican presidential candidates through the 1980s. Wallace, with increasing skill, defined politics in terms of populist conflict, pitting an elite Democratic establishment against working men and women struggling to make a decent living and decent lives for themselves. Nixon, for his part, developed strategies essential to capitalizing on the issue of race, while avoiding the label of racism.

Nixon in 1968 was among the first Republicans to understand how the changing civil rights agenda could be made to offer a politically safe middle ground to candidates seeking to construct a new conservative majority—or what turned out to be, in 1968, a plurality. The Nixon strategy effectively straddled the conflict between growing public support for the abstract principle of racial equality, and intensified public opposition to government-driven enforcement mechanisms. Nixon found a message that encompassed the position of a growing majority of white Americans who had come to believe that denial of basic citizenship rights to blacks was wrong, but who were opposed to the prospect of substantial residential and educational integration imposed by the courts and by the federal regulatory bureaucracy through involuntary mechanisms, especially busing.

The dominant civil rights issues of 1968 were school integration and open housing. On April 10, six days after the assassination in Memphis of Martin Luther King, Jr., Congress enacted legislation barring discrimination in the sale or rental of houses and apartments—although powers of enforcement were purposefully kept weak. The following month, the Supreme Court ruled in *Green v. County School Board of New Kent County, Va.* that the original remedy to school segregation—"freedom of choice"—had failed to end dual school systems in the South. The decision held growing implications for the North, where housing patterns, and in some cases school board policies, had produced extensive de facto segregation that could not be remedied by the simple replacement of neighborhood schools with a system of voluntary cross-district registration.

For Nixon and his campaign, these issues were highly problematic: whites opposed to open housing and school integration were a potential source of enough new votes to win the presidency; but any direct attack on the principle of racial equality risked the loss of millions of traditional Republican voters likely to be repelled by the taint of overt racism. Nixon broke new ground in finding a resolution for this kind of conflict, establishing a politically safe terrain by simultaneously affirming his belief in the principles of equality while voicing opposition to the use of federal intervention to enforce compliance.

In a closed meeting with southern delegates to the 1968 Republican convention in Miami, Nixon demonstrated that it was possible to affirm respect for the law, signaling at the same time that he would relieve pressure on beleaguered whites. Asked about open housing, Nixon said: "I feel now that conditions are different in different parts of the country . . . [and] ought to be handled at the state level rather than the federal level." The Supreme Court and school integration? "I want men on the Supreme Court who are strict constitutionalists, men that interpret the law and don't try to make the law. . . . I know there are a lot of smart judges, believe me—and probably a lot smarter than I am—but I don't think there is any court in this country, any judge in this country, either local or on the Supreme Court—any court, including the Supreme Court of the U.S.—

that is qualified to be a local school district and to make the decision as
your local school board."[1]

This was just the kind of message that the ascendant conservative
majority in the presidential wing of the GOP—the wing that had been
established during the Goldwater campaign—wanted to hear. Throughout the nomination process, Nixon carefully wooed key leaders of the
Goldwater insurgency over to his side, gathering the backing of such
figures as Strom Thurmond; political strategist Harry Dent, from South
Carolina; Mississippi GOP chairman Clarke Reed; and Howard "Bo" Cal-
laway of Georgia, who later ran unsuccessfully for governor.[2]

In a September 1968, television interview in Charlotte, North Carolina,
broadcast in the South six weeks before the election, Nixon clearly established the gulf between abstract principle and the reality of enforcement.
After reaffirming his support for the 1954 Supreme Court decision, *Brown
v. Board of Education*—"I believe that the decision was a correct one"—
Nixon added the critical caveat:

> But, on the other hand, while that decision dealt with segregation and said that
> we would not have segregation, when you go beyond that and say it is the
> responsibility of the federal government, and the federal courts, to, in effect,
> act as local school districts in determining how we carry that out, and then to
> use the power of the federal treasury to withhold funds or give funds in order
> to carry it out, then I think we are going too far. In my view, that kind of
> activity should be scrupulously examined and in many cases, I think, should
> be rescinded. . . . I think that to use that power on the part of the federal
> government to force a local community to carry out what a federal administra-
> tor or bureaucrat may think is best for that local community—I think that is a
> doctrine that is a very dangerous one.[3]

Nixon's development of a strategy that staked out a position lending
comfort to racial conservatives, while remaining publicly committed to
racial equality, was one of crucial importance to the Republican party.
Through the 1970s and 1980s, this strategy provided a politically viable
approach to such issues as busing, affirmative action, and racial quotas.
Through those years, the overwhelming majority of white Americans
came to support the right of blacks to go to the same schools as whites and
to have access to the same job market; but those same white Americans
decisively opposed and continue to oppose the use of racial preferences in
hiring and in education, and to oppose the use of court-ordered busing to
achieve integration.[4]

Nixon's strategic contribution in 1968 to the politics of race and to the
formation of a Republican presidential majority was less crucial, however,

in forging that new conservative majority than was the contribution of George Wallace—both in terms of Wallace's assault on liberalism and in terms of his successful effort to confer moral legitimacy upon political conservatism.

In the final count of the 1968 election, Wallace won only 9.9 million voters, 13.5 percent of the total cast, and failed to achieve his goal of denying an electoral vote majority to either Nixon or to Humphrey and of forcing the House of Representatives to pick the new president. Wallace did succeed, however, in rupturing the Democratic moorings of millions of voters, including many of those who cast their ballots for him, and countless others who wavered until voting for Nixon on election day.

Often dismissed as marginal and as a reflection of the temporary social upheavals of the late 1960s and early 1970s, the Wallace campaign in fact captured the central political dilemma of racial liberalism and the Democratic party: the inability of Democrats to provide a political home for those whites who felt they were paying—unwillingly—the largest "costs" in the struggle to achieve an integrated society.

Wallace provided a desperately sought-after moral justification to those whites who saw themselves as most victimized and most displaced by the black struggle for civil rights. This struggle had in many ways became a contest for limited resources—for a city's quality schools and teachers, for union jobs and apprenticeships, for the first layer of housing outside rusting urban centers, and for social status and community standing in an economy that increasingly devalued working-class employment. For these voters, Wallace transformed the terms of the debate, placing the issue of civil rights in a new, reassuring, and opportune moral context.

Wallace portrayed the civil rights issue not as the struggle of blacks to achieve equality—a goal increasingly difficult to challenge on a moral basis—but as the imposition on working men and women of intrusive "social" policies by an insulated, liberal, elitist cabal of laywers, judges, editorial writers, academics, government bureaucrats, and planners:

> They [judges, federal regulators, liberal intellectuals] have looked down their noses at the average man on the street too long. They look down at the bus driver, the truck driver, the beautician, the firemen, the policeman, and the steelworker, the plumber, and the communications worker, and the oil worker and the little businessman, and they say, 'We've gotta write a guideline. We've gotta tell you when to get up in the morning. We've gotta tell you when to go to bed at night.' "[5]

Wallace, in effect, sought to turn the charge of racism on its head—anticipating the rallying cry of conservatives for the next twenty years:

"reverse discrimination." "You know who the biggest bigots in the world are—they're the ones who call others bigots," Wallace declared at a Milwaukee rally as he struggled to be heard over the shouts of protesters.[6] "Well, it's a sad day in the country when you can't talk about law and order unless they want to call you a racist. I tell you that's not true,"[7] Wallace repeatedly told audiences.

The Wallace campaign shaped a new right populism and a new symbolic language for the politics of race, a symbolic language allowing politicians to mobilize white voters deeply resentful of racial change without referring specifically to race. Wallace created a new demonology and defined a new political symbol, an adversary of the public will that would for the next twenty years compete with, if not replace, the Republican "establishment" of big business and corporate America. The Republican corporate establishment had been stigmatized by countless Democratic candidates in order to win elections. The Wallace populist message created a countervailing Democratic "establishment" determined to impose its liberal authoritarian, statist agenda on an unwilling electorate, a Democratic establishment made up of the government itself and of "a select elite cult" including "some professors, some newspaper editors, some preachers, some judges and some bureaucrats."[8]

To voters who felt besieged by the heavy hand of the new liberal establishment, Wallace said: "You are one man and one woman, and your thoughts are just as good as theirs."[9]

The Wallace campaign set in motion the broadening of the conservative anti-government coalition to include a large segment of moderate and low-income whites. Wallace's anti-government message undermined the allegiance of many working-class white voters to the federal government and to the Democratic party, an allegiance that had been constructed on the basis of such New Deal–era programs as unemployment and workman's compensation, the National Labor Relations Act, the Federal Housing Administration, the G.I. Bill, public works spending, and Social Security. For these voters, Wallace held up as an object of derision a federal government "triflin' with children, tellin' 'em which teachers have to teach in which schools, and busing little boys and girls half across a city just to achieve 'the proper racial mix'."[10]

In the course of the 1968 campaign, Wallace helped to put in place the foundation of what ten years later would become a groundswell of discontent over tax burdens among working and lower-middle-class voters, a development essential to the strengthening of Republican presidential prospects. Wallace called for an end to government spending on the "Great Society," which was seen as concentrating benefits on poor blacks.

Most importantly, Wallace focused public attention on the financial costs of integration: "We don't need half a billion dollars being spent on bureaucrats in Washington of your hard-earned tax money to check every school system, every hospital, every seniority list of a labor union. And now after the election they're going to check even on the sale of your own property."[11]

Wallace, in effect, structured the political debate in 1968 to facilitate for millions of working and lower-middle class Democratic voters a Republican vote four years later. Wallace's conservative populism placed his supporters in opposition to an elitist Democratic establishment intent on collecting higher taxes in order to conduct what he described as liberal social experiments; Wallace was able to establish a common ground between besieged working-class voters and their traditional Republican adversaries—corporate America, the well-to-do, and the very rich—a common bond in opposition to federal regulation and to high taxes.

---

Wallace won only five states in 1968—Alabama, Mississippi, Arkansas, Georgia, and Louisiana—almost precisely replicating the victories in the deep South of Strom Thurmond running on a segregationist ticket in 1948, and Goldwater's southern victories in 1964. More than either Thurmond or Goldwater, however, Wallace provided the Republican party with tools for reaching Democratic working-class voters. Wallace's conservative populism, his conceptualization of a privileged, coercive liberal Democratic establishment, and his redefinition of racial conflict—painting the opponents of integration as victims of an overbearing, dictatorial, and arbitrary central government—proved essential to the building of a new, conservative Republican presidential majority.

---

In 1968, Richard Nixon barely won the presidency—drawing 31.79 million votes (43.4 percent) to Humphrey's 31.25 million (42.7 percent), although Nixon won the electoral college vote by 301 to Humphrey's 191 and Wallace's 46. The 9.9 million votes (13.5 percent) cast for Wallace became central to Nixon's blueprint for reelection four years later. From 1969 to 1972, Nixon sought to tap the Wallace vote, incorporating many of Wallace's strategems into his own tactical repertoire and encouraging his vice president, Spiro T. Agnew, to become, in effect, the Republican counter to Wallace.

At the same time, in the grasp of a very different—but parallel—vision of populist empowerment, the Democratic party initiated reforms of the presidential nomination process with the express purpose of increasing the leverage of "average" Democratic voters and activists, while reducing the power of elected officials and city and state party bosses. Power within the presidential wing of the Democratic party abruptly shifted to those liberal activist groups that had spearheaded the left flank of the drive of the 1960s for broad-based rights and for greater social democratization. These liberal activist groups included, among others, the civil rights leadership, the Vietnam Moratorium Committee, Americans for Democratic Action, the National Welfare Rights Organization, and the National Women's Political Caucus.

New Democratic party rules enacted between 1969 and 1972, requiring proportional representation of blacks and women, mandating open-slating processes, and making popularly elected delegates subject to a wide range of procedural challenges, lent themselves to liberal, college-educated rights-oriented reformers. The new ground rules set up a form of competition more advantageous to the articulate and well-educated than to the traditional blue-collar holders of precinct and ward-based power. The competition to become a candidate for delegate to the Democratic convention—competition preceding the primary or caucus—shifted to a forum under the control of reformist regulation.

The most aggressive seekers of power under these new rules were activists with roots in the civil rights and anti-war movements—as well as in the growing women's movement. These constituencies saw as their major adversary the traditional, old-guard, white, male Democratic leaders who had pushed through the nomination of Hubert Humphrey in 1968, despite Humphrey's failure to enter a single primary. The new base of power in Democratic presidential selection was decisively liberal on race issues, deeply committed to the civil rights agenda, and to an unprecedented degree, it was distant both physically and ideologically from the more socially and morally conservative white working and lower-middle class voters who had been a mainstay of the party. These new holders of power were, moreover, liberal not only on race, but also on foreign policy, women's issues, sexual conduct, drugs, religion, and a host of other cultural matters; finally, they were strongly in favor of the extension of a range of expanded rights to previously disadvantaged or disregarded groups across American society.

———

As the two parties diverged on civil rights and on race—and on what came to be seen as a nexus of broader rights-related and social/moral issues—the competition between the Democratic and Republican parties became less a forum for the reduction of racial tensions in the struggle over schools, jobs, and housing, and more a forum for the partisan expression of racial conflict. The Republican party developed a vested interest in the conflict itself, as voter support for the GOP grew with the intensification of busing controversies and housing integration disputes, and as the Democratic coalition continued to splinter. The realigning potential of a politics of race was most clearly and openly recognized by Nixon strategist Kevin Phillips. In the South, Phillips wrote in 1969, "maintenance of Negro voting rights is essential to the GOP. Unless Negroes continue to displace white Democratic organizations, the latter may remain viable as spokesmen for Deep Southern conservatism."[12]

On a national scale, the 1968 Wallace campaign, according to Phillips, had served as a "way station . . . for Democratic traditionalists following party realignment into the Republican party," a realignment driven by race. "The principal force which broke up the Democratic (New Deal) coalition is the Negro socioeconomic revolution and the liberal Democratic ideological inability to cope with it. 'Great Society' programs aligned that party with many Negro demands, but the party was unable to defuse the racial tension sundering the nation," Phillips wrote after the 1968 election in his book, *The Emerging Republican Majority*. "The Democratic Party fell victim to the ideological impetus of a liberalism which had carried it beyond programs taxing the few for the benefit of the many (the New Deal) to programs taxing the many on behalf of the few (the Great Society)."[13]

The emergence of race as a central issue dividing the parties posed troubling political questions for Nixon once in office. As chief executive, Nixon was charged with carrying out the law, and Supreme Court rulings as well as the body of civil rights legislation on the books placed inescapable responsibility for enforcing integration goals on the chief executive. It was Nixon's political gift, however, to mine conflict for profit: Just as he had staked out, during the campaign, a middle ground between endorsement of the principle of integration and opposition to forceful implementation, Nixon as president developed the strategy of staying within the letter of the law, while making abundantly clear wherever possible his reluctance to aggressively enforce it.

On July 3, 1969, six months after Nixon took office, the Department of Justice and the Department of Health, Education and Welfare (HEW) jointly announced that strict compliance with timetables for integration would be dropped: "A policy requiring all school districts, regardless of the difficulties they face, to complete desegregation by the same terminal date is too rigid to be either workable or equitable." The announcement paid immediate political dividends in the South. The *Columbia State* in South Carolina headlined its story, "School Deadlines Scrapped," and the Montgomery, Alabama, *Advertiser* simply declared, "Nixon Keeps His Word."[14] In September 1969, Nixon told reporters: "There are those who want instant integration and those who want segregation forever. I believe that we need a middle course between those two extremes."[15]

In filing the July 1969 motion to delay desegregation, the Justice Department for the first time since the start of the modern civil rights revolution placed itself on the side of the white South against black plaintiffs. When the Supreme Court on October 29 in an unsigned brief rejected the administration position and ordered immediate adoption of desegregation plans, Nixon declared: "[W]e will carry out the law," but stressed that he did "not feel obligated to do any more than the minimum the law required" and he made clear that he "disagreed" with the Court.

The Court ruling, Nixon warned, should not be viewed by "the many young liberal lawyers [in the Justice Department] . . . as a carte blanche for them to run wild through the South enforcing compliance with extreme or punitive requirements they had formulated in Washington."[16] Nixon, in effect, succeeded in defining forced desegregation as the responsibility of the courts, not of his administration, and simultaneously declared that he supported a far more slow and cautious approach to integration than did the Supreme Court—a critical step in wedding 1968 Wallace voters to Nixon's own 1972 re-election bid.

Rebuffed by the Supreme Court, Nixon sought to change it, nominating in succession two conservative southern members of the federal bench, Clement F. Haynesworth, Jr., of South Carolina, and G. Harrold Carswell, of Florida, to fill the vacancy created by the resignation in 1969 of Abe Fortas. Among other things, both nominees were burdened with controversial records on racial issues—Haynesworth with a series of votes against civil rights interests in key cases before the Fourth Circuit Court; and Carswell with his involvement in the conversion of a public golf course (under court order to desegregate) into a private, whites-only club. The nominations mobilized the civil rights lobby, organized labor, as well as a host of other liberal interests, and both judges were rejected by the Senate.

On April 9, 1969, the day after the Senate voted down the Carswell nomination, Nixon personally read a statement in the White House press room:

I have reluctantly concluded, with the Senate presently constituted, I cannot nominate to the Supreme Court any federal appellate judge from the South who believes as I do in the strict construction of the Constitution. . . . I understand the bitter feeling of millions of Americans who live in the South about the act of regional discrimination that took place in the Senate yesterday. They have my assurances that the day will come when men like Judges Carswell and Haynesworth can and will sit on the high Court.[17]

Nixon, in effect, extracted from his battles with the Supreme Court, the Senate, and the civil rights bureaucracy three political advantages. The first was to separate himself and his administration from the inexorable momentum of evolving civil rights law in the area of school integration, publicly and credibly disassociating himself from the wrenching process of desegregation that he was in fact powerless to stop. The second was to secure a grip not only on the South for the 1972 election, but also on the growing number of white northerners, many of them urban Democrats, who were beginning to feel they were bearing the brunt of school and job integration. The third was to make a case to voters disturbed by the liberal civil rights policies of the Supreme Court and of a Democratic Congress that the way to change those policies was to elect conservative Republicans to the presidency—including Nixon himself for a second term.

Nixon further strengthened his credentials as a racial conservative when his administration sought in 1969 to weaken the Voting Rights Act. The bid of the Nixon administration to eliminate provisions in the act requiring officials in the South to obtain "preclearance" from the Justice Department for local election law changes, although ultimately unsuccessful, served to demonstrate to the concerned electorate that a Democratic Congress, rather than the Nixon administration, was behind the singling out of the South as the target of the most stringent enforcement provisions.

Largely overlooked when the Voting Rights Act was passed in 1965, the preclearance provision (Section Five) had emerged by 1969 as a powerful federal tool to prevent states and local jurisdictions in the South from adopting ostensibly race-blind strategies that in fact had racially discriminatory effects. These seemingly neutral tactics included the conversion of single-member city council or state legislative districts into city-wide, at-large elections for the purpose of continuing to bar blacks from office in white-majority cities. In a key 1969 decision, *Allen v. Board of Elections,* the Supreme Court affirmed that all election law changes in the jurisdictions covered by the Voting Rights Act must be cleared by the Justice Department.

For the white South, the requirements of the Voting Rights Act had represented a direct and pervasive federal assault on the deeply-rooted practice of controlling the local political process in order to maintain the economic and social subordination of blacks. The immediate effect of the act—the enfranchisement of millions of southern blacks—was to challenge white political power in the deep South, within such states as Georgia, Alabama, Mississippi, and Louisiana in a host of counties where blacks were in the majority.

Faced with an ongoing surge in black voter registration—in Mississippi, the percentage of the black population registered to vote had exploded from 6.7 percent in 1964 to 59.4 in 1968—white politicians increasingly turned to changes in election laws and practices to protect their power. In Mississippi, for example, the legislature in 1966 enacted measures allowing county boards of supervisors to replace single-member districts, which in many communities effectively guaranteed black representation, with at-large elections, which could be used to maintain exclusive white control of county boards.

The preclearance provision brought these maneuvers to a halt. The civil rights division of the Justice Department effectively held veto power over every alteration in election law and administrative practice in the South, from precinct locations to municipal annexations to legislative and congressional district boundaries. Through the preclearance provision, the federal government, in effect, took control of what had, before 1965, been a centerpiece of white rule—the management of state and local elections.

Nixon's 1969 proposal to weaken the Voting Rights Act initially carried in the House, the 208 to 204 vote demonstrating once again the distinctions between the two parties on race: Republican members voted 129 to 49 to eliminate the preclearance requirement, and Democrats voted 155 to 79 in favor of retaining it. Ultimately, in a confrontation with the more liberal Senate (which backed retention of the preclearance provision) the House reversed its position and included preclearance measures in legislation extending the Voting Rights Act for another five years. Nixon, however, had realized his central goal, clearly aligning himself with the white South in a battle with the Democratic Congress, and distancing his own administration from a program of stringent federal enforcement.[18]

While the highly visible legislative, administrative, and judicial battles over civil rights enforcement provided Nixon with the opportunity to court Wallace voters for 1972, Nixon's selection of Spiro Agnew as vice president constituted a more frontal appeal. One of the most insistent demands of southern delegates to the 1968 GOP convention had been for a vice presidential running mate "acceptable" to the region, and Nixon met this demand with his choice of the Maryland governor.

Agnew had won national attention on April 11, 1968, when, in the aftermath of Baltimore rioting triggered by the assassination of Martin Luther King, Jr., he summoned fifty black elected officials and community leaders to a meeting at the state office building. With the city police chief and the state police chief standing behind him, Agnew accused the black leaders of cowardice for refusing to renounce such radicals as Stokely Carmichael and H. Rap Brown: "You were beguiled by the rationalization of unity; you were intimidated by veiled threats. You were stung by insinuations that you were Mister Charlie's boy, by epithets like Uncle Tom. . . . The looting and rioting which has engulfed our city during the past several days did not occur by chance. It is no mere coincidence that a national disciple of violence, Mr. Stokely Carmichael, was observed meeting with local black power advocates and known criminals in Baltimore three days before the riots began." After more than half the blacks stalked out and the meeting came to an end, Agnew told reporters that his purpose had been to "separate the leaders from the lunatic fringe", adding "[Y]ou can't talk around problems forever, even though it shocks people."[19]

Once in office, Agnew became the purveyor of a strain of public rhetoric pioneered at the national level by Wallace. Just as Wallace in 1968 had denounced the "permissive attitude of the executive and the judiciary," "anarchists," "pointy headed intellectuals," "guideline writers," "pseudo-intellectuals," "bearded professors, "scum," and "punks"—two years later Agnew as vice president toured the country in behalf of Republican candidates, denouncing "permissivists," "avowed anarchists and communists," "misfits," the "garbage" of society, "thieves, traitors and perverts," and "radical liberals."[20]

Agnew became the standard-bearer of a Republican party in the grip of a new awareness: that transformation of the GOP's minority status would require breaking the hold of the Democratic party on white working and lower-middle-class voters. Agnew's explicit strategy was to achieve what he called a "positive polarization" of the electorate. In a 1971 speech describing his role in the 1970 elections, Agnew declared that "dividing the American people has been my main contribution to the national political scene since assuming the office of vice president. . . . I not only plead guilty to this charge, but I am somewhat flattered by it."[21]

———

During the first two years of his administration, Nixon's attempts to retard the pace of southern desegregation, to weaken the Voting Rights

Act, to appoint racial conservatives to the Supreme Court, and to ally himself with the fractious tactics of his vice president functioned to over-shadow far less visible early administration efforts in support of black economic advancement. These efforts were grounded, in Nixon's view, in legitimate, market-oriented mechanisms. In 1969, opposition to affirmative action and minority contracting setasides had not yet become integral—as they soon would—to the policy strategy of the Republican party; on the contrary, the GOP still saw business-centered programs as the engine for pulling blacks into the private-sector mainstream. To that end, Nixon lent his support to the development of a government-led "black capitalism," actively promoting three racially preferential programs that would before long become controversial: 1) activation of a minority contracting pro-gram known as "Eight-A," setting aside fixed percentages of federal con-tracts for minority-owned businesses; 2) the establishment within the De-partment of Commerce of an Office of Minority Business Enterprise (OMBE) to assist minority businesses in securing government contracts[22]; and, 3) the so-called "Philadelphia Plan"—designed to increase black ac-cess to high-paying union jobs.

The Philadelphia Plan (named for the five-county Philadelphia area where bidders on federal construction projects fell under the plan) estab-lished the authority of the federal government to require companies doing business with the government to set up "goals and timetables" for the hiring and promotion of minorities. The plan set specific percentage "ranges" for hiring blacks and other minorities for craft union jobs. Plum-bers and pipefitters, only twelve out of 2,335 of whom in Philadelphia were black (0.5 percent), were given a hiring goal of 5 to 8 percent in 1970, a range that would rise to 22 to 26 percent by 1973.

"Visible, measurable goals to correct obvious imbalances are essential," declared Arthur A. Fletcher, the assistant secretary of Labor for Wage and Labor Standards under President Nixon.[23] In 1969, both minority seta-sides and "goals and timetables" were seen by Republicans as effective in attracting blacks to the exigencies of market competition. By 1970, the "goals and timetables" mechanism was incorporated into the regulations governing all federal procurement and contracting—involving a universe of corporations that employed over a third of the nation's workforce.[24]

For the still strong wing of the Republican party committed to racial liberalism—a tradition extending back to the abolitionist movement—black capitalism seemed to offer a counterbalance to administration efforts to build support among Wallace voters by capitalizing on the racial ten-sions resulting from desegregation. Nixon in 1969 did not anticipate that the affirmative action provisions of his Philadelphia Plan or that the promotion of black capitalism through minority contracting setasides would become, in the course of the next twenty years, essential to a Republican strategy of polarizing the electorate along lines of race and thus key to constructing a partisan realignment.

Nixon did, however, recognize the political advantage in proposing a program that would exacerbate the already deep tensions between two core Democratic constituencies: "Nixon thought that Secretary of Labor George Schultz had shown great style in constructing a political dilemma for the labor union leaders and the civil rights groups," wrote Nixon aide John Ehrlichman in 1982, looking back on the White House years. "The NAACP wanted a tougher requirement; the unions hated the whole thing. . . . Before long, the AFL-CIO and the NAACP were locked in combat over one of the passionate issues of the day and the Nixon administration was located in the sweet and reasonable middle."[25]

———

The ambiguities of an administration and of a party seeking, on the one hand, to develop a clear-cut southern strategy predicated to a significant degree on white resistance to black gains, and seeking, on the other hand, to build support for black economic advancement, were swept away during the second half of Nixon's first term. The emergence of a single issue—busing—came to dominate the administration's racial strategies.

During the four years of Nixon's first term, court-ordered busing in northern as well as southern cities became the most controversial and racially charged matter before the nation. Over the objections of the Nixon administration, and later of Congress, busing was the remedy developed by the courts to attack the problem of school segregation in residentially segregated communities. Busing transformed the politics of city after city, both in the North and in the South, in much the same way that the Civil Rights Act of 1964 had transformed the presidential voting habits of whites across the states of the old Confederacy. No other issue brought home so vividly to whites the image of the federal government as intruder and oppressor—the same government which for millions of voters had for nearly forty years been seen as relatively benign, and often as benefactor and protector.

Busing was by no means the only issue to alter the structure of white voting behavior, but it was busing that drove home with most clarity the realization that the new liberal agenda would demand some of the largest changes in habit and custom from the working-class residents of low and moderate-income enclaves within the big cities—enclaves with often heavily Irish, Polish, Italian, or Slavic populations: Los Angeles, South

Boston, Dayton, Denver, New York's Canarsie, and Cleveland's west side. Busing provided Nixon with an anvil on which to forge a link for the receptive voter between an intrusive federal government, liberalism, and the national Democratic party.

The combination of the Civil Rights Act of 1964 and of subsequent Supreme Court rulings gave the legal system a momentum of its own, initially invulnerable to conservative pressures from inside or outside the Oval Office. At the same time, the enforcement staffs of the Civil Rights Division within the Department of Justice and of the Office for Civil Rights within HEW—filled with generally liberal lawyers committed to pressing integration cases in every section of the country, lawyers with the weight of federal legislation and case law behind them—added critical energy to that momentum.

In February 1969, a federal court ordered substantial busing in Los Angeles and in Pasadena; and in April, the Office for Civil Rights in HEW moved to cut off federal funds to a noncompliant Ferndale, Michigan. By 1971, angry public protests against busing orders were held in San Francisco, Indianapolis, Pontiac, Michigan, and Detroit. The same year, in *Swann v. Charlotte-Mecklenburg Board of Education,* the Supreme Court ruled 9–0 that busing was a permissible remedy for school segregation, notwithstanding Nixon's appointment of Warren Burger to replace Earl Warren as Chief Justice. Burger, in fact, wrote the opinion.

In January 1972, the busing issue took on an entirely new and, to many, a threatening dimension, when a federal district court judge in Virginia ordered the busing of students across county lines between the largely black Richmond school system and two surrounding, predominately white counties. On July 10, 1972, it became clear that the threat of city-suburban busing was not going to be limited to the South: federal judge Stephen J. Ross ordered the state of Michigan to buy 295 buses for the cross-county busing of students between Detroit and fifty-three surrounding districts.[26] By 1974, when the Supreme Court rejected busing between different governmental jurisdictions, key segments of the white electorate had already either abandoned their reflexive loyalty to the national Democratic party or had switched altogether to the GOP.

Nixon proved adept at disassociating himself and the office of the presidency from the enforcement efforts that the executive branch was under court and legislative mandate to carry out. The theme of containing the efforts of the more or less "permanent" civil service to enforce integration objectives—a containment attempt directed from the Republican-controlled Oval Office—would run through the remaining years of the Nixon presidency.

When HEW in 1971 ordered an extensive busing plan for Austin, Texas, Nixon publicly repudiated the proposal, declaring: "I am against busing as that term is commonly used in school desegregation cases."[27] Ronald Ziegler, Nixon's White House press secretary pointedly warned later that year that government workers "who are not responsive will find themselves involved in other assignments or quite possibly in assignments other than the federal government."[28] When Herbert G. Klein, White House director of communications, told Nixon on July 3, 1971, that civil rights "laws are being over-enforced," Nixon shot off a memo to John Ehrlichman, domestic affairs advisor: "E—I want you personally to jump [Elliot] Richardson and Justice and tell them to *Knock off this Crap*. I hold them personally accountable to keep their left wingers in step with my express policy—Do what the law requires and not *one bit more.* "[29]

On March 17, 1972, as Nixon prepared for the general election nine months away, he began an all-out assault on busing. In a message to Congress calling for legislation to end the practice of busing, the president declared that the school bus, "once a symbol of hope," had become a "symbol of social engineering on the basis of abstractions. . . . In too many communities today, it has become a symbol of helplessness, frustration and outrage—of a wrenching of children away from their families, and from the schools their families may have moved to be near, and sending them arbitrarily to others far distant."[30]

The announcement provoked a hostile reaction—heaven-sent in the Republican view—in just the quarters of the bureaucracy Nixon sought to separate himself from. Ten black lawyers in the Civil Rights Division at Justice released an open letter accusing the administration of yielding to "racist pressure groups and political expedience. . . . What we have been witnessing," they wrote, "[is] a camouflaged effort to resurrect the concept of 'separate but equal' ".[31]

———

While busing served as a mobilizing issue for the Republican party throughout Nixon's first term, it fell like an axe through the Democratic party, severing long-standing connections and creating a new set of troubled alliances: white, blue-collar northerners with southerners against blacks and upper-middle-class liberals. A dwindling band of northern liberals found that they were defending a policy with no real constituency: poll after poll found decisive white opposition to busing, and only lukewarm support in the black community, which was generally split down the middle on the issue.[32]

Northern Democrats representing predominantly white working-class districts, voters who until the mid-sixties were firm supporters of civil rights, began to defect in droves on the issue of busing. Democratic Representative John Dingell of Michigan, for example, had voted in favor of the 1964 Civil Rights bill, despite the threat of a tough primary challenge in his Dearborn district. His vote was taken at the time to demonstrate that a politician representing white working-class and ethnic voters could back civil rights. Nine years later, Dingell was a leader of anti-busing forces, successfully sponsoring a House amendment barring the use of federal money to buy gasoline "for the transportation of any public school student to any school farther than the public school closest to his home"—over the bitter objections of black members of the House. During the debate on the Dingell amendment, Parren Mitchell, a black congressman from Baltimore, said he had been recently asked by a young black student, " 'Why do they hate us so?' " "Mr. Chairman," Mitchell continued, "that question will be raised on the floor today, and I do so raise it."[33]

By 1972, the number of northern Democrats in the House opposed to busing had grown nearly fivefold, from twelve in 1968 to fifty-eight. All five of the white Democrats from metropolitan Detroit voted against busing on amendments to the 1972 HEW appropriations bill. Four out of seven white Chicago Democrats, all four Democratic members of the Connecticut delegation, and all three of the white representatives from metropolitan Baltimore joined the anti-busing coalition that year.[34]

---

In devising a political strategy for capturing white working-class and southern voters, the Nixon administration in 1972 would have had difficulty designing a scenario more advantageous to the GOP, and more damaging to the Democratic party, than the scenario the Democrats devised for themselves.

In the aftermath of the 1968 defeat of Hubert Humphrey, the most pressing issue for the presidential wing of the Democratic party was to begin the process of reconciling the three major conflicting factions within the party. The first faction was a broad intra-party left driven by the anti-Vietnam War movement and committed to a social agenda of expanded rights for women, minorities, and once-excluded groups such as homosexuals—a wing represented by the candidacy of George McGovern, and liberal on racial, cultural, and economic matters. The second faction was an intra-party right committed to resisting cultural and racial change, but still liberal on economic matters—represented by George Wallace; the third faction was a party center caught between the two—

liberal on economics, and to a degree on race, but disturbed by emerging cultural trends—represented by Humphrey.

The 1972 nomination fight marked the final attempt of the Democratic party to contain in one tent the range of interest groups that had previously found common ground in support of traditional Democratic economic liberalism—interest groups that were now affiliated with one or another of the three warring factions as the agenda shifted to such matters as civil rights, black empowerment, women's rights, abortion rights, criminal rights, and issues of personal and sexual liberation.

The critical battleground for fundamental conflicts within the Democratic party—conflicts that may well have been impossible to reconcile under any circumstances—became party reform, hammered out on the Democratic party rules commission that had drastically restructured the procedures for the selection of presidential convention delegates between the elections of 1968 and 1972. Democratic party reforms had been initiated as a result of the passage of two little-noted resolutions at the tumultuous 1968 Chicago convention, resolutions which were carried in a modest effort to assuage the feelings of angry delegates who had supported the failed presidential bid of Minnesota Senator Eugene McCarthy. Over the objection of McCarthy delegates, the party-controlled nomination process had allowed Hubert Humphrey to become the Democratic presidential candidate in 1968 without having entered any primaries. The 1968 resolutions called for the creation of a special Commission on Party Structure to insure that "all feasible efforts have been made to assure that delegates are selected through party primary, convention, or committee procedures open to public participation within the calendar year of the National Convention."[35]

No one, neither Democratic party regulars nor the press, had any notion of the scope of what had been set in motion by the reform drive at the 1968 convention. "There was not much attention to the Rules Committee reports. Our objective was to get a nominee," Max Kampelman, one of Humphrey's major strategists, recounted later. "We said to ourselves, if you are going to study it, you can control it. If you get the nomination, you'll have control of the DNC [Democratic National Committee]. If you have the DNC, then you'll control any study. A study commission could be a way of harmonizing the issue."[36] Few judgements have proved more incorrect.

With the presidency in Republican hands, Democratic party regulars and centrists were in fact unable to control the work of the reformist rules commission. Mobilized by the McCarthy and Robert Kennedy campaigns, frustrated by Humphrey's 1968 nomination, and swollen by the first wave of the postwar baby boom (many of whom were veterans of the civil rights and student peace movements) the liberal-reform wing of the Democratic party dominated the commission and achieved a radical alteration of the presidential delegate selection process.

The new rules shifted the power to nominate presidential candidates from the loose alliance of state and local party structures, which had in the past been empowered to use party control to pick delegates, to the universe of generally liberal reform activists who were now granted direct access to the machinery of delegate selection. Beginning in 1972, delegates were chosen under rules requiring either open party conventions and caucuses, or primaries. With the exception of such rare cities as Chicago and Albany, where Democratic party organizations remained strong, reform activists aligned with the anti-war, women's, and other rights movements—as well as with procedural "good-government" types, advocates of the elderly and the disabled, and a host of other liberal interests—far outnumbering party regulars, whose bases were generally in the lower-income blue-collar and ethnic neighborhoods.

The resulting shift between 1968 and 1972 in the political makeup of Democratic convention delegates was dramatic. In 1968, 57 percent of the delegates were chosen through procedures controlled by state parties, largely independent of presidential candidates, and 43 percent were picked through primaries or caucuses where their affiliation with a specific candidate was more important than their ties to the state or local party. By 1972, the percentage of state party-based delegates fell to 18 percent, while the number of candidate-based delegates grew to 82 percent. The loose and decaying collection of state Democratic parties had lost control of the presidential nomination process.[37]

Elected officials—from governors to senators to congressmen to city councilmen—who in the past had generally enjoyed automatic selection as delegates, were now required to run for slots in open primaries and caucuses, an option most chose not to exercise. Local organizations were forced to pick delegate slates at open meetings, publicized in advance. Perhaps most important, organizations running slates had to pick candidates who reflected proportionately the racial and gender makeup of the political jurisdiction; a failure to do so was considered *prima facie* evidence of a rules violation in any credentials challenge.

The development and application of the rules themselves became such an arcane and complex operation that the competitive advantage shifted to well-educated, upper-middle-class elites who understood how to control and manipulate the process.

Party reform and the new Democratic party rules not only severely

restricted the muscle of state-based party organizations, but they also produced a class shift in terms of the makeup of Democratic presidential
convention delegates. "Before reform, there was an American party system in which one party, the Republicans, was primarily responsive to
white-collar constituencies and in which another, the Democrats, was
primarily responsive to blue-collar constituencies. After reform, there
were two parties each responsive to quite different white-collar coalitions,
while the old blue-collar majority within the Democratic Party was forced
to try to squeeze back into the party once identified predominately with its
needs," Byron Shafer wrote in his book *Quiet Revolution.* [38]

Party reforms as expressed through rules changes in fact produced a
substantive, ideological upheaval. Before 1972, Democratic presidential
delegates were only slightly more liberal than the public at large, according to delegate surveys, while Republican delegates were considerably
more conservative than the electorate. Delegates to the 1972 Democratic
convention, however, were significantly farther to the political left of the
electorate at large than the GOP delegates that year were to the right. [39]

No development better summarized the shift in intra-party power than
the decision of McGovern forces at the 1972 Democratic convention to
oust the 59-member Cook County delegation under the control of Chicago
Mayor Richard Daley. Since 1932, the Chicago organization had been
more important to the success or failure of Democratic presidential candidates than any other city machine. Without Daley in 1960, for example,
John F. Kennedy would not have carried Illinois by an 8,858-vote margin;
and without Illinois and just one other state carried by less than a percentage point, New Jersey, Kennedy would not have been elected in 1960.

The 1972 Chicago–Cook County delegation, elected in the March 21
Illinois primary, was vulnerable to challenge because Daley's machine had
slated candidates in closed meetings, and the composition of the Chicago
delegation did not have the proportionally required numbers of women
and blacks.

Pro-McGovern reformers successfully voted out the Daley delegates
and replaced them with a slate "chosen," Theodore H. White wrote, "no
one knew quite how. In the First Congressional District of Chicago, for
example, a group of people had met at the home of one James Clement and
decided that only ten of those present might vote for an alternate to Mayor
Daley's slate; those ten had chosen seven delegates, including the Rever-
end Jesse Jackson. This rival hand-picked alternate slate offered the exact
proportion of women, blacks and youth required by the McGovern reform rules. Yet the elected slate in the First Congressional had been voted
in by the people of Chicago, and these had not." [40]

In an open letter to Alderman William Singer, the leader of the Chicago reformers, *Chicago Sun-Times* columnist Mike Royko wrote:

> I just don't see where your delegation is representative of Chicago's Democrats. . . . About half of your delegates are women. About a third of your delegates are black. Many of them are young people. You even have a few Latin Americans. But as I looked over the names of your delegates, I saw something peculiar. . . . There's only one Italian there. Are you saying that only one out of every 59 Democratic votes cast in a Chicago election is cast by an Italian? And only three of your 59 have Polish names. . . . Your reforms have disenfranchised Chicago's white ethnic Democrats, which is a strange reform. . . . Anybody who would reform Chicago's Democratic Party by dropping the white ethnic would probably begin a diet by shooting himself in the stomach.[41]

After the credentials committee voted 71 to 61 to oust the Daley delegation, Frank Mankiewicz, spokesman for the McGovern campaign, dryly noted: "I think we may have lost Illinois tonight."[42]

When the general election was held, McGovern was crushed, 62–38 percent, losing by 17.99 million votes. For the long-run future of the capacity of the Democratic party to nominate and elect presidents, the central issue was not just the magnitude of McGovern's defeat. It was the inability of the Democratic party to absorb competing factions and to mediate the differences between them. The new rules removed from the presidential selection process those white, elected party officials who were closer to the racial and cultural conflicts that were plaguing the party than were the liberal reformers who dominated the proceedings. Among those who did not attend the 1972 convention were 225 of 255 Democratic congressmen, the Democratic mayors of Los Angeles, Detroit, Boston, Philadelphia, and San Francisco, Mayor Daley and his Chicago loyalists, as well as uncounted city councilmen, state legislators, and leaders of Democratic ward organizations.[43]

By the end of the 1972 primary season, on June 6, there was no stronger evidence of the bitter divisions within the Democratic party than the distribution of 3.76 million votes to Wallace on the right, 4.12 million to Humphrey in the center, and 4.05 million to McGovern on the left.[44] The ideological spectrum of the majority Democratic party had become too broad to survive the nomination process intact.

The McGovern delegates who came to control the process in 1972 were committed to continuing the rights revolution—a revolution that many working and lower-middle-class white voters saw as threatening to traditional, deeply valued, if inequitable, social arrangements. The 1972 Democratic platform had separate planks on the rights of the poor, American Indians, the physically disabled, the mentally retarded, the elderly, veterans, women, and children, as well as—in the language of the platform— "the right to be different, to maintain a cultural or ethnic heritage or lifestyle, without being forced into a compelled homogeneity." At a time when crime was rising at an unprecedented rate, the Democratic platform devoted more attention to the restoration of constitutional rights to released convicts than to efforts to combat street violence.[45]

Party activists, most of whom were white, were shaping a new liberalism that applied a number of the principles, strategies, and objectives of the civil rights revolution to the quest for a broader set of rights for individuals and groups. This new rights revolution called for a substantial redistribution of power, privilege, wealth, status, cultural authority, government resources, and legal protection. But unlike the economic liberalism of the New Deal, the beneficiaries of the new rights revolution were specific, previously discriminated against and often outcast groups—not the broad classes (with the exception of women) of earlier progressive movements.

---

By 1972, there was already clear evidence that the Democratic party, which had historically represented those in the bottom half of the income distribution, needed to give serious consideration to revising its traditionally redistributional strategies if its goal was to win majorities in general elections. Growing numbers of voters, including many Democrats, had left the working class and entered the middle class during the years following the Second World War. In the two decades between 1952 and 1972, median family income, in inflation-adjusted 1977 dollars, nearly doubled, from $8,881 to $16,102, and the percentage of families making more than $25,000 a year increased more than six-fold, from 3.2 percent to 20.5 percent.[46]

Without a ready-made 'have-not' majority, the advocates of the new liberalism of the 1960s and 1970s were hampered by the fact that they sought to build a center-left coalition on the basis of a redistribution of power and benefits to groups that many traditional Democratic voters did not identify with.

The authors of the Democratic 1972 platform wrote:

It is time now to rethink and reorder the institutions of this country so that everyone—women, blacks, Spanish-speaking, Puerto Ricans, Indians, the young and the old—can participate in the democratic heritage to which we aspire. We must restructure the social, political and economic relationships throughout the entire society in order to ensure the equitable distribution of wealth and power.[47]

In the case of poor people, the platform read:

Welfare rights organizations must be recognized as representative of welfare recipients and be given access to regulations, policies and decision-making processes, as well as being allowed to represent clients at all governmental levels.[48]

In the area of criminal rights, the 1972 platform committed the Democratic party to policies that resulted, a decade and a half later, in the furlough of Willie Horton:

Recognition of the constitutional and human rights of prisoners, realistic therapeutic, vocational, wage-earning, education, alcoholism and drug treatment programs; emergency, educational and work-release furlough programs as an available technique; support for 'self-help' programs; and restoration of civil rights to ex-convicts after completion of their sentences, including the right to vote, to hold public office, to obtain drivers' licenses and to public and private employment.[49]

The party was caught in a dilemma: the dominant faction in control of the presidential nomination process had made a moral decision to commit the party and its nominee to work in behalf of an expansion of legal and citizenship rights to those who had been on society's margins. In making such a commitment, the liberal wing of the national party guaranteed that the field on which presidential politics were fought—the field of majoritarian public opinion—would tilt in favor of the Republican party. This course of action raised a second, more complex, moral issue: at what point in a two-party system does a political party abdicate its responsibility to seek power in behalf of its constituents; and at what point—if ever—does its commitment to a substantive moral position supersede its obligation to win?

———

For Richard Nixon, the commitment of the Democratic party in 1972 to an expanding rights revolution provided the ideal opportunity to enlarge upon the strategies he—and George Wallace—had pioneered in 1968. Focusing public attention on the costs of the new liberalism, Nixon sought to provide positive moral and ideological legitimacy to those who did not want to pay those costs. Of the worker concerned about high taxes, Nixon said: "I don't think it is right to charge him with selfishness, with not caring about the poor and the dependent." To the mother concerned about court-ordered busing, he declared: "When a mother sees her child taken away from a neighborhood school and transported miles away, and she objects to that, I don't think it's right to charge her with bigotry."[50]

In a critically important expansion of these arguments Nixon set out to establish positive grounds for the rejection of the kinds of social responsibilities that were raised by the civil rights movement—presaging the conservative ideological framework articulated far more consistently by Ronald Reagan. Nixon concluded an October 21, 1972, radio address with a direct assault on the demand for middle-class sacrifice in behalf of the most disadvantaged that had become an integral aspect of the liberal position:

> There is no reason to feel guilty about wanting to enjoy what you get and what you earn, about wanting your children in good schools close to home or about wanting to be judged fairly on your ability. Those are not values to be ashamed of; those are values to be proud of. Those are values that I shall always stand up for when they come under attack.[51]

Nixon in 1972, seeking to secure the shifting loyalties of the white working class, turned presidential rhetoric against the major civil rights initiative of his own first administration—the Philadelphia Plan. Although Nixon had fought for the plan in 1969, by 1972 he sought to reap political reward from stockpiled blue-collar resentments: "When young people apply for jobs . . . and find the door closed because they don't fit into some numerical quota, despite their ability, and they object, I do not think it is right to condemn those young people as insensitive or even racist."[52]

In retrospect, two elements of Nixon's 1972 campaign strategy are striking: 1) the degree to which the underlying theme of race is repeatedly stressed, in the references to busing and to affirmative action; and, 2) the extraordinary degree to which Nixon anticipated the social-issue agenda of the conservative Republican revolution that swept Ronald Reagan into office in 1980. Nixon, expanding on themes introduced into national politics by Wallace, effectively established the groundwork for the anti-tax ideology of the 1980s, repeatedly rejecting a "liberal" paradigm centered around "social responsibility," in favor of a conservative paradigm centered around "legitimate self-interest."

Nixon saw the polarizing power of racial issues such as busing and affirmative action—issues that came to dominate the civil rights agenda in the wake of the demolition of legal barriers to equal opportunity. In the process of both provoking and responding to voter concerns about race, Nixon, and a handful of strategists within the Republican party, recognized the catalytic power of race to transform the content of the political debate. Race facilitated the beginning of an ideologically conservative conversion of the electorate, as the social costs of programs such as housing integration, busing, and affirmative action became indissolubly fused in the minds of crucial numbers of voters with steeply rising taxes, cultural metamorphosis, increases in violent crime, expanding welfare rolls, greater numbers of illegitimate children, and evidence of the deterioration of both black and white family structures.

Race gave new strength to themes that in the past had been secondary—themes always present in American politics, but which had previously lacked, in themselves, mobilizing power. Race was central, Nixon and key Republican strategists began to recognize, to the fundamental conservative strategy of establishing a new, non-economic polarization of the electorate, a polarization isolating a liberal, activist, culturally-permissive, rights-oriented, and pro-black Democratic Party against those unwilling to pay the financial and social costs of this reconfigured social order.

Nixon in 1972 advanced an emerging conservative strategy, using new techniques and tactics to insure his own landslide re-election; but the circumstances were not yet ripe to bring these techniques and tactics to bear on the task of deliberately building a broadened Republican party. In 1972, the post–World War II economic boom had not quite come to a halt, and the Democratic party still dominated the legislative agenda.

# 5
# The Conservative Ascendance

IN the aftermath of Richard Nixon's 1972 landslide victory over George McGovern, the investigation of the Republican break-in at the Democratic party headquarters—the scandal known as Watergate—provided the besieged forces of liberalism with an opportunity to stall the conservative ascendance. Watergate replenished forces on the liberal side of the political spectrum—the Democratic Congress, organized labor, civil rights groups, and the network of public-interest lobbying and reform organizations—supplying new leverage in what was otherwise rapidly becoming, in political terms, a losing ideological battle.

The central conflict between liberalism and conservatism since the late sixties had focused on the aggressive expansion of constitutional rights to previously disfranchised, often controversial groups. These included not only blacks, but others in relatively unprotected enclaves (mental hospitals, prisons, ghettos) as well as homosexuals (who increasingly resented being cast as deviant), ethnic minorities, and women—who had the strongest base of political support but whose movement, nonetheless, engendered substantial political reaction. Just as this expansion of rights had run into growing public and political opposition, the Nixon administration was itself caught flagrantly violating the core constitutional rights of "average" citizens—rights for which there was, in general, broad consensual support.

The official Republican sanction of the break-in of Democratic National Committee headquarters, the secret wiretapping of fourteen government officials and three newsmen, the burglary of anti-war activist

Daniel Ellsberg's psychiatrist, and the extensive White House cover-up, constituted government-authorized violations of fundamental constitutional guarantees: due process, protection from illegal search and seizure, the separation of powers, and freedom of speech.[1] The second article of impeachment against Nixon (the article receiving the greatest number of votes in the House Judiciary Committee, 28–10, in July 1974,) charged that in directing the FBI, CIA, IRS, and Secret Service to attack political adversaries, Nixon "repeatedly engaged in conduct violating the constitutional rights of citizens, impairing the due and proper administration of justice, and the conduct of lawful inquiries, or contravening the laws governing agencies of the executive branch."[2]

The outcry against the actions of the Nixon White House effectively stifled for the moment public expression of the growing resentment toward the liberal revolution. Watergate "is the last gasp of . . . our partisan opponents," Nixon told his aide, John Dean.[3] The Nixon administration had already been damaged by the forced resignation in October 1973 of Spiro Agnew, who, facing the possibility of a substantial jail term, resigned from the vice presidency, pleading *nolo contendere* to charges of accepting illegal payments from Maryland contractors.

For many liberal constituencies, Watergate provided the grounds to attempt to indict and convict the snowballing conservative counteroffensive. For Democratic members of Congress, and for the larger Democratic establishment, the procedural ruthlessness of the Nixon administration— the enemies lists, the attempts to use the IRS and Justice Department to harass political adversaries, the burglaries, and the illegal wiretapping— was part and parcel of a much broader and more threatening administration drive to assault the constitutional underpinnings of the liberal state.

For liberal interest groups, the appeal of Watergate was even more direct: "The election of Richard Nixon as President sent a shiver through the civil rights and anti-war movements—and the ACLU. A symbol of the cold war of the 1950s, Nixon appeared hostile to civil rights and to virtually all the recent gains in civil liberties," wrote Samuel Walker, in his 1990 book, *In Defense of American Liberties: a History of the ACLU*. After the national board of the American Civil Liberties Union (ACLU) voted to endorse impeachment of the president on September 29, 1973, when Congress was still very tentatively exploring the process, membership in the organization shot up. Ads, financed by such liberal bankrollers as General Motors heir Stewart Mott declared that "Richard Nixon has not left us in doubt . . . if he is allowed to continue, then the destruction of the Bill of Rights could follow," and produced a flood of cash and support. "Over 25,000 new members joined in 1973 alone, driving the ACLU's membership to an all-time high of 275,000."[4]

The Watergate-inspired re-invigoration of the left effectively choked off the growth of conservatism from 1973 through 1976, but the suppression meant that instead of finding an outlet within the political system, right-ward pressure built throughout the decade to explosive levels. The Democratic party experienced a surge of victory in 1974 and 1976, while developments in the economy, in the court-enforced enlargement of the rights revolution, in the expansion of the regulatory state, in rising middle-class tax burdens, and in the growth of crime and illegitimacy were all in fact working to crush liberalism.

Watergate resulted in a political system out of sync with larger trends. A host of groups on the left of the spectrum—Democratic prosecutors, the media, junior congressional Democrats, new reform organizations, and traditional liberal interest groups—gained control over the political agenda just when a selection of other key indicators suggested that the power of the right should be expanding:

• Family income after 1973 abruptly stopped growing, cutting off what was left of popular support for government-led redistributional economic policies. Inflation (driven in part by the first OPEC oil shock) simultaneously pushed millions of working and middle-class citizens into higher tax brackets, encouraging them to think like Republicans instead of Democrats. As low and middle-income voters began to view the taxes deducted from their weekly paychecks with rising anger, the number of welfare and food stamp clients continued to grow at record rates, forcing a conflict between Democratic constituencies that would lead, by the end of the decade, to a racially-loaded confrontation between taxpayers and tax recipients.

• In courts across the country, the drive by a wide range of civil liberties organizations—from the ACLU to the Mental Health Law Project to the National Gay and Lesbian Task Force—reached its height. These organizations were committed to winning new rights for recreational drug users, the mentally ill, gays, American Indians, illegal aliens and the dependent poor. Their success produced not only benefits for targeted populations, but also conservative reaction in communities in every region of the country.

• Crime rates continued to surge, intensifying public discontent with liberal Democratic support of defendants' and prisoners' rights.

• The movement to liberalize abortion laws, which had been making substantial political progress in state legislatures, succeeded with the Supreme Court's 1973 decision, *Roe v. Wade;* that decision, in turn, produced a political counter-mobilization that rapidly became a mainstay of the conservative movement. Equally important, *Roe* reflected the growing depen-

dence of liberalism on court rulings. The legal arena provided liberal interest groups with a host of victories through the mid-1970s. Court rulings
frequently lacked the political legitimacy and support, however, that
comes from public debate and legislative deliberation. Liberal court victories reduced incentives for the left to compete in elective politics to win
backing for its agenda, while sharply increasing the incentives for the
right—both social and economic—to build political muscle.

• The Arab oil embargo of 1973 resulted in gas lines across the country,
intensifying in some sectors hostility toward liberal foreign-policy positions seen as supportive of Third World interests. Covert and explicit
hostility towards Third World countries intensified and fueled, in some
cases, a resurgence of domestic nativism, and even a degree of racism.

• Legislation passed in the civil rights climate of 1965, liberalizing previously restrictive, pro-European immigration policies, produced a surge
of Hispanic, Asian, and other non-European immigration; created new
competition for employment and housing; increased pressure for public
services; and generated a revival of pressures to restore restrictions on
immigration.

• The Justice Department, the Equal Employment Opportunity
Commission (EEOC), and the Office of Federal Contract Compliance
Programs (OFCCP) all capitalized on a sequence of legislative mandates,
court rulings, and executive orders to sharply expand enforcement of affirmative action programs in the public and private sectors, increasing the
saliency of the issue of quotas, an issue beginning to match busing in terms
of the depth of voter reaction.

• Busing, in turn, by the early and mid-1970s, had become a legal
remedy frequently imposed to correct school segregation in the North as
well as in the South. The 1973 Supreme Court decision in *Keyes v. Denver
School District No. 1* significantly increased the likelihood that a northern
school system would be found guilty of illegal discrimination, and therefore subject to busing orders.

• In a number of major cities, black political gains were translating
into the acquisition of genuine power. An inevitable outcome of the process of enfranchisement, the ascendancy of black politicians meant the loss
of power for some white politicians, and in an increasing number of major
cities competition for control of City Hall turned into racial confrontation. In 1967, Richard Hatcher and Carl Stokes won the mayor's offices in
Gary, Indiana, and Cleveland, Ohio, respectively; in 1970, Kenneth Gib-
son became mayor of Newark; in 1974 Coleman Young and Maynard
Jackson won in Detroit and Atlanta. These contests involved sharply polarized electorates (the only exception being the 1973 election of Tom
Bradley, a black, in Los Angeles, where the mayoralty was won with more

white than black votes). As Democratic black political power grew in the cities, Republican voting in white suburbs began to intensify, accelerating the creation of what political strategists would term "white nooses" around black cities.

————

There were forces at work in the 1970s, combining to produce an explosive mix—forces pitting blacks, whites, Hispanics, and other minorities against each other for jobs, security, prestige, living space, and government protection. As weekly pay fell, and as the market for working-class jobs tightened, government intervention in behalf of employment for minorities intensified; the doors opened for a wave of Latinos and Asians legally seeking jobs, at the same time that illegal immigration from across the Mexican border increased. Simultaneously, former civil rights lawyers and activists turned their attention to continuing the extension of rights to the ranks of the once-excluded.

This sequence of developments engendered a form of backlash within key sectors of the majority white electorate, backlash generating conservative pressures on an ambitious and threatening liberalism, conservative pressures which were only temporarily held in check by Watergate. The immediate political consequences of the investigation and prosecution triggered by the Watergate break-in lulled Democratic Party leaders into ignoring the outcome of the 1972 presidential election—into thinking that their majority party status was secure, and that the ability of the Republican Party to dominate presidential elections with a racially and socially conservative message had been washed away in the outcry for official probity and reform.

Politicians, academics, and the media remained largely ignorant of the direction the country would, in fact, take by the end of the decade. Patrick Caddell, who had conducted polls for both McGovern in 1972 and Jimmy Carter in 1976, wrote in a post-1976 election memorandum to President-elect Carter: "When we turn to the Republicans, we find them in deep trouble. Their ideology is restrictive; they have few bright lights to offer the public. Given the antiquated machinery of the Republican Party, the rise of a moderate, attractive Republican in their primary process is hard to imagine. The Republican Party seems bent on self-destruction."[5] Everett Carll Ladd, a political scientist expert in assessing the balance of power between the two parties, wrote in 1977:

[W]e are dealing with a long-term secular shift, not just an artifact of Watergate. The Republicans have lost their grip on the American establishment, most notably among young men and women of relative privilege. They have

lost it, we know, in large part because the issue orientations which they manifest are somewhat more conservative than the stratum favors. . . . The [Repub-
lican] party is especially poorly equipped in style and tone to articulate the
frustrations of the newer, emergent American *petit bourgeoisie*—southern
white Protestant, Catholic, black and the like."[6]

In fact, it was the Democratic party that was continuing to lose its
class-based strength. The forces pushing the country to the right exerted
the strongest pressures on whites in the working and lower-middle class,
and it was among these voters that Democratic loyalty was continuing to
erode. Party leaders failed to perceive these trends because losses among
low-to-moderate-income whites during the mid-1970s were compensated
for by momentary gains among upper-income, normally Republican
white voters who were most insistent on political reform in response to
Watergate.

Among middle and low-status whites, voter turnout for Democratic
congressional candidates in 1974, and for the Democratic presidential nominee in 1976, was lower than it had been in the 1960s, when the
New Deal coalition was stronger. The following table shows the percentage of white support for Democratic congressional candidates in 1964
and 1974, both years producing major gains for Democratic House candidates.

TABLE 5.1

Percentage of Vote Received by Democratic Congressional Candidates
from Low, Medium, and High Status Whites

|  | 1964 | 1974 | Gain (+) or Loss (−) |
|---|---|---|---|
| High Status whites | 48 | 57 | +9 |
| Middle Status whites | 65 | 62 | −2 |
| Low Status whites | 74 | 67 | −7 |

SOURCE: Everett Carll Ladd, Jr., *Transformations of the American Party System* (New
York: Norton, 1978), 245.

Democrats at the height of Watergate had lost substantial levels of
support among low-status whites, and had experienced a modest decline
among middle-status whites. Only a surge of support among upscale
whites compensated for the difference. A very similar pattern emerges in
the comparison of the white Democratic vote for president in two very
close elections, both won by Democrats, John Kennedy in 1960 and
Jimmy Carter in 1976:

TABLE 5.2

Percentage of Vote Received by Democratic Presidential Nominees
from Low, Medium, and High Status Whites

|  | *1960* | *1976* | *Gain (+) or Loss (−)* |
|---|---|---|---|
| High status whites | 38 | 41 | +3 |
| Middle status whites | 53 | 49 | −4 |
| Low status whites | 61 | 53 | −8 |

SOURCE: Ladd, *Transformations of the American Party System*, 289.

In effect, Democrats were winning in 1974 and 1976, just as the core of their traditional base among whites was crumbling. The party became dependent on upscale, traditionally Republican voters whose new found loyalty would disappear as economic and foreign-policy issues regained their saliency, and as the memory of Watergate faded.

In the buildup of conservative, anti-liberal sentiment in the electorate, the most important development was the fact that 1973, the year the Senate set up a special committee to investigate Watergate, was also the year that marked the end of a sustained period of post–World War II economic growth. Hourly earnings, which had grown every year since 1951 in real, inflation-adjusted dollars, fell by 0.1 percent in 1973, by 2.8 percent in 1974, and by 0.7 percent in 1975.[7] Weekly earnings fell more sharply, by 4.1 percent in 1974 and by 3.1 percent in 1975. Median family income, which had grown from $20,415 (in 1985 inflation-adjusted dollars) in 1960, to $29,-172 in 1973, began to decline in 1974, when family income fell to $28,145, and then to $27,421 in 1975.[8]

Steady economic growth, which had made redistributive government policies tolerable to the majority of the electorate, came to a halt in the mid-1970s, and, with stagnation, the threat to Democratic liberalism intensified. In a whipsaw action, the middle-class tax burden rose with inflation just as the economy and real-income growth slowed. The tax system was losing its progressivity, placing a steadily growing share of the cost of government on middle and lower-middle-class voters, vital constituencies for the Democratic party. In 1953, a family making the median family income was taxed at a rate of 11.8 percent, while a family making four times the median was taxed at 20.2 percent, nearly double. By 1976, these figures had become 22.7 percent for the average family, and 29.5 percent for the affluent family.[9] In other words, for the affluent family, the tax burden increased by 46 percent from 1953 to 1976, while for the average family, the tax burden increased by 92.4 percent. Not only were cumulative tax burdens growing, but they were also shifting from Republican constituencies to Democratic constituencies.

At the same time, one of the most painful elements of the federal income-tax structure, the marginal rate system, had begun to impinge on the vast majority of voters, not just on the affluent. As recently as the early 1960s, 90 percent of the population was effectively exempt from steeply rising marginal tax rates that applied only to those in the top 10 percent of the population. For 90 percent of the population, there were only two marginal rates, 20 percent for nearly half of all taxpayers, and 22 percent for a quarter of the entire population, as the bottom fifth paid no taxes whatsoever. By 1979, however, this same 90 percent of the population faced ten different marginal tax rates.[10] Routine pay hikes regularly pushed taxpayers into higher marginal brackets and, worse, rising infla-tion meant higher marginal rates without any increase in real income. At the same time, Congress also approved steadily higher Social Security taxes. From 1960 to 1975, the maximum annual Social Security tax liability grew from $144 to $825, a 473 percent increase. During the same period, per capita income grew by only 166 percent, so that the Social Security tax was taking an increasingly large bite out of wage and salary income.

In political terms, the damage was most severe to the Democratic party. Democratic-approved Social Security tax hikes fell much harder on those making less than the median income, voters who had traditionally tended to vote Democratic by higher margins than those above the me-dian. In 1975, for example, a worker with taxable income of $14,100 paid $825, or 5.85 percent of his income, to Social Security, while someone making $75,000 paid the same $825, or just 1.1 percent of income.[11]

These economic developments became one-half of an equation that functioned to intensify racial divisions within the traditional Democratic coalition. The other half of the equation was that taxpayer-financed wel-fare, food stamps, and other expenditures for the poor were growing expo-nentially. In the decade from 1965 to 1975, the number of families receiving benefits under Aid to Families with Dependent Children (AFDC), grew by 237 percent. Until that point, the national caseload had been growing at a *relatively* modest pace—from 644,000 households in 1950 to 787,000 in 1960 to 1,039,000 in 1965, an increase over fifteen years of 61 percent.

From 1965 to 1970, the number of households on welfare more than doubled to reach 2,208,000, and then grew again by more than one million, reaching 3,498,000 families in 1975.[12] The Food Stamp program, which was initiated on a small scale in 1961 and then greatly enlarged in 1970, provided benefits to 400,000 people in 1965, 4.3 million in 1970, and in-creased four-fold, to 17.1 million recipients in 1975.[13] Throughout the 1970s, the illegitimacy rate for both blacks and whites grew significantly, but for blacks, the decade saw illegitimate births begin to outnumber legitimate births. For whites, the illegitimacy rate rose from 5.7 percent of all live births in 1970, to 7.3 in 1975, to 11.0 in 1980; for blacks, the rate went from 37.6, to 48.8, to 55.2 percent in the same period.[14]

The tensions growing out of these economic and social trends were compounded by the substantial conflicts growing directly out of the expansion of the civil rights movement into the broader rights revolution. Lawyers who had been trained in the trenches of the South—often funded by liberal, tax-exempt organizations and foundations, just as civil rights litigation projects had been—moved, in the late 1960s and early 1970s, into the broader rights arena. They developed litigation strategies designed to remedy the longstanding denial of rights to groups in unprotected enclaves (psychiatric hospitals, immigrant detention camps, Indian reservations, jails), and also to social "victims" (homosexuals, the disabled, the indigent). Particularly powerful was the evolving idea that conditions of birth or chance—ranging from gender to race to skin color to sexual orientation to class origin to ethnicity to physical or mental health—should not place any American at a social or economic disadvantage, insofar as it was possible for the state to offer protection and redress. "The rights revolution was the longest-lasting legacy of the 1960s," writes Samuel Walker in his history of the ACLU. "Millions of ordinary people—students, prisoners, women, the poor, gays and lesbians, the handicapped, the mentally retarded and others—discovered their own voices and demanded fair treatment and personal dignity. The empowerment of these previously silent groups was a political development of enormous significance."[15]

The rights movement had already found political expression within the Democratic party, which had not only endorsed a broad spectrum of human rights at its 1972 convention, but which was granting specific recognition to a network of separate caucuses for blacks, women, and homosexuals within the Democratic National Committee. It was not until the mid-1970s, however, that the rights revolution reached its full power, changing some of the most fundamental patterns and practices of society. As these changes began to seep into public consciousness, the political ramifications slowly became felt throughout the majority electorate—an electorate under economic siege and rapidly losing its tolerance for the rapid redistribution of influence, as well for the redistribution of a host of economic and social benefits.

Just as the economy was beginning to stagnate, as oil producing countries were demonstrating their power to hold the energy-hungry United

States hostage (with the price of imported oil rising from $1.80 a barrel in 1970 to $14.34 in 1979),[16] and as the shift from manufacturing to services was forcing major dislocations in the job market, the rights revolution assaulted the traditional hierarchical structure of society, and in particular the status of white men.

The strongest of the rights movements was, in fact, the drive for the equality of women, who were included as beneficiaries of the equal employment provisions of the original 1964 Civil Rights Act. Political support for women's rights remained strong, symbolized by the congressional approval in 1972 of the Equal Rights Amendment (ERA) and by a series of legislative victories throughout the 1970s. At the same time, the women's movement—in combination with financial pressures making the one-earner family increasingly untenable—produced a major alteration in family structure, as labor force participation among married women grew steadily, from 35.7 percent in 1965, to 41.4 in 1970, to 45.1 percent in 1975, to 50.7 percent in 1980.[17]

The changes that were taking place in the workplace, in family relationships, and in the balance of power between men and women were not cost-free. The number of divorces, which had remained relatively constant from 1950 through 1967, began to escalate sharply. In 1967, the divorce rate for every 1,000 married women was 11.2; by 1975, the rate had grown to 20.3; and in 1979, the divorce rate reached its height, 22.8—more than double the 1967 level.[18] At the same time, the annual number of children of parents getting divorced grew from 701,000 in 1967, to 1.12 million in 1975, to 1.18 million in 1979.[19]

The more outspoken leaders of the women's rights movement, many of whom cut their teeth in the civil rights and anti-war movements, adopted rhetoric and tactics that exacerbated the anxieties of a host of men already facing diminished job prospects, eroding family incomes, and a loss of traditional status in their homes. "Lesbian sexuality could make an excellent case, based on anatomical data, for the extinction of the male organ," Anne Koedt wrote in "The Myth of the Vaginal Orgasm," an essay subsequently reprinted in an estimated twenty different anthologies of feminist writings.[20]

The women's rights movement was reinforced by the Supreme Court in *Roe v. Wade,* as the Court took the expanded right to privacy established in *Griswold v. Connecticut,* a case involving the sale of contraceptives, and extended the reasoning to establish a woman's right to terminate pregnancy during the first trimester. The sum of these developments—the entry of women into the workforce, the rising divorce rate, and the doubling of the number of reported abortions, from 586,800 in 1972 to 1.2

million in 1976[21]—as well as the halving of the fertility rate between 1960 and 1975[22]—contributed to the building of a conservative response.

The anti-abortion movement and the massive growth of parishioners attending fundamentalist Christian churches during the 1970s were in many ways powerful reactions to the emergence of the women's rights movement. "[T]he danger signs are quite evident: legislation on the national level reflects widespread acceptance of easy divorce, abortion-on-demand, gay rights, militant feminism, unisex facilities, and leniency towards pornography, prostitution and crime. . . . In short, many religious leaders believe that America may soon follow the footsteps of Sodom and Gomorrah," wrote Tim LaHaye, organizer of fundamentalist Christian voters, in his book, *The Battle for the Mind.*[23]

The surge of women newly entering the job market, women now empowered with unprecedented control over their reproductive and sexual lives, coincided with the opening of the nation to another source of competition for employment and, in the Southwest and West, for political power: Hispanic and Asian immigration. Legislation enacted in 1965, growing out of the general climate surrounding the civil rights revolution, ended the racially restrictive immigration policies that had been on the books since the Immigration Act of 1924. The 1965 law opened the door to a wave of new immigration, primarily from Mexico and the Caribbean. The total number of legal immigrants and refugees from Central and South America, rose from 183,717 in the 1950s, to 751,060 in the 1960s, to 1,555,697 in the 1970s. These figures do not include the movement of United States citizens in Puerto Rico to the mainland, nor do they include illegal immigration, nor do they reflect the population growth following immigration—with the total Hispanic population of the United States growing from 9.07 million in 1970 to an estimated 22.4 million in 1990. The rising tide of legal Hispanic immigration was matched by Asian immigration, which grew from 186,671 in the 1950s, to 447,537 in the 1960s, to 1,798,861 in the 1970s. Overall, the Asian population in the United States also grew rapidly—from 1.34 million in 1970 to 7.3 million in 1990.[24]

The drive to achieve equality for women and the abandonment of racially exclusionary immigration policies, in tandem with the civil rights movement, were consistent with the evolution of an egalitarian American political culture. But each evolutionary development contributed in turn to a growing conservative backlash or reaction, which was strengthened in turn by the increasing momentum of the more controversial rights movements. In 1974, the gay rights movement persuaded the American Psychiatric Association to remove homosexuality from its list of mental illnesses; between 1973 and 1975, the movement won approval of gay rights ordinances in eleven cities and counties, barring discrimination on the basis of sexual orientation; by 1989, the drive had produced legal prohibitions against discrimination against gays in housing, employment, and in the provision of other services in sixty-four municipalities, sixteen counties, and thirteen states.[25]

The early 1970s also produced a movement to win legal rights for the mentally ill and for the mentally retarded, accelerating the nationwide process of deinstitutionalization. In 1975, the mental health rights movement won, in *O'Connor v. Donaldson,* a decision by the Supreme Court barring involuntary institutional confinement of non-dangerous patients.[26] *Donaldson* was followed by a series of decisions in state and federal courts establishing stringent procedural safeguards for those facing forced commitment, including the right to a formal hearing, the right to appeal, the right to be represented by a lawyer, and proof from committing authorities that confined individuals were dangerous either to themselves or to others.[27] The general public approved these rights in principle, but the practical reality—particularly the lack in every jurisdiction of taxpayer support for costly community-based alternative care—led to the abandonment of large numbers of emotionally fragile men and women to the streets, subways, parks, and storefronts of the nation, where routine commuting, recreational, and shopping experiences became disturbing and often frightening for significant numbers of voters.

---

Perhaps the most controversial of all the major rights movements identified with liberalism over the past twenty-five years were the initiatives in behalf of criminal defendants and prisoners. In a series of decisions between 1957 and 1966, including *Mallory v. United States, Gideon v. Wainwright, Escobedo v. Illinois, Mapp. v. Ohio,* and *Miranda v. Arizona,* the Supreme Court found criminal defendants, many of them poor and black—and some clearly guilty—entitled to a range of fundamental protections and rights in state as well as federal courts. These included protections against illegally obtained evidence, self-incrimination, deprivation of due process, and cruel and unusual punishment; and called for rights to counsel, to silence, and to a speedy trial. The prisoners' rights movement grew out of both the civil rights struggle and the Supreme Court decisions affirming defendant protections. Proponents of inmate rights took up the issues of prison overcrowding, restrictions within prisons on political activity and free speech, and the authority of prison officials to punish inmates.

The *Miranda, Gideon,* and *Escobedo* rulings, enlarging the rights of defendants and often restricting the activities of police and prosecutors, were issued just as the nation's crime rate began to shoot up. The reaction of much of the public, of the law enforcement community, and of a host of moderate to conservative politicians was intense—and almost invariably hostile. In a 1972 Gallup poll, the percentage of city residents naming crime as the most important issue rose from 4 percent in 1949 to 22 percent; more strikingly, 74 percent said that the courts were not tough enough with defendants.[28]

What was widely seen as a judicial assault on the criminal justice system extended, in addition, to the prison system. In a precedent-setting decision, a federal district court found in *Pugh v. Locke* in 1976 that the entire Alabama prison system was in violation of the eighth amendment prohibition against cruel and unusual punishment. Judge Frank M. Johnson found that "prison conditions are so debilitating that they necessarily deprive inmates of any opportunity to rehabilitate themselves or even maintain skills already possessed."[29] By the late 1980s, thirty-seven states, the District of Columbia, Puerto Rico, and the Virgin Islands were operating prisons under court order, almost all because of overcrowding and inmate violence, lack of medical care, unsanitary conditions, and absence of rehabilitation programs.[30]

Following the reforms of the criminal justice system and at the beginning of the prisoners' rights movement, were a sequence of Supreme Court decisions that rendered the death penalty illegal. In three related 1972 cases, *Furman v. Georgia*, *Jackson v. Georgia*, and *Branch v. Texas*, the Court overturned all existing death penalty statutes on the grounds that there was a "wanton and freakish" pattern in their application; the decisions effectively took an estimated 600 people across the country off death row.[31] The prohibition against the death penalty stood until 1976, when the court in *Gregg v. Georgia*, *Profitt v. Florida*, and *Jurek v. Texas*, restored its use.

The expansion of defendants' rights, the prisoner rights movement, and the four-year prohibition on the death penalty coincided with a sharply increasing crime rate and ran headlong into increasingly conservative public opinion on crime—all of which had marked consequences for domestic politics and for race relations. Popular support for liberal policies on crime and rehabilitation had grown steadily from the mid-1930s, when polls were first taken, to the mid-1960s. At that juncture, public opinion shifted in a decisively rightward direction, as crime rates rose sharply. In 1965, a substantial minority of survey respondents, 36 percent, said that the courts treated criminals "about right" or "too harsh[ly]," while 48 percent said the courts were not harsh enough. By 1977, the percentage describing court treatment of criminals as too harsh or about right had fallen to a minimal 11 percent, and those who said the courts were not harsh enough had risen to 83 percent.[32]

For one brief period, 1965–66, a plurality of Americans opposed the death penalty for those convicted of murder (47 percent opposed, 42 percent in favor, 11 percent no opinion in May 1966).[33] Since then, support for the death penalty has steadily grown. By late 1972, the year of the Supreme Court decisions barring capital punishment, 60 percent of those surveyed favored the death penalty, and only 30 percent opposed it; by the end of the 1970s, the ratio stood at 67 percent in favor, 27 percent opposed; and by 1988, 79 percent were in favor, 16 percent opposed.[34]

Increasingly conservative public opinion on the death penalty was a reflection of a much broader and growing base of support for tough sentencing. By 1987, mandatory sentencing laws were adopted in forty-six states, and presumptive sentencing requirements restricting judicial discretion in twelve states.[35] Even more striking evidence of transformed sentencing policy is found in the sharp increase in the nation's prison population, which started to rise sharply in 1974. For the previous fifteen years, the number of people in prisons had held steady at roughly 200,000. From 1974 to 1979, judges began imposing longer sentences, parole releases dropped sharply, crime rates themselves rose, and the prison population shot up to 300,000; it reached 400,000 by 1982 and 755,425 by 1990.[36]

The criminal rights and the prisoner rights movements strengthened the linkage between the rights revolution and one of the most emotionally charged areas of American life: crime. The crime rate, which had surged in the 1960s, continued to grow in the 1970s. The following table compiled from Federal Bureau of Investigation data, traces the pattern.

TABLE 5.3

The Increase in All Reported Crime and Violent Crime (Murder, Robbery, Assault, and Rape) from 1960 to 1980

(The figures are in 1,000s, so that, for example, in 1960, 3.38 million crimes, and 288,000 violent crimes, were reported to police, and in 1980, 13.4 million crimes and 1.3 million violent crimes were reported.)

|  | *1960* | *1965* | *1970* | *1975* | *1980* | *% Increase* |
|---|---|---|---|---|---|---|
| All Crime | 3,384 | 4,739 | 8,098 | 11,292 | 13,408 | 296% |
| Violent Crime | 288 | 387 | 738 | 1,040 | 1,345 | 367% |

SOURCE: Table supplied by the FBI, *Index of Crime, United States, 1960–1988*; and *Crime Index Rate, United States, 1960–1988*.

The sharp rise in reported violent crime had major consequences for both politics and race relations across the country. There are a number of ways to measure differences between crime rates for blacks and whites—the three most common being 1) an annual victimization survey conducted by the Department of Justice from 1973 to the present; 2) FBI arrest rate statistics from 1965 onward; and, 3) the makeup of the prison population.[37] All three show a much higher crime rate among blacks than whites, with the ratio significantly higher for violent crime (murder, robbery, assault, and rape) than for property crimes (larceny, motor vehicle theft, burglary). From 1960 to 1986, the prison population shifted from 38 percent to 43.5 percent black.[38] In terms of the victimization surveys, which suggest lower rates of crime for blacks than does the FBI compilation of arrest rates, and are thus less subject to charges of racial bias, the 1974 survey found that while blacks made up 11 percent of the total U.S. population,[39] victims of aggravated assault said 30 percent of their assailants were black, victims of robbery said 62 percent of their attackers were black, and victims of rape said 39 percent of the offenders were black.[40]

The gap between the races has consistently been widest of all for robbery, (muggings, stick-ups, purse-snatches), one of the most threatening and most common of the violent crimes. It is threatening because it the crime committed most often by strangers; it involves the use of force or the impending use of force; and it is the crime that occurs most often where the victim feels most vulnerable, outside of the home, on the streets and sidewalks. Robbery is the one crime in which the victim survey and the arrest rates show almost identical ratios between black and white offenders, suggesting that the arrest rates are a relatively accurate reflection of the rate of commission of robbery. The annual criminal victimization surveys conducted by the Department of Justice consistently show that more robberies are committed by blacks than whites.

The robbery figures throughout the 1960s, 1970s, and 1980s reflect at the extreme the challenge posed to Democratic liberalism by rising rates of social disorder in the wake of civil rights legislation and following upon substantial growth of federal expenditures in behalf of the poor. This is a dilemma that the Democratic party and liberals have been reluctant to address, a reluctance motivated by compassion, by fear of provoking backlash, and by the desire to preserve a basis for more effective policy interventions. This reluctance, no matter how understandable, has nonetheless eroded the political credibility of liberalism and of the Democratic party.

For many members of the black leadership class, and for much of the white liberal community, examination of divisive racially freighted issues has been seen as having the potential to produce damaging results. These include the encouragement of a racist and "victim blaming" analysis of black poverty; a disproportionate focusing on black dysfunction, downplaying white criminality and white drug abuse; and failure to recognize the emergence of white underclasses in other highly industrialized and competitive societies, including a largely white underclass in England.[41] A focus on so-called social pathology or on a "culture of poverty" among the most disadvantaged, some liberals argue, can be used to shift the burden of responsibility for institutionalized discrimination from the perpetrators to those who suffer social and economic ostracism at society's hands; to shift to blacks blame for an aberrant culture, rather than holding accountable their historic victimizers. A focus on "social deviance" or on an underclass subculture leaves unaddressed, according to this perspective, the oppressive economic and social structures which make inevitable the set of behavioral responses then labeled pathological. Finally, a number of liberals feel that the public naming of patterns of social disorder, including the use of the word "underclass,"[42] draws undue attention to such patterns, attention which can be manipulated by conservative ideological antagonists for political gain. The successful election in 1989 of Republican State Representative David Duke in Louisiana, the president of the National Association for the Advancement of White People, whose campaign stressed with striking success black crime, illegitimacy, and welfare dependency, and Duke's 44 percent vote in the 1990 Louisiana senatorial primary, can be seen as a confirmation of these fears.

Conversely, pointed liberal avoidance of these issues has its own liabilities. First of all, these issues are inescapably in the political arena: voters are seeking a resolution to the violence and social disorder expressed in crime, drug use, and illegitimacy. Secondly, the failure of the left to address such issues has permitted the political right to profit from explicit and covert manipulation of symbols and images relying upon assumptions about black poverty and crime—as in the Republicans' 1988 campaign focus on the death penalty, Willie Horton, and the "revolving prison door" television commercials.

The liberal failure to convincingly address increasingly conservative attitudes in the majority electorate, attitudes spurred in part by crime and welfare rates, has damaged the national Democratic party on a variety of counts. Perhaps most important, it has signaled a failure to live up to one of the chief obligations of a political party: to secure the safety and well-being of its own constituents, black and white. Secondly, self-imposed

Democratic myopia has in no way prevented the majority public from forming "hard" opinions on crime, drug use, chronic joblessness, and out-of-wedlock births—nor from judging the national Democratic party as excessively "soft" in its approach to contemporary social issues—nor from voting for politicians whose conservative attitudes on crime and social disorder more completely mirror its own.

# 6

# The Tax Revolt

THE COSTS of liberalism—highly visible, and often exploited by the right in the course of political competition—have obstructed public recognition of the achievements of the federal government, of the Democratic party, and of the civil rights movement. The trends on crime, drug use, chronic joblessness, welfare, and out-of-wedlock births in the decades following the Civil Rights Act of 1964 contrast sharply with the unprecedented development of a black working and middle class. During the years following passage of the Civil Rights Act, an expanding economy, legal prohibitions against racial discrimination, and growing private support and public-sector backing for new education and employment opportunities for blacks joined to become powerful sources of social transformation.

With the federal judiciary, Congress, and the government regulatory apparatus acting together as an engine of change, blacks surged into higher education and into professional and managerial employment. In 1973, the income of young (aged 25–29) black college graduates actually exceeded that of young white college graduates by nine percent;[1] by the mid-1970s, the percentage of black high school graduates going on to college matched, and in some years surpassed, the percentage among whites.[2]

Clifton Wharton, chancellor of the State University of New York, himself black, pointed out in 1978: "Blacks who make up 11 percent of America's population, now make up 10 percent of the 10.6 million college students. In one year, 1974, the percentage of black high school graduates actually exceeded the percentage of white high school graduates going to college."[3] The number of blacks holding managerial, professional, and technical jobs grew from 474,060 in 1960 to 781,369 in 1970 to 1,564,914 in

1980, with private-sector managerial jobs held by blacks growing by 222 percent between 1970 and 1980, from 87,765 to 282,488; with the number of black engineers growing by 163 percent, from 13,679 to 36,019; and with the number of black lawyers and judges growing by 262 percent, from 3,728 to 15,277.[4]

During these years, the mandate of the federal regulatory structure to force change in both public- and private-sector employment policies was expanded exponentially. From 1966 to 1979, the budget of the Equal Employment Opportunity Commission (EEOC) grew from $3.25 million to $111.4 million; and between 1970 and 1979, the budget of the Office of Federal Contract Compliance Programs (OFCCP) grew from $570,000 to $43.2 million.[5] By 1972, every cabinet-level department in the federal government had an equal employment office.[6]

The power of the civil rights enforcement process was most apparent in the changing composition of municipal police forces in cities that were either placed under court-enforced consent decrees to boost the hiring of minorities, or that had elected black mayors who initiated affirmative-action hiring programs. In Atlanta, the percentage of black officers rose from 10 in 1968 to 29.9 in 1975 to 47.2 in 1985; in Detroit, for the same time periods, the percentages rose from 5 to 22.3 to 41.2; in Oakland, California, from 4 to 12.4 to 22.8 percent.[7]

The substantial gains in economic and job status were heavily concentrated among working blacks and among intact black families. From 1940 to 1970, family income for all black families (both intact and single-parent families) as a percentage of white family income grew from 41.1 percent to 61.2 percent. But from 1970 to 1980, there was almost no growth, with black family income as a percentage of white family income rising only 1.7 percent over ten years to reach 62.5 percent. The income of *intact* black families, however, not only had grown at a faster pace in the earlier period—from 41.6 percent of white income in 1940 to 71.4 percent in 1970—but continued to grow through 1980, when it reached 82 percent of white family income.[8] The following Table 6.1, based on the work of James P. Smith, of the Rand Corporation, and Finis R. Welch, of UCLA, traces these trends in terms of the distribution of white and black families, intact and female-headed, between the poor, middle class, and affluent, from 1960 to 1980.

What this chart demonstrates is that while racial disparities in income remained huge in 1980, the rate of reduction of poverty among blacks from 1960 to 1980 was much faster than that among whites, and the near doubling in the percentage of affluent black families far outpaced the rate of growth of affluent white families—although the absolute percentage of

TABLE 6.1

The Income-Group Status of Families from 1960 to 1980*

|  | 1960 | 1970 | 1980 |
|---|---|---|---|
| *All Families* | | | |
| White | | | |
| Poor | 12% | 9% | 9% |
| Middle Class | 62 | 66 | 61 |
| Affluent | 25 | 25 | 30 |
| Black | | | |
| Poor | 48 | 32 | 30 |
| Middle Class | 49 | 59 | 59 |
| Affluent | 6 | 9 | 11 |
| *Intact Families* | | | |
| White | | | |
| Poor | 10 | 7 | 6 |
| Middle Class | 64 | 67 | 64 |
| Affluent | 26 | 26 | 30 |
| Black | | | |
| Poor | 39 | 21 | 15 |
| Middle Class | 54 | 69 | 68 |
| Affluent | 7 | 7 | 17 |
| *Female-Headed Families* | | | |
| White | | | |
| Poor | 34 | 32 | 30 |
| Middle Class | 52 | 58 | 52 |
| Affluent | 14 | 10 | 8 |
| Black | | | |
| Poor | 69 | 58 | 53 |
| Middle Class | 29 | 40 | 44 |
| Affluent | 2 | 2 | 3 |

*The figures are the percentage of the group that is either poor, middle class, or affluent.

SOURCE: James P. Smith and Finis Welch, "Race and Poverty: A Forty-Year Record," *The American Economic Review* (May 1987), Tables 2 and 3, pp. 154 and 155.

affluent white families remained far higher than that of blacks. The most striking development within the black community, however, was the huge drop in poverty among intact families, from 39 percent in 1960 to 15 percent in 1980, and the more than doubling of the percentage described as affluent. This stands in sharp contrast to the far slower decline in poverty among black female-headed households, dropping from 69 to 53 percent, and the effective stagnation in the already minimal number of black female-headed households described as affluent (from 2 to 3 percent).

Although the poverty rates of both intact and female-headed black families improved during the 1970s, there was very little improvement in the overall rate of black family poverty. This seeming anomaly grows out of the fact that the distribution of intact and female-headed households changed dramatically in the 1970s: the percentage of black family households headed by women—more than half of whom were poor in both 1970 and 1980—grew from 28 to 40 percent between 1970 and 1980, while the percentage of intact black family households—among whom poverty rates sharply improved—declined from 68 to 55 percent.[9]

In addition, while working black men and women made substantial gains relative to whites (the income and wages of black women reached virtual parity with those of white women by 1979–80), the percentage of blacks who were working fell significantly from 1970 to 1980. In that period, the percentage of black 24-year-old men who were productively engaged in work, in school, or in the military fell from 78.9 to 71.8 percent, while the percentage who were either unemployed, out of the labor force altogether, or in jail grew from 21.1 to 28.2 percent. For 35 and 36-year-old black men, the percentage who were unemployed, out of the workforce, or in jail grew from 13.7 percent to 20.3 percent.[10]

The growing bifurcation within the black community, between the better-off and the worse-off, and the close links of this bifurcation to family structure, class, and to the changing job marketplace, produced a partial revival among some liberals of the study of factors other than—or in addition to—direct racial discrimination in determining the social and economic well-being of blacks. Influential works seeking explanations of black poverty looking beyond racial discrimination included Richard B. Freeman's *Black Elite: The New Market for Highly Educated Black Americans,* and the work of William Julius Wilson, including *The Declining Significance of Race: Blacks and Changing American Institutions.* Both Freeman and Wilson argued that the achievements of the civil rights movement in outlawing discrimination and in establishing affirmative action programs in the public and private sectors had worked well for educated blacks from upper-working-class or middle-class intact families, but that the successes of the civil rights movement had done little for less-educated blacks from low-income, single-parent homes who were poorly positioned to take advantage of newly created opportunities.

Wilson, a liberal social democrat and a black, contended that "many blacks and white liberals have yet to recognize that the problem of economic dislocation is more central to the plight of the black poor than is the problem of purely racial discrimination. . . . As the black middle class rides on the wave of political and social changes, benefitting from the growth of employment opportunities in the growing corporate and government sectors of the economy, the black underclass falls behind the larger society in every conceivable respect."[11]

Wilson, in effect, laid down the gauntlet, arguing that: "The black elites' definition of the current problems of black Americans is embodied in an ideology of culture and politics which obscures class differences—an ideology which therefore stresses a single or uniform black experience. . . . The issues are being defined by the articulate black intelligentsia—the very group that has benefited the most in recent years from anti-discrimination programs."[12]

The reaction among black sociologists to Wilson, a MacArthur Prize Fellow and professor of Sociology and Public Policy at the University of Chicago, was intense. In 1978, the Association of Black Sociologists passed a resolution declaring: "It is the position of this organization that the sudden national attention given to Professor Wilson's book obscures the problem of the persistent oppression of blacks. . . . The Association of Black Sociologists is outraged over the misrepresentation of the black experience. We are also extremely disturbed over the policy implications that may derive from this work and that, given the nature of American society, are likely to set in motion equally objectionable trends in funding, research and training."[13]

In 1984, six years after the publication of *The Declining Significance of Race*, Alphonso Pinkney, a black and a professor of sociology at Hunter College, wrote that black sociologists like Wilson "who support the conservative movement are not unlike government officials in (formerly) South Vietnam who supported American aggression against their own people."[14] In 1989, eleven years after publication of Wilson's book, Charles V. Willie, a black professor at the Harvard School of Education, contended: "By spatializing the problem of poverty in his structural analysis of the urban poor, Wilson is an accomplice to whatever harm is visited upon this population in the deadly 'game' of power politics."[15]

Even as the controversy over the causes of black poverty raged, the widening split within the black community and the worsening conditions of the underclass lent themselves to increasingly influential conservative analyses that attacked both the incentives created by the welfare state and the social consequences of the rights revolution. The most detailed and broadly circulated of these analyses was produced by Charles Murray in his 1984 book *Losing Ground,* and in numerous subsequent articles. Murray argued that the best way out of poverty for those with little education and few skills was to get a poorly paying job, to acquire skills, and to move up the training ladder

> . . . and thereby eventually to move into a relatively secure job with decent wages. [But] The reforms of the 1960s . . . discouraged poor young people, and especially poor young males, from pursing this slow, incremental approach in four ways. First, they increased the size of the welfare package and transformed the eligibility rules so as to make welfare a more available and attractive *temporary* alternative to a job. Second, the reforms in law enforcement and criminal justice increased access to income from the underground economy. By the 1970s, illegal income (including that from dealing in drugs, gambling, and stolen goods, as well as direct predatory crime) had become a major source of income in poor communities. Third, the breakdown in inner-city education reduced job readiness. Acculturation to the demands of the workplace—arriving every day at the same time, staying there, accepting the role of a subordinate—diminished as these behaviors were no longer required in the schoolroom. Fourth, the reforms diminished the stigma associated with welfare and simultaneously devalued the status associated with working at a menial, low-paying job—indeed, holding onto a menial job became in some poor communities a *source* of stigma.[16]

The dilemma posed to liberalism by the rise of illegitimacy, crime, and long-term joblessness is part of a much broader political and ideological dilemma. In pressing egalitarian goals, in seeking to advance the rights of disenfranchised groups (groups often lacking broad popular support) as well as the rights of blacks and Hispanics, liberalism itself has resorted to covert strategems, strategems at once anti-democratic and anti-intellectual. Public debate within the Democratic party and among liberal thinkers and activists has been heavily censored by the fear of harm to minorities at the hands of the majority public, as well as by the fear of exacerbated conflict within the party, and within the broader ranks of the left.

The unwillingness of liberalism and of the Democratic party to engage in painful debate has, in turn, led to a reluctance to examine the effectiveness and costs of programs and of legal remedies adopted to implement liberal ends. This reluctance has made impossible a well-conceived strategy focusing on how best to bear and to mitigate such costs—particularly the political costs.

The dependence of liberalism on the courts and on the regulatory and bureaucratic structures of government reflects the staggering difficulties of maintaining majority support for a liberal agenda. Even the dependence of liberalism on Congress, as opposed to the White House, reflects the need to turn to an institution where intense special-interest pressure can supersede less vociferous majority opinion.

The result has been the undermining of the once-powerful ability of liberalism to speak for "the little guy," the average working man and woman. Reluctance to debate the liberal agenda vigorously in public has, furthermore, intensified the public perception of an anti-democratic liberal elite—and has increased the ability of conservatism and of the Republican party to claim to represent so-called traditional community values: of family, neighborhood, church, school, and the workplace—values endorsed by the voting majority. This polarization places liberalism in the difficult, and at times intolerable, position of defending minority rights against majority values, the consequences of which will be explored in more detail in the last chapter.

If the increasing political isolation of liberalism was spurred by the use of court-ordered busing to desegregate northern schools, it was further aggravated by the expansion, in the late 1960s and early 1970s, of racial preferences in hiring and in education.

In June 1965, Lyndon Johnson had argued that unlike blacks, other immigrant groups "did not have the [American] heritage of centuries to overcome, and they did not have a cultural tradition which had been twisted and battered by endless years of hatred and hopelessness, nor were they excluded, these others, because of race or color—a feeling whose dark intensity is matched by no other prejudice in our society."[17]

The competitive disadvantage borne by blacks, as well as the realization that the removal of legal barriers to integration was by itself insufficient to remedy the legacy of disadvantage sown by three centuries of slavery and of formal segregation, led to an unprecedented set of government policies. Federal directives and regulations—developed by the Equal Employment Opportunity Commission (EEOC) in the late 1960s and early 1970s, and then endorsed by the Supreme Court in 1971 in *Griggs v. Duke Power Co.* and in later decisions—provided for racial preferences in hiring and promotion. These policies created, in turn, new conflicts and polarizations within the electorate, as affirmative action, by its nature, required whites to give up both customary privileges and substantial material rewards. If discrimination had produced a job marketplace tilted significantly in favor of whites, racial preferences deliberately tilted the marketplace to favor minorities. Affirmative action required whites, who in many cases had not individually practiced discrimination, to absorb the penalties for past discrimination by other whites, ceding opportunities for employment and promotion to competing blacks.

These were costs that would have been difficult to absorb under any circumstances, but the constricting economy of the 1970s and early 1980s sharply raised the costs. What made the issues of rising crime, illegitimacy, drug use, joblessness, and welfare dependency so incendiary and so politically charged in these circumstances, was the questions they raised in the minds of white voters—voters from a broad range of ideological backgrounds—about the worth and legitimacy of such sacrifice.

Many of the most aggressive efforts to provide jobs for blacks were directed by the Justice Department between 1967 and 1974 at the building trades unions; the next round of affirmative action remedies was targeted at city, county, and state agencies, especially at police and fire departments. White men working as carpenters, plumbers, sheetmetal workers, iron workers, steamfitters, cops, and firemen—jobs that had been largely white preserves—became the focus of the anti-discrimination drive waged by the Civil Rights Division of the Justice Department.[18]

From the start, the Justice Department challenged established hiring and promotion practices seen as barring blacks from full participation in the job market, practices such as seniority, ability testing, educational requirements, union membership, and nepotism (the choosing of apprentices from among the relatives of union members). These practices had long been integral to the union movement, as well as to corporate hiring and to most mechanisms of promotion. In 1967, a federal district court in Louisiana ruled illegal practices of Local 53 of the Asbestos Workers Union, outlawing both the limiting of membership to the close relatives of those in the union and the requirement of majority membership support— by vote—for all new union admissions. These practices clearly had discriminatory consequences, but they were also practices core to a host of craft unions across the country, unions that had been built not only as labor organizations, but as family and ethnic associations structuring community life.[19]

Cases involving these issues slowly worked their way through the legal system in the 1970s toward a Supreme Court generally sympathetic to minority claims. At stake in these cases were issues often involving the life work of both individuals and of groups. Discrimination had resulted in the denial of jobs to blacks for several hundred years, but the remedies often involved zero-sum solutions in which the gains of one group were losses for the other. Even worse, these losses were occurring just when the market in unskilled and semi-skilled jobs was declining.

Part of the dilemma posed by employment discrimination cases is reflected in the majority opinion by Justice William Brennan, upholding the award of retroactive seniority to discriminated-against blacks in the 1976 case *Franks v. Bowman Transportation Co., Inc.*, and in the dissenting opinion of Justice Lewis Powell.

Brennan wrote that retroactive seniority was essential for the victim of discrimination because without it, he "will never obtain his rightful place in the hierarchy of seniority according to which these various employment benefits are distributed. He will perpetually remain subordinate to persons who, but for the illegal discrimination, would have been, in respect to entitlement to the benefits, [ie., longevity of employment] his inferiors." Powell, in dissent, contended that the discrimination in question had been committed by the company, not its employees. Consequently, the award of retroactive seniority would penalize "the rights and expectations of perfectly innocent employees. The economic benefits awarded discrimination victims would be derived not at the expense of the employer, but at the expense of other workers [who would be leapfrogged on the seniority roster by subsequently hired victims of employment discrimination]."[20] In fact, both justices were correct.

The power of the federal government to bring suit against unions and private companies was extended through amendments to the Civil Rights Act by a Democratic Congress in 1972, bringing under the jurisdiction of the Justice Department terrain traditionally crucial to the vote-gathering efforts of the Democratic party: municipal employment in major cities, particularly in police and fire departments, many of which had been controlled for generations by white ethnic groups, predominantly by Irish-Americans and Italian-Americans.

From 1972 to 1980, the Justice Department took fifty-one city, county, and state governments to court, including both the police and fire departments of Los Angeles, Chicago, Miami, and St. Louis; the fire departments in Boston, Dallas, Buffalo, Atlanta, and San Francisco; and the police departments in Philadelphia and Cincinnati. At the same time, private suits moved toward agreement under consent decrees in such cities as Detroit and Birmingham just as the first black mayors were elected to office there.[21]

Police, firemen, unionized skilled craftsmen, and their families were the mainstays of white, working-class precincts in America's cities; precincts that from the 1930s to the mid-1960s had produced decisive Democratic margins. These voters had little if any cultural sympathy for the rights revolution in the first place, and in the 1970s, they became defacto defendants (through their unions and employers) in the most controversial of all federal policies targeted at calcified patterns of inequality: affirmative action.

No issue has captured the fundamental tension between two basic American goals—the maintenance of an egalitarian society and the elimination of the consequences of illegal discrimination—better than racial preferences and affirmative action. No issue more clearly divides public opinion between white and black America, and few issues are more sharply disagreed upon by the Republican and Democratic parties.

Not until 1968—103 years after the end of the Civil War—did the Birmingham Fire Department hire its first black fireman. Throughout all those years, blacks were systematically denied the opportunity not only of employment, but of building seniority and of learning the promotional ropes. Legal proceedings were initiated against the city in 1974, the year that the second black fireman was hired, and, seven years later in 1981, after the election of Richard Arrington, Birmingham's first black mayor, the city agreed to a consent decree providing that every white hire or promotion would be matched, one for one, by a black hire or promotion, as long as blacks were available who had fulfilled basic test requirements.

In 1983, James Henson, a white fireman, and Carl Cook, a black fireman, both took the Birmingham Fire Department test for lieutenant. Both passed, but Henson ranked sixth among all who took the test, with a score of 192, while Cook ranked 86th, with a score of 122. Under the consent decree, Cook was promoted to lieutenant, and Henson was not.

In 1990, Henson became part of a group of whites attempting to challenge the consent degree, arguing: "I can understand that blacks had been historically discriminated against. I can also understand why people would want to be punitive in correcting it. Somebody needs to pay for this. But they want me to pay for it, and I didn't have anything to do with it. I was a kid when all this [discrimination] went on." Cook, on the other hand, contended that the white firemen "don't have anything to gripe about because they're still living off what their forefathers did. . . . I look at that [white complaints of reverse discrimination] like I would look at a bank robber, and this guy has taken the money and he's gone and he's bought a house in one of the exclusive sections of town, and he's bought his teenager a Mercedes or Jaguar. And then all of a sudden the law comes and says, 'Wait a minute, we've got your picture. You're the one that robbed the bank. So we're going to confiscate your house, your car, your clothes.' And then the family stands there and says, 'Well, you can't do that. We didn't rob the bank. You got him; he robbed the bank.' "[22]

The example of the Birmingham Fire Department represents an extreme: pitting white and black workers against each other in a competition for government-controlled jobs and employment benefits. Over time, these racial divisions reverberated into Birmingham's political system. Once a city where every elected official was a Democrat, racial conflict has begun to translate into partisan realignment. By the end of the 1980s, Jefferson County, which encompasses Birmingham, had eighteen seats in the state House of Representatives split evenly between nine blacks and nine whites. In partisan terms, there were nine black Democrats, eight white Republicans, and one white Democrat. Among the white Republican state representatives was Billy Gray, former president of the Firefighters Union. Race had become central to establishing partisan difference.

While at one end of the labor-market spectrum affirmative action rulings were affecting blue-collar men and their families, at other points on the spectrum government support for remedial racial, and gender, preferences were forcing a major restructuring of traditional patterns of white-collar employment and of university admissions. In addition, just as Department of Justice lawsuits forcing court-ordered hiring and promotion in unions and in police and fire departments were driving a wedge between formerly Democratic white workers and increasingly Democratic black competitors, affirmative action was forcing divisive conflicts between two once-firmly allied Democratic groups, Jews and blacks.

In 1978, when the Supreme Court took up the issue of Paul Allen Bakke's challenge to the policy of the medical school at the University of California, Davis, to set aside sixteen of one hundred openings for "disadvantaged" (in practice, minority) applicants, the case placed at loggerheads Jewish organizations such as the Anti-Defamation League, and civil rights groups such as the NAACP. For Jews and blacks, quotas have had entirely different historical meanings: serving for Jews to exclude them from professional and educational opportunities, and thus fiercely resisted, while serving for blacks as a means of inclusion, useful in opening up opportunities.

The Supreme Court ruled in favor of the white applicant, Bakke, ordering his admission to medical school, although the important opinion written by swing Justice Powell found that race could be used as a "plus" factor in admissions by universities seeking a diversified student body. A decade later, Dr. Robert G. Petersdorf, president of the Association of

American Medical Colleges, contended that the "Supreme Court [*Bakke*] decision actually encouraged affirmative action goals by allowing the use of race and other determinants . . . as acceptable admissions policy". From 1978 to 1988, the percentage of blacks enrolled in medical schools remained firm at six percent.[23]

The zero-sum element of affirmative action in higher education is evident from the statements of officials who endorse the policy. "We are committed to a program of affirmative action, and we want to make the university representative of the population of the state as a whole," James A. Blackburn, dean of admissions at the University of Virginia, said in 1988. "That means fewer spaces for the traditional mainstream white students who have come here from around the county. . . . If you were looking at the academic credentials, you would say Virginia has it upside down. We take more in the groups with weaker credentials and make it harder for those with stronger credentials."[24]

In the workplace, the employment provisions of the Civil Rights Act of 1964, as enforced by the EEOC upon all employers of one hundred or more, and the affirmative action hiring requirements applicable to all federal contractors with contracts exceeding $50,000 and with fifty or more employees—employment provisions enforced through the Office of Federal Contract Compliance Program (OFCCP)—have produced a major restructuring of employment patterns across the country. Together, the EEOC and the OFCCP regulate private-sector companies employing about one-half of all the nation's workers. Since the enactment of the Civil Rights Act, there has been a massive shift of black workers from companies that are not covered by either the EEOC or the OFCCP to firms that are—particularly to federal contractors who do not want to lose access to continued business with the U.S. government. The shift to EEOC and OFCCP-covered companies has been significant because these are the nation's larger companies with better pay and fringe-benefit packages and with wider opportunities for advancement than, for example, retail companies, one of the most exempt industries.[25]

In 1966, when the EEOC first set requirements that firms under its jurisdiction file reports annually, just under half, 48 percent, of all black workers were employed by these companies; sixteen years later, 60 percent of all black workers were employed by EEOC-covered companies. "As large as those changes in total employment seem, they pale next to changes within the manager and professional jobs," according to a Rand Corporation study. "Black managers and professionals were half as likely as white managers and professionals to work in [EEOC] covered firms in 1966. By 1980, black managers were equally likely to be found in covered firms."[26] Along similar lines, Jonathan S. Leonard, professor of Industrial Relations in the School of Business of the University of California, Berkeley, found that in companies covered by the OFCCP, the employment growth rate from 1974 to 1980 for black men was 3.8 percent faster than in non-covered firms; 7.9 percent faster for other minority males (primarily Asian-American and Hispanic); 2.8 percent faster for white women; and 12.3 percent faster for black women. In contrast, the employment of white men grew at a rate 1.2 percent slower in covered firms than in non-covered companies.[27]

———

Although the original impetus of the federal equal-employment and contract-compliance provisions was to remedy discrimination against blacks and other racial minorities, critical political support for sustained congressional backing of such provisions was provided by the inclusion of women in the 1964 legislation. Later, the base of political support was further strengthened by adding the elderly and the handicapped, with passage in 1967 of the Age Discrimination in Employment Act and, in 1973, of the Rehabilitation Act, barring discrimination against the physically and mentally handicapped.

Together, organizations representing blacks, women, the elderly, and the handicapped represented a powerful lobby in behalf of legislation and executive orders barring discrimination and requiring affirmative action programs in the private and public sectors. The addition of groups other than blacks, and the rising political muscle of women, significantly altered enforcement patterns. In the late 1960s, the ratio of actionable charges brought by the EEOC on the basis of race outnumbered those brought on the basis of sex by three to one, 9,562 race cases to 2,689 sex cases in 1969; 15,396 race cases to 5,820 sex cases in 1971. With the political signals sent by congressional passage of the Equal Rights Amendment in 1972, however, the number of sex discrimination cases grew—by 413 percent between 1971 and 1981, from 5,820 to 30,925—while the number of race discrimination cases grew by 186 percent, from 15,394 to 44,085.[28] In terms of court suits filed by the EEOC, the pattern is even more striking. In 1986, for example, the EEOC issued a press release declaring that in the first quarter of the year it had set a record for filing "lawsuits on behalf of job discrimination claimants." Of those suits, many more were filed in behalf of persons claiming sex discrimination (forty-one suits) and age discrimination (28 suits), than for racial discrimination (21 suits). (The EEOC does not represent the handicapped in private-sector cases.)[29]

———

The political support provided to blacks by organizations representing women, the elderly, and the handicapped has not, however, reduced the division between whites and blacks on the issue of racial preferences. In the early to mid-1970s, as affirmative action become an acute source of friction between once-loyally partisan white and black Democrats, conflict over the issue that caused the most severe racial divisions in city after city—court-ordered busing to remedy urban school segregation—reached a high point.

From 1969 to 1976, desegregation plans—many of which required busing—were ordered in forty-seven of the country's one hundred largest school districts, thirty-three of them in the South, and the remaining fourteen in such northern cities as Detroit, Boston, Denver, San Francisco, Minneapolis, and Dayton. In many of these school districts, white enrollment plummeted. From 1968 to 1976, the percentage of white students in Boston public schools fell from 68.5 to 44; in Detroit from 39.3 to 18.6; in Dade County (Miami) from 58.3 to 41; in Atlanta from 38.2 to 11.7; in Denver from 65.6 to 48.1; in San Francisco from 41.2 to 27.6; and in Birmingham from 48.6 to 31.2.[30]

————

While Democrats basked in the reflected glow of Watergate, the momentum behind conservatism continued to build, until by the late 1970s it reached levels that knocked the legs out from under liberalism and, to a lesser extent, out from under the national Democratic party. The effects of racial schisms in the Democratic coalition during the second half of the 1960s and early 1970s—schisms created by urban riots, by rising crime rates, by pressures to end segregated housing, by affirmative action, and by busing—were further reinforced in the mid and late 1970s by inflation, by income stagnation, rising welfare and food stamp costs, and by ever-growing tax burdens.

Watergate had served briefly to mask the conflicts of Democratic liberalism; by the 1978 elections, however, Democratic liberalism ran into a brick wall. That year, the political debate shifted in a direction that would prove to be debilitating to the presidential wing of the Democratic party for at least the next decade. With brutal force, the tax revolt—which erupted in California in 1978 with the passage of property-tax-cutting Proposition 13—moved across the country. The tax revolt opened up a new schism in American politics, pitting taxpayers against tax recipients.

For the Democratic party, the party of government activism, this new division was a major threat, creating fault lines across Democratic constituencies; fault lines often coinciding with, or running closely parallel to, the party's racial fissures. Proposition 13 established the groundwork for an anti-tax ethic that would sustain Republicans in presidential campaigns—and in many state and local contests—through at least the next decade.

The tax revolt, in tandem with sustained partisan conflict over racial policies—and over social/moral issues ranging from gun control to school prayer to abortion—catalyzed the mobilization of a conservative presidential majority. California became the testing ground for this new conservatism—California with its soaring property taxes, especially in the Los Angeles area (which already faced a school busing order); with its Democratic legislature and its Democratic governor both unwilling to use revenue surpluses to provide tax relief; and with its easy access to the ballot for almost any group seeking a statewide referendum.

The battle over Proposition 13—passed by a margin of 65 to 35—split the electorate along lines that reinforced and widened the divisions that had already begun to appear over race. Polls taken during the campaign for Proposition 13 show that there were only two groups providing consistent opposition to the property tax rollback: blacks and public employees.

Polls conducted in May and August of 1978 showed 67 percent of whites supporting Proposition 13, while only 29 percent of blacks supported it, and only 42 percent of public employees. At the same time, the central focus of public hostility to government spending in California was on programs providing a significant share of benefits to minorities: welfare and, to a lesser extent, public housing. California voters in three polls conducted from July 1977 to November 1979 favored cuts in welfare over increases by a margin of 73–27. Cuts in public housing were favored over increased expenditures by a more modest 54–46 margin. In contrast, increased spending on police was favored over cuts by a 71–29 margin, on public schools by a 58–42 margin, on public transportation by a 66–34 margin, and on environmental protection by a 53–47 margin.[31]

The tax revolt provided, in addition, a new means for conservatives to identify and define an "establishment" attempting to thwart the populist will of the electorate—an establishment closely linked to the pro–civil rights establishment demonized by Wallace and Nixon in 1968 and in 1972. The array of groups opposing Proposition 13 lent itself to characterization as a liberal establishment: labor unions, the League of Women Voters, Common Cause, feminist and civil rights groups, the Chamber of Commerce, the California Teachers' Association, and a host of powerful corporations. When Democratic State Assembly Speaker Leo McCarthy sought to paint Proposition 13 as a "Landlords' Enrichment Act," Howard Jarvis, the leading proponent, countered with a list of the companies pouring money into the drive to defeat the anti-tax measure, including $25,000 contributions from Southern California Edison, Pacific Mutual Insurance Company, the Bank of America, Atlantic Richfield; and $15,000 donations from Southern Pacific Railroad and Standard Oil of California.[32]

The California victory of Proposition 13 produced a wave of tax-cutting and tax-limitation referenda in at least eighteen other states over the next four years, with victories in states as diverse as Massachusetts, Alaska, Washington, Missouri, Montana, Maine, and Utah.[33] The tax revolt brought to fruition the phenomenon that Kevin Phillips had seen in the election results of 1968, a "great political upheaval . . . a populist revolt of the American masses who have been elevated by their prosperity to middle-class status and conservatism. Their revolt is against the caste, policies and taxation of the mandarins of Establishment liberalism."[34]

The tax revolt was a major turning point in American politics. It provided new muscle and new logic to the formation of a conservative coalition opposed to the liberal welfare state. The division of the electorate along lines of taxpayers versus tax recipients dovetailed with racial divisions: blacks (along with the growing Hispanic population) were disproportionately the recipients of government programs for the poor, disproportionately the beneficiaries of government-led efforts to redistribute rights and status, and the black middle and working classes were far more dependent on government programs and jobs than their white counterparts.[35] Race melded into a conservative-driven agenda that sought to polarize the public against the private sector. The tax revolt provided conservatism with a powerful internal coherence, shaping an anti-government ethic, and firmly establishing new grounds for the disaffection of white working- and middle-class voters from their traditional Democratic roots.

———

The fusion of race and taxes reflected in the tax revolt was mirrored in another, far-less publicized development of 1978, a development that proved equally critical to the rising fortunes of the American right: the political mobilization of the white fundamentalist Christian community. The activation of the organized Christian right was the culmination of one current of conservative reaction to the events of the post-*Brown* civil rights era, a mobilization that began to achieve organizational coherence in the 1970s, reflecting the complex interweaving of race, taxes, rights, and broader social and cultural conflicts as they contributed to the growing national strength of the Republican party.

The seeds of the full-blown Christian right can be said to have been sown on May 21, 1969, when the Lawyers Committee for Civil Rights

Under Law filed suit challenging the federal tax exemption granted to segregated private schools in Mississippi. The suit was the centerpiece of a civil rights drive to eliminate government subsidies to those private schools that had been created, in the era of "massive resistance," in order to evade integration orders. Many of these schools, known as "segregation academies," were set up across the south in cooperation with the White Citizens Council. William Green, a black parent from Holmes County, Mississippi, and his lawyer from the Lawyers Committee for Civil Rights, Frank Parker, won their case in 1971; but litigation dragged on for the next five years as initial Internal Revenue Service (IRS) regulations proved inadequate. Private schools, barred by the federal courts from receiving free state textbooks because of their discriminatory policies, continued to hold on to tax exemptions simply by inserting in their charters a pro forma nondiscrimination clause. Parker and Green went back to the courts in 1976 to force tougher regulation.

Initially, the IRS prepared to fight the suit, but with the election in 1976 of Democrat Jimmy Carter, and the appointment of Jerome Kurtz as IRS Commissioner, administration policy shifted. "I became convinced they [the Lawyers Committee] were right," said Kurtz. "I didn't know what the service was doing resisting the case. There were whole [new] school systems formed in Mississippi [in the wake of desegregation rulings]."[36] Kurtz ordered the creation of tough guidelines and shifted the burden of proof of nondiscrimination to private schools seeking tax exemptions in the years immediately following a desegregation order if, as was commonly the case in the South, there were no black students in the school or if the percentage of black students was suspiciously low.

Kurtz's announcement of the proposed regulations on August 22, 1978—largely unnoticed by the general public and by the media—sounded a thunderbolt through the fundamentalist and evangelical communities. "It kicked the sleeping dog," Richard Viguerie, a conservative, direct-mail fundraising specialist, declared. "It galvanized the religious right. It was the spark that ignited the religious right's involvement in real politics."[37]

Kurtz's proposed regulations produced an estimated 126,000 letters of protest to the IRS. Kurtz, who as IRS commissioner had regularly received threats, was so alarmed by the warnings in anonymous letters and phone calls that he obtained Secret Service protection for himself and his wife.[38]

The Christian school movement expanded rapidly in the 1970s, with the number of children attending fundamentalist academies growing from a negligible figure in the early and mid-1960s, to an estimated 1.45 million by 1986, with most of the growth occurring during the 1970s, when multiple public school desegregation orders were initiated.[39]

In many cases Christian schools were set up in response to integration orders; in other cases they were a response to the far more complex perception that violence and drugs had become commonplace in the public schools, that the schools no longer taught sexual restraint, that Supreme Court decisions prohibiting prayer in the schools amounted to an assault on the teaching of basic values, and that what had become known as "secular humanism" was corrupting the minds of the young. These concerns meshed and overlapped with issues of race and in many cases were racially driven, but the motivations involved were far too complex to be categorized as exclusively racist. In many respects, the Christian school movement was a reaction to social and cultural conflict that prominently included, but was by no means limited to, issues of race.

Before 1978, the rise of Christian fundamentalism, while generally beneficial to the Republican party, had not taken on an overt and specific partisan character. If anything, partisan politics had traditionally been anathema to church leaders. The proposed IRS regulations directed at private schools, however, turned what had been a loose confederation of Christian school associations, more concerned with textbooks and accreditation than with politics, into the core of a deeply political movement; the Moral Majority was created in 1979 in large part out of the structure of the Christian school movement, drawing from that movement key staff and organizational resources for the establishment of state chapters across the country.

Robert Billings, Sr., who as director of the National Christian Action Coalition led the 1978 fight against the IRS, became the first executive director of the Moral Majority. At least twenty-five of the first fifty state chairmen of the Moral Majority were affiliated with fundamentalist churches that sponsored Christian academies.[40] "The Christian school issue was the one thing that turned everyone on," Billings observed. "Moral Majority came on the heels of that. The reason we could do chapters for Moral Majority was that there were already chapters in existence."[41] In 1979 Billings declared, "Jerome Kurtz has done more to bring Christians together than any man since the Apostle Paul."[42]

The Republican party, in turn, recognized the partisan potential of the IRS controversy. Two Republican House members, Bob Dornan of California and John Ashbrook of Ohio, won passage of a rider to the IRS appropriation in 1979 barring enforcement of the regulation. When the Republican party gathered in July, 1980 in Detroit to nominate Ronald Reagan, writers of the platform section on education included a sentence declaring: "We will halt the unconstitutional regulatory vendetta launched by Mr. Carter's IRS Commissioner against independent schools."[43]

Within a matter of two years, the Republican party had gained a new ally: the leadership of the white fundamentalist and evangelical communities, a leadership with access to a ready-made organization through the huge, and rapidly growing, network of church schools. In 1976, white fundamentalists had voted for Jimmy Carter over Gerald Ford by a margin of 56–44. In 1980, 61 percent of white, born-against Protestants voted for Ronald Reagan. Among white Protestants falling into the "most fundamentalist" category, a category making up 15 percent of the total electorate, Reagan won 85 percent of the vote.[44] Reagan in 1980, running against a born-again Southern Baptist, barely carried seven southern states—Alabama, Arkansas, Kentucky, Mississippi, North Carolina, South Carolina and Tennessee—by a total of 108,799 votes out of 8.73 million cast, or 1.2 percent, votes that were more than accounted for by the switch among white fundamentalists.

———

The year 1978 marked not only the passage of Proposition 13 and the beginning of the surge of fundamentalist Christians towards the Republican party, but also the beginning of a decisively rightward shift in the outcome of elections for federal office, with a series of Republican victories more significant than their numbers might suggest: three in the Senate and fifteen in the House. The Senate that year moved decisively in a conservative direction, with the defeat of such Democratic liberals as Colorado's Floyd Haskell, Iowa's Dick Clark, and New Hampshire's Thomas McIntyre by, respectively, such spokesmen for the new right as Bill Armstrong, Roger Jepsen, and Gordon Humphrey.

The 1978 election signalled the resurgence—after a Watergate-triggered hiatus—of conservatism, a pent-up rightward force that gained momentum over the next two years and turned the 1980 election into a Democratic rout. From 1978 to 1980, during the Carter years, the central claim of the post–New Deal Democratic party—that it could manage the economy and produce sustained growth—collapsed under the combined weight of inflation, escalating oil prices, unemployment, high interest rates, and industrial stagnation. Instead of inflation serving to dampen unemployment, and unemployment serving to slow inflation, the two occurred simultaneously, deeply alarming the public and challenging trust in Democratic competence.

In a nation accustomed to a steadily improving standard of living, median family income continued the slide started in 1973, falling by $1,352 between 1978 and 1980, from $29,087 to $27,735, a 4.6 percent drop in infla-tion-adjusted dollars; average gross weekly earnings fell by $16.57, from $189.31 to $172.7, an 8.8 percent decline in inflation-adjusted dollars; and the unemployment rate increased from 6 to 7.1 percent. The rate of inflation rose from 7.7 percent in 1978 to 13.5 percent in 1980. The cost of buying a house or car on time became prohibitive as the prime rate rose from 9.06 percent in 1978 to a high of 21.5 percent in late 1980.[45]

The domestic image of Democratic economic incompetence was com-pounded on the international front, first by the seizure of sixty-six hos-tages at the American embassy in Iran on November 4, 1979, and then by the December 29, 1979, Soviet invasion of Afghanistan. In Iran, a revolu-tionary Third World government—prominently featured in the United States on the nightly news—humiliated the nation with impunity for 444 days, releasing the hostages just hours after Carter's term in office came to an end.

The invasion of Afghanistan provoked an acknowledgment from Carter of striking naiveté concerning Soviet intentions, as the president admitted that the invasion "has made a more dramatic change in my opin-ion of what the Soviets' ultimate goals are than anything they have done in the previous time that I have been in office."[46] Carter's imposition of a grain embargo on the Soviet Union and of a U.S. boycott of the 1980 Olympic Games in Moscow damaged American interests as much or more than they did Soviet interests.

The economic and foreign policy failures of the Carter administration drove home to a majority of the electorate an image of the Democratic party as imposing increasing costs on American voters without adequate compensating rewards. The years from 1964 to 1980 had, in fact, produced an accumulation of pressures and grievances—creating a chain reaction pulling together the interactive issues of race, rights, and taxes, a reaction fueling an evolving Republican presidential realignment.

Liberalism had produced a climate in which key segments of the white electorate felt besieged in the preserves they had built, in their homes, neighborhoods, jobs, schools, and unions. Middle-class mobility, social status, and homeownership were threatened by stagnant incomes and ris-ing taxes. The constant struggle by many Americans to maintain so-called traditional values—of self-discipline and hard work—was perceived to be under attack by a liberal credo revolving around a different set of ideals— of human potential, self-expression, personal freedom, and individual ful-fillment. Finally, liberalism had produced a climate in which court rulings were seen by many voters as undermining traditional authority and tradi-tional patterns of conduct—in spheres as diverse as the country's media, its cultural organs, its concert halls, its parks, its offices, its fire houses, its classrooms, and its prisons.

The fusion of race with other issues—cultural, social, and moral—was critical to this chain reaction, defining and shaping the conflicts of the 1970s. While the civil rights movement achieved, by many measures, a substantially more equal society, and provided many white and black Americans with experiences of deep pride and satisfaction, the fusion of race with more divisive issues inescapably bore grave costs for the political institution most closely associated with racial, and increasingly cultural, liberalism: the Democratic party. Throughout the sixties and seventies, the momentum behind the conservative reaction built steadily, as voters began to associate the Democratic party with a redistributive liberalism, with accelerating social change, with big government, with rising tax burdens, and with stagnant middle-class incomes.

The collapse of the economy during the Carter presidency suggested to key voters that Democratic party government carried heavy burdens. Crucial segments of the white electorate responded to rising tax burdens and to the economic slowdown by focusing their anger on two pillars of the Democratic party: domestic government spending and the concept of collective social responsibility. "In the late 1970s when the tax revolt started, people started linking government spending to inflation," said Frederick Steeper, of Market Opinion Research (MOR), which conducts polls for the Republican National and Congressional Committees. "Instead of unions, or corporate price gouging, they were saying government spending. It was a major change. They saw government spending as out of hand." At the same time, MOR poll data showed a growing public rejection of the argument that society was responsible for the problems of the poor, and revealed public support for a "return back to individual responsibility, that the poor had to help themselves." These two attitudes—blaming government spending for inflation, and renewed belief in individual responsibility—focused the hostility of many whites on means-tested programs for the poor, particularly on welfare and food stamps.[47]

The liberal brake on conservative ideas no longer functioned. The opportunity to firmly establish a conservative presidential majority, and perhaps a conservative majority that would determine the outcome of elections in House and Senate contests, was at hand. By 1980, a decade and a half after passage of the Civil Rights bill and the Voting Rights Act, sixteen years after the first presidential election pitting a Democratic racial liberal against a Republican racial conservative, the political arena had been decisively reconfigured in favor of the Republican party, especially in those elections that lent themselves to polarization along liberal-conservative ideological lines.

# 7
# Race, Rights, and Party Choice

THE CONSERVATIVE REVOLUTION that took root within the Republican party in the early 1960s, the revolution that first coalesced around the 1964 Goldwater campaign, did not reach its full development until the election of 1980. Conservative ideologues, especially in the South, slowly consolidated their power over the Republican presidential nomination process in the years following Goldwater's 1964 defeat, as their own political philosophy became increasingly viable in—and salable to—an electorate turning to the right. Ronald Reagan, breaking into national politics with a televised speech in support of Goldwater in 1964, went on to spend the eight years between 1966 and 1975 cutting his political teeth—and honing his conservative edge—as governor of California.

Reagan's years in the California governor's mansion were a training ground in the politics of race, rights, and taxes. His tenure in office was dominated by fair-housing controversies, the free-speech and anti-war movements on campuses, by the aftermath of the massive black riots in Watts, by unprecedented Hispanic (and later Asian) immigration, by battles to reduce exploding welfare rolls, and by the birth of the citizen tax revolt. The enormous suburban growth of the state, providing a demographic base for a selectively expanding conservatism, and California's advanced involvement in competitive trade with Asia's industrial-technological sector, placed the state in the forefront of developments that would dominate national politics throughout the late 1970s and the 1980s.

During his two terms as governor, Reagan became a spokesman for a political and governing philosophy in which the insulation of the private sector, and the insulation of private citizens, from an intrusive government—whether a government seeking to regulate industry and commerce or a government seeking to shape the behavior of individual citizens—was seen as essential to the functioning of a healthy, autonomous economic and social order. Government regulation of industry, in this view, inevitably hampered productivity and growth. Government intervention in the job market (through affirmative action or such wage-setting mechanisms as the Davis-Bacon Act), or government intervention in patterns of family and work organization (through welfare or other social-service arrangements),[1] undermined the balance of incentives and disincentives necessary to create an efficient work force and to integrate into a prosperity-generating economic order all of America's diverse citizens.

In articulating a politics of generalized government restraint, Reagan mastered the excision of the language of race from conservative public discourse. In so doing, Reagan paralleeld Nixon's success in constructing a politics and a strategy of governing that attacked policies targeted toward blacks and other minorities without reference to race,—a conservative politics that had the effect of polarizing the electorate along racial lines and of weakening traditional economic divisions between Democrats and Republicans.

The importance of excising the language of race from American right-wing politics—a politics long burdened with a history of explicit racism and a politics that had often had, particularly in the South, a race-conscious intent—cannot be overestimated. In facing an electorate with sharply divided commitments on race—theoretically in favor of egalitarian principle but hostile to many forms of implementation—the use of a race-free political language proved crucial to building a broad-based, center-right coalition.

Reagan, like Goldwater, articulated a public philosophy directed at drawing into the Republican party citizens with the kinds of economic, social, and racial concerns that could be addressed in terms of a free-market conservative doctrine. In his October 1964 speech for Goldwater—a speech that established before a national audience the future president's ideological credentials—Reagan declared: "It is time we realized that socialism can come without overt seizure of property or nationalization of private business. It matters little that you hold the title to your property or business if government can dictate policy and procedure and holds life and death power over your business."[2]

Reagan's commitment to the insulation of business and of property rights from government intrusion, first voiced in 1964 when the dominant issue before the nation was civil rights, carried an unmistakable message to those who were keyed into the conservative terms of discourse: that Reagan stood in philosophical opposition to government interventions, those that threatened "your property or business," and those that "dictate[d] policy and procedure," including, it went without saying, the basic provisions of the 1964 Civil Rights Act.

Reagan had found an ostensibly neutral language that would become a powerful tool with which to advocate stands that polarized voters on race-freighted issues—issues ranging from welfare to busing to affirmative action. He did so without communicating overt bigotry or anti-black affect *to whites,* while large numbers of blacks perceived his policies as anti-black; by 1986, fully 56 percent of blacks saw Reagan as racist.[3]

Reagan, in turn, saw his own philosophy and policies, despite their clearly polarizing consequences, as race-neutral. Campaigning for governor in 1966, Reagan attacked state fair-housing legislation as "an infringement of one of our basic individual rights . . . which threatens individual liberty." When his primary opponent contended that the opposition of Reagan and Goldwater to the Civil Rights Act of 1964 "still plagues the Republican Party, and unless we cast out this image, we're going to suffer defeat," Reagan angrily replied: "I resent the implication that there is any bigotry in my nature. . . . Don't anyone ever imply I lack integrity. I will not stand silent and let anyone imply that."[4]

Reagan, an out-and-out proponent of the business ethic, salaried for many years by General Electric—Reagan, whose 1966 campaign for California governor was organized by a "handful of millionaires" who ran the former movie-star as "the man who can enunciate our principles to the people"[5]—became by 1980 the leading proponent of a new *conservative egalitarianism,* an egalitarianism that became a critical weapon in fracturing what remained of the New Deal coalition. Building on the growing hostile public reaction to the liberal agenda on race, social reform, expanding rights, and escalating taxes, conservative egalitarianism became the ideological basis for the formation of a new presidential majority. This new majority—a top-down, conservative coalition—was dominated by the affluent and by the upper-middle class, but it reached down the economic ladder to include smaller margins of less well-off white voters. The top-down coalition established common ground on a wide range of policies between corporate chief executive officers and segments of the white working and lower-middle class, groups that had been adversaries—often bitter adversaries—in an earlier era.

---

Reagan had sought, but failed to win, the GOP presidential nomination in both 1968 and 1976. It was not until 1980 that the ground was prepared for the increasingly dominant ideological right wing of the GOP, for much of the business community, for key sectors of the white working and middle classes, for the newly mobilized Christian right, and for the heir apparent to the Goldwater movement to join together to successfully claim voter allegiance for a new conservative politics. This was a politics clear in its determination to avoid overtly segregationist, anti-black, or anti-minority rhetoric, but a politics determined at the same time to roll back the domestic arm of the federal government.

By the 1980 campaign—a decade and a half after his Goldwater speech—Reagan had himself become a catalytic factor in the potent political mix of race, rights, and taxes, producing a reaction that turned the 1980 election into a watershed in American politics. The 1980 election produced the following major developments:

• Not only did the voters elect the most ideologically conservative president in the nation's history, but with the election of conservative majorities in the House and Senate, the voters effectively released the liberal "brake" on public policy that had in effect controlled the shape of spending, regulatory, and tax legislation for most of the previous forty-eight years.

• The Reagan candidacy—with its anti-government, states' rights, law and order, anti-liberal, and anti-welfare rhetoric—drove public perceptions of the racial conservatism of the Republican party to levels matching those set during the 1964 campaign. Instead of resulting in across-the-board Republican defeat, however—as had happened in 1964 in contests ranging from the presidency to state legislative races—the Reagan candidacy led a racially conservative Republican party to victory at every level.

• The Reagan campaign secured the white South for the Republican party in presidential elections, providing the GOP with a solid base of at least 141 electoral votes in the next two elections. Equally important, the 1980 election accelerated the decline of Democratic loyalties in white working and lower-middle-class communities surrounding the large northern cities with their increasingly black ghettos.

• The shift during the late 1960s and 1970s in the agenda of the civil rights movement to such government-directed redistributive efforts as busing and affirmative action allowed the Republican party to establish as its counter-position a philosophical high ground: conservative egalitarianism. Advocacy of *equal opportunity*—the original clarion call of the civil rights movement—became the center-right position. Just as the white South had moved during the 1960s from opposing school desegregation to supporting the principle of "freedom of choice," in order to check the tougher alternatives of court-ordered school assignments and busing, conservatism by 1980 had adopted "equal opportunity" as the alternative to civil rights remedies that called for various forms of racial and gender preference, remedies focused on equality of results.

• For the first time, the fragile alliance between traditional Republican constituencies—the affluent and business on the one hand, and traditionally Democratic working and lower-middle-class whites on the other—went beyond an election-day majority, such as the one Nixon had established in 1972, to become a governing majority in support of conservative policy outcomes, a goal no Republican administration had been able to achieve for fifty years.

• Under the aegis of conservative principle, the Reagan administration produced an agenda that placed the interests of a substantial segment of black America against the interests of a substantial segment of white America. Above and beyond the fact that blacks were disproportionately affected by Reagan administration cuts in such means-tested programs as AFDC, Supplemental Security Income (SSI), and food stamps, the administration's assault on the domestic arm of the federal government sliced into a vital source of quality employment far more important to blacks than to whites. The political and policy polarization of tax recipients versus taxpayers inherently pitted a disproportionately black minority of the electorate against an overwhelmingly white majority.

———

As Reagan and his strategists prepared for the 1980 election, they aimed at putting together an alliance of the Republican party and dissident factions of the New Deal. At a speech before the American Conservative Union in February 1977, Reagan argued that

> the so-called social issues—law and order, abortion, busing, quota systems—are usually associated with the blue collar, ethnic, and religious groups who [*sic*] are traditionally associated with the Democratic Party. The economic issues—inflation, deficit spending, and big government—are usually associated with Republican Party members and independents. . . . The time has come to see if it is possible to present a program of action based on political principle that can attract those interested in the so called 'social' issues and those interested in 'economic' issues. In short, isn't it possible to combine the two major segments of contemporary American conservatism into one politically effective whole?[6]

Departing from the populist strategy of George Wallace, a strategy that placed the steelworker, fireman, beautician, and union foreman at the core of his constituency, Reagan recognized that in a conservative majority, working-class voters would be a part of a larger coalition, not the centerpiece. Such voters would, according to Reagan, share power and centrality with—and sometimes cede power to—traditional Republican business interests: "The New Republican Party I am speaking about is going to have room for the man and woman in the factories, for the farmer, for the cop on the beat, and for the millions of Americans who may never have thought of joining our party before, but whose interests coincide with those represented by principled Republicans."[7]

———

By 1980, the opportunity to merge the interests of the white working man with those of traditional Republican pro-business, free-marketeers had arrived in full force. The issues of taxes, of an ailing economy, and of the collective set of grievances closely linked to race and rights—including crime, affirmative action, welfare spending, busing, IRS regulation of the Christian school movement, women's liberation, homosexual rights, abortion, etc.—had reached an unprecedented level of intensity among key segments of the white electorate. This intensity provided Reagan and the Republican party with the opportunity to activate a new set of polarizing issues to rupture the frayed class base of a traditional, economically-oriented Democratic liberalism.

Inflation, spiraling interest rates, and rising taxes during the last two years of the Carter administration effectively ensured a Republican presidential victory in 1980—and insured as well substantial GOP House and Senate gains. But the scope of the conservative victory depended heavily on an underlying ideological shift: the Republican party and an emerging populist-conservative ideology, for the first time in fifty years, captured from the Democratic party and from liberalism a piece of the moral high ground, staking out a new conservative claim by key segments of the white electorate to the long-standing tradition of an idealized American egalitarianism.

The political equation was relatively straightforward. Democratic liberalism by the end of the 1970s was judged by many voters to have failed to live up to a basic political obligation: that of rewarding and protecting its own constituents. At the height of Democratic liberal ascendancy—between 1974 and 1980—core Democratic voting blocs suffered from the consequences of economic stagnation and, in many sectors, from outright economic decline.

At the same time, the national Democratic party became more closely associated with a rights agenda that had moved past equal opportunity to support for overtly remedial and redistributive measures—particularly for busing and racial preferences. These preferential measures, seeking to rectify the effects of past discrimination against one group, now inevitably imposed substantial costs on another.

Racially preferential remedies, particularly those created by the federal judiciary, were largely instituted without being subjected to the political or legislative process. Court-established remedies, in consequence, regardless of their moral justifiability or of their merits in creating an enlarged black middle class, not only lacked firm public support, but were, in fact, opposed by decisive majorities of white voters.

The positions adopted by the national Democratic party in favor of racial preferences and busing were critical in allowing the national Republican party to take over the political and philosophical center. Sixteen years earlier, in the 1964 election, Goldwater's conservative stands on privacy, property, and states' rights had served as an umbrella sheltering and protecting from the taint of an explicit ideology of white supremacy Southern voters seeking to avoid integration.

In the context of the civil rights issues of 1964—at a time when a majority of the northern public, moved by the nonviolent, church-based struggle of blacks, was in favor of the relatively modest goals of the early civil rights movement—Goldwater was widely perceived as being *against* "equality of opportunity." By 1980, the content of the civil rights agenda had shifted so that Ronald Reagan—who in 1964 had shared Goldwater's views—was able to become the *advocate* of "equal opportunity," and to remain at the same time firmly in the conservative camp.

As racial battles were fought less over legally prohibited *access* to opportunity—prohibitions institutionalized under legal segregation—and fought more, as the sixties and seventies unrolled, over such affirmative remedies as minority preferences in hiring and busing, "equal opportunity" became a Republican standard, and included among its supporters racial conservatives, including those who were in fact anti-black, as well as much of the moderate center, and the ideological right.

In terms of public opinion among whites, the Republican stand, focused on "opportunity"—however illusory—was backed by the overwhelming majority of voters. As early as 1972, 97 percent of whites polled said blacks should have "as good a chance" to get any job as whites, and by 1980, 88 percent of whites said black and white students should go to the same schools.[8] Whites, however, sharply opposed out-and-out racial preferences. The number of whites in a 1980 poll opposed to the government providing "special help" to minorities outnumbered those favoring such help by a margin of 65–35.[9] By 1985, when tougher questions asked respondents specifically about racial preference in hiring, whites were opposed by a margin of 87–13; in the case of college and university admissions, whites were opposed to racial preferences by a margin of 74–26.[10]

The changing politics of civil rights permitted the Republican party to achieve its central goal—the establishment of a putatively egalitarian, ideologically respectable, conservatism. In 1980, Reagan and the GOP portrayed *opposition* to central elements of civil rights enforcement—opposition to the use of race and sex preferences in hiring and in college admittance, to court-ordered busing, and to the introduction of means-tested programs for the poor—as deriving from a principled concern for fairness: as a form of populist opposition to the granting of special privilege.

"The truths we hold and the values we share affirm that no individual should be victimized by unfair discrimination because of race, sex, advanced age, physical handicap, difference of national origin or religion, or economic circumstance," the 1980 Republican Platform declared. "However, equal opportunity should not be jeopardized by bureaucratic regulation and decisions which rely on quotas, ratios and numerical requirements to exclude some individuals in favor of others, thereby rendering such regulations and decisions inherently discriminatory."[11]

Together with opposition to rising taxes on the working and middle classes, conservatism—with its new "anti-discriminatory," meritocratic, and egalitarian rhetoric—became a powerful political weapon.

The racial basis of conservative egalitarianism served as a key factor in the diversion of populist resentment away from the rich and toward the poor, toward minorities, and toward the federal government. Unlike liberal egalitarianism, which focused public attention on the regressive distribution of income, on the need for a progressive tax system, and on the exploitation of working men and women by a political and social system controlled by and for an economic elite, conservative egalitarianism focused on the inequities imposed by liberalism.

The fundamental strategy developed by George Wallace, of creating the specter of a coercive Democratic liberal establishment—a powerful centralized, bureaucratic, and unresponsive government imposing its regulatory will and its tax collectors on a hard-pressed electorate—reached its full dimensions in the Reagan campaign of 1980.

"If you look at American politics, what you've always had is an anti-establishment thing out there. For about 150–160 years, the establishment was always business. You go back to the agrarian revolt, the establishment was always business. [Franklin] Roosevelt comes in and established another establishment and it was government. And so you have for the first time two establishments," explained Lee Atwater, who served as deputy campaign manager for Reagan, as campaign manager for George Bush, and as chairman of the Republican National Committee.

"In the 1980 campaign, we were able to make the establishment, in so far as it is bad, the government. In other words, big government was the enemy, not big business. . . . If the people are thinking that the problem is that taxes are too high and government interferes too much, then we [Republicans] are doing our job. But, if they get to the point where they say the real problem is that rich people aren't paying taxes, that Republicans are protecting the Realtors and so forth, then I think the Democrats are going to be in pretty good shape. The National Enquirer readership is the exact voter I'm talking about. . . . There are always some stories in there about some multimillionaire that has five Cadillacs and hasn't paid taxes since 1974, or so-and-so Republican Congressman hasn't paid taxes since he got into Congress. And they'll have another set of stories of a guy sitting around in a big den with liquor saying so and so fills his den with liquor using food stamps. So it's which one of those establishments the public sees as a bad guy [that determines whether conservative or liberal egalitarianism is ascendant].[12]

The effectiveness of this new populist-egalitarianism in promoting a conservative agenda was four-fold.

• It provided moral legitimacy to a broad offensive against the policies and programs developed by Democratic liberalism to serve constituencies of the left. Conservative egalitarianism and its emphasis on equal opportunity could be taken beyond the attack on racial preference to permit an assault on the network of special preferences, in public policy and in party rules, that the Democratic party had developed to offer a degree of protection from competition to labor unions, to the poor, and to women. The prevailing wage provisions of the Davis-Bacon Act, designed to protect union contractors in competition for federal work with non-union shops; the provision of welfare, food stamps, and other benefits paid out of the general tax-financed treasury for the benefit of designated, means-tested groups; party rules and caucuses that established automatic representation rights to groups consequently exempt from intra-party competition: all of these distributive arrangements became vulnerable to "egalitarian" challenge on the grounds that each had granted a special privilege unavailable to the "ordinary" citizen on a democratic basis.

• Conservative egalitarianism, with its anti-government cast and its emphasis on equal opportunity, and conservative economic theory, with its emphasis on untrammeled markets free from government interference, served as mutually reinforcing ideologies, and forged between themselves a powerful weapon with which to challenge modern liberalism. Insofar as modern liberalism has come to be associated with the mobilization of government in behalf of the disadvantaged and in behalf of those ill-equipped to prevail in unrestrained market competition, it has become a doctrine championing public policies that offer protection to the vulnerable (individual, groups, and select sectors), public policies that seek to alleviate market-imposed hardship, and that attempt to remedy gross distributional inequities.

Such policies include the progressive income-tax rate structure to reduce regressive income distribution; increased government spending, to break the cycle of poverty; affirmative action, to remedy the consequences of past discrimination; the creation of a regulatory structure to protect the organizing and bargaining rights of unions; and the subsidization and protection of new industries seeking to gain a foothold in the market, and of older industries facing the threat of extinction.

By the late 1970s, the protective and remedial character of liberalism became subject to challenge under a newly attractive formulation: the characterization of liberalism as *inegalitarian*, as in fundamental violation of the American tradition of equality, as causing market distortions, as creating inefficiencies, as constituting a costly burden on the economy, and even as spurring newly virulent social pathologies.

• The concept of conservative egalitarianism in combination with laissez-faire and "supply side" economic theory provided intellectual justification for the abandonment of the interventionist and redistributive government policies that had characterized the New Deal order. By this reasoning, once legal barriers to market participation by minorities had been removed (as they were with the overthrow of Jim Crow in the mid-1960s), the state had no business attempting to "micromanage" institutional or human behavior. It was beyond the competence of the state to concern itself with the lingering effects of historic discrimination on the present competitive position of blacks, other minorities, or women; just as it was beyond the responsibility of the state to strengthen the bargaining position of worker against management.

Equal opportunity and market efficiency became, in conservative hands, concepts dealing in the present tense. While modern liberalism saw the virtually 100 percent white Birmingham Fire Department of 1968 as clear evidence of an historic pattern of discrimination that justified numerically based hiring of blacks and whites on a one-for-one basis until the consequences of *past discrimination* were eliminated, the new egalitarian conservatism had a different goal. It sought instead to eliminate all *contemporary hiring discrimination*, viewing such steps as one-for-one hiring as discrimination against those (whites) who should by standardized merit-oriented criteria, such as ability tests, be preferred.

- By shifting the obligation of government from the correction of past discrimination against groups, to the prevention of contemporary discrimination against individuals (always in the context of minimum government regulation), conservative egalitarianism undermined two basic tenets of modern liberalism. The first was the belief that not only in the case of civil rights issues, but on a broad range of economic and social matters generally, a key function of government is to protect the interests of broad classes of people. Such a class-oriented, protectionist, and essentially redistributionist view of government obligation is based on the assumption that in a free-market system, the balance of private power will otherwise inherently favor the most powerful groups and classes—the affluent, the owners and managers of corporate enterprise, large property holders, etc. In the modern liberal view, government intervention in behalf of less well-positioned classes and groups such as the poor, workers, blacks, and women can help to mitigate some of the more glaring inequities which will otherwise inevitably arise in the course of unrestrained market competition.

A second basic tenet of modern liberalism has been the belief that government intervention in the operation of markets is justified by long-range benefits: that, for example, housing subsidies and education assistance to the working and lower-middle classes in wake of World War II, or programs specifically geared to enlarge the black middle class, function to establish the *multi-generational development of skills*—of new job proficiencies, of professional expertise, and of socialization into a modern work ethic—skills and values that are essential not only to a stable social order but to a broadly productive and internationally competitive society.

The power of conservative egalitarianism—based on an idealized concept of "equal opportunity" and reinforced by free-market economic theory—is that it affirms basic American principles of equality while protecting, and in some cases reinforcing, the very unequal distribution of racial and economic benefits challenged by liberalism. Conservative egalitarianism provides the ideological framework for the protection of their own interests to those who are challenged by insurgent groups—an ideological framework generally consonant with American ethical traditions.

The national Republican party, which in the aftermath of the Great Depression had become identified by much of the public with economic privilege and with "royalists of the economic order," was able during the course of the civil rights era to successfully recast itself as the proponent of a new and more 'genuine' egalitarianism. This egalitarianism was not only largely cost-free to core constituencies of the top-down GOP coalition—the coalition that gained full ascendancy in 1980—but provided a tool for the further protection of the interests of elites as well, particularly the opportunity which 'egalitarianism' offered to attack both the progressive tax structure and federal regulation of the corporate sector.

———

In the debate over the rights and responsibilities of both government and of its citizenry that emerged out of the intensified conflict between liberalism and conservatism in the late 1970s and early 1980s, the role of race in helping to build a working conservative political majority should not be underestimated. Race was embedded in conflicts surrounding tax, spending, education, welfare, regulatory, and industrial policy. The racial consequences of policy alternatives—inescapable because of racial differences in income, in reliance on government benefits, in job and family patterns, in rates of criminality, in demographics, in suburban versus urban residential trends, as well as in a host of other measures—became integral to the structuring of the political debate, sometimes explicitly, sometimes implicitly. In the construction of a conservative ideological edifice, race served, in effect, to increase the bonding power of brick to mortar.

———

In making the case in 1980 for his own presidential candidacy and for a major retrenchment in domestic spending, Ronald Reagan made explicitly clear that the target of his planned assault on government would be the means-tested programs serving poor constituencies, heavily black and Hispanic, that had become the focus of much public hostility to government. One of Reagan's favorite and most often-repeated anecdotes was the story of a Chicago "welfare queen" with "80 names, 30 addresses, 12 Social Security cards" whose "tax-free income alone is over $150,000."[13] The food stamp program, in turn, was a vehicle to let "some fellow ahead of you buy T-bone steak" while "you were standing in a checkout line with your package of hamburger."[14]

These campaign appeals and strategies on the part of Reagan and the Republican party revived the sharply polarized racial images of the two parties—a polarization that had characterized the Johnson-Goldwater contest. By 1980, the racial polarization of the two parties was to prove highly profitable to Republicans, with racial conservatism contributing decisively to the GOP advantage.

This shift in the marketability of racial conservatism to the majority electorate reflected the degree to which public attitudes toward civil rights had changed in a matter of sixteen years. If, in 1964, Goldwater's racial conservatism had been catastrophic for his party, by 1980, the white public had become far more ambivalent—torn between support for the principle of racial justice, but opposed to aggressive mechanisms to remedy discrimination. In 1980, the majority public saw Reagan and the Republican party as conservative on matters pertaining to minority America, but this was no longer a liability; it had, in fact, become an advantage.

In 1964, as noted above (page 36), 60 percent of respondents said that the Democratic party was more likely to provide fair employment treatment of blacks, while only 7 percent said the GOP was more likely. This gap between the parties narrowed somewhat after 1964, when the GOP presidential banner was carried by Richard Nixon and Gerald Ford, each more moderate on civil rights than Goldwater. In 1972 and in 1976 (in response to a slightly different question), the number of voters who saw the GOP as unlikely to help minorities outnumbered, by a very small 4–3 margin, those who saw the Republican party as supportive of minority interests.[15] In 1976, for example, with Carter and Ford as the presidential nominees, 33 percent of poll respondents described the GOP as likely to help minorities, and 40 percent described the party as unlikely to do so, for a net 7 percent point balance on the conservative side of the ledger (with the remainder placing the party in the center or holding no opinion). The Democratic party throughout this period remained the party of racial liberalism: 64.8 percent of those surveyed in 1976 said the Democratic party was likely to adopt policies favoring minorities, while only 14 percent said the Democratic party was unlikely to help minorities, for a liberal tilt of 50.8 percentage points.

In 1980, with Reagan at the top of the ticket (Reagan's record included opposition to the Civil Rights Acts of 1964 and 1965, opposition to fair-housing legislation, and opposition to a holiday honoring Martin Luther King, Jr.), the public image of the Republican party became again sharply more conservative on racial issues. That year, by a margin of better than 6 to 1, the electorate saw the GOP as unlikely to help minorities.[16] Table 7.1 shows these trends.

With Reagan heading the ticket, the racial conservatism of the GOP matched the racial liberalism of the Democratic party. The racial polarization of the parties coincided with the larger fusion of race, partisanship, and ideology that had been building throughout the 1970s, a process that culminated in the sharp turn to the right in domestic politics in 1980. Liberalism, which before the civil rights revolution had been seen by a majority of voters as largely race-neutral—as primarily an economic philosophy of government intervention in behalf of the nation's "have-nots" —became, in the wake of the civil rights movement, closely associated with issues linked to race.

TABLE 7.1

The Racial Polarization of the Political Parties

The public perception of the racial liberalism of the Democratic party
and of the racial conservatism of the Republican Party in 1972, 1976,
and 1980.

|  | 1972<br>Nixon-<br>McGovern | 1976<br>Carter-<br>Ford | 1980<br>Reagan-<br>Carter |
|---|---|---|---|
| *Public Perception of the Democratic Party* | | | |
| Democrats likely to aid minorities | 59.4% | 64.8% | 68.8% |
| Democrats not likely to aid minorities | 12.4% | 14 % | 11.9% |
| *Public Perception of the Republican Party* | | | |
| Republicans likely to aid minorities | 27 % | 33 % | 11.4% |
| Republicans not likely to aid minorities | 37.2% | 40 % | 65.8% |

Source: National Election Studies (NES) data supplied by Arthur Miller, of the
University of Iowa, by telephone to the author, January 17 and 19, 1990.

Analysis of 1972 and 1976 National Election Studies (NES) data by
political scientists Edward G. Carmines and James A. Stimson shows that
some of the strongest divisions between voters identifying themselves as
liberals and conservatives were over attitudes toward black protests and
urban unrest, attitudes toward segregation and integration, and attitudes
toward protecting the rights of criminal defendants, and that these divisions paralleled the more traditional liberal-conservative conflict over the
responsibility of government to provide employment and fair wages. In
both 1972 and 1976, racial issues were more important in defining differences between liberals and conservatives than stands on the question of the
progressivity of tax rates—a traditional centerpiece of economic liberalism.[17]

The growing salience of racial issues in determining liberal-conservative differences applied even more strongly to the parties themselves. John

Petrocik of UCLA, found that through the 1970s, "Republican identifiers became less sympathetic toward blacks, Democratic identifiers adopted a distinctly pro-black posture compared with the 1950s, and the size of the interparty difference [on race] began to rival Democratic-Republican disagreement" on such traditionally partisan economic issues as domestic government spending.[18]

Carmines and Stimson, in turn, have tracked this growing divergence on racial policy between self-identified Democratic and Republican voters. On the basis of responses to a range of questions (including, "Are civil rights leaders pushing too fast, too slow or about right?" "Should the federal government prevent discrimination in housing, schools and public accommodations?" and "Do you support segregation, desegregation or something in between?") Carmines and Stimson found that the racial attitudes of Republicans and Democrats began to diverge sharply in 1964, with Republicans becoming decisively conservative and Democratic decisively liberal.[19]

In other words, in the years following the civil rights legislation of the 1960s, racial attitudes, became a central characteristic of both ideology and party identification, integral to voters' choices between Democrats and Republicans, and integral to choices between policy positions on a range of non-racial issues traditionally identified with liberalism and conservatism. At the same time, a wide range of social developments, including the emergence of a growing urban underclass and the associated problems of crime, joblessness, and urban school failure, were becoming, in the public mind, indelibly associated with race through the growing body of statistical information demonstrating disproportionate black involvement; through media coverage of crime, of declining labor-force participation among black males, and of a long-term (sometimes multi-generational) welfare clientele; and through increased public policy and academic interest in the intractable persistence of black and Hispanic poverty.

The intensified racial polarization of the two parties coincided with a shift to the right in public opinion—a shift with strong racial overtones and one that made the electorate more receptive to the Reagan administration's 1981 budget-cutting and tax-cutting proposals. The intensified conservatism of the majority public by 1980 on policy issues relating to race should not be misread as an across-the-board movement to the right or towards economic conservatism in general: within overall trends showing increased opposition to government spending and to federal tax levels, the focus of the electorate's ire was measurably on programs serving the poor and blacks.

One of the strongest signals of a rising anti-government form of conservatism lay in the response to questions asking whether government was getting too powerful. In 1980, 49 percent of the polled electorate viewed government as too powerful, more than triple the 15 percent who thought government was not too strong. This was the highest anti-government ratio since the question was first asked in 1964. Similarly, support for government action to reduce income inequality fell to a low point in 1980, while the percentage of voters who thought their federal income taxes were too high reached 68 percent that year.[20]

On close examination, the anti-tax, anti-government view of the electorate in 1980 was very specifically directed. It did not, for example, reflect diminished support for higher government spending on education, health, Social Security, crime control, drug addiction control, and environmental protection—all of which retained unstinting, and in some cases growing, majority support. In the case of the military, public support for increased spending grew decisively after the Soviet invasion of Afghanistan and after the seizure of hostages in Iran. While the percentage of the electorate saying that "too little" was being spent on defense had remained in the range of 23 to 31 percent through most of the 1970s, in 1980, it shot up to 56 percent.[21]

Public anger at government in 1980, in fact, was directed at programs serving heavily minority and poor populations. This closely paralleled the findings of surveys of California voters during the tax revolt debate of the late 1970s, when the only programs that a majority of voters sought to cut were welfare and public housing. In 1978 and 1980, national support for increased spending to improve the condition of blacks fell to a record low, 24 percent. Opposition to welfare spending reached its highest level in 1976, and remained there through 1980.[22] The percentage of respondents in 1980 saying that blacks and other minorities should help themselves, 41 percent, versus those saying that government should improve the social and economic position of blacks, 19 percent, was at an all-time high, compared to 37–29 in 1976, and 38–31 in 1972.[23]

A significant segment, a "swing" sector, of the white public had come to make a distinction between what Republican pollsters called "good welfare"—Social Security, education, health, police—and "bad welfare"—food stamps, Aid to Families with Dependent Children, and other means-tested programs favoring poor or near-poor heavily black and Hispanic constituencies.[24] This distinction provided the ideal wedge for the Republican party to use to further divide the Democratic coalition, a wedge that Reagan was ideally situated to exploit to maximum advantage.

One trend in public opinion that illuminated the politics of race in the 1980 election was the gulf between blacks and whites on a fundamental aspect of economic policy. In 1980, blacks who believed that it was the responsibility of government to provide jobs outnumbered those who contended that "government should just let every person get ahead on his own" by a margin of 70–30. Whites, however, split in the opposite direction, contending by a 62–38 margin that government should just let "every person get ahead on his own" instead of guaranteeing work.[25]

This question revealed the extent to which ideology, voting patterns, and race had become comingled. In addition to polarizing blacks and whites, the question polarized Reagan and Carter voters, white and black, with Carter getting 80 percent of those who strongly supported government intervention to provide work, and Reagan winning 79 percent of those most opposed to such intervention.[26]

In a parallel split, Carter received 93 percent of the vote from those citizens, white and black, who most strongly supported government efforts "to improve the social and economic position of blacks," while Reagan got 71 percent of those who felt most adamantly that "the government should not make any special effort to help because they should help themselves."[27] Race and ideology by the end of the 1970s had become inextricably linked, threatening the viability of liberalism and of the Democratic party.

# 8

# A Conservative Policy
# Majority

THE INCREASING ideological and racial polarization of the electorate had as early as 1968 and 1972 demonstrated the power of a strong emphasis on social issues to produce a conservative election-day majority. In the second half of the 1970s, social and racial issues meshed with the tax revolt and with the political mobilization of the corporate sector to produce a powerful engine propelling substantive change in economic and regulatory policy.

Working-class whites and corporate CEOs, once adversaries at the bargaining table, found common ideological ground in their shared hostility to expanding government intervention; these former antagonists joined forces across traditional class lines to form the core of a center-right majority that survived past election day to become a driving force in support of conservative policy retrenchment.

The ideological convergence between, on the one hand, free-market doctrine promoted by the business-financed conservative movement and, on the other hand, the goals of whites seeking a roll-back of civil rights policies (such as affirmative action and busing), and of costly means-tested programs (such as welfare and food stamps)—together created the circumstances for a vigorous cross-class alliance. Business interests and key elements of the white, working and middle classes sought a major retraction of the regulatory state, with economic conservatives viewing government intervention as a source of market inefficiencies, and with segments of the lower and middle-class white community viewing government intervention as a threat to schools, jobs, unions, neighborhoods, families and to a range of cherished values.

Both factions of the cross-class coalition sought lowered tax burdens, and joined in the ongoing polarization of taxpayers versus tax recipients. Both factions of the coalition shared a common vision of the federal government as the source of costs and burdens—unjustifiable on either economic or social grounds—and both factions saw the liberal federal judiciary serving as the coercive agent of government and as the linchpin of social change, imposing resented, unjust, and unnecessary burdens.

This ideological convergence permitted the Republican party to expand beyond its traditional base, a base which had been dominated by the affluent, and beyond a temporary election-day majority to establish a sustained *policy majority*. In direct contrast to the Democratic party's New Deal "bottom-up" coalition, in which voters in the bottom third of the income distribution voted Democratic by the strongest margins, the new Republican presidential majority was a "top-down" coalition, in which voters in the top third cast the strongest margins for the GOP.

This Republican cross-class alignment laid the foundation for the enactment in 1981 of the first major retrenchment of the liberal government policies of the New Deal and of the Great Society. The alignment of business, the affluent, and moderate-income whites produced a right-leaning coalition that established a political base of support for the adoption of upwardly redistributive tax and spending policies.

Substantial segments of the white working and lower-middle class found common ground with business and with the well-to-do in support of an agenda that not only shifted government benefits from those at the bottom of the income distribution to those at the top (benefits valuable to the traditional constituencies of the GOP); but, equally important, an agenda that addressed the concerns of the lower and middle-income white voting majority, by slowing, and sometimes reversing, the "downward" redistribution of benefits to blacks, minorities, and to other previously excluded or disadvantaged groups, many of which had recently emerged into the competition for public goods under the aegis of the rights revolution.

———

The Republican drive to curtail government intrusion in the conduct of American business, and to curtail the "anti-corporate" and pro-regulatory bias of the Democratic party, dovetailed with Republican determination to end "reverse discrimination." This determination became emblematic of policies designed not only to halt the redistribution downwards of *tangible* benefits, including income and job access, but also of *intangible* benefits, including cultural hegemony, prestige, authority, and social space—in civic life, in schools, in the workplace, in residential neighborhoods, and in the broader society.

At the same time, the surge in urban-ghetto crime rates, illegitimacy, drug abuse, and welfare dependency served as a sledge hammer, crushing liberal instincts among many voters. At the extreme, in a white community like New York's Canarsie, surrounded by the slums of Brownsville, Flatbush, and East New York, once liberal Jews together with more conservative Italians shifted sharply to the right in the years leading up to the 1980 election. Racial tension in Canarsie produced open expression of bitterness over threatened values, neighborhoods, community, and perceptions of well-being—expression that, if manifested and experienced less virulently elsewhere, nonetheless characterized a common aspect of white backlash.

Yale sociologist Jonathan Rieder described the climate of opinion he found in the late 1970s when he lived and worked among residents of Brooklyn's white urban ethnic enclaves:

> Canarsie's image of ghetto culture crystalized out of all the visual gleanings, fleeting encounters, and racist presumptions. Lower class blacks lacked industry, lived for momentary erotic pleasure, and, in their mystique of soul, glorified the fashions of a high-stepping street life. The hundreds of thousands of female-headed minority households in New York City, and the spiraling rate of illegitimate births, reinforced the impression that ghetto women were immoral. . . . Racism, which primed whites to select fragments of reality that confirmed their prejudgments, accounts for a good measure of such distorted and mean-spirited claims. But that interpretation suffers from at least three drawbacks. First, it neglects the social forces that shape racial judgments. Canarsians' obsession with the worst in ghetto life reflected ghetto realities: a high proportion of lower-class blacks and soaring rates of drug addiction, family breakdown, and criminality. . . . A second problem with the emphasis on racism is that it neglects the cultural rule that breaches of moral norms must be punished. When provincial Jews and Italians recoiled from the riven families of the ghetto, they were prisoners of ancient notions of right as well as vituperative passion. "The blacks have ten kids to a family," the Italian wife of a city worker observed. . . . "Bring up a few, give them love and education." . . . The final drawback of the emphasis on racism is that it downplays the desire, which was contained in all the racial classifying, to decipher enigmas. It is hard to exaggerate the bewilderment Canarsians felt when they considered the family patterns of the ghetto. To be without a family in southern Italy "was to be truly a non-being, *un saccu vacante* (an empty sack) as Sicilians say, *un nuddu miscatu cu niente* (a nobody mixed with nothing). . . .

The immediacy of the dangers of place was ominous for the vitality of the New Deal coalition. Even where the new obsessions did not undermine liberal economic beliefs, closeness to the ghetto created new concerns which overshadowed the old ones or made them seem dreamily remote. . . .

A city worker, practically beside himself, exploded, "These welfare people get as much as I do and I work my ass off and come home dead tired." . . .

Canarsians spoke about crime with more unanimity than they achieved on any other subject, and they spoke often and forcefully. Most had a favorite story of horror. A trucker remembered defecating in his pants a few years earlier when five black youths cornered him on an elevator and placed a knifeblade against his throat. "They got $200 and a gold watch. They told me, 'Listen you white motherfucker, you ain't calling the law.' I ran and got in my car and set off the alarm. A group of blacks got around the car. If anybody made a move, I'd have run them over. The police came and we caught one of them. The judge gave them a fucking two-year probation." The experience left an indelible imprint. He still relived the humiliation of soiling himself.[1]

An unbridgeable gulf separated the residents of Canarsie from the continuing agenda of the Democratic party and of key black leaders. The intensely held belief among Carnarsians, that they were the victims of black oppression and of a government favoring blacks over whites, rendered impossible even consideration of the views of many black leaders that white racism was the central fact of life determining ghetto outcomes. "[R]acial discrimination is deeply rooted in the structure of American institutions. In many cases those in power in these institutions profit from the maintenance of racial discrimination, for it is to their economic advantage," wrote Alphonso Pinkney, a black sociologist at Hunter College, in 1984, "[that] the long-standing problems of poverty, unemployment, job discrimination, inadequate housing and barriers to education continue to reinforce the subordinate position of Afro-Americans. Deeply ingrained white racism serves to justify the oppression of blacks."[2]

The divide was even wider between white Canarsians and more radical black thinkers. Manning Marable, director of the African and Hispanic Studies Program at Colgate University, wrote in 1985:

At the heart of Black politics is a series of crimes: the brutal exploitation of human and natural resources of the African continent; the perpetuation of chattel slavery and the transatlantic slave-trade for nearly four centuries; the sexual abuse, rape and physical oppression of Black women; the lynching, assassination and castration of Black men; the denial of basic human rights and simple dignity which have been given to others without question; the imposition of educational institutions which fetter the mind and crush the spirit; the confiscation of billions of hours' worth of unpaid or low-paid labor-power in the process of capitalist production; the attempted obliteration or distortion of indigenous cultural, religious and social institutions among African people; the expropriation of our land and economic institutions.[3]

Conservative economic doctrine and an ascendant right-populism provided the ideological foundation used by the Reagan administration to define and win approval of an agenda that effectively joined the interests of business and of moderate-income whites—two groups that had often been at loggerheads in the politics of the New Deal—behind policies that simultaneously shifted benefits back from the bottom to the top and from blacks to whites. Race provided conservatism with an essential ingredient in overcoming class differences between segments of the white electorate, in establishing an ideologically coherent structure of rewards in actual policy, and in creating, for the first time in fifty years, a sustainable national majority.

Racial polarization, in effect, helped create a political climate receptive to an economic agenda based on the conservative principle that sharply increasing incentives and rewards for those people and interests at the top of the economic pyramid and decreasing government support for those at the bottom would combine to spur economic expansion and growth. To the degree that divisions between blacks and whites overlapped divisions between the poor and the affluent, between the dependent and the successful, and between city and suburb, race became an ally of conservatism.

Insofar as those in the bottom quintile of the income distribution can be identified as disproportionately black and Hispanic—making possible the isolation of the poor as conceptually separable from the white majority—racial polarization facilitates the enactment of regressive redistributional policies. And insofar as the government programs serving those in the bottom of the income distribution simultaneously divide the poor from the working class and black from white, those programs are highly vulnerable to conservative assault.

The intensity of white opposition to government programs associated with the poor and minorities, to rising tax burdens, and to a civil rights regulatory agenda imposing costs on whites had profound consequences for both elective politics and for public policy. In elective politics, the growing identification of government intervention and activism with racial intervention and activism helped to splinter the economic base of the Democratic coalition. In terms of policy, these racial divisions helped to open the door for the Republican party to enact a conservative economic agenda and to reward its own establishment constituencies, the affluent and business.

For the two generations before the 1980 election, the underlying strength of the New Deal coalition, of the Democratic loyalties of the electorate, and of economic liberalism had created an insurmountable obstacle to conservatism. In the sixteen years during which the GOP had control of the White House between the elections of Herbert Hoover and Ronald Reagan (1953–1961 and 1969–1977, including two years of Republican control of both branches of Congress in 1953–1955) the GOP was effectively barred by the liberal tilt of the electorate from making any substantial effort to cut social spending, to reduce the power of the regulatory state, or to make the tax system less progressive.

The liberal "brake" within the electorate acted, until 1980, as a constraint on conservatism. Nixon not only acceded to a wide range of liberal Democratic initiatives regulating the environment and the workplace, for example, but he very explicitly recognized, in 1972, the underlying strength and appeal of liberalism and of the traditional Democratic party—while ducking the liabilities of the Republican label—when he ordered campaign aides to "avoid 'Republican' everywhere," to never use the words "Republican" and "Democrat"—"Don't blame the Democrats. . . . Call them McGovernites."[4]

In the first year of the Reagan administration, there were no such constraints—on language or on policy. Changes in federal law enacted under the direction of the Reagan administration dramatically reshaped the tax burden for different income and racial groups. From 1980 to 1985, the combined effective tax rate—including federal income, Social Security, excise, and corporate taxes—rose sharply for the bottom 20 percent of all households, going from 8.4 to 10.6 percent; and dropped most precipitously for those in the top 20 percent, from 27.3 to 24 percent. For those in between—the middle 60 percent—tax rates changed by much smaller percentages.

In dollar terms, these changes meant that by 1985, the average family in the bottom quintile making $6,320 paid $137 more in taxes under the laws of that year than it would have if the 1980 law had remained unchanged. Those families in the top quintile, with an average income of $76,137 in 1985, paid $2,531 less in 1985 taxes as a result of changes in the tax law.[5] This regressive redistribution was achieved in large part through enactment of the 1981 tax cut—the centerpiece of the Reagan revolution. The 1981 measure, cutting taxes by $749 billion over five years, was skewed in favor of the affluent and corporations, and allowed taxes on the working poor to rise by failing to adjust for inflation two key elements of tax law designed to help those on the bottom rungs: the earned income tax credit and the standard deduction. This regressivity was then compounded by increases in the Social Security payroll tax, which not only has no progressive rate structure but which provides no standard deduction.

Looking at these figures in terms of their racial impact, the 1981–82 changes in federal tax burdens meant that in 1985, 36.4 percent of all black households and 28.7 percent of Hispanic households fell into the category forced to pay higher federal taxes—the bottom quintile—compared to just 18.2 percent of white households. Conversely, 21.4 percent of white households were in the top quintile getting the largest tax cuts, compared to only 9 percent of all black households and 10.9 percent of Hispanic households.[6]

When these figures are tabulated against actual voting and voter turnout patterns for different racial and income groups, the partisan advantage to the GOP of reducing the progressivity of the tax structure becomes apparent. In 1980, a total of 85.5 million people voted, but, because 78 percent of the registered well-to-do voters turned out and only 54 percent of the registered poor turned out, the top quintile of the income distribution produced an estimated 20.1 million votes, and the bottom quintile produced only 13.9 million votes, a difference of 6.2 million. Taking the Reagan administration's tax policies from 1980 to 1985, and calculating the partisan allegiances of whites, blacks, and Hispanics in the top and bottom quintiles, then produces the results shown in Tables 8-1 and 8-2.

Tables 8.1 and 8.2 illustrate how a policy of raising tax rates on the bottom quintile and lowering rates on the top quintile helps Republicans and hurts Democrats. Such a policy, in addition, hurts both blacks and Hispanics, while helping whites. For Democrats, the policy is a net setback, because there are 1.14 million more "losers" among Democratic voters than winners (7.14 million "winners" in the top quintile subtracted from 8.28 million "losers" in the bottom quintile). For the GOP, the policy

TABLE 8.1

The Losers—The Racial and Partisan Makeup of Those Who Paid Higher Taxes

(These people fell into the bottom quintile of the income distribution with an average family income in 1985 of $6,230. They paid a tax *increase* of $137 as a result of legislative action.)

|  | *Democrats* | *Republicans* |
|---|---|---|
| Whites | 5.3 million | 5.1 million |
| Blacks | 2.5 million | 0.2 million |
| Hispanics | 0.48 million | 0.32 million |
| Total | 8.28 million | 5.62 million |

TABLE 8.2

The Winners—The Partisan and Racial Make-up of Those Who Received Tax Cuts

(These people fell into the top quintile with an average family income in 1985 of $76,137. They received a tax *cut* averaging $2,513.)

|  | Democrats | Republicans |
|---|---|---|
| Whites | 6.0 million | 12.7 million |
| Blacks | 0.9 million | 0.1 million |
| Hispanics | 0.24 million | 0.16 million |
| Total | 7.14 million | 12.96 million |

produces 7.34 million more "winners" than "losers" (12.96 million taxpayers in the top brackets and 5.62 million in the bottom rungs of the income distribution). In a reflection of how race, partisanship, and policy all work together, the table also demonstrates that 1.7 million more blacks are further into the red than those who come out ahead, as are 400,000 Hispanics. In contrast, a net of 8.3 million whites come out ahead under the tax changes enacted between 1980 and 1985. The adoption of redistributional policies transferring tax benefits from blacks to whites, simultaneously transfers benefits from Democrats to Republicans.

The politics of the Reagan administration's budget cuts paralleled administration policy on taxation. At the simplest level, it is clear that by targeting cuts at such programs as AFDC and food stamps, the Reagan administration was able to place the burden of spending reductions most heavily on minority populations.

There are a number of ways to look at the racial composition of the groups that faced the most severe budget cuts. In terms of the race of those receiving welfare and food stamps, whites constitute fewer than 50 percent of recipients, in both cases. As of 1988, 47 percent of food stamp recipients were white, 36.1 percent black, and 12.7 percent Hispanic. The rest were Asian, Pacific Islanders, American Indians, and other minorities.[8] Families receiving AFDC in 1988 were 40 percent black, 39 percent white, 16 percent Hispanic, and the remaining 5 percent were Asian, American Indian, and other minorities.[9]

These data are often used by liberal proponents of social service programs to show that whites comprise a substantial portion of the recipients of means-tested programs, contrary to the perception of many that such programs serve overwhelmingly black and Hispanic clienteles. For the

Republican party, however, which receives almost no support from blacks, a different political calculus comes into play. While roughly equal numbers of black and white households receive welfare, the 1.54 million black households receiving AFDC are a major percentage of the black community: 15.5 percent of the 9.9 million black households, with the proportion of black households receiving food stamps being even larger, 26 percent. Conversely, the 1.5 million white households receiving AFDC make up just 2 percent of all white households, and just 4.6 percent of all white households get food stamps. Hispanic households fall onto a middle ground between blacks and whites: 9.7 percent of Hispanic households receive welfare, and 15.2 percent get food stamps, based on 1988 data.[10]

Cuts in welfare, then, affect only two of every 100 white households, but fifteen of every 100 black households, and ten of every 100 Hispanic households. Food stamp cuts affect nine in 100 white households, but twenty-six of every 100 black households, and fifteen of every 100 Hispanic households. Among whites, receipt of food stamps is the exception, and an attempt to cut the number of recipients is of no direct economic consequence to the overwhelming majority of white voters. A cut in welfare or food stamps may prick the conscience of some whites, but for the overwhelming majority, it does not touch their wallets. Among blacks, food stamps are a source of support for over a quarter of the population, and welfare provides income to more than a seventh of all black households.

Cutting welfare and food stamps, then, is a very low-cost proposition to the Republican party which in 1980 presidential election received only 1.3 percent of its votes from blacks. Such cuts, however, impose a high cost on Democratic constituents; in the 1980 presidential contest, Jimmy Carter got 25.5 percent of his votes from blacks.[11]

———

The same racial-political calculus can be applied to the overall strategy of the Reagan administration to cut back the size of the domestic arm of government and to increase the size of the defense sector. As a basic source of employment, government at the city, state, and federal level is far more important to blacks than to whites, especially for good, high-wage jobs. Overall in 1980, a significantly larger percentage of working blacks, 22.5 percent, had government jobs than whites, 15.3 percent. This disparity becomes even sharper when the racial pattern of employment in managerial and professional jobs—the best paying and most prestigious jobs—is examined. Of all blacks with jobs at this level in 1980, fully 53.5 percent were employed by government, at the federal, state, or local levels; for whites, the percentage was just 27.5 percent.[12]

These figures reflect one aspect of the strong economic basis for the exacerbated ideological and political conflict that characterized the relationship of the Reagan administration with blacks. For Reagan to propose cutting the size of the federal government represented a direct assault on a core source of quality employment for blacks. The assault is all the more sharply defined by the employment patterns of key federal agencies and departments: the major departments in which the Reagan administration sought to make cuts employed blacks at higher rates than the federal government as a whole; while the Defense Department, which received major budget increases under Reagan, employs blacks in civilian jobs at a rate well below the federal average.

In 1982, for example, the overall rate of black employment in the federal government was 16.97 percent. At the Department of Defense, however, the civilian rate of black employment was 12.5 percent. In contrast, in departments that experienced staff reductions, the rate of black employment was far above average: Education, 35.9 percent black; General Services Administration, 34.1 percent; Health and Human Services, 24.7 percent; Housing and Urban Development, 25.1 percent; and Labor, 22.5 percent.[13]

The consequences of public policy during the Reagan administration for the employment of blacks spilled over to the private sector. One of the major sources of quality, private-sector employment for blacks at management levels in large corporations has been in running equal employment opportunity and personnel divisions. The reduction by the Reagan administration of equal employment opportunity enforcement efforts prompted many companies, faced with tougher international competition and with the need to reduce costs, to cut back or eliminate altogether their equal employment divisions. "The ranks of blacks in corporations [have been] . . . decimated," said John N. Odom in 1987, executive director of Black Agency Executives, an association of black management and social services executives.[14] The same year, Mary Anne Devanna, research director of Columbia Business School's Management Institute, pointed out that "for years, blacks and women were steered into jobs that were not central to the organization. Now those jobs are precisely the jobs that are being eliminated."[15]

---

Beyond the fact that the cuts of the Reagan administration in welfare, food stamps, Medicaid, housing subsidies, and other means-tested programs for the poor had little political cost for Republicans, the spending reductions met the tacit demands of a substantial number of those Democrats who provided Reagan's margin of victory. A disproportionately large percentage of the white Democrats who cast Republican ballots in 1980 were voters seeking to reverse what they saw as a federal government tilt in favor of blacks and other minorities.

In the 1980 contest, 22 percent of all Democrats defected from their party to vote for Reagan. This defection rate shot up to 34 percent among those Democrats who believed civil rights leaders were pushing "too fast"; to 31 percent among those Democrats opposed to special government aid to minorities; and to 38 percent among those opposed to government intervention to insure that everyone has a job and a good standard of living.[16] Cutting welfare, food stamps, housing subsidies, and other efforts to integrate blacks into the social and economic mainstream fulfilled an implicit Republican campaign promise to these disaffected white Democratic voters.

For Reagan, conservative racial policies were more important in his appeal to white Democrats than they were in securing his Republican base. Results from a Washington Post/ABC survey in March 1981 of 12,767 white voters showed that on a number of key questions, Democratic whites who voted for Reagan in 1980 were more conservative on racial issues than were Republican voters. White Democrats who stayed loyal to Carter, in contrast, were more liberal than were Republicans.

Among whites, Democrats voting for Reagan (Reagan Democrats) believed, by a margin of 71 (agree) to 25 (disagree), that blacks have worse jobs, income, and housing than whites because they "don't have the motivation or will power to pull themselves out of poverty." In contrast, white Republicans supported this view by a more moderate 57–38 margin, and white Carter voters by a 55–41 margin.

Reagan Democrats clearly held more conservative stands on racial issues than other voters. Reagan's ability to pry this group loose from the Democratic coalition was critical not only to his election but also to the enactment of a conservative legislative and regulatory agenda. For a substantial percentage of defecting Democrats—all of them white—the redistributive policies of the Democratic party were no longer seen as benefiting their own families, friends, and neighborhoods, but were seen rather as benefiting minorities at the expense of the working and middle class. Along similar lines, these Reagan Democrats believed that the major emphasis of the regulatory role of the federal government had shifted away from the provision of such essential goods as job safety and the policing of monopolies to the imposition of forced busing and of racial preferences.

———

On a broader scale, the emergence of the Reagan Democrats was a reflection of how the issues of race and poverty, along with the moral cultural and values issues raised by the rights movement, ran head-on into a populist, conservative "egalitarianism"—and into an *egalitarian defense* constructed along traditional meritocratic lines. Paradoxically, at the same time that efforts to ensure new rights to once-marginal groups were defined by the left in egalitarian terms, the means and the costs of these efforts were judged by many voters to impose burdens vulnerable to an *egalitarian challenge.*

For the white patrolman passed over for promotion to sergeant in favor of a black or Hispanic who scored lower on a test; for the elderly Catholic landlady required by law to lease the apartment on her third floor to a homosexual couple; for the night worker in New York who must ride the subway with the no longer confinable deranged; for the nurse assaulted in the hospital parking lot by a criminal out on bail; for the divorced secretary whose children were bused by court order to a school in a distant and unfamiliar neighborhood, the logic of social and racial liberalism was difficult, if not impossible, to grasp.

Conservative populism gave the Republican party—once effectively defined by a majority of voters as the party of the rich—a coherent response to the anguish of the white patrolman, the night worker, the nurse, and the Catholic landlady.

———

These once-Democratic voters, now drawn to a conservative politics with an egalitarian cast—egalitarian in terms of access rather than of outcomes—shared in common with the business community the belief that they were victims of a runaway liberalism, of a mushrooming rights revolution, and of an overly ambitious state. Just as the rights granted to minorities, criminal defendants, pornographers, homosexuals, and the mentally ill imposed certain redistributive costs, the business community had been the target of another outgrowth of the rights movement, the surge in corporate regulation enacted a decade before the 1980 election.

The network of corporate regulatory structures and of regulatory legislation established by the federal government in the late 1960s and the early 1970s—the Occupational Health and Safety Administration (OSHA), the 1970 amendments strengthening the Clean Air Act, the Environmental Protection Agency (EPA), the Consumer Product Safety Commission, the Federal Water Pollution Control Act of 1972, the Mine Safety and Health Administration—"represented kind of a Great Society for the private economy," David Vogel, of the School of Business Administration at the University of California, Berkeley, wrote in 1988. The expansion of corporate regulation gave public-interest lawyers leverage to replicate the tactics of the civil rights bar. "Just as the courts had defined and enforced civil 'rights,' so now they could be used to extend to the public the 'right' to clean air and water, a safe workplace, and food free from dangerous chemicals," wrote Vogel.[17]

For a brief period, roughly 1981 through 1983, the intense opposition to regulation shared by business and by many middle and working-class white voters established a hospitable climate for a substantial policy retrenchment. For the industries most opposed to regulation—particularly mining, chemicals, oil, lumber and paper—the Reagan administration appointed such industry sympathizers as James Watt as Secretary of the Interior and Anne Burford as head of the Environmental Protection Agency, along with lesser known, but similarly committed, anti-regulatory appointees to run OSHA, the National Labor Relations Board (NLRB), the Federal Trade Commission (FTC), the Consumer Product Safety Commission, and the rest of the federal regulatory apparatus.

Reagan administration roll-backs of the regulatory state ranged from a reduction of the budget of EPA's water and air quality, hazardous waste, and toxics divisions—from $968 million in 1980 to $674 million in 1982 (in 1982 dollars); to the placement of severe restrictions on the discretionary inspection power of the field enforcement personnel of OSHA.[18] The Department of the Interior under Watt increased the acreage leased out for coal mining to 120,000 acres in 1981 and 1982, compared to a total of 20,000 acres in 1979 and 1980.[19] Although by late 1983, public antipathy to the policies of Watt and Burford forced their replacement with more moderate appointees, the general relaxation of regulatory vigor continued. Reflecting the overall reduction of corporate regulation, the number of pages describing pending regulatory proposals published annually in the Federal Register, which had grown from 14,479 pages in 1960 to 87,012 pages in 1980, fell to 47,418 in 1986.[20]

----

The race, rights, and tax-driven merger of the ideological interests of working and middle-class whites with those of corporate America laid the groundwork for the fulfillment of an additional set of conservative goals, goals that did not, in fact, have broad popular support: the rewarding of the bankrollers of the conservative revolution. The financial backing for the surge of GOP House and Senate victories in 1978 and 1980 had been spearheaded by the network of industries—oil, chemical, lumber, paper, pharmaceutical, fabricated metals, rubber, and machinery[24]—industries that had borne the brunt of the sharp expansion of corporate regulation in the late 1960s and early 1970s.

By the end of the 1970s, the political action committees (PACs) of these heavily regulated industries along with such foundations as the John M. Olin Fund, established by the chairman of the board of the Olin Mathieson Chemical Corporation, the J. Howard Pew Foundation, created by the former chairman of Sun Oil Company, and the Noble Foundation, set up by Oklahoma oilman Edward E. Noble, became the advance guard of a drive to finance the political and intellectual resurgence of the right.[22] It was this movement that provided the cash to turn such conservative think tanks as the American Enterprise Institute (AEI) and the Heritage Foundation into influential promoters of lowered taxes of down-sized government, and of scaled-back business and social regulation.

Throughout the 1970s, the political rearmament of the business community constituted one of the most comprehensive and effective efforts to force an ideological shift in national policy in the country's history. Major corporations organized management-level employees and stockholders into armies of "grassroots" lobbyists to pressure Congress. The Chamber of Commerce was converted from a nearly moribund organization, viewed with disdain in Washington, into an articulate national spokesman for corporate interests, a source of detailed analysis of the economic costs of legislation, and a meeting ground for alliances of businesses and trade associations. In 1972, the Business Roundtable was established as an organization for the chief executive officers of Fortune 500 companies to pressure the federal government. From 1974 to 1980, the number of corporate PACs grew from 89 to 1,251, and from 1972 to 1980, the cash flow to the campaigns of House and Senate candidates grew from $8 million to $39 million.[23] Behind the lure of cash was the growing threat of assault by the independent, right-wing PACs, which by 1980 included the National Congressional Club affiliated with Republican Senator Jesse Helms of North Carolina, $7.9 million; the National Conservative Political Action Committee (NCPAC), $7.7 million; the Fund for a Conservative Majority, $3.2 million; and Citizens for the Republic, $2.3 million.[24]

In 1979 and 1980, these ideological, corporate, and trade association PACs poured money into the defeat of liberal Democrats Birch Bayh of Indiana, George McGovern of South Dakota, Gaylord Nelson of Wisconsin, Frank Church of Idaho, and John Culver of Iowa—defeats that were critical to the 1980 GOP take-over of the Senate. Regulation-averse industries not only financed Republican challenger and open-seat candidates, but they magnified their support by channeling additional cash to the Republican National, Congressional, and Senatorial Committees, and to such pro-Republican "independent" PACs as NCPAC and the Fund for a Conservative Majority.

Independent oilmen alone gave more money to the Republican party and to Republican candidates—conservatively estimated at $25.7 million—than all of the money raised in 1980 by the Democratic National, Congressional, or Senatorial Committees.[25] The importance of this flow of cash is reflected by the fact that six of the twenty GOP Senate victories that year were achieved by margins of less than one percent; without the willingness of these industries to provide large, early contributions to Republicans challenging incumbent Democratic senators, the GOP take-over of the Senate in 1980 might not have taken place.

With the absence of a liberal brake on right-wing policy initiatives, the Reagan administration was in a position to reward hardcore business supporters of the conservative revival. For the corporate sector, the 1981 tax cut included the most generous business tax reduction—$164 billion—in the history of the nation. The legislation provided for $11.6 billion in reduced taxes for the industry that had led the charge in financing Republican candidates: independent oil. Estate and gift taxes, which fall most heavily on the very wealthy, were cut by $22.1 billion over six years. In contrast, the average working family getting the median income received an income tax cut worth about $255 a year (by 1984), most of which (about $177), was taken back in increased Social Security taxes.[26]

The 1981 tax bill was modified by legislation enacted in 1982 and 1986, but overall the Reagan administration oversaw a major restructuring of the distribution of the tax burden. The following table shows the pattern of the distribution over the past twenty years:

### TABLE 8.3
The Percentage of Total Federal Receipts Contributed by the
Individual Income, Corporate, and Social Security Taxes in 1980 and
1989
(The remaining percentages are contributed by excise, estate, and other
miscellaneous tax sources.)

|  | 1970 | 1975 | 1980 | 1989 |
|---|---|---|---|---|
| Individual income taxes | 46.9% | 43.9% | 47.2% | 45.6% |
| Corporate taxes | 17 % | 14.5% | 12.5% | 10.5% |
| Social Security taxes | 23 % | 30.3% | 30.5% | 36.7% |

SOURCE: Congressional Budget Office, *The Economic and Budget Outlook: Fiscal Years 1990–1994* (Washington, D.C., 1989); *Economic Report of the President, 1990*, tables on federal receipts.

In effect, if the tax burden had been distributed in 1989 in the same way that it was in 1970, corporations would have paid an additional $59.1 billion.

The individual income tax burden in 1989 was $11.8 billion less than it would have been under the 1970 distribution, but the Social Security tax—the tax that falls most heavily on working and lower-middle-class employees—was $124.5 billion higher in 1989 than it would have been under the 1970 distribution.

———

Overall, the formation of a top-down conservative coalition with the interests, the will, and the cohesion to recast broad areas of federal policy, produced a substantial retrenchment of those redistributive policies that particularly benefit minorities. In the course of the first two years of the Reagan administration, the top-down coalition was able to secure as a reward for its working and lower-middle-class white constituencies cutbacks both in means-tested programs and in civil rights enforcement and for those in the dominant, upper-income ranks of the coalition, to secure as a reward a huge transfer of tax benefits and significantly lessened business regulation.

The period of most intense political conservatism was brief, lasting only three years: from 1978, with the tax revolt and the first clear election results showing active anti-liberal sentiment, to the beginnings of the recession in late 1981. But the underlying political change in the ideological composition of the electorate would prove to have substantial staying power. It was during the period of intense conservatism that opposition to federal taxes, to programs benefiting minorities, and to a range of downwardly-redistributive government policies reached its height.[27]

The conservative presidential majority was at that time, however, still fragile and newborn. Reagan had pieced together a majority vote of just 50.7 percent in 1980, and the decisive Republican takeover of the U.S. Senate that year, with the GOP winning twenty of the thirty-four seats at stake, masked the fact that many more votes had been cast for Democratic senatorial candidates, (30.39 million), than for Republican ones (27.33 million)—in large part because of the huge Democratic majorities in Senate contests in California (1.6 million), Illinois (619,006), and Ohio (1.6 million), in contrast to the razor-thin margins of Republican victors.[28]

The economic recession of 1981–82, however, produced a hiatus in the conservative ascension, and the strong pro-Democratic tilt in the midterm elections of 1982 ended the immediate prospect of a full-fledged Republican realignment. Democrats picked up twenty-six House seats, and the southern Democratic-Republican alliance that had controlled House deliberations in 1981 could not be revived. The recession itself gave the Democratic party grounds to attack the upwardly redistributional policies of the Reagan administration. Reagan's approval rating collapsed in the course of the most serious economic downturn since the Second World War, reaching a low-point of 35 percent approval, versus 56 disapproval at the start of 1983, according to the Gallup poll.[29] Congressional Democrats, in turn, learned to exercise the power of incumbency to bring to a halt the financial commitment of corporate and trade association PACs to a Republican takeover of Congress.

Representative Tony Coelho of California, then the chairman of the Democratic Congressional Campaign Committee (DCCC), went to the leaders of Washington's business lobbying community and told them: "You people are determined to get rid of the Democratic Party. The records show it. I just want you to know we are going to be in the majority of the House for many years and I don't think it makes good business sense for you to try to destroy us and support the Republicans. . . . We are going to keep records."[30] The hardball tactics paid off. From 1980 to 1984, the percentage of corporate PAC contributions going to Republicans challenging Democratic House incumbents, and to GOP candidates in open-seat contests, fell from 29 percent to 17 percent.[31]

On the surface, then, the 1984 election had the earmarks of a contest that should have been at least relatively competitive. Working to the advantage of the Republicans was the fact that the country had pulled out of recession at the end of 1982, and the recovery was nearly two years old by November 1984. In addition, individual demographic realignments were continuing among such groups as fundamentalist Christians and Cuban-Americans, along with a slower, but large-scale and sustained shift to the GOP among southern whites. Conversely, the Democrats had made gains on a number of fronts: the recession had discredited some of the more grandiose claims of supply-side economics; attitudes on a wide range of public policy issues (such as spending for education, health, and the environment) had become more liberal; the corporate cash spigot for GOP candidates had begun to dry up; the Democratic majority in the House was secure; and Republican attempts to cut Social Security payments during Reagan's first term had revived perceived GOP liabilities as the rich man's party, hostile to the interests of the average voter.

In fact, however, the 1984 presidential election produced a landslide victory for Reagan. In that election, the defection of white, working-class northern Democrats turned into a hemorrhage. Reagan's success in 1984 grew out of, first, a continuing and strengthened convergence of issues surrounding economics, culture, and race, a convergence that had been building throughout the 1970s to support a coherent conservative ideology. The Democratic defection grew, secondly, out of the sustained nurturing and rewarding of the conservative majority by a Republican party in control of the White House.

The Democrats, deluded by the short-term gains of the 1982 election, misjudged the significance of the 1982 recession. The recession, as the next chapter will explore, in fact accelerated and intensified a restructuring of the nation's economy, a long-term, wrenching process that caused massive suffering and dislocation to core Democratic constituencies, suffering which left the presidential wing of the Democratic party—at least for the time being—scarred, powerless, and ineffective.

# 9
# The Reagan Attack on
# Race Liberalism

Traditional Democratic Liberalism reached a political nadir in the election of 1984. For the first time in twenty years, the leadership of core Democratic party constituencies—from organized labor to feminists, from old-line city clubs to reform liberals, along with much of the black leadership—coalesced behind the nomination of one candidate, Walter F. Mondale. The intention and the fundamental strategy of these core constituencies was to restore the Democratic coalition, to capitalize on the recession of 1981–82, and to revive Republican liability as the party of Herbert Hoover and of the Great Depression. When the ballots were counted on November 6, 1984, however, it was Mondale, the Democratic standard bearer, who replicated Hoover's performance—losing the majority-party vote to Reagan by exactly the same margin that Hoover lost to Franklin Delano Roosevelt in 1932, 59.2 percent to 40.8 percent.[1]

The 1984 election marked a major shift in the movement toward the Republican party in presidential elections. From 1968 to 1980, the white South had been the driving force in the realignment of presidential politics, the leading indicator of a national trend. In 1984, the precincts in white, working-class neighborhoods in the urban North joined the South in propelling a presidential realignment, as the eroding Democratic loyalty of these voters transformed itself from ambivalence to outright rejection. The 1984 election demonstrated that the policy agenda developed by the Reagan administration once in office—an agenda designed to sustain the racial and economic polarization that had emerged in force in the 1980 election—had worked to nurture and enlarge the Republican presidential voting base established in 1980.

For the Democratic party, Reagan's success in expanding his support in northern, working-class white neighborhoods was a body blow. Mondale was the incarnation of the traditional New Deal Democratic party, unlike either Carter or McGovern, but his candidacy produced a severe Democratic setback among precisely those constituencies to which a regular Democrat ought to appeal.

Among white blue-collar workers, once the core of the party, Democratic identification fell 15 points between the 1980 and 1984 elections, four more points than among professionals and managers; among white high school graduates, Democratic identification fell by 18 percentage points, twice the nine percentage point drop among college graduates.[2] Hostility to the Democratic party and its nominee had grown most among just those voters essential to the restoration of an economically based, biracial coalition of the center-left.

For the Republican party, the 1984 election was an opportunity to test the degree to which the conservative revolution of 1980 had become institutionalized. The election affirmed not only that the GOP had reinforced the loyalty of key elements of the new voting majority in presidential elections—through governance and through political strategy—but also that the Reagan administration and the GOP had restructured the terms of the political debate to establish a contrast debilitating to the Democratic party, a contrast that the Democratic party in some instances actively reinforced despite the damaging consequences.

At the core of this restructured debate was the adamant opposition of the Republican party to raising taxes, a stand that in both real and symbolic terms carried a much broader message: that the GOP would stand as a bulwark against, and as an adversary of, all costs imposed by the liberal agenda of race, rights, and taxes. The symbolic significance of the anti-tax message was repeatedly given specific reinforcement by the drive of Reagan loyalists, particularly those in the Justice Department, to end racial preferences, to end affirmative action, to take the government out of the business of enforcing racial integration, and to define "reverse discrimination" as the symbol of liberalism run amok.

Throughout his tenure in office, Reagan explicitly and implicitly affirmed this broad commitment to stand tall against redistributive liberalism: in his successful repopulation of the federal judiciary with ideological conservatives; in his racially conservative appointments to the Department of Justice; in his pointed efforts to force a retrenchment of the welfare and regulatory state; and in the major alteration of the federal tax code during his years in office. Even when the specifics of Reagan's policies were opposed by majorities of the electorate—his attack on environmental protection, for example, or his acceptance of a tax hike in 1982—Reagan's larger commitment to block the tide of liberalism, and the conversion of this commitment into Republican orthodoxy, prevented majority public opinion from turning against him.

More importantly, this broader commitment by both the president and the Republican party established the basis for the strengthening and servicing of the conservative, top-down majority coalition that had come to dominate presidential elections. One of the most consistent themes of the politics of the 1980s was the qualitative difference between the capacities of the Republican and Democratic parties to strengthen their bases of constituent support; to modify strategies to accommodate changing public opinion, ideology, and demography; and to develop strategies to reward the loyal and to penalize the opposition. The Republican party had an inherent advantage in this contest. Rising international economic competition undermined the ability of the Democratic party to service such constituencies as labor and blacks through traditional protective programs—mandatory union-scale wages on federal contracts, and affirmative action hiring, for example—programs that worked best when competition was limited by national borders.

Continued suburbanization, in turn, strengthened natural Republican voting bases, while the share of the national vote cast in Democratic urban strongholds declined. Throughout these transitions, the huge resource advantage of the GOP in terms of money, poll data, consultants, computerized voter lists, phone banks etc.—particularly in the new technology of politics—provided information and material essential to the fine-tuned tactical and strategic adjustments necessary to staying ahead of the opposition.

In the aftermath of the Democratic defeat in 1984, Reagan received much of the credit for producing the radical shift of voter allegiance reflected in the 1984 outcome. In fact, while Reagan's role was indisputably critical, he was more a principal agent within—rather than the prime mover of—a sea change involving forces substantially more profound and extensive than the fortunes of the two political parties or of their candidates. To see Ronald Reagan as the cause of an ascendant conservatism minimizes the significance and consequence of large-scale social and economic transformations—developments beyond the power of any single political player to determine. Major elements of this sea change include the following:

• For many white voters who had experienced severe hardship in the economic upheaval of the prior decade, and who had also been on the front lines of racial conflict, the Democratic Party in 1984 virtually lost its voice. For these voters, particularly in and surrounding major northern cities, Democratic party messages began to be read and interpreted through a "racial filter"—a filter changing the meaning of traditional Democratic messages and destroying their effectiveness. "Working class voters were persuaded that if you hitched your wagon to the poor, every time the poor moved up a rung on the ladder, they are going to take you down a rung. If you hitched your wagon to the rich, every time they move up a rung, they'll take you up a step. It was a sea change in American politics," contended Mondale campaign manager Bob Beckel, looking back on the 1984 race.[3] Among these voters, Reagan administration policies restricting the scope of affirmative action, busing, and other civil rights remedies; the concerted administration drive to reconstruct a once-liberal judiciary; the consistent administration effort to cut back the means-tested programs of the welfare state; and the encompassing Republican anti-tax stand, all worked as powerful coalition-building tools to produce higher Republican voting margins in 1984 than in 1980.

• The power of the Democratic party to revive the Herbert Hoover–Great Depression image of the GOP—as the party of the rich and of an unraveling economy—was eclipsed in 1984 when many voters perceived the collapse of key sectors of American industry as rooted in the Democratic administration of Jimmy Carter. This collapse had become visible for the first time to the public during the late 1970s, at a time when Democrats were in full control of Congress, and when organized labor was dominant in both the steel and auto industries. For crucial groups within the industrial working class, the period from 1978 through 1982 represented a second Great Depression, a depression whose inception was associated not with Republicanism, but with Democratic party rule, and with a period of trade union hegemony. For ranks of workers in heavy industry, the 1981–82 recession was not a discrete event tied to the Reagan administration, but a continuation of the industrial decline begun under Carter. For the Republican party and the Reagan administration, the success in assigning responsibility for the economic deterioration of 1978–1982 to a history of misguided Democratic policy decisions represented a major ideological victory, strengthening public—and elite—receptivity to the conservative argument for restricting and reshaping domestic interventions by the federal government.

• The divergence in the underlying values and images associated with the two parties—a divergence driven by the agenda of race, rights, and taxes—reached new heights in 1984. For the GOP, religiosity (measured by church attendance) took its place, by 1984, within a loose alliance of other conservative or "traditional" values, now increasingly clustered on the right and claimed by the Republican party: belief in hard work, in the nuclear family, in self-reliance, in personal restraint, in thrift, foresight, and self-denial; belief in doctrines of individual responsibility, in obedience to the law, in delayed gratification, in respect for authority, and in a more repressive (or less self-expressive) sexual morality. This fusion of values, beliefs, reactions, and commitments—increasingly perceived by key segments of the white electorate to be more persuasively upheld by the party of the right—served, in turn, to strengthen the powerful advantage of the Reagan campaign in television-spot dominated campaigning—a form of campaigning far more amenable to the triggering of submerged values and fears than to the presentation of substantive issues or policy positions.

• Conversely, the identification of the Democratic party with previously subordinate groups—groups making new claims and demands on the majority for rights, for authority, for status, for centrality, for political power, and for money—intensified in 1984. This identification strengthened the perception of the Democrats, by crucial numbers of voters within the white electorate, as the party of victims, of redistribution to victims, and of a public ethos skirting the issues of individual responsibility, fiscal discipline, and social obligation. The accumulated history of Democratic ties to the rights revolution—particularly as amplified and exploited by the campaign messages of the GOP in 1984 (and in 1988)—produced a linkage in public perceptions between the national Democratic party (whose most famous spokesman was now Jesse Jackson) and such benefit-hungry groups as welfare recipients, feminists, black militants, illegal immigrants, gays, addicts seeking drug treatment, AIDS victims, and members of the underclass. The word "groups" in GOP hands would soon come to connote just these constituencies.

The complex of connections between the national Democrats and these newer entrants to the competition for public resources severely restricted the competitive ability of the Democratic party and of its presidential nominee in the mainstream "values marketplace" of politics.

• Benefiting from demographic and ideological trends—and from access to a huge reservoir of financial support—the presidential wing of the Republican party in 1984 in addition moved a quantum jump ahead of the Democratic party in terms of its mastery over the technology, over the nuts-and-bolts tactics, and over the broader strategy of national elections. Vast quantities of Republican cash financed the maintenance of a semi-permanent cadre of campaign specialists who were either employed by the three major Republican committees or served as consultants to them. These specialists became, in turn, increasingly adept in the control and manipulation of a tri-level strategy for victory: the "air war" on television; the "ground war" of high-tech direct mail, phone banks, polls, focus groups, and computerized voter lists; and the effective political use of government policy itself to build election-day majorities. The careful separation of the air and ground wars permitted the Reagan campaign to conduct an essentially centrist campaign on television, while using the far less visible tactics of the ground war to mobilize support among groups with more divisive, and potentially threatening, agendas—including fundamentalist Christians and anti-abortion activists.

This ability to keep some constituencies off of center stage was in sharp contrast to the Democrats, whose negotiations, jousting, and mobilization of minorities, peace activists, feminist organizations, homosexual-rights groups, and a host of other controversial interests were generally conducted in full public view, often on the evening news. In the arena of government policy itself, the Reagan administration was committed to stressing, consistently and visibly throughout its first term, adamant opposition to Democratic-endorsed racial preferences, quotas, goals, and time-tables. The repeated raising of the issue of affirmative action—and the high profile of the Reagan Justice Department in this effort—gave added power to Reagan's campaign theme in white, working-class neighborhoods and in the South, a theme captured by the slogan aired repeatedly throughout the 1984 campaign: "You haven't left the Democratic Party, the Democratic Party left you."

———

The isolation of the national Democratic party during the 1984 campaign was dramatically reflected in the ease with which the Reagan team and the Republican party were able to polarize the electorate along racial and economic lines through simple assertions of "middle-class values and goals." The political success of such Republican assertions signaled that the public perceptions of the two parties had become dangerous to Democratic ambitions. For a crucial segment of the white electorate, to be middle class, to hold traditional values, to endorse work, family, responsibility, achievement and the like, meant not supporting the presidential wing of the Democratic party.

The insularity of the national Democratic party—its ignorance of the power and potential for conservative exploitation of the "values" issue—grew out of the coexistence of its liberalism and idealism with its distance from the concerns of pivotal numbers of working and middle-class white voters. These pivotal voters felt that public resources once securely within their own province were being rapidly diluted, stretched, and redirected—redistributed to people often unfamiliar, "different," and often sharply critical of or dissident from majority values. This Democratic insularity provided a point of attack for the 1984 Reagan campaign. Among the principal Republican strategic responses to Democratic vulnerability was the initiation of a major extension of the language of politics—the enlargement of a television language empowering the Republican party and its candidate to reach voters through a set of majoritarian "values-oriented" images and phrases that, for key segments of the electorate, set the GOP apart from the Democratic party. This television language was most fully expressed in 1984 in the series of campaign commercials collectively known by the phrase from one of them, "It's morning again in America."

Two sets of forces combined to provide the Republican party with the opportunity to dominate the values marketplace, the first of which were the schisms within the Democratic coalition. The second was the adoption by the GOP of a comprehensive, resilient ideology focused on conservative egalitarianism, an ideology revolving around "equal opportunity" rather than "equal outcomes"; around the idea that market mechanisms functioned most effectively to allocate scarce resources; and around the linkage of merit and status, and of reward and effort. It was an ideology that used opposition to federal tax burdens to unite the rich and the working class, as opposed to the use of federal spending to unite the poor with the middle class, an ideology purged of overt bias, tinged—in the wake of twenty years of unprecedented social change—with nostalgia, and with an implicit but stern admonition to life's losers.

"You persuade by reason, but you motivate people by tapping into values that run much deeper," said Richard Wirthlin, Reagan's pollster, in discussing the strategy underpinning both the conduct of the 1984 election and the conduct of the Reagan presidency: "[You] measure attitudes toward the issues and attitudes toward the candidate, but go beyond that and see if those could be linked in any reasonable rational fashion to people's values. And again it's in this higher level of values and emotions that you really do understand what things are driving behavior."[4] This appeal to values and emotions was conducted both in the campaign, through superficially "inclusive" messages, and through governance, where policy and programs helped to polarize the electorate by race and by class.

At the core of the 1984 campaign strategy was the recognition that televised images—Reagan filmed at the Daytona 500, surrounded by bleachers of white working-class southerners; Reagan, beer in hand, among the working-class regulars in a Boston bar—could now be used to project the values Republicans were successfully appropriating. These

painstakingly staged television events, in combination with phrases carefully tested in focus groups for voter resonance—"ours is a chosen land,"
"a triumph of hope and faith," "a celebration of the new patriotism"—
were used to focus viewer/voter attention on a value-laden conception of
both conservatism and of the Republican party. This conception was designed to contrast sharply with a Democratic party painted as estranged
from the mainstream; a party which, in Reagan's words, "sees people only
as members of groups."[5]

---

The success of Republican strategy required not only the complicit, if
unknowing, cooperation of the Democratic party and of its own liberal
cadre, but, even more importantly, it depended on a genuine resonance
with the voters. The Republican party by 1984 had gained a powerful
internal coherence based on factors far more substantial than the manipulation of televised images. By 1984, Republican identification with "traditional values" and with the advocacy of a conservative egalitarianism had
significantly increased working and middle-class support for a party already closely associated by many voters with the so-called "Protestant
ethic."

The 1984 election marked the solidification of a parallel trend functioning to the advantage of the GOP: the voting patterns of the religious and
the non-religious. Religiosity (defined in terms of regular church attendance) became by the mid-eighties an identifying characteristic of white
voters who aligned themselves with the Republican party. Among Catholics, union members, southerners, and white northern Protestants, regular
churchgoers in 1984 were 11 percentage points more Republican than
Democratic, while those who never attended church were 8 points more
Democratic.[6] In a parallel finding, when voters in 1984 were asked about
the degree of their belief in the authenticity of the Bible, the only group of
those surveyed who said they intended to cast a majority of their votes for
Mondale, 55–45, were those who agreed that the Bible "was written by
men who lived so long ago that it is worth very little today." Mondale lost
by a slim, 49–51, margin among those who agreed that the Bible "is a good
book because it was written by wise men, but God has nothing to do with
it," and he was crushed, 40–60, among those who believed either that the
Bible "is God's word and all it says is true," or that the Bible was "inspired
by God but it contains some human errors."[7]

Republican dominion over the terrain where religious conviction, the
work ethic, backlash over social reform, conservative egalitarianism, anti-
black feeling, and racial conservatism met, gave the GOP, by 1984, a deci-

sive advantage in the competition over values, providing access to both a general election majority and to those specific groups of white voters most directly affected by conflicts over race. This complex interaction is best reflected in the contrast between the central public themes of the 1984 Reagan campaign on the one hand, and the actual perception of the content of the political conflict by key segments of the electorate on the other. While the 1984 campaign ostensibly portrayed competition between Democratic and Republican agendas and values in race-neutral terms, in actuality, urban, working-class whites saw (or read) those same partisan divisions as structuring a race-freighted competition for the "direction of the country," as well as for increasingly contested diminishing national resources. In a sense, *explicitly* accessing or tapping voter convictions and anxieties about values and economic status allowed *implicit* access to anxieties and resentments about race.

Reagan campaign strategists sought to define the choice in 1984 as between two alternative visions of America, one Republican, the other Democratic. In a heavily used 1984 commercial—devoid of explicit racial content, but with strong implicit messages about "the kind of country" Democrats were responsible for—pictures of rusting farm and factory equipment, and a shot of an elderly woman walking bent with a cane, alone are first shown with a Reagan voice over

> This was America in 1980. A nation that wasn't working. Huge government spending gave us the worst inflation in 65 years, interest rates were at an all-time high. The elderly were being forced out of their homes. People were losing faith in the America dream.

The picture then changes to scenes of farmers loading seed, an arc welder at work in a machine plant, autoworkers entering a factory gate, and a family bringing home a newly purchased living room rug, with Reagan's voice now extolling a restored America:

> So we rolled up our sleeves and showed that by working together there is nothing Americans can't do. Today, inflation is down and interest rates are down. We've created six and a half million new jobs. Americans are working again. So is America. If the dream that built America is to be preserved, then we must not waste the genius of one mind, the strength of one body or the spirit of one soul. Now it's all coming together. With our beloved nation at peace, we are in the midst of a springtime of hope for America.

The Reagan television spot was notable not only for the utter absence of bias, but for its conflation of an idealized, homogeneous Republican "hometown" with an evocation of economic success—reminding voters of what was arguably the most important dimension to them of the first Reagan administration: that the country had entered the second year of a substantial economic recovery after experiencing the most severe recession since the 1930s. Simultaneously, the portrayal in the T.V. spot of two visions of America, one Democratic, the other Republican, reinforced a far more conflict-ridden perception of America held by key swing voters.

———

The central battleground in 1984 was in fact for the support of beseiged members of the most vulnerable sector of what remained of the New Deal coalition, the white working and lower-middle class. Not quite the balance of power, these voters were, rather, at the fulcrum of power: not only were their votes important numerically, but they were essential to the ideological coherence of each party. For the Democratic party, their support was critical to the maintenance of an economically based coalition made up of majorities of voters at or below the median income. For the Republican party, these voters were essential to the strengthening of the doctrine of conservative egalitarianism that had become the hallmark of the GOP.

Macomb County, for example, is a largely white, working-class suburb on the northeast border of Detroit, a bastion of United Auto Workers and assembly-line retirees, one of the constituencies that had absorbed the brunt of the collapse of the auto industry in the late 1970s and early 1980s. Before the civil rights revolution moved north, this county had been bedrock for the Democratic party. In 1960, Macomb County voters cast one of the highest margins of any major suburban county for the Democratic candidacy of John F. Kennedy, 63 to 37 percent. Even in the midst of the civil rights and anti-war battles of 1968, Macomb County voters cast a solid 55 percent of their votes for the Democratic nominee, Hubert Humphrey, compared to just 30 percent for Nixon, and 14 percent for Wallace. Democratic allegiance was severely eroded in the early 1970s, not only by the conversion of Detroit to a black-majority city, but also by the threat of forced busing between Macomb County and Detroit, a proposal rejected by the Supreme Court in 1974, but one that significantly altered established voting patterns. In 1976, Gerald Ford, a Michigan native son, carried the county by a 52–48 margin; four years later, Reagan beat Carter countywide by a 56–44 margin.

In 1984, however, the bottom fell out for the Democratic party in Macomb county. In a working-class area hard-hit by the recession, in neighborhoods with a deep tradition of union loyalty, Mondale, a labor stalwart, lost to Reagan by a margin of 67–33, precisely reversing

Kennedy's 1960 victory over Nixon. Even worse for the Democrats, the GOP picked up half of the county's state legislative seats. The outflow of Democratic defectors, which had accelerated in 1980, became, by 1984, a flood—not only in Macomb County, but in similar areas across the country, areas like Southwest Chicago; Parma, Ohio, outside of Cleveland; and Northeast Philadelphia, where precincts that twenty years earlier had yielded decisive Democratic majorities, voted for Reagan over Mondale in 1984 by 2–1 margins.

The Michigan Democratic party, facing the prospect of losing its base not only in Macomb County but in all of the state's white, working-class suburbs, financed a study of Democratic defectors in the county. The study, conducted by a major Democratic polling firm, was based on five separate focus-group sessions in early 1985. Stanley Greenberg, president of the Analysis Group, summarized the findings:

> These white Democratic defectors express a profound distaste for blacks, a sentiment that pervades almost everything they think about government and politics. . . . Blacks constitute the explanation for their [white defectors'] vulnerability and for almost everything that has gone wrong in their lives; not being black is what constitutes being middle class; not living with blacks is what makes a neighborhood a decent place to live. These sentiments have important implications for Democrats, as virtually all progressive symbols and themes have been redefined in racial and pejorative terms. . . . The special status of blacks is perceived by almost all of these individuals as a serious obstacle to their personal advancement. Indeed, discrimination against whites has become a well-assimilated and ready explanation for their status, vulnerability and failures. . . . Ronald Reagan's image [was] formed against this [Democratic] backdrop—disorder and weakness, passivity, and humiliation and a party that failed to speak for the average person. By contrast, Reagan represented a determined consistency and an aspiration to unity and pride.[8]

While extreme in their willingness to make their views known, the voters of Macomb County were not exceptional among the white working class. Findings parallel to those of the Analysis Group were produced by a $250,000 study commissioned by the Democratic National Committee in 1985, a nationwide poll involving 5,000 voters and thirty-three separate focus groups targeting key Democratic constituencies, including white liberals, blacks, public employees, white urban ethnics, and white southern moderates. The DNC study, conducted by CRG Communications of Washington, D.C., found that race was a divisive issue among all of these groups, but that it was most intense among the white ethnic voters (primarily Irish and Italian) and among southern Democratic moderates. These white voters, according to the CRG study, believed "the Democratic Party has not stood with them as they moved from the working to the middle class. They have a whole set of middle-class economic problems today, and their party is not helping them. Instead it is helping the blacks, Hispanics and the poor. They feel betrayed." These voters "view gays and feminists as outside the orbit of acceptable social life. These groups represent, in their view, a social underclass. . . . They feel threatened by an economic underclass that absorbs their taxes and even locks them out of the job, in the case of affirmative action. They also fear a social underclass that threatens to violate or corrupt their children. It is these underclasses that signify their present image of the Democratic Party. . . . The Democrats are the giveaway party [and] 'giveaway' means too much middle-class money going to blacks and the poor. . . ." Affluent liberals and such groups as "blacks, gays, hispanics, feminists and labor" were effectively "trad[ing] the party between themselves, leaving the 'common man' out of the picture."[9]

The attitudes among white voters found by the CRG study were diametrically opposite to the views found among a substantial majority of black voters, as expressed in other contemporary surveys. The divide between blacks and whites on the issue of government responsibility to provide jobs and a decent standard of living remained huge in 1984, with a massive 58-percentage point spread between black support for government intervention and white opposition to such intervention.[10] In response to a related question—whether government should provide fewer services, even in health and education, in order to cut spending, or whether government should provide more services—whites were effectively split down the middle, while blacks were in favor of expanded services by better than a two to one margin, 69–31.[11]

"The issues that concern working-class minorities comprise the traditional 'fairness' agenda of jobs, housing, welfare, and education. They want more benefits for themselves and their children," the CRG voter study found. These working-class minority voters *"strongly assert the validity of the 'fairness' theme.* [emphasis added]. They believe that they are entitled to certain governmental benefits and view the diminishment of those benefits as a betrayal of a trust." For the white voters of Macomb County, in contrast, the Analysis Group found that *"conventional Democratic themes, like opportunity and fairness, are now invested with all the cynicism and racism* that has come to characterize these sessions [emphasis added]. In effect, the themes and Party symbols have been robbed of any meaning for these Democratic defectors. On hearing the term 'fairness,' these voters recall, on the one hand, 'racial minorities' or 'some blacks kicking up a storm,' and on the other hand, 'only politics' or politicians who are 'lying.' It never occurred to these voters that the Democrats were referring to the middle class."[12]

In essence, the Democratic message by 1984 was viewed by one sector of the white electorate—a crucial sector in terms of presidential votes— through what might be called the prism of race; traditional liberal messages were passed through a racial filter; the word "fairness" was read in racial terms, even when no explicitly racial content was intended. For the Democratic message to be heard by key numbers of white voters as favoring blacks and as preempting the rights and customary privileges of whites was fatal to the Mondale candidacy; the more so since "fairness" by the 1980s, had become a central Democratic theme. The 1980 Democratic platform declared that "In all of our economic programs, the one overriding principle *must be fairness.*"[13] Four years later the 1984 platform asserted that "A nation is only as strong as its commitment to justice as equality. Today, *a corrosive unfairness* eats at the underpinnings of our society."[14]

————

While the tensions between factions of the Democratic party made it possible for Reagan and for the Republican party to establish in 1984 a seemingly race-neutral political language which in fact accessed—that is, implicitly evoked—submerged racial and cultural conflict, that year's election represented the clearest signal that the voice of the national Democratic Party no longer resonated with a voting majority. For one segment of the old Roosevelt coalition—10 to 15 percent of the white voters, by rough estimate—the "fairness" message of the Democratic party now jarred, incongruent in the context of a harsh worldview. In this view, life was dominated by a bitter struggle for limited resources; in this view, blacks, like whites, were responsible for their own well-being. This view held that the history of legal oppression and discrimination against blacks had been remedied, and was no longer to be compensated for by government "handouts"; and that if blacks wanted the rewards of American society, they would have to compete, unaided, as whites felt they themselves did, armed only with whatever advantages or disadvantages were dealt to them at birth. For white voters who construed fairness in this manner, braced before what they regarded as a grueling social and economic competition, the Democratic party had come, in the course of twenty-five years, to represent, not their own interests, but instead, those of their adversaries.

The worldview of such white voters—voters vital to a party dependent on lower-income biracial majorities—had the effect of scrambling Democratic messages, of superimposing 'racial' interpretations on traditionally

liberal economic messages. Mondale's call for a tax hike on workers earning more than the median income in order to finance a restoration of
Reagan budget cuts, and Mondale's promise to revive "fairness" in the
distribution of the tax burden, were not heard by these white voters in
terms of a Democratic candidate seeking to improve the lot of the average
white working man and woman. Instead, Mondale and the Democratic
party were heard by these key voters as advocating a redistribution—*from*
whites *to* the black and Hispanic poor. By the time of the 1984 presidential
election, the national Democratic party had lost its encompassing voice for
this key constituency.

———

The gap between the largely race-neutral explicit messages of the Reagan-Bush 1984 campaign and the deeply racial view of politics among
those voters who became known as "Reagan Democrats" was bridged by
the actual content of specific policies and programs pressed for by the
Reagan administration throughout its tenure. The goals of the Reagan
administration were most sharply defined during its first year in office, a
year marked by major successes in winning approval of tax and budget
legislation. In 1981, the Reagan administration established its credentials as
the adversary of the liberal redistributive state, making it abundantly clear
to both the beneficiaries of liberalism, and to those who felt that they were
paying the costs of the liberal state, where the administration stood.

While the Reagan administration was forced, over the seven remaining years, to compromise on almost every front, the conservative commitment was sustained in principle, and there was never any doubt in the
minds of concerned voters where the Reagan administration would take
the nation if it were free of congressional and bureaucratic restraint. The
annual submission of a budget calling for continued decimation of subsidy
and regulatory programs, dismissed by the leaders of Congress and by the
press as "dead on arrival," was in fact a signal of an unbending, if largely
symbolic, commitment to conservative principle, geared towards slashing
government spending on domestic social programs. Until the forced resignation of Edwin Meese in 1988, the Justice Department remained a bastion
of conservative ideology and practice, insistently challenging liberal policy, liberal programs, and liberal legal precedent. The Justice Department
became, in fact, the heart and mind of the Reagan revolution, as Reagan
himself was forced by political reality to bend in his appointments to such
other departments and agencies as Labor, the Environmental Protection
Agency, and Interior. In tandem with the ideological transformation, by
executive appointment, of the federal judiciary, from Supreme Court to

district court, the Justice Department attack on the legal underpinnings of the liberal rights revolution—including attacks on policies established in the late sixties and seventies on affirmative action, busing, voting rights cases, employment discrimination, and abortion—began to bear real fruit with a series of Supreme Court decisions handed down in 1989 (the year after Reagan left office), decisions paring back affirmative action remedies and restricting minority set-aside programs.[15]

The Reagan administration repeatedly brought to the attention of the public the gulf between the two parties on issues of government-led redistribution—especially redistribution with a racial cast. The centerpiece of this assault was the highly publicized, sustained Republican attack on affirmative action; on race-based quotas, goals, and timetables; on minority set-asides; on race-norming (race-based scoring) in employment testing; on race-based university admissions policies; and on other forms of racial preference. Through these attacks, the executive branch under Reagan, and the Republican party, nourished and stimulated racial interpretations of both public policy and of governance. The Reagan administration consistently established not only its opposition to quotas, goals, and timetables, but also demonstrated that it would challenge these practices whenever possible—in the courts, in the enforcement policies adopted by regulatory agencies, and in the negotiation of consent decrees and other agreements with private and public-sector employers.

———

For white and black workers who felt that they could no longer depend on their unions, on their employers, on their country, or on their political party to protect their wages, for workers who faced exacerbated competition for well-paying jobs and for security in the middle class, affirmative action gained increased salience, in the eyes of *both* its beneficiaries and its opponents.

Of all the civil rights issues, none proved to be more racially polarizing than race-based affirmative action. Unlike busing, for example, which in 1980 was opposed among whites by a 90-10 margin, and split blacks by a 49-51 margin,[16] affirmative action pits a strong majority of blacks in favor of preferences (to correct for past discrimination) against overwhelming majorities of whites deeply opposed to such programs. In public opinion polls, whites are opposed to black preferences in hiring and job promotion by a margin of 81 to 11, and are against reserving openings for blacks at colleges by a margin of 69 to 22. Blacks favor these programs by, respectively, margins of 57 to 36, and 73 to 24.[17] For a Republican party seeking to divide the electorate along lines giving the GOP a huge advantage, few issues are as attractive as affirmative action.

Opposition to race-based affirmative action became for the Reagan regime a matter not only of principle and of policy, but of partisan strategy. Republicans delineated two competing visions of America: one of individual initiative and equal opportunity (Republican), the other of welfare dependence and anti-egalitarian special preference (Democratic).

In a process paralleling the system of rewards targeted to the "top" of the top-down coalition (rewards focusing on benefits valuable to business and to the rich, such as government deregulation and tax cuts), the Reagan administration, on every front, from the Equal Employment Opportunity Commission to the Justice Department to the Civil Rights Commission to the Legal Services Corporation, made clear—to the workers of McComb County, as well as to the rest of the country—where the administration's loyalties lay. The administration went on to demonstrate how the loyalty of those lower-income white citizens who voted Republican would be rewarded: by the arrest and, if possible, the rollback of the downwards redistribution that had been triggered by the civil rights agenda and by the rights revolution. The core issue of race-based affirmative action, the issue of compensation for historic discrimination, was reformulated; those blacks who had not themselves *personally* suffered *illegal discrimination* were to be considered by government as uninjured by the legacy of discrimination, and were to be redefined as "non-victims."

In 1981 the new Republican administration selected William Bradford Reynolds, an Andover and Yale-educated corporate lawyer with no background in civil rights, to head the Civil Rights Division of the Justice Department. Reynolds repeatedly stressed his opposition to the use of goals, timetables, and quotas to provide contemporary remedies to past discrimination. His position went to the heart of the egalitarian issues raised by racial preference: "I am, most candidly, offended by all forms of discrimination; I regard government tolerance of favoring or disfavoring individuals because of their skin color, sex, religious affiliation or ethnicity to be fundamentally at odds with this country's civil rights policies. . . . I subscribe to individual rights. . . . I embrace the doctrine of 'equal opportunity.' "[18]

The assault on affirmative action—an assault portrayed as a matter of principle—involved both policies and budgets. From 1981 to 1983, the budgets of the two major agencies pressuring the private sector to adopt affirmative action programs to hire minorities and women, the Equal Employment Opportunity Commission (EEOC) and the Office of Federal Contract Compliance Programs (OFCCP), were, respectively, reduced by 10 and 24 percent, with staff reductions of 12 and 34 percent. Back-pay awards won through actions by the OFCCP—the body responsible for eliminating job discrimination among federal contractors, a massive universe of corporations employing nearly 40 percent of the nation's work-force—fell from $9.3 million paid to 4,336 recipients in 1980, to $3.6 million paid to 1,758 recipients in 1983.[19]

The Justice Department under Reynolds immediately began to challenge both existing and prospective remedies in employment discrimination cases that called for racial preference in hiring or promotion. "We no longer will insist upon or in any respect support the use of quotas or any other numerical or statistical formulae designed to provide *non-victims* [emphasis added] of discrimination [current black applicants for employment, for example] preferential treatment based on race, sex, national origin or religion," Reynolds told Congress in 1981.[20]

This stand illuminated the core of the administration position on affirmative action and school desegregation: the function of government intervention was not to correct contemporary employment, or contracting, or student assignment patterns that grew out of historic discrimination—by requiring, for example, quotas in the hiring practices of 95-percent-white police forces, or by requiring the busing of children in northern school districts. Instead, the function of government was to protect *individuals* from *specific* acts of discrimination. A black man applying to become a policeman in Birmingham was not, in this view, a member of a historically discriminated-against group who deserved special favorable treatment in order to redress the wrongs of the past; instead, he was a "non-victim of discrimination" as long as no specific action was taken to treat his application for a job in any way differently from white, Hispanic, or other applicants. (Individual discrimination cases, unlike "disparate impact" suits, usually involve a single plaintiff, and lead to far less sweeping remedies.) In school desegregation cases, similarly, Reynolds declared in 1981 that the department would "refrain from seeking race-conscious remedies, such as court-ordered busing, solely for the purpose of achieving a particular racial balance."[21]

One of the clearest signals of administration civil rights policy sent to both conservative and liberal networks was Reagan's 1988 veto of legislation overturning the Supreme Court ruling in *Grove City College v. Bell* (1984). The measure, which Congress enacted over Reagan's veto, restored the power of the federal government to end subsidies to institutions with records of discrimination. The Grove City veto was part of a much more wide-ranging administration strategy on matters of race, a strategy that included opposition to strengthening the Voting Rights Act, lax enforcement of civil rights regulations by both the Justice and Education Departments, and the active, systematic encouragement of efforts by local school boards to modify or to seek dismissal of court orders requiring mandatory busing.[22]

In line with this strategy were the repeated attempts by the Reagan administration to eliminate the Legal Services Corporation (LSC)—in seven out of eight years, the Reagan budget attempted to cut all funding for the agency—reflecting the broader goals of an ascendant race-and-rights-conscious conservatism. From the vantage point of the right, much of the work of legal-aid programs—funded with public tax dollars—had been to represent *groups and classes* such as the poor, minorities, migrant workers, single mothers, the mentally ill, tenants, and so on, in what amounted to a government-sponsored use of the legal system to intervene in the private marketplace, to influence the political process, and to create and expand the rights revolution.

When Reagan was governor of California, the California Rural Legal Assistance program and other state branches of the legal-aid program had repeatedly frustrated his administration by filing class action suits that successfully challenged, for example, the governor's attempt to cut Medicaid spending by $200 million in 1967, and his repeated efforts to establish restrictive welfare regulations. At the same time, the California Rural Legal Assistance program took on one of Reagan's core bases of support, agribusiness, using class action suits to compel enforcement of sanitary regulations and wage and hour laws for farm workers, and to prevent the illegal importation of foreign migrant labor.

On a national scale, the LSC had become, in part, the embodiment of the rights revolution, funneling grants to such organizations as the National Center on Women and Family Law, the Migrant Legal Action Center, the National Legal Center for the Medically Dependent and Disabled, the National Senior Citizens Law Center, and the Indian Law Support Center. The initial attempt by the Reagan administration in 1981 to kill the entire LSC appropriation paralleled the original conservative opposition in the mid-1960s to *all* civil rights legislation: the initial assault on Legal Services went, in political terms, too far, challenging the generally accepted principle of government-funded legal representation for the very poor. Congress, even at the height of the conservative revolution in the early 1980s, rejected the administration position, compromising instead by cutting the appropriation from $321 million to $241 million.[23]

In the following years, the assault on the Legal Services Corporation by the Reagan and Bush administrations was brought much more into line with the principles of conservative egalitarianism. A sequence of legislative actions and regulatory decisions, both by Congress and by the Reagan-appointed LSC board, resulted in procedural limitations on the autonomy of legal services lawyers, particularly on their authority to bring class action suits; it also resulted in a virtual prohibition on legislative lobbying in behalf of LSC clients, and created more establishment management of individual legal-aid programs by giving local bar associations control over a majority of appointments to the boards overseeing local programs. The central thrust of these reforms has been to restrict and inhibit class and group-based representation of the poor and minorities in the economic and political arenas, and to focus instead on the representation of individual clients in such matters as divorce, credit disputes, rent and eviction proceedings, and the host of civil legal cases that affect the day-to-day lives of most citizens, including the poor. Just as the focus of Reagan-era civil rights enforcement was shifted to individual cases of discrimination, so too was legal aid redirected away from class and group action to individual representation.

———

The overall conservative strategy of the 1980s was to substantively challenge the underlying legal arguments that since 1964 had been accepted by much of the federal judiciary and by earlier Justice Department officials. Reynolds's predecessor as assistant attorney general for Civil Rights during the Carter years, Drew Days, III, writing in 1984 in the *Harvard Civil Rights-Civil Liberties Law Review,* argued that there were "two basic premises" underlying civil rights enforcement that the Reagan administration fundamentally reversed: "First, that America has yet to fulfill the promises of 'life, liberty and the pursuit of happiness' on an equal basis for large *groups* of its citizens; and second, that the federal government should play a major role in *vindicating* civil rights [emphasis added]."[24]

To bring home its challenge to such liberal premises, the Reagan Justice Department filed a sequence of suits (unsuccessfully) in 1983 and 1984 asking the Supreme Court, and lower courts, to declare unconstitutional affirmative action agreements in Detroit, Boston, and New Orleans (agreements under which police and fire departments had hired equal numbers or fixed percentage ratios of blacks and whites) on the grounds that such agreements violated the Fourteenth Amendment guarantee of equal protection for white applicants and for white police seeking promotion, and amounted to illegal "reverse discrimination."[25]

Soon thereafter the Justice Department sought, again unsuccessfully, to abrogate affirmative action plans with strict goals and timetables in fifty-one cities, counties, school districts, and state agencies.[26] These challenges by the Reagan Justice Department were the opening guns in a prolonged offensive against race-based affirmative action, an offensive which did not produce substantial results until 1989. By that time, the appointment by Reagan of Anthony Kennedy to replace Lewis Powell gave the conservative wing of the Supreme Court an effective majority, and the concerted effort to roll back or curtail civil rights remedies began to pay off: in *Wards Cove Packing Co., Inc. v. Atonio,* which shifted much of the burden of proof in disproportionate-effects-based discrimination cases from employer to employee; in *City of Richmond v. J. A. Croson Co.,* which set stringent rules for the establishment of minority contracting set-aside programs in state and local government; in *Martin v. Wilks,* which permitted white firefighters to file suit challenging a consent decree several years after its terms had been implemented; in *Patterson v. McLean Credit Union,* which limited employment law applications of the 1866 Civil Rights Law to violations based on racial discrimination in hiring and in certain kinds of major promotions, but excluded harassment and other forms of racial discrimination on the job; and in *Lorance v. AT & T Technologies,* which sharply restricted the rights of plaintiffs to file bias suits protesting discriminatory seniority systems.

The selection of Reynolds to lead the charge against quotas, goals, and timetables was backed up by a wide range of administration appointments in other agencies. The Reagan White House chose as chairman of the Civil Rights Commission, Clarence M. Pendelton, Jr., an outspoken opponent, by his own account, of "quotas, proportional representation or the setting aside of government contracts for minority businesses."[27] To run the EEOC, Reagan selected Clarence Thomas, a conservative black who was "unalterably opposed to programs that force or even cajole people to hire a certain percentage of minorities. I watched the operation of such affirmative action policies when I was in college and I watched the destruction of many kids as a result."[28] On October 25, 1983, Reagan fired three Democratic members of the Civil Rights Commission who supported quotas, after issuing an earlier statement declaring that opponents of his plans for the commission "really want to have racial quotas. The President is opposed to quotas and so are his nominees."[29]

The anti-quota, anti-goals and timetables, and anti-busing policy stands taken by key administration officials were part of a much broader conservative shift in the direction of government, a shift that carried with it a powerful message of allegiance to the white voters of Macomb County and other similar regions aross the nation. The focus of public discontent over government spending as revealed in surveys in California during the tax revolt, and in national surveys between 1978 and 1980, had been very specifically directed toward welfare, public housing, and other means-tested programs; the Reagan administration responded to that public demand.

In federal social spending, the largest percentage cuts during the Reagan years were made in means-tested programs serving heavily black populations, programs staffed, in many cases, by black personnel. The basic welfare programs, AFDC and food stamps, were cut by 17.4 percent and 14.3 percent, with the result that at least 400,000 families lost their eligibility for welfare, and nearly one million individuals lost eligibility for food stamps.[30] The Social Service Block Grant and the Community Services Block Grant—two sources of funding for local social welfare programs—were cut respectively by 23.5 and 37.1 percent; and, if the Reagan administration had been able to persuade Congress, the cut in the Social Service Block Grant would have been 41.2 percent, and the Community Service Block Grant would have been eliminated altogether, a goal the administration achieved in the case of the defunded Comprehensive Employment and Training Act (CETA), a public service employment program.[31]

---

The concerted drive to pare back civil rights remedies and means-tested programs was a critical part of a much larger political and ideological strategy of the right: an unrelenting drive to use the popular appeal of certain conservative ideas—particularly those with the effect of "giving" less to blacks—to maintain and enlarge a right-of-center majority coalition. The political genius of conservatism, and of the Republican party, in the 1980s lay in the ability to repeatedly find ways to, first, reinforce the tenuous cross-class alliance behind Republican presidential politics; and, secondly, to nurture the loose consensus behind a right-leaning national policy—a consensus between the affluent and the nation's corporate leadership on one side, and substantial slices of the white working and lower-middle classes on the other. Through all three presidential elections of the decade, the successful implementation of these strategies prevented a restoration of the Democratic presidential coalition.

For those in the lower strata of the top-down coalition, the core message was that under Republican direction, the federal government was no longer tilted in favor of minority competitors for jobs, schools, union apprenticeships, or college entrance; that the executive branch of the federal government was no longer going to invest itself in forcing the introduction of blacks into white environments; and that both means-tested programs, and the taxes to pay for such programs, had been decisively cut. The wedges driven into core constituencies of the Democratic coalition—the wedge issues of race, rights, and taxes (some driven in by the GOP, others self-directed by the Democratic Party)—created fissures among the Democrats, fissures critical to the political reconfiguration of the presidential electorate, and to the establishment of a conservative presidential majority. This new presidential majority would, in turn, accept policy changes providing by far the largest immediate *economic* benefits to those on the highest rungs of the income ladder.

For those at the top of the top-down coalition, the rewards of loyalty were tremendous. In terms of income alone, those at the high end of the distribution experienced huge gains during the decade of the 1980s, as the top one percent saw average family income grow by 75 percent, from $313,206 in 1980 to $548,970 in 1990 (both figures in 1990 dollars); while all those families falling in the bottom 90 percent saw average income grow by just 7 percent, from $27,451 to $29,334 (in 1990 dollars).[32]

This surge in income for those at the top grew out of a host of economic developments, strengthened and reinforced by Reagan administration policies governing taxes, wages, unions, antitrust and environmental regulation, and energy production. This political commitment to the affluent—a principled commitment, in Republican terms, to the affluent as the prime movers of economic growth—is most clearly reflected in changes in the federal tax code during the 1980s when the GOP controlled the White House. From 1980 to 1990, the combined effective federal tax rate (income, Social Security, corporate, excise, etc.) rose by 16.1 percent for families in the bottom quintile of the income distribution, by 6 percent for those in the second lowest quintile, and by 1.2 percent for those in the middle quintile. For those in the second highest quintile, taxes were cut by 2.2 percent, and for those in the top quintile by 5.5 percent, steadily rising to a 7.3 percent cut for those in the top ten percent, to a 9.5 percent cut for those in the top five percent, and a 14.4 percent cut for those in the top one percent of the income distribution.[33]

At the same time, the Reagan administration—acting to secure profits and success for American business, as well as to keep American labor competitive in low-wage world markets—pressed policies that kept wages down for those in the bottom half of the income distribution. Throughout Reagan's tenure, the minimum wage was kept at $3.35 an hour so that those workers who were paid the minimum, and those whose pay scales were keyed to the minimum, experienced an overall, inflation-induced salary cut.

On a broader scale in its efforts to support and reinvigorate American business, the Reagan administration significantly weakened the bargaining power of organized labor, a traditional source of pressure to raise wages, not only for its own members, but also for a host of non-union workers whose pay grows as union pay grows. Already facing declining membership, organized labor was dealt a devastating blow when Reagan in 1981 fired 11,500 striking professional air traffic controllers in an action that sent a strong message to private-sector management and established presidential sanction for the essentially new practice in the 1980s of hiring replacement workers for those out on strike, gutting labor's basic bargaining tool.

During the Reagan years, the number of strikes involving 1,000 or more employees fell below 50 a year, compared to over 200 in all but three of the years between 1947 and 1980. Before Reagan's firing of the controllers, "there was always a sense that people would eventually say, 'Enough, let's sit down and get serious'," said Robert M. Baptiste, a union lawyer, but "now, companies just want to get rid of unions."[34]

As private-sector management intensified the use of hardball tactics, taking on labor in organizing fights and in union decertification efforts, the trade union movement lost a key institutional governmental ally, the National Labor Relations Board (NLRB), which, in the past, had often intervened in behalf of labor, as the Reagan administration appointed pro-business members to the board and staff. Under the chairmanship of Reagan appointee Donald L. Dotson, the percentage of unfair labor practice findings by the NLRB against management in complaints filed by unions fell to 50 percent, compared to 84 percent in 1974–75, the previous period of Republican control.[35] By 1988, the share of the work force represented by unions fell to 16.8 percent, the lowest level since the start of the Great Depression, down from the high of 35.5 percent in 1945, and a sharp fall-off from even 1980, when 23 percent of the workforce belonged to unions.[36]

Reagan labor policies were, in effect, a blow to the solar plexus of a union movement already reeling from the effects of international competition and the evolution of the American labor market away from heavy industry towards high technology and services. For management, Reagan administration policies were a bonanza in the drive to keep labor costs down. During much of the 1980s, wage gains won by organized labor failed to set the pace for all wage scales, and the percentage gains won by unions fell slightly behind those granted in the non-union sector: from 1983 to 1989, non-union compensation grew by 29 percent, while union compensation grew by 28 percent.[37] The Reagan administration's wage and labor policies contributed to the reversal in the 1980s of what had been a steady pattern of rising average hourly earnings in every decade from 1950 to 1979. From 1980 to 1989, hourly earnings, in 1977 dollars, fell from $4.89 to $4.80, after rising from $3.36 in 1950 to $4.20 in 1959, from $4.27 in 1960 to $5.02 in 1969, and, more modestly, from $5.04 in 1970 to $5.14 in 1979.[38]

While the executive branch under Reagan advanced the interests of management in helping to keep workers' wages down, the administration in both symbolic and very practical terms encouraged massive income growth for those at the top end of the income distribution. In this respect, the tax measures described above were only one part of a comprehensive set of policies and regulatory strategies that promoted, during the 1980s, both the pre- and after-tax gains of those in the highest brackets.

At a symbolic level, President Reagan at the head of the Republican party was uncritical in his endorsement of wealth and of material acquisition. "What I want to see above all is that this remains a country where someone can always get rich," he declared on June 28, 1983.[39] The first Reagan inauguration, in January 1981, was a spectacular display of conspicuous consumption, a celebration of ostentatious affluence new to the nation's capital—a weekend when Lear Jets, limousines, and exotic furs clearly identified the loyalties of the president and of his wife, Nancy—a celebration abandoned only when the recession of 1982 turned such display into a potential political liability.

George Gilder's *Wealth and Poverty* (1981), and Jude Waninski's *The Way the World Works* (1978), provided intellectual and economic rationale for government protection of private enterprise, and along with a raft of supply-side economists preaching the virtues of deregulation, conservative economic popularizations became ideologically and practically influential.

At a more workaday level, the administration lifted antitrust restraints[40] to establish a sympathetic legal climate for the surge of corporate buyouts, takeovers, acquisitions, and mergers, the total value of which exceeded two-thirds of a trillion dollars between 1980 and 1988, the year corporate takeover activity reached $311 billion.[41] This surge helped drive, in turn, the stock market rise from 946.25—on the day Reagan first to office—to 1.879.14 on the day he left office, and produced income and transaction fees that reached as much as $550 million for Michael Milken, of Drexel Burnham, and over $50 million in 1988 for at least eleven other financial negotiators. From 1979 to 1987, when the income of American workers fell behind the increase in the Consumer Price Index (CPI) by 8 percent, the income of corporate chief executive officers grew 76 percent faster than the CPI, and the income of investors grew 176 percent faster. From 1982 to 1989, the average net worth of those on the Forbes 400 list rose from $230 million to $672 million, a 192 percent increase, while the CPI rose by only 18 percent.[42]

Reagan policies, in effect, encouraged a transformation of income patterns that revealed a growing disparity between the incomes of the rich and of the less well off. For those in the top one percent of the income distribution, the single most important factor was a massive increase in capital gains realizations from stocks, bonds, real estate, and other investments. For this elite group, annual income realized from capital gains grew by $92,590, or 112 percent from $82,946 in 1980 to $175,536 in 1990. Wage and salary income for this group grew by $89,013, or 81 percent, from $109,439 in 1980 to $198,452 (all in 1990 dollars), with the rest of the income growth coming from scattered sources. For the bottom 90 percent of the income distribution—wage and salary income grew by $825, or 3.9 percent, from $20,917 to $21,742, while capital gains realizations rose by an average of $12, or 4.2 percent, from $287 to $299.[43]

Broad government encouragement of growing income and wealth concentration among the affluent, and of corporate liberation from federal regulation, was integral to public policy at almost every level. The 1981 tax bill, for example, encouraged the concentration of wealth by raising the inheritance tax exemption from $175,625 to $600,000, by raising from $3,000 to $10,000 the annual gift tax exclusion, and by lowering the maximum estate tax rate from 70 to 55 percent on the portion of estates that exceeds $2.5 million. By 1986, these tax changes meant a reduction of $4.7 billion annually in the tax burdens paid primarily by the very wealthy.[44] On a smaller scale, the 1981 tax bill exempted from taxation the first $75,000 made by anyone working in a foreign country, a step designed primarily to benefit American-based, multi-national corporations and their executives on assignment overseas.[45]

———————

The power, over the past decade, of the ascendant conservative wing of the Republican party to adopt policies marketed as fostering economic growth in general, but which indisputably fostered the striking growth in the concentration of income and wealth among the affluent, required the breakup of a once-strong Democratic coalition, a coalition which had represented, since the New Deal, the traditional constellation of interests of those in the bottom half of the income distribution.

Racial conflict and tension, and the consequent disruption of class alliances, were essential to this breakup; openings for the political right created by racial, values, and rights conflicts, conflicts susceptible to the mobilization of generalized anti-liberal and anti-government sentiment, were key to the formation of a top-down coalition. But these conflicts would have been insufficient for Republican victory without the devastating economic upheaval that faced much of the black and white working class by the late 1970s and early 1980s. For the white working class, eager for a return to the rapid improvement in its standard of living that had characterized the post–World War II era, these upheavals meant that traditional Democratic and union policies, which had functioned effectively for fifty years to support both industry and the work force, abruptly lost political and economic legitimacy.

Traditional economic alliances that had been grounded in the presumption of an inherently adversarial relationship between workers and management, were superceded by alliances based on values and racial interests joining, in presidential elections, lower and working-class whites with management, against low-income blacks and other minorities. These new alliances had at least three major components.

The first was the desire of key sectors of the white electorate to return to an era in which blacks and other minorities had far less power and visibility and did not compete with whites for either tangible or intangible goods. The second was the perceived economic *ineffectiveness* of the old Democratic class-based coalition. Thirdly, new alliances were based on an increasing fear on the part of American voters that to tie the hands of business and of the wealthy meant to undermine the ability of American business to generate increasing levels of wealth (some of which would surely trickle down the income ladder), and revealed an emerging acceptance among key American workers of the business argument—that is, of the necessity of government acquiescence to the demands of an evidently besieged corporate sector. The consequences for liberalism and the Democratic party were devastating.

# 10

# Coded Language:
## "Groups," "Taxes," "Big Government," and "Special Interests"

THE EMERGENCE of a *policy-based*, right-of-center presidential majority grew out of the conflation of intensified racial tension, the tax revolt, and one of the most significant developments since the Great Depression—a major economic downturn clearly associated with the Democratic party. Not only was the Depression securely identified with Herbert Hoover's Republican party, but the recessions of the 1950s and early 1970s were tied to the Eisenhower and Nixon-Ford administrations, reinforcing a twentieth-century link between the GOP and periods of high unemployment.

In the late 1970s, the Democratic party was in full command of the federal government and fully empowered to set the public agenda. Organized labor, a major ally of the Democratic party, was firmly entrenched in the nation's steel mills and auto plants. Neither the Democratic party nor the nation's most powerful unions were able, however, to stop the loss of 207,000 jobs in the primary metals industries, the loss of 182,000 jobs in fabricated metals, or of 280,000 jobs making motor vehicles and equipment—a combined total loss between July 1979 and July 1980 of 669,000 jobs in these industries alone.[1]

In this context, the recession of 1981–82 was an integral part of a larger industrial and social upheaval—an upheaval accompanied by a decade in the 1970s of unprecedented rates of unemployment, inflation, interest, and taxation—all defying traditional Democratic interpretation or solution.

For many white voters, this upheaval threatened, rather than reinforced, party loyalty. At a symbolic level, the specter of "Black Tuesday"—October 29, 1929—the day that marked the start of the Great Depression and planted the seeds of the New Deal Democratic realignment, had become, for many voters, obsolete. Instead, in the industrial heartland of the nation—in steel-based communities like Sparrows Point, Buffalo, Lackawanna, Johnstown, Pittsburgh, McKeesport, Aliquippa, Gary, East Chicago, Cleveland, Warren, and Youngstown—the electorate was haunted by a "Black Monday": September 19, 1977, the day on which Youngstown Sheet and Tube Co. announced the shut-down of its Campbell Works, throwing 4,500 people out of work in the heart of Ohio's Mahoning Valley.

The Campbell Works was the first major United States casualty in an international war that left strewn on the American battlefield the hulks of well over 600 steel and auto plants, from USX's Cuyahoga Works to Chrysler's Dodge Main to General Motors' Assembly Plant No. 8. "It's all wrong, but I don't know who's wrong," Francis Peeples, a Youngstown steelworker said on the day in 1977 that the Campbell Works closure was announced, reflecting the economic and political dilemma of the suddenly unemployed.[2]

The economic deterioration of the domestic automobile and steel industries, the industries that had provided the basis for the most striking gains by working-class America and by organized labor in modern history, was devastating to liberalism in general, and to racial liberalism in particular. Blue-collar workers who had been under pressure by the civil rights movement to share the benefits of high wages and middle-class status felt that they had less and less to give to their own families, let alone to new groups seeking apprenticeships, jobs, and seniority.

In 1975 and 1976, just at the beginning of a period of rapid industrial retrenchment, the steel industry and the United Steelworkers were ordered by federal courts to establish plant-wide seniority systems to eliminate practices that restricted blacks to the dirtiest, lowest-paying jobs in the coke ovens and on janitorial crews. As it happened, however, the major effect of the order was not to integrate promotion by company-wide seniority, but to integrate the order of company-wide lay-offs.[3] Similarly, in 1974, a white steelworker named Brian Weber filed suit charging that he was a victim of "reverse discrimination" under an agreement between Kaiser Aluminum and the United Steelworkers, an agreement setting aside 50 percent of in-plant training slots for minorities. By the time the Supreme Court rejected Weber's claim in the landmark 1979 decision, *Kaiser Aluminum & Chemical Corp. v. Weber,*[4] however, there were almost no chances for advancement for either blacks or whites in the basic metal industries. By the election of 1982, at the height of the recession, total job losses in the auto and metals industries over three years had reached 1.19 million. On a broader scale, the number of jobs in the private, goods-producing sector fell, between July 1979 and election day in November 1982, by a cumulative total of 3.67 million, from 26.62 million to 22.95 million—the loss of nearly one out of every seven jobs.[5]

For the United Steelworkers of America and for the United Automobile Workers, plant closures—which had begun to accelerate during the Carter administration—represented the end of an era. These two giant unions had been the crown jewels of the labor movement, with proud histories of setting new standards in contract negotiations, unions that had won pay scales and fringe benefits allowing blue-collar workers for the first time in American history to enter the middle class, to send their children to college, to buy homes, and to provide their families with medical care. The Steelworkers in 1949 had established for the first time the right for all organized labor to put pensions on the bargaining table; in the 1950s, the union won extra vacation time for older workers[6]; in 1955 the UAW had won supplemental unemployment benefits guaranteeing laid-off workers cash income equivalent to 95 percent of their after-tax working pay.[7]

By the early 1980s, however, the debilitated United Steelworkers was forced to swallow repeated wage cuts and fringe benefit "give-backs." The union's primary mission in large sections of the Midwest and in Pennsylvania's Monongahela Valley was now to set up soup kitchens, emergency food supplies, and employment offices for the out-of-work. In 1984, Lynn R. Williams, president of the Steelworkers, told Congress that in the industrial heartland, "proud men and women, many of whom are highly skilled industrial workers, are reduced to a permanent underclass of structurally unemployed."[8]

Broad shifts in industrial employment forced American workers and voters who had once been committed to a vision of economic liberalism within the Democratic party to give far more consideration to the strength and importance of often brutal market forces, to accede to decisions and commitments dictated by emerging global competition, and to view with increasing distrust prescriptions from what seemed to be an extinct era of liberal politics and labor-management detente—an era during which the United States had been largely insulated from rivalry with modern overseas industry and low-wage foreign labor.

The ability of the United Steelworkers to win high wages—compensation packages that reached $19.42 an hour by 1982—shocked the American public and fed anti-union sentiment.[9] Union workrules, high hourly pay, and the accommodation between labor and management in the automobile and steel industries were regularly identified in the media and by business analysts as central factors in the failure of America to prevail in international competition. At the same time, the Democratic alliance between labor and liberal reformers in Washington was strained, as the regulatory structure imposed on business by a Democratic Congress, particularly environmental legislation, which was forcing high corporate costs, came under repeated attack by both labor and industry.[10]

Conservative economic analysis gained increased leverage as doubts about—if not full-scale disbelief in—traditional Democratic and labor strategies began to emerge. "An industry or company that today operates at a blue-collar cost of more than 15% is already way behind. GM still has blue-collar cost of nearly 30%—in part because of restrictive work rules in its union contracts. But Toyota and Honda in their U.S. plants, paying the same wage rates, operate at labor costs of less than 20% and expect to reduce to 15% within a decade," wrote Peter Drucker, one of America's leading business analysts, reflecting the increasingly prevalent economic thinking that challenged the assumptions and the legitimacy of both the dominant liberal wing of the Democratic party and of organized labor.[11] "There is no parallel in history to the rise of the working man in the developed countries during this century," Drucker wrote in another article. "[T]he rise in social standing, and especially in political power, has been greater still. And now it is all over. There also is no parallel in history to the abrupt decline of the blue-collar worker during the past 15 years."[12]

Caught in a downward spiral that first came to the attention of American workers during the Carter administration, many traditional Democratic voters were torn from their partisan moorings. This downward spiral was provoked by an inability to consistently prevail in international competition, fed by—so it was argued—Democratic regulatory practices and by successful union wage negotiations rather than by labor's traditional culprit, management exploitation.

Industrial workers, black and white, in the steel and auto sectors proved to be the shock troops of a much broader, highly disruptive international economic war. Global competition intensified just as American productivity rates began to fall; higher levels of competition and lower levels of productivity forced a sudden end to the modestly paternalistic corporate practices of the 1950s and 1960s—an epoch during which American businesses had been able to cement for a lifetime the loyalty of their white-collar employees, and a period during which business had the wherewithal to negotiate wage settlements beneficial to both labor and management. By the 1970s and 1980s, not only was job continuity threatened by competitive pressure, but the wave of corporate takeovers and mergers ended management continuity for millions of employees. By 1984, major reductions of white-collar work forces had become a commonplace in large corporations. In contrast to blue-collar layoffs, which were carried out on the basis of seniority, management-level reductions fell almost entirely on those in their fifties, a universe made up almost exclusively of white men. These cutbacks, estimated by *Business Week* magazine at 500,000 in 1984 and 1985, forced an expanded recognition among the voting populace of market pressures, and fed a continuing deterioration of support for liberal social and economic policies. "The social compact is breaking down," said Nella G. Barkley, president of Crystal-Barkley, a career counseling firm. "We had paternalism only when we had strong growth." The erosion of corporate paternalism led in turn to an intensification of individualism, fueling support for conservative government policies.[13]

At the most basic level, economic pressures on individual workers functioned to obstruct the generosity of spirit essential to the support of liberal economic and social policies. Middle-class status became increasingly difficult to achieve and maintain throughout the 1970s and the 1980s, more and more often requiring two wage earners in a family. Average gross weekly earnings were lower in every year between 1980 and 1984, ranging from $168.09 to $173.48 (in 1977 inflation-adjusted dollars), than in any year between 1963 ($175.17) and 1979 ($183.41), with the high mark falling in 1973 at $198.41.[14]

By 1984, the pervasive dislocations within the job market, within American families, within individual communities, and within the industrial economy proved to be devastating to the national Democratic party and to the Mondale campaign. Job displacement, loss of security, new family configurations, changing neighborhoods, dangerous streets, crime, dizzying global transformations, and rapidly intensifying competition undermined the capacity of ordinary citizens to tolerate modest sacrifices in behalf of the less well off—a toleration essential to the implementation of liberalism.

———

While the Reagan administration for its first four years in power maintained a steady public drumbeat of opposition to government benefits targeted to blacks, to affirmative action, and to all race-based special preferences, the 1984 Democratic nomination process became the ideal foil for a realignment-hungry GOP. The primary contest between Walter Mondale, Gary Hart, Jesse Jackson, and John Glenn forced onto center stage public awareness of the dependence of Mondale on the network of Democratic constituencies known as "special interests"—the same interests pejoratively characterized by Reagan as "groups."

"Special interests" were increasingly perceived by key sectors of the voting public as allied or interrelated, and as pressing the claims of minorities, including trade unionists, blacks, Hispanics, feminists, homosexuals, AIDS victims, etc., for government special preferences. These special preferences, in turn, were potentially damaging, in the minds of a significant number of voters, not only to America's overall international competitive position, but detrimental as well to the moral fibre, the personal well-being, and the security of individual "ordinary" citizens.

Mondale's long struggle to win the nomination made the Democratic party, and Mondale himself, vulnerable to exactly the negative, special-interest tainted portrayal most advantageous to the GOP. The Democratic primary election process pushed the Mondale campaign in directions that proved fatal for the general election—a danger recognized in advance by Mondale's campaign staff, but one which they were unable to prevent. On January 18, 1983, as the campaign prepared to seek to lock up the nomination early, Richard Moe, Mondale's former chief of staff, wrote a memorandum that warned:

> Handling the traditional [Democratic] constituencies presents a serious dilemma. On the one hand we need their active organizational and financial help to get the nomination. On the other hand being perceived as a "captive" of the constituencies can have very damaging consequences. The goal should be to get as much support as possible from these groups while at the same time appearing to be your own man and independent of any special interests. . . . Most people see special interests as part of the problem, not part of the solution. It follows that they see candidates who pander to these groups for support—saying everything they want to hear, giving them everything they want—as very un-presidential. It really turns them off because they know that's not what the country needs; the country needs someone who has the courage to say no occasionally.[15]

In the year and a half between the writing of that memo and Mondale's nomination in San Francisco in July 1984, the former vice-president was repeatedly wounded in precisely the ways foreseen by Richard Moe. Mondale's strong ties to the AFL-CIO, an organization which took the unprecedented step of endorsing his candidacy in October 1983, well before the beginning of the primary process, and Mondale's backing of organized labor's agenda—including highly controversial protectionist "domestic content" legislation (requiring imported cars to have a percentage of their parts and material made in America)—made the vice-president vulnerable to being painted as the captive of trade unions, a charge repeatedly made by his Democratic opponents during the long, exposed competition for the nomination.

In a Des Moines debate on February 11, 1984, Gary Hart sought to turn Mondale's labor backing into a liability, asking Mondale if he could "cite one major domestic issue where you have disagreed with organized labor." Mondale failed to identify any differences, replying instead that the AFL-CIO "came to me in support of my proposals. This was not a deal. They trust me and they have a reason to be in this campaign."[16] As the primary campaign progressed, Mondale's dependence on labor became increasingly problematic. Faced with a cash shortage in his battle with Gary Hart in the Illinois, New York, and Pennsylvania primaries, strategists for Mondale created a subterfuge to escape the restrictions of federal campaign finance law: special "delegate committees" that served as conduits for contributions, mostly from labor PACs, over and above campaign limits, and in violation of Mondale's own claim that he would reject all PAC contributions. In a later settlement with the Federal Election Commission, Mondale admitted accepting "at least $299,215" in PAC contributions, and at least $47,402 in individual contributions from these delegate committees. Mondale, for all intents and purposes, looked increasingly like a politician deeply in hock to organized labor.

The pattern of perceived co-optation by labor was, in some respects, repeated with regard to organized feminists. The most innovative move of the Mondale campaign, the selection of Representative Geraldine Ferraro, of Queens, New York, as his running mate, was tainted by the public impression that Mondale acted in response to pressure applied by "special interest" feminist "groups." In the summer of 1984, shortly before the Democratic convention, when Mondale was attempting to pick his vice-president, the National Organization for Women (NOW) and other women's organizations conducted a highly visible lobbying campaign to persuade Mondale to select a women as his running mate. NOW passed a resolution declaring that its members would nominate a woman from the floor "if necessary," and there was much publicized talk of a feminist walk-out from the convention if Mondale chose a male running mate.[17] A damaging special-interest aura was created around the selection of Ferraro, compounding the image of a Democratic nominee who bent to the will of constituent groups.

At the July convention in San Francisco, Mondale supporters sought to extricate the candidate and the Democratic party from the most debilitating aspect of the "special interest" debate: the conflict over affirmative action and quotas. Quotas went to the heart of the liability of the Democratic party as the advocate of minorities and of special preferences in behalf of separate "groups." The Mondale campaign sought to defuse this issue by attempting to include an explicit rejection of quotas in a section of the platform that supported less stringent affirmative action measures. Jesse Jackson, however, pressed for a plank explicitly backing quotas, except those "inconsistent with the principles of our country." In the final compromise, Jackson effectively won the struggle. The 1984 platform as adopted by the convention declared that the Democratic party "reaffirms its longstanding commitment to the eradication of discrimination in all aspects of American life through the use of affirmative action, goals, timetables *and other verifiable measurements* to overturn historic patterns and historic burdens of discrimination in hiring, training, promotions, contract procurement, education and the administration of all Federal programs." [Emphasis added.][18] There was little question that "other verifiable measurements to overturn historic patterns" of discrimination amounted to an endorsement of quotas.

Nothing, however, drove home to working-class voters the liabilities of the national Democratic party—a party now perceived by many as championing an expanding government committed to imposing costly redistributive burdens—more effectively than the issue of taxes. Mondale declared in his acceptance speech that he would raise taxes by $85 billion annually,[19] and immediately reinforced for the voters of Macomb County, and of working and lower-middle class precincts across the nation, the image of his candidacy and of his party as advocating "give-away programs, that is, programs aimed primarily at minorities," in the words of the Analysis Group Study.[20]

The Mondale tax proposal signaled to key white voters that not only was the Democratic party aligned with those have-not Americans who belonged to disadvantaged "groups," but that the party was prepared to impose higher dollar costs on white working men and women in order to advance its commitment to targeted minorities. Mondale proposed to use $30 billion of the new revenues for spending to "promote fairness,"[21] a phrase that had come to be interpreted in a number of white working-class neighborhoods, contrary to Democratic intentions, as a proposal to redistribute revenues to the black and Hispanic poor, to tax the many for the benefit of the few—a "few" seen by many as increasingly undeserving.

Mondale's tax proposal provided the perfect foil for the Reagan campaign. In August 1984, at the Republican convention in Dallas—and throughout the remainder of the election—Reagan built campaign momentum with a series of chanted questions:

> Reagan: "Is there any doubt that they will raise our taxes?" Audience: "No!" "That they will send inflation into orbit again?" "No!" "That they will make government bigger than ever?" "No!" "And deficits even worse?" "No!" "Raise unemployment?" "No!" . . . "We're here to see that government continues to serve the people and not the other way around. Yes, government should do all that is necessary, but only that which is necessary. We don't lump people by groups or special interests."[22]

For disaffected white voters, Reagan drew the connection between taxes and "groups" and "special interests"—adding to Republican rhetoric phrases and words that now bore a new meaning—signifying for many working and middle-class voters the reliable opposition of Reagan and the Republican party to benefits targeted at blacks, feminists, homosexuals, and others seeking new rights, protections, or preferences from government.

---

The growing belief in key white precincts that the Democratic party's advocacy of fairness was actually a cover for party favoritism directed towards minorities was compounded, in the course of the 1984 Democratic presidential nomination process, by a historic development: the emergence of the first fully competitive black candidate, Jesse Jackson. While Jackson mobilized the black electorate during the Democratic primaries—reviving black voter registration and election day turnout drives—his message sent a chill of fear down the spines of many white voters buffeted by racial resentments and by twenty years of cataclysmic racial and cultural change—voters who already questioned whether the Democratic party could represent their pocketbook interests at a time of economic retrenchment.

"Our time has come," Jackson declared in his announcement on November 4, 1983, at the Convention Center in Washington, D.C. Setting out a campaign theme that lent itself to very different interpretations by white television viewers and live black audiences, Jackson repeatedly declared to cheering and applauding gatherings of overwhelmingly black crowds: "We're not asking for welfare, we're asking for our share."[23]

Jackson, by the end of the 1984 nomination fight, was well on his way toward replacing Senator Edward Kennedy of Massachusetts as the leading spokesman for the liberal wing of the Democratic party. Kennedy—defeated in his bid for the Democratic nomination in 1980, damaged by

Chappaquiddick and by his divorce, and plagued by continuing reports of
unruly personal behavior—had become no longer credible as a presidential candidate. The shift from Kennedy to Jackson sharpened the racial
character—the racial "reading"—of liberalism. Jackson himself at the
Democratic convention articulated a liberal vision paradoxically coinciding with the one attacked by Reagan, a vision portraying the country in
terms of groups:

> My constituency is the damned, the disinherited, the disrepected, and the
> despised. . . . America is not like a blanket, one piece of unbroken cloth—the
> same color, the same texture, the same size. It is more like a quilt—many
> patches, many pieces, many colors, many sizes, all woven and held together by
> a common thread. The white, the Hispanic, the black, the Arab, the Jew, the
> woman, the native American, the small farmer, the businessperson, the envi-
> ronmentalist, the peace activist, the young, the old, the lesbian, the gay and the
> disabled make up the American quilt.[24]

The Jackson message reinforced a changing public perception of the
Democratic party and of liberalism, a shift that had been evolving steadily
over twenty years out of the cumulative records of the two parties, their
candidates, the rights revolution, busing, affirmative action, global competition, and the upheaval in the domestic job market. This shift in the
perspective of the voting majority on the national Democratic party can be
seen by comparing the kinds of groups and interests that the public associated with the party in 1972, and twelve years later in 1984.

"In 1972, a wide range of groups were commonly perceived to comprise the Democratic coalition, including the middle class, blacks, Catholics, the poor, liberals, and labor unions—the same groups that have long
been recognized as the major elements of the traditional Democratic coalition," Arthur Miller and three other political scientists wrote, on the basis
of an evaluation of National Election Studies (NES) poll data. However,
Miller and his colleagues found that, by 1984, "a major shift had occurred
in the relationship between groups and party evaluations, particularly for
the Democrats." In effect, blacks, the middle class, poor people, and Catholics were no longer identified by significant numbers of those polled with
the Democratic party. Instead, and to some degree taking their place, were
black militants and feminists—two groups that were not linked in the
public mind to either party in 1972—along with people on welfare (as
opposed to poor people) and gays and lesbians. In other words, for many
voters, the Democratic party in 1984 had lost its identification with groups
that have broad, consensual support and sympathy, and had gained identification with far more controversial groups.[25]

While Mondale wore the special interest character of his candidacy on his sleeve, the Reagan campaign demonstrated that it was possible to separate, and to a certain extent to isolate and conceal, the special interest aspects of the Republican coalition. Money, as much as anything else, made this separation possible, and money is a campaign resource in which, at the party and presidential level, the GOP has a decisive advantage.

Money becomes critical because it is essential to the financing of a war *beyond* the already prohibitively expensive television "air war"—essential to a costly "ground war," the most effective method of appealing to controversial constituencies without exposure in the mass media. The operation of an effective "ground war" in a presidential campaign is crucial if the candidate is to avoid the danger, in Richard Moe's words, of "being perceived as a 'captive' of the constituencies." The mechanics of the political ground war—targeted direct mail, phone banks, mobilization of members of controversial groups, and so on—perform two functions. The most important is raising the highest possible levels of support in "leverageable" groups. The second is achieving these raised support levels without alienating voters who strongly disagree with the policy agendas of the "leverageable" groups. Ground war tactics amount, in effect, to separate campaigns, conducted far from television's eye.

On the Republican side, two critically important constituencies carrying heavy political baggage in general election contests in the 1980s were fundamentalist Christians and anti-abortion activists. The politicized fundamentalist Christian movement, in particular, was a vital element of the expanded Republican coalition, but the extremely high negatives of its leaders posed dangers to a GOP seeking to broaden its voter base and build support among younger, more libertarian voters. Even in Virginia, Jerry Falwell's own state and home to his Moral Majority, 53 percent of the polled electorate in 1985 said they would be more likely to vote against a candidate who had Falwell's endorsement; only 8 percent said they would be more likely to vote for a Falwell-backed candidate.[26]

In this context, the drive of the Reagan campaign to mobilize the fundamentalist Christian community is a case study in a constituency kept shielded from broad public attention. The Reagan campaign itself, and the Republican National Committee (RNC), financed a number of carefully targeted appeals to the conservative Christian community. In a mailing to 45,000 evangelical and fundamentalist ministers, Senator Paul Laxalt of Nevada, general chairman of the Reagan-Bush '84 Committee, wrote: "As leaders under God's authority, we cannot afford to resign ourselves to idle neutrality in an election that will confirm or silence the president who has worked so diligently in your behalf."[27]

The quiet financing by the GOP of narrowly targeted, judiciously worded mass mailings was accompanied by the development of convoluted mechanisms to discretely finance another key element of the ground war, the voter registration and get-out-the-vote drives among conservative Christians.[28]

As soon as the Reagan-Bush '84 campaign had raised the $20.2 million maximum allowed by law, Joe Rogers, the campaign's finance chairman, resigned to form a private fundraising company, Leadership '84. Leadership '84 then solicited from Republican donors (many of whom had already given to the Reagan campaign) tax deductible contributions for a Rogers-run foundation, Americans for Responsible Government. During this same period, key leaders of the conservative Christian political movement, many of them serving on a Christian Advisory Committee to the Reagan-Bush campaign, set up a new, separate organization, the technically non-partisan American Coalition for Traditional Values (ACTV), to conduct voter registration and voter participation drives in the fundamentalist Christian community. Leadership '84 raised money from the universe of largely Republican donors for its client, Americans for Responsible Government, which then channeled the money to ACTV, the staff of which became the ground troops in the Christian voter registration and turnout operation, all of which helped to produce a massive, white Christian fundamentalist vote for the GOP in November.

At the same time that the Democratic party and a network of liberal foundations were openly pouring money into a highly publicized drive to register black voters in the South, the conservative ACTV—operating in technical independence of the Reagan-Bush campaign, in tandem with an organizationally discrete $11 million registration drive conducted jointly by the Reagan-Bush Committee and the RNC—more than matched black registration with newly registered whites, many of them southern evangelicals. In Louisiana, for example, black Democratic registration grew by 9,427 between early 1984 and late 1985, while white Republican registration shot up by 75,215.[29] In North Carolina, the number of blacks registered to vote increased by 53,805 between early 1984 and the close of registration on October 8, 1984, while white registration grew by nearly five times that amount: by 252,558.[30] Following the November election, Joe Rogers was rewarded with the ambassadorship to France.

Money not only provided the leverage to mobilize vital constituencies, it was essential for the acquisition of information and expertise. By 1984, the Republican party had assembled an unparalleled combination of technical competence, fundraising mastery, research material, demographic data, and a trained cadre of strategists and tacticians to promote presidential, Senate, House, and gubernatorial campaigns. Between 1977 and 1984, the major Republican party committees—the National, Congressional, and Senatorial—raised a total of $766.9 million, compared to $201.4 million raised by their Democratic counterparts. The difference, in practical terms, was in fact even greater than these figures suggest, because virtually all Democratic money went to pay basic operating costs: staff, travel, office rental, and equipment.

Republican money, in contrast, was plentiful enough to finance not only basic costs, but also to underwrite 1) the acquisition of the most sophisticated available data on the electorate, gathered through polls, focus groups, voter list development, and demographic studies; and 2) the maintenance costs of a cadre of election specialists either directly employed by the major Republican committees or serving as paid consultants to them. This cadre—composed of skilled operatives such as Charles Black, Richard Wirthlin, Roger Ailes, Roger Stone, Lee Atwater, Robert Teeter, Lance Tarrance, Stuart Spencer, and Richard Bond—have been mainstays of Republican presidential campaigns for the past decade and, in some cases, for the past two and a half decades.

"I basically think that in any given campaign crisis, there are only six or seven ways a thing can play out," Atwater said in 1990, looking back on his experience running the South for Reagan in 1980, his service as deputy manager of the Reagan-Bush '84 campaign, and his experience as manager of the Bush-Quayle campaign in 1988. "So at some point, if you have been in enough campaigns, any crisis you face, you know there are six or seven ways that it can turn out. I've got my own theory, the one-inch adjustment theory. In a crisis situation, you have one inch to move in, and you have to synthesize from your personal experience and your historical knowledge—you have to figure out that one inch or other."[31] On the Democratic side of the aisle there has been virtually no one on tap with knowledge to match that of Republicans Atwater, Black, Wirthlin, Teeter, Ailes, Spencer, or Bond.

In terms of information acquisition, the Democratic National Committee (DNC) financed fewer than one poll every two years between 1977 and 1984[32]; in contrast, the RNC paid just one company, Richard Wirthlin's Decision Making Information, a regular retainer of $68,000 a *month,*[33] and double that in election years, to track the most minute shift in public opinion on every pending controversy, and to evaluate through extensive focus-group testing the emotional reaction to every phrase in Reagan's speeches, and to every nuance of the presidential debates. The

RNC in addition financed periodic polling by such firms as Market Opinion Research and Tarrance and Associates in order to track state-by-state shifts in public opinion—a critical source of information in a presidential election in which the outcome is determined by separate, winner-take-all contests for the electoral votes of each state.

In contrast, when DNC chairman Paul Kirk decided to spend $250,000 on a 1985 *post-election* poll, and on a series of focus groups, the move was unprecedented for Democrats in terms of the size of the expenditure. The Democratic party, in effect, learned of the high saliency of racial issues in key working-class precincts only after the election was over, while the combined Republican committees spent an estimated total of $8.8 million on *pre-election* polls and related research during the 1983–84 cycle, and were fully abreast of voter attitudes in every segment of the electorate well before the 1984 election reached full swing.[34]

What this meant was that the Republican party went into the 1984 election fully cognizant of the continuing racial tensions within crucial segments of the electorate, sensitive to how the ideas of "big government" and of "special interest" interacted for key voters with divisive issues of race and "values," and fully aware of deep public aversion to paying for the privilege of big government with high—let alone higher—taxes.

The Democratic party and its nominee, in contrast, went into the general election with their understanding of the mood and views of the general electorate based almost entirely on the distorted information gained from campaigning among liberal primary and party activist constituencies. Mondale, his strategists, and party officials were out of touch with disturbing aspects of voter sentiment on race, unaware of the depth of the national anti-tax mind-set, blind to the hidden costs of a rights-oriented liberalism, unable or unwilling to formulate strategies effective in countering those costs, and outmatched by their GOP rivals in the techniques of "encapsulating" special interests. The Democratic National Committee had no money to invest in polling in 1983 and 1984, and, up until shortly before the Democratic convention, all of Mondale's polling was geared to his battle to win Democratic primaries. There was, for example, virtually no polling done to analyze the potential ramifications of Mondale's tax proposal. "I had no idea of its [the tax proposal's] existence until I saw a draft of the acceptance speech in San Francisco [at the convention]," Peter Hart, Mondale's pollster, said. "It came to me as a bolt out of the blue."[35]

In short, the Democrats approached November, 1984 without the depth of political knowledge or skill essential for the conduct of an ideologically intricate and technically demanding general election campaign, relying instead on understanding and skills based disproportionately on the experience of Democratic intraparty primary and caucus competition.

———

The presidential wing of the Democratic party in 1984 helped maintain a Republican strategy of polarization of the electorate based on race, on 'values', on taxpayer versus tax recipient, and on the conflict between those classes and groups seeking government protection and those who do not get such protection. This polarization was essential for the maintenance of a Republican presidential majority willing to back the network of wage, tax, anti-trust, and regulatory policies which accelerated trends in the distribution of income working to the immediate advantage of the most well-to-do.

The structure of this polarization by 1984 clearly aligned blacks (as tax recipients, as heavily employed by government, and as advocates of preferential treatment in civil rights enforcement, affirmative action, and federal spending on means-tested payments to the poor) with other key Democratic constituencies. Organized labor by the mid-1980s was falling into a position of increasing vulnerability to the polarizing strategies of the right: unions were becoming blacker, more dependent on tax-paid (public sector) wages, and more insistent on special government protection. From 1970 to 1984, the union movement became steadily more dependent on blacks as a source of membership, as the number of whites in unions declined from 16.9 million to 14.4 million, while the number of blacks grew slightly from 2.4 to 2.5 million, and would grow to 2.6 million by 1988. At the same time, between 1968 and 1984, the percentage of union members employed by government—and whose income was therefore dependent on tax dollars—grew from 17.5 percent, or 3.86 million, to 32.6 percent, or 5.64 million, and would reach 6.23 million, or 37 percent of union members in 1988, relegating this sector of the trade union movement to the 'tax recipient' category.[36] Finally, the beleaguered union movement by 1984 was seen less as the advocate of worker-management parity at the bargaining table, and more as seeking special protection in trade legislation (domestic content) and in contract law—using Davis-Bacon to mandate union scale on all government contracts.

———

The 1984 presidential election produced the consolidation, and in some cases the institutionalization, of the often chaotic forces that had produced the conservative revolution of 1980. The Democratic party had come increasingly to represent—to an important swing sector of the electorate—a liberal agenda that imposed costs on the majority for the benefit of those seeking special preference, and key white constituencies had begun to view the party and its message of "fairness" through a racial filter. Jesse Jackson had replaced the Kennedy dynasty as the national symbol of Democratic liberalism, reinforcing the association of liberalism with interest group representation of victims.

Meanwhile, the Republican party from 1981 to 1984 had fashioned strategies to combine a populist appeal with free-market economics—strategies highlighting sustained opposition to raising taxes, and continuous antagonism to government regulation, to government-led civil rights enforcement, and to the use of racial preferences. The liability to the GOP represented by the recession of 1981–82 lessened as many voters associated that recession with the larger economic downturn that had become visible to the public during the most recent period of Democratic party rule in the late 1970s. The growing focus of public attention on the social dysfunction of the underclass and the continued growth in the illegitimacy rate created what many members of the middle class saw as an expanding class of the *undeserving* poor. For many voters, these developments among the poor cast increasing doubts, on the efficacy of domestic programs that had been fashioned over the years by a liberal-activist intelligentsia, by an expanding social service government bureaucracy, by Democratic presidents, and by Democratic Congresses. Doubts about the efficacy of Democratic party antipoverty strategies—in spite of the striking success of many government programs in helping to create a black middle class—were strengthened by the groundswell, in the late 1970s and 1980s, of conservative critiques targeted at liberal social initiatives, a groundswell represented perhaps most forcefully by Charles Murray's *Losing Ground,* putting forward an influential, if disputed, challenge to the core programmatic arrangements of the welfare state. (See discussion in chapter 6.)

New forces gave new meaning to the coded language of politics. "Fairness," championed by Mondale and stressed in the Democratic platform, no longer symbolized the Democratic struggle to achieve tax equity for "average" working men and women, to provide access to middle-class homes and incomes, or to insure the right to bargain with management for just compensation; "fairness" now meant, to many voters, federal action to tilt the playing field in favor of minorities, government unions, feminists, criminal defendants, the long-term jobless, never-wed mothers, drug addicts, and gays. A liberal, in turn, was no longer regarded, by key voters, as a proponent of progressive government action fueling an expansive economy that would provide an equitable dispersion of increasing national wealth; a liberal was now looked upon as the harbinger of a stagnant economy, forcing a zero-sum competition in which the gains of one group were the losses of another. The word "group" in Republican rhetoric came to signify all Democratic claimants for special preference: those who—in this view—sought to enlarge their share of the pie by taking portions of what others had earned through hard work, diligence, and self-denial.

The meaning of "taxes" was also transformed. No longer the resource with which to create a beneficent federal government, taxes had come for many voters to signify the forcible transfer of hard-earned money away from those who worked, to those who did not. Taxes had come to be seen as the resource financing a liberal federal judiciary, granting expanded rights to criminal defendants, to convicted felons, and, in education and employment, to "less qualified" minorities. Federal taxation had become, in the new coded language of politics, a forced levy underwriting liberal policies that granted enlarged rights to those members of society who excited the most negative feelings in the minds of other, often angry voters.

The continuing vitality of this coded language—a language of "groups," "taxes," "big government," "quotas," "reverse discrimination," "welfare," and "special interests"—became critical to the maintenance of the conservative presidential majority in the latter half of the 1980s, as the utility of other weapons in the Republican populist arsenal diminished, as the doctrine of "conservative egalitarianism" began to lose its popular appeal, and as the early momentum behind the revolution of the right began to lose its force.

# 11

# White Suburbs
# and a Divided Black
# Community

IN PREPARING for the 1988 election, Republican strategists planning
the campaign of George Bush faced a new set of problems: the fires that
had fueled the conservative revolution had been banked; the combustibil-
ity of the issues of race, rights, and taxes had been reduced—in large part
because the Reagan administration had fulfilled many of its implicit promises to key white constituents. The anger and resentment in the white
working and lower-middle class, which had helped the GOP in the elections of 1980 and 1984, had been blunted by the successes of the Reagan
revolution. It was not difficult, however, to reignite those fires.

By 1988, the perception of a link between the Democratic party and
controversial government policies on race, rights, and taxes had become
imbedded in the conscious and unconscious memory of American politics—a perception still close enough to the surface to be accessible to
political manipulation. This perception often exerted influence on an
unarticulated level, a level at which the national Democratic party was still
tied, in the minds of many voters, to the problems of crime, welfare, school
failure, family dissolution, spreading urban squalor, an eroding work
ethic, and global retreat.

In 1988, the Bush campaign assembled and deployed a range of symbols
and images designed to tap into these submerged concerns—concerns
often clustering around the nexus of racial, ethnic, cultural, and "values"
anxieties that had helped to fuel the conservative politics of the post-civil

rights era. The symbols of the Bush campaign—Willie Horton, the ACLU, the death penalty, the Pledge of Allegiance, the American flag, "no new taxes," the "L-word," and "Harvard boutique liberal"—conjured up the criminal defendants' and prisoners' rights movements, black crime, permissive liberal elites, a revenue-hungry state, eroding traditional values, tattered patriotism, and declining American prestige. Themes and symbols tapping these issues became for the Republican party the means of restoring the salience of associations damaging to Democrats, and the means of maintaining the vitality of the majority conservative coalition.

The 1988 Bush campaign strategy essentially looked backwards, organized around the conflicts and schisms of the previous twenty-five years. The campaign was fought on the battleground of the civil rights and the broader rights movements, focusing on the liabilities that had accumulated around the liberal wing of the national Democratic party.

The 1988 Bush campaign masked, in many respects, what were, in fact, far more complex social developments. Some of these developments suggest the potential for a *lessening* of racial isolation in the next decades, and include not only the sustained growth of the black middle class, but include also the continued ascension of increasing numbers of blacks to positions of power and authority in the public and private sectors; the increased willingness of whites to vote for a black candidate; and the possibility that partisan competition for black support will break the logjam now impeding black economic and social advancement. Developments springing from the increasing upward mobility of large numbers of black Americans have the potential to release each party from calcified positions in a fixed ideological debate, and from rigid policy alternatives lacking in innovation and vigor.

Conversely, however, there is another set of forces at work in America *intensifying* racial separation, particularly the separation, if not segregation, of poor blacks—and these forces have the potential to institutionalize racially separate structures in the political and economic spheres. Such forces could well make superfluous the divisive tactics of Republican political strategists. There may prove to be enough internal logic and cohesion to a right-of-center, top-down coalition that explicit polarizations over issues of race, rights, and taxes—such as those characterizing the 1988 Bush campaign—will no longer be necessary.

If this set of trends continues, racial and other, parallel divisions may become so ingrained in the composition and organization of American society that explicit political strategies to bring them to the surface will be unneeded.

The most important of these segregating forces is the ascendance of the suburban electorate to virtual majority status, empowering an overwhelmingly white segment of the voting population to address basic social service needs (schooling, recreation, libraries, roads, police and fire protection) through local suburban government and through locally generated revenues, and to further sever already weak ties to increasingly black urban constituencies.

In addition, just as the job market is placing an ever-higher premium on advanced skills and on college-level education, black college enrollment has declined and rising college tuitions pit whites against blacks over basic policy choices—over, for example, student aid awards in the form of grant or loan assistance.

International economic competition has also, in turn, become an inexorable force, allowing conservative economists to argue that, for besieged American corporations, the costs of racial preferences in hiring and promotion threaten American industrial flexibility and strength—an argument adding an economic rationale to the "principled" opposition to affirmative action characterizing the now-dominant conservative majority on the Supreme Court.

Demographic and economic forces that cumulatively intensify racial separation and conflict reinforce political polarization and serve the purposes of those on the right and those on the left who seek to sustain divisions in which race supersedes income, class, and status in the formation of competing coalitions.

———

In mid-summer 1988, long-range historical developments were far from the thinking of campaign operatives staffing the battle between Vice-President Bush and Massachusetts Governor Dukakis. With Dukakis far ahead in the polls, the central goal of the Bush campaign was to reignite social issue conservatism, and to counteract the successes of the Reagan revolution—success in quieting the most insistent demands of those seeking insulation from liberal government and success in deflating the pressures on working and lower-middle class whites—the very pressures that had led such voters to join in a top-down coalition with the conservative right.

The successes of the Reagan administration on the social issues front had been substantial. From 1981 to 1988, the Reagan White House had altered the ideological thrust of the federal court system, once the mainstay of the civil rights movement and of the rights revolution. By the end of his second term, Reagan had appointed 290 of 571 district court judges,

78 of 156 appeals court judges, and three members of the Supreme Court, enough to establish a 5–4 conservative Court majority.

"The Reagan administration was engaged in the most systematic philosophical screening of judicial candidates ever seen in the nation's history, surpassing Franklin Roosevelt's administration," wrote legal scholar Sheldon Goldman, of the University of Massachusetts, describing the effort, orchestrated in large part by Attorney General Edwin Meese, to appoint a judiciary that would roll back the earlier liberal rights revolution.[1]

The Reagan administration had successfully slowed or halted the social regulation, the spending trends, and the rising income tax levies that had produced the sharpest white resentment. The Justice Department had abandoned busing orders and the imposition of stringent goals and timetables to remedy school desegregation and employment discrimination cases.[2] The rapid growth of the welfare caseload from 1965 to 1980 was brought to an end, with the number of households on AFDC increasing by less than 1 percent from 1980 to 1988, from 3,712,00 to 3,748,235.[3]

In the area of crime, the Reagan administration was more the beneficiary of demographic trends than the instigator of effective policy. The post–baby-boom decline in the number of people between the ages of 16 and 24—ages at which people commit the most crimes—produced a 10.2 percentage point drop in the victimization rate for violent crimes from 1980 to 1988, although rates began to rise sharply again in 1987 and 1988, with the onset of the crack cocaine epidemic.[4]

The administration succeeded in quieting the vehemence of the tax revolt—the popular uprising that had given the conservative movement ready access to electoral majorities. Federal income tax burdens fell from 9.6 percent of the Gross National Product in 1981 to 8.4 percent in 1988.[5] At the same time, the number of brackets in the marginal tax-rate structure—a second source of discontent with the tax system—were reduced in 1986 from fourteen to four, and the bracket structure was indexed to prevent inflation from driving up taxes.

The accomplishments of the Reagan administration created a climate of lessened white tension over race, rights, and taxes, a climate modestly favorable to the restoration of Democratic loyalties. This dovetailed with the decline in support for the Reagan-Bush administration that followed disclosures in 1986 and 1987 of the Iran-Contra, arms-for-hostages scandal, and the growing list of allegations and charges of corruption and profiteering among Reagan-era Republican officials—charges that ultimately affected two of Reagan's closest aides, Michael Deaver (convicted of lying to Congress about lobbying activities), and Edwin Meese (who resigned his position as attorney general just days before the release of a report highly critical of his involvement in the Wedtech contracting scandal).

In terms of the economy, the Reagan administration had produced—or benefitted from—a sustained recovery after the recession of 1981–82, but the rewards of this recovery were not spread evenly across the society. Most importantly, the white working and lower-middle class voters who had provided critically important levels of support for the GOP in the elections of 1980 and 1984 did not experience significant improvement in either pre- or post-tax income during the 1980s. While pre-tax family income grew substantially from 1980 to 1990—from $35,814 to $41,369, or 15.5 percent—by far the largest gains were concentrated among those in the upper brackets. The following Table 11.1, using Congressional Budget Office (CBO) data, shows the changes in inflation-adjusted dollars.

The growing regressiveness in the distribution of income was even sharper when calculated in terms of after-tax income, a far more accurate measure since this is the amount of money people actually have to spend. The differences between the distribution of pre-tax and after-tax income

TABLE 11.1

Changes in Pre-tax Income, for the U. S. Population Ranked by Income Decile, with Additional Figures for the Top 5 Percent and the Top 1 Percent, 1980–1990

|  | *1980* | *1990* | *Percent Change* |
|---|---|---|---|
| First Decile (poor) | $5,128 | $4,695 | −8.4% |
| Second | 10,388 | 10,154 | −2.3 |
| Third | 16,298 | 16,363 | 0.4 |
| Fourth | 21,932 | 22,492 | 2.6 |
| Fifth | 27,354 | 28,123 | 2.8 |
| Sixth | 32,674 | 33,760 | 3.3 |
| Seventh | 38,213 | 40,651 | 6.4 |
| Eighth | 44,833 | 49,049 | 9.4 |
| Ninth | 55,008 | 63,663 | 15.7 |
| Tenth | 105,611 | 144,832 | 37.1 |
| Top 5% (rich) | 142,133 | 206,162 | 45.0 |
| Top 1% (very rich) | 312,826 | 548,969 | 75.5 |
| Everyone (average) | 35,814 | 41,369 | 15.5 |

SOURCE: House Ways and Means Committee, *Tax Progressivity and Income Distribution* (Washington, D.C., 26, March 1990), Table 10, p. 28, using data from the Congressional Budget Office Tax Simulation Model.

reflect the consequences of tax policy during the Reagan administration. The following Table 11.2 shows this pattern.

Diminished white discontent over race and taxes combined with administration corruption, the Iran-Contra scandal, and growing income disparities to set the stage for an election in which the Democratic party had a chance at presidential victory. The size of the 17-percentage point lead in the polls held by Dukakis in July 1988 was unsustainable through the general election, but it reflected a restoration of Democratic loyalty that strategists for the presidential campaign of George Bush recognized as a substantial threat.

Lee Atwater, manager and central strategist of the 1988 Bush campaign, was acutely aware of the danger of economic discontent to the GOP and to his candidate:

> You see a new group who are not quite of age, they are 32–37. They grew up same time I grew up. My parents taught me that if I got a college degree, I've got it made. I was taught that the whole world was an oyster. These people believe all that and grow up. . . . All of a sudden these people who grew up thinking they'd get the white collar college jobs, all of a sudden they really are

TABLE 11.2

Changes in After-tax Income, for the U. S. Population Ranked by Income Decile, with Additional Figures for the Top 5 Percent and the Top 1 Percent, 1980–1990

|  | 1980 | 1990 | Percent Change |
|---|---|---|---|
| First Decile (poor) | $4,785 | 4,295 | −10.3% |
| Second | 9,445 | 9,119 | −3.4 |
| Third | 14,063 | 13,886 | −1.3 |
| Fourth | 18,146 | 18,482 | 1.8 |
| Fifth | 22,078 | 22,608 | 2.4 |
| Sixth | 25,932 | 26,741 | 3.1 |
| Seventh | 29,725 | 31,767 | 6.9 |
| Eighth | 34,258 | 37,798 | 10.3 |
| Ninth | 41,202 | 48,037 | 16.6 |
| Tenth | 75,568 | 106,638 | 41.1 |
| Top 5% (rich) | 100,209 | 151,132 | 50.8 |
| Top 1% (very rich) | 213,416 | 399,697 | 87.3 |
| Everyone (average) | 27,484 | 31,840 | 15.8 |

SOURCE: Ibid., 30.

getting [what amount to] blue collar jobs. They say, 'I can see where I end up. Here I am the number two guy in my hometown Rexall Drugs, I'm making 28 grand, and I know if I stay here another 20 years, I can be the number one guy making 36 grand. For the first time in my life, I realize, Boy, it ain't going to happen.'[8]

Atwater, who cut his political teeth in ex-Democrat, ex-segregationist Strom Thurmond's 1970 South Carolina Republican senatorial campaign, derived his strategies from the race-driven politics of the South, a region of hardball race-coded campaigning where Atwater—and other native politicians, including top Republican strategist Charles Black of North Carolina—learned to use racial and social issues to break the partisan loyalties of white Democrats and to fracture their decisive majority. "Republicans in the South could not win elections simply by showing various issues and talking about various issues. You had to make the case that the other guy, the other candidate is a bad guy and I'm a good guy. You simply could not get out in a universe where 60 percent of the people were Democrats and 28 percent Republican, and win by talking about your issues. The more you can make a Democrat a 'national Democrat' and a symbol of the national Democratic Party, the better off you are," said Atwater in 1984, looking back on his South Carolina experience.[7]

In developing a strategy to break the 17-point advantage held by Dukakis in mid-summer, 1988, Atwater drew on his understanding of the dynamics of Southern voting, an understanding that had become increasing applicable to national contests. In a 1984 analysis of domestic politics Atwater wrote:

"We have as the main voting groups in Southern politics 1) country clubbers ['reliably Republican'], 2) populists, 3) blacks ['reliably Democratic']. . . . The class struggle in the South continues, with the populists serving as the trump card. . . . Populists have always been liberal on economics. So long as the crucial issues were generally confined to economics—as during the New Deal—the liberal candidate would expect to get most of the populist vote. But populists are conservatives on most social issues. . . . As for race, it was hardly an issue—it went without saying that the populists' chosen leaders were hardcore segregationists. . . . After Carter's defeat [in 1980], the Democrats backed away from their Great Society rhetoric and diverted public attention from busing, affirmative action, etc., and toward clear economic issues. In 1982, we discovered we could not hold the populist vote on economic issues alone. When social and cultural issues died down, the populists were left with no compelling reason to vote Republican. . . . When Republicans are successful in getting certain social issues to the forefront, the populist vote is ours. The trick we must master is choosing those social issues that do not alienate the country clubbers since, again, we need their votes and the populists' to win in the South.[8]

In 1988, the Bush campaign, under Atwater's guidance, mastered the trick of selecting racial/social issues that achieved the fundamental goal of maintaining the election-day alliance between the country clubbers and the populists on a national scale. Facing off against Dukakis, who was a committed reform Democrat, a liberal lawyer, a card-carrying member of the American Civil Liberties Union, a Harvard Law School graduate, an early civil rights activist, a governor who had vetoed a bill mandating the Pledge of Allegiance, and a Greek ethnic with a Jewish wife, the Bush campaign used the American flag, Willie Horton, the ACLU, the death penalty, the Pledge of Allegiance, and a dramatic emphasis on no new taxes ("read my lips") to drive a wedge right into the heart of the Democrats' 17-point advantage.

When the top staffers of the Bush campaign met on the morning after Dukakis's Atlanta acceptance of the Democratic nomination, Atwater declared: "I'm going to scrape the bark off that little bastard."[9]

———

Few events could be better suited to focus public attention on the liabilities of Democratic liberalism than the crimes of William R. (Willie) Horton, Jr.,—a black felon featured in a barrage of Republican television commercials, speeches, and leaflets throughout the 1988 campaign. Convicted of the first-degree murder of a 17-year-old gas station attendant and sentenced to life in Massachusetts prison without possibility of parole, Horton was granted ten weekend furloughs under a program first initiated in 1972 in the early stages of the prisoners' rights movement.

That was the year the national Democratic party platform committed the party to "Recognition of the constitutional and human rights of prisoners; realistic therapeutic, vocational, wage-earning, education, alcoholism, and drug treatment programs. . . . Emergency, educational and work-release furlough programs as an available technique."[10]

In 1976, Dukakis, two years into his first term as Massachusetts governor, vetoed a bill that would have prohibited furloughs of first-degree murderers, contending that such a bill would "cut the heart out of efforts at inmate rehabilitation." Ten years later, on June 6, 1986, Horton, on his tenth weekend furlough, disappeared.[11]

In eight months, Horton resurfaced in Maryland. On April 3, 1987, Horton forced his way into the Oxon Hill, Maryland, home of Clifford Barnes and his financée, Angela Miller, who was out that evening. Horton beat Barnes with a pistol, cut him twenty-two times on his stomach and chest, tied and gagged him in the cellar. When Angela Miller returned home, Horton tied her up and raped her twice over a four-hour period. Barnes, in the cellar, broke free and called the police from a neighbor's house. After a car chase, Horton was captured and tried in Maryland where he was sentenced to two consecutive life terms plus 85 years. The judge refused to send him back to Massachusetts, saying, "I'm not prepared to take the chance that Mr. Horton might again be furloughed or otherwise released. This man should never draw a breath of free air again."[12]

The Dukakis administration dealt with the furor that developed after Horton's 1987 arrest in Maryland with evasion.[13] Dukakis did not apologize to Miller or to Barnes, rejected the requests of the press, particularly of the Lawrence *Eagle-Tribune,* for information on the records of Horton and other furloughed prisoners, and continued to defend the furlough program. "Don't forget that Mr. Horton had nine previous successful furloughs," Philip Johnston, Dukakis's secretary of Human Services, told reporters.[14]

Atwater, who had assigned a campaign staffer to unearth weaknesses in the Dukakis record, could not contain himself on learning the details of the Horton case. At a meeting with southern Republicans in Atlanta on July 9, two weeks before the Democratic convention, Atwater held forth in a gleeful stream of consciousness:

> I can't wait until this Dukakis fellow gets down here [the South]. There are quite a few questions he ought to have to answer every day he's down here, and every time he gives the answer, there's going to be votes coming up just like in a cash register. Can you imagine him trying to answer how in the world as governor, a responsible position like governor, he was in favor of this furlough program that allowed first-degree murderers and drug pushers to go on weekend vacations where they could murder, sell drugs and do all the rest of this stuff? There is a story about a fellow named Willie Horton who for all I know may end up to be Dukakis' running mate. Dukakis is making Hamlet look like the rock of Gibraltar in the way he's acted on this [Atwater was referring to Dukakis' procedure for selecting a running mate.] The guy [Dukakis] was on TV about a month ago and he said you'll never see me standing in the driveway of my house talking to these candidates [referring to Mondale's protracted search in 1984 for a running mate, interviewing prospects at his Minnesota home]. And guess what, on Monday, I saw in the driveway of his [Dukakis's] house? Jesse Jackson. So anyway, maybe he'll put this Willie Horton guy on the ticket after all is said and done. And Willie Horton is the fellow who was a convicted murderer and rapist who got let out

on eight [Atwater got the figure wrong] of these weekend furloughs, and on
the ninth one, he brutally and wantonly raped this woman. . . . And do you
know what the response was from the Dukakis crowd: 'Well he didn't do
anything on the other eight.[15]

With Horton creating a case study, at the extreme, of the costs of
Democratic liberalism, the more abstract issues of Dukakis's membership
in the ACLU, his veto of legislation requiring teachers to lead the Pledge
of Allegiance, his opposition to the death penalty, his wife's confession to a
history of amphetamine abuse, and his generally rights-oriented, liberal
stance provided the means for the Bush campaign to wrap the collective
agenda of race, rights, and values around the neck of the Democratic
presidential nominee.

Willie Horton represented for key sectors of the electorate the consequences of an aggressively expansive liberalism, a liberalism running up
against public opinion, against "traditional" values, and, to a certain degree, against common sense. In the mind of many voters, the Willie Horton case came to stand for the blurring by liberalism of legitimate goals,
such as modest help for prisoners judged suitable for rehabilitation (prisoners, for example, without long records of violence), with the *il*legitimate goal, in the majority view, of "coddling" violent and dangerous
criminals whom much of society judged irredeemable.

Republican strategists correctly perceived that the furlough of Willie
Horton epitomized an evolution of the far-reaching rights movement and
of post-war liberalism, an evolution that was resented and disapproved of
by significant numbers of voters who saw crime as existing on a *continuum*
with other social and moral problems aggravated by liberalism. For these
voters, the evolving rights movement was seen as extending the same
public access to hard-core pornography as to *Lady Chatterley's Lover;* as
allowing welfare recipients to avoid the responsibility for supporting their
own children; as fostering drug use, illegitimacy, homosexual promiscuity, and an AIDS epidemic—all leading to demands on taxpayers to foot
skyrocketing health-care and social service bills—bills traceable, in this
view, to behavior commonly judged "immoral," and incurred disproportionately by blacks and Hispanics.

Crime became a shorthand *signal,* to crucial numbers of white voters,
of broader issues of social disorder, tapping powerful ideas about authority, status, morality, self-control, and race. If criminal defendants in the
years preceding the rights revolution had been, like many other beneficiaries of that movement, in fact subject to arbitrary authority and to random
cruelty, by the 1980s they had completely lost their public status as victims.
Populist legitimacy and sympathy had shifted decisively from victims of

law enforcement to the victims of criminal violence, and in general to those who felt themselves to be victimized by the rights revolution and by social change—"average" citizens whose own rights seemed to them to be unprotected by the liberal state.

"On no other issue is the dividing line so clear, on no other issue is my opponent's philosophy so completely at odds with mine, and I would say with the common sense attitudes of the American people, than on the issue of crime," Bush declared in a October 7, 1988, campaign speech to police officers in Xenia, Ohio. "There are some—and I would list my opponent among them—who have wandered off the clear-cut path of common sense and have become lost in the thickets of liberal sociology. Just as when it comes to foreign policy, they always 'Blame America First,' when it comes to crime and criminals, they always seem to 'Blame Society First.' . . . [Criminal justice under Dukakis is] a 'Twilight Zone' world where prisoners' 'right to privacy' has more weight than the citizen's right to safety."

---

There has been considerable debate over the degree to which the furlough-pledge-ACLU-death penalty-and flag themes used by the Bush campaign effected the presidential election of 1988. A number of economists and political scientists have argued that the outcome, 54 percent Bush to 46 percent Dukakis, closely approximated the predicted outcome based on models using the historic effects of income trends, GNP growth, unemployment, inflation, and interest rates.[16] At the same time, however, a series of polls that tracked voter shifts through the campaign clearly suggest that the social/moral and racial issues played a critical role in moving voters from support of Dukakis to support of Bush between June and November of 1988. What in fact appears to have taken place is that the set of social/moral/racial issues raised by the Bush campaign functioned to push specific segments of the electorate toward the GOP, with the final result meeting the standards that would be expected from the general economic climate surrounding the election.

A series of seven polls conducted from April 1987 to November 1988 by the Times Mirror company and by the Gallup Organization, surveying a total of 16,403 voters, found "that the success of the Bush campaign was based on making liberalism, the Pledge of Allegiance, and the prison furlough controversies salient, while at the same time making Bush vulnerabilities of less relative importance to key voter groups. . . . Bush succeeded in neutralizing the economic discontent" of these groups.[17] Using a unique set of "typology" groups to analyze the electorate, the survey found that the Bush campaign themes were most effective among whites in the groups described as: a) "the disaffected," 95 percent of whom are white, "alienated, pessimistic, and financially pressured. . . . skeptical of both big government and big business"; b) "New Dealers: older, blue-collar, and religious [88 percent white] . . . although supportive of many social spending measures . . . are intolerant on social issues"; and c) "God and Country Democrats: older, poor, disproportionately black [63 percent white, 31 percent black, 6 percent Hispanic and other groups] . . . have a strong faith in America and are uncritical of its institutions [whites in this group supported Bush]."[18]

These 1988 white defectors from the Democratic party closely resemble the voters of Macomb County, and the urban ethnics and white southerners examined in the post–1984 election studies by the Democratic National Committee and by the Michigan Democratic party. In a series of post–1988 voter studies and focus groups, Ed Reilly, who conducted polling for the unsuccessful presidential campaign of Democratic Representative Richard Gephardt of Missouri, found that

> The race issue, affirmative action, the sense of subsistence programs from the government all going 'to people other then myself,' to state it politely, is a very prevalent theme with Democrats around the country, especially with those more culturally conservative, northeast Catholics and southern white males. What you hear is their hostility to a giveaway agenda for minority groups. When you get underneath all the layers of code words, the emerging definition of where working class Democrats fit is they talk about themselves as 'the people who work.' People who don't work, that describes [their perception] of the black-white problem in our society right now. . . . Crime and drugs, and a sense of the mobility of crime right now, that it doesn't stay in that neighborhood over there, that it's a real threat to me and my children, that's added a real dimension to black-white relations.[19]

Down in the precincts of the Twenty-Third in southwest Chicago in 1988, the terms of the debate over race were even more blunt. "Every night I sit at home and watch the news. I see Jesse [Jackson] up there talking about 'black empowerment, our people,' and that's sending a message out there that no Democratic precinct captain can possibly overcome," said Michael Caccitolo, a Republican committeeman. "When the Dan Ryan [Expressway] was being rebuilt, the old lady from Operation Push [Rev. Willie Barrow, president at that time of Jackson's Operation Push] comes out and says 'we are going to close the Dan Ryan down unless we get more blacks on construction.' The people in the neighborhood remember that. Nobody threatened to close the Dan Ryan down to get Polish people on. And they [city and state officials] backed down and they gave a bunch of black guys entry level jobs. And look who they threw off and got sent back to the neighborhood and told get on unemployment. All it takes is two or three of them. . . . Would you define them as Republican precinct captains? No. Is it advantageous for the Republicans to watch a guy like that sitting in a tavern drinking his beer and telling the story about how he got bumped? And then all of a sudden it's 6 o'clock and [on TV] it's Jesse. It's bad and it ain't going to get better."[20]

---

Caccitolo's assessment, that the race-dominated politics of the Twenty-third Ward "ain't going to get better," may prove accurate; but at the same time, the politics of white, working-class neighborhoods in city wards and precincts like those of the Twenty-third are likely to become increasingly less critical to the outcome of presidential elections, as Reagan Democrats lose their pivotal stature. The political demography of the country is changing in ways that prompted John Morgan, a Republican voting analyst who serves as a consultant to the Republican National Committee, to suggest in the aftermath of the 1988 election, "We don't need their votes any more."[21]

In a critical development in presidential elections, the 1992 contest will mark the first time that suburban (and exurban) voters cast an absolute majority of ballots. This reflects the continuation of a trend that will have profound implications for the strategies of both parties, for the role of race in national elections, and for the formulation of policy at the federal and local levels.

From 1970 to 1986, the overwhelmingly white suburbs grew from 40.8 percent of the nation's total population to 44.9 percent.[22] In the same period, central cities, where the black population—particularly the poor black population—is concentrated, held a declining percentage of the total American population, from 35.2 to 31.6 percent.[25] These figures in fact underestimate racial and class trends, because the sharpest population declines over the past two decades have resulted from an exodus of whites from the most heavily black cities, including Detroit, Baltimore, New Orleans, Atlanta, Cleveland, Gary, Newark, and St. Louis. Conversely, many of the cities experiencing high growth have very small black populations, like Arlington, Texas, 2.9 percent black, 56 percent growth from 1970 to 1980; Glendale, Arizona, 1.9 percent black, 29.5 percent growth; and Modesto, California, 2.1 percent black, and 24.3 percent growth.[24]

In terms of partisanship, in terms of the racial implications of local spending policies, and in terms of the formulation of strategies to build majority presidential coalitions, these and other "growth" cities should be included with the suburbs, and not with New York, Chicago, Baltimore, Washington, Birmingham, and the host of heavily black, older cities.

The older-city/suburban-exurban trends have significant consequences both for politics and for policy. While public opinion polls show

228 · *Chain Reaction*

increasing support for expenditures on education, health, recreational facilities, and a range of other desired public services, a growing percentage of white voters are discovering that they can become fiscal liberals at the local level. They can satisfy these demands through increased suburban and county expenditures, guaranteeing the highest possible return to themselves on their tax dollars, while continuing to maintain policies of fiscal conservatism at the federal level. Suburbanization has permitted whites to satisfy liberal ideals revolving around activist government, while keeping to a minimum the number of blacks and the poor who share in government largess.[25]

The residents of Gwinnett County, Georgia, for example—one of the fastest growing suburban jurisdictions in the nation, heavily Republican (75.5 percent for Bush), affluent, and white (96.6 percent)—have been willing to tax and spend on their own behalf as liberally as any Democrats. County voters have in recent years approved a special recreation tax, all school, library, and road bond issues, a one percent local sales tax, and have re-elected local officials who have imposed the highest property tax rate in the Atlanta metropolitan area.[26]

The accelerated growth of suburbs has made it possible for many Americans to fulfill a basic drive toward civic participation—involvement in schools, cooperation in community endeavors, a willingness to support and to pay for public services—within a smaller universe, separate and apart from the consuming failure, crime, welfarism, decay—and blackness—of the older cities.

If a part of the solution to the devastating problems of the underclass involves investment in public services, particularly in the public school systems of the nation's major cities, the growing division between city and suburb lessens white self-interest in making such an investment. In 1986, fully 27.5 percent of all black school children, and 30 percent of all Hispanic school children, were enrolled in the twenty-five largest central-city school districts. Only 3.3 percent of all white students were in these same twenty-five districts.[27]

Even within major cities, there is a growing divergence of interests between blacks and whites. The more affluent (i.e., the more white) citizens in racially mixed cities are in many cases turning to privatized services. These services include independent and parochial schools, which serve high percentages of whites in cities such as New York, Washington, Chicago, Boston, Philadelphia, and Baltimore, along with even higher percentages in the deep South; private police and security services in apartment buildings, malls, and office complexes; proliferating private clubs providing tennis, racquetball, gymnastic, swimming, and other recreational facilities; and private transportation services in crime-ridden cities like New York, where banks, law firms, and major businesses contract with livery services to provide transportation for employees and customers and sidestep whenever possible local public transit.

This privatization functions as a disincentive to the middle class and the affluent to support raised taxes for improved public services in cities—the services most needed and most supported by the black and Hispanic urban populations. In Chicago's Twenty-third Ward, Mike Caccitolo, the GOP committeeman, recounted a poll the Cook County Republican party conducted in 1988. "We asked the question [in a survey of the Ward's voters] if a tax increase were dedictated to the improvement of the education system, would you be opposed or would you support it? 82 percent are opposed to taxes to improve the school system. I don't need a truck to hit me in the face. Now why? Very simple: all these people put their kids in parochial school."[28]

On a much larger scale, the nation is moving steadily toward a national politics that will be dominated by the suburban vote. From 1968 to 1988, the percentage of the presidential vote cast in suburbs grew from 35.6 percent to 48.3 percent. The rural vote declined from 34.8 percent in 1968 to 22.2 percent in 1988, while the central city on the surface remained stable, 29.6 percent and 29.5 percent of the vote respectively, with declines in heavily black cities off-set by increases in cities with much higher white populations.[29]

The suburban vote is becoming the core of the Republican base, and that trend will in all probability reshape the nature of the partisan competition between Democrats and Republicans.

If the GOP becomes increasingly secure in its suburban base, the most probable scenario is that its candidates will be free to lessen their dependence on divisive tactics and on the accentuation of social, moral, and racial issues, an accentuation designed particularly to capitalize on racial tensions within and surrounding urban areas. The Republican party under George Bush has already begun to move in this direction, developing a far less divisive strategy of governance than under Reagan, governance combining a moderate degree of civic responsibility with an underlying disengagement from the turmoil of the cities—beneficence without fiscal substance—a kinder, gentler America, in Bush's phrase.

During the first two years, the Bush presidency has struggled through what may well come to be seen as a period of fundamental Republican transition. After winning election in a campaign dominated by issues and signals rooted firmly in the traumas of the 1960s and 1970s—Willie Horton, the death penalty, the ACLU, the flag, and "no new taxes"—the most visible early domestic direction of the Bush administration has in fact been towards a muted conservatism, pressing aggressively for a cut in the capital-gains tax rate but abandoning the overall GOP anti-tax stance, encouraging volunteerism, meeting with civil rights leaders, moving toward a modest degree of conciliation with black America, generating from the White House a discreet display of public sympathy for the victims of AIDS—seeking at the same time to sustain the shift of fiscal responsibility from the federal government to state and local governments, and placating both business interests and discontent whites with the veto of the Civil Rights Act of 1990.

This form of politics is designed to accommodate the power shift to the suburbs and the declining role of Reagan Democrats in determining the outcome of national elections. On the one hand, Bush toned down conservative rhetoric, ameliorating the discomfort of white voters disturbed by the more calculated efforts of the Reagan Republican party to splinter the electorate around racial and social issues. Bush took care, for example, to urge support for civil rights per se, defining objections to the 1990 and 1991 legislation strictly in terms of "quotas". On the other hand, Bush imposed minimal "costs" for social responsibility. In Bush's case, the risk to an ascendant conservatism and to a broad Republican voter realignment lies not just in the president's abandonment of the "no new taxes" pledge, but in his lack of understanding that maintaining a highly publicized opposition to tax hikes—with all the "meaning" that such opposition entails—has been essential to the maintenance of a majority conservative coalition.

———

The rise of Republican suburbs in a "white noose" around declining cities with majority, or near-majority, black and Hispanic populations is becoming the central characteristic of politics in such key states as New York, Michigan, Illinois, and Ohio. From 1968 to 1988, the total vote cast by the heavily Democratic New York City counties of Queens, the Bronx, Kings (Brooklyn), and New York (Manhattan) has fallen from 2.4 million to 1.9 million, while the surrounding Republican-leaning counties (Westchester, Nassau, Suffolk, and Richmond) have risen from 1.5 million to 1.6 million, for a net gain of just under 600,000 votes in favor of the Republican counties. In Illinois during the same twenty-year period, the 1.9 million-vote advantage in 1968 of Democratic Cook County (Chicago and environs) over the surrounding GOP counties of DuPage, Will, and Lake, dropped by 1988 to a 1.4 million vote advantage. In Michigan, Wayne County (Detroit and surrounding communities) in 1968 cast 1.03 million votes, 470,000 *more* than the 560,000 cast in neighboring Oakland and McComb counties; by 1988, Wayne county (62 percent white, 38 percent black and Hispanic) cast 748,156 votes, 5,448 *less* than the 753,604 voters who went to the polls in McComb (97 percent white) and Oakland counties (93 percent white). In terms of actual vote outcomes, Humphrey in 1968 came out 433,096 votes ahead in these three counties; Dukakis in 1988 lost the three counties by 13,164 votes.[30]

What all this suggests is that a politics of suburban hegemony will come to characterize presidential elections. With a majority of the electorate equipped to address its own needs through local government, not only will urban blacks become increasingly isolated by city-county boundaries, but support for the federal government, a primary driving force behind black advancement, is likely to diminish.

For those seeking to maintain and nurture a right-of-center coalition, suburban hegemony provides the ideal setting for the repeated mobilization of an election-day majority without depending upon divisive 'wedge' issues to prevent the restoration of the more economically-based Democratic coalition.

---

The development of a Republican presidential coalition based, to a large extent, in the nation's suburbs has been facilitated by series of developments within the black community. The past two decades have produced an economic bifurcation among blacks far more extreme than that among whites. For black families, those in the top quintile of the income distribution by 1987 had average incomes sixteen times larger than that of those in the bottom quintile, compared to a nine-to-one parallel ratio among whites.

The bifurcated economic pattern among black Americans presents sharply contrasting images to both races of black advancement and of black deterioration, of the success of the civil rights movement and of its failure, of competitive strength under adversity and of withdrawal from competition. The clear majority (over 60 percent) of black Americans are living conventional work lives. Between a third and two-fifths (30 to 40 percent) of black America, however, exists at or below the margin of regular employment, minimal income, and personal security.

From 1973 to 1987, the rate of income growth for the top 60 percent of all black families has been significantly greater than that for the top 60 percent of white families, and this pattern held true in the shorter period from 1979 to 1987, covering most of the Reagan years. Income in the top fifth of black families grew by 33.3 percent from 1973 to 1987, while growing by only 24.5 percent among the top fifth of white families. Among the bottom 40 percent of black Americans, however, the movement relative to their white counterparts has been backwards. The following Table 11.3 describes changing patterns of income for different quintiles over the period from 1973 to 1987.

A majority of black families are slowly moving toward relative income equality. The bottom 40 percent are, however, falling behind, and dangerously so for those in the very bottom quintile. For the average-sized family in the late 1980s, the official poverty level was $7,886, or just $152 dollars a week, nowhere near enough to live on by any standard. For black families with children, in the bottom quintile, *average annual income* (measured by after-tax income and including housing assistance and food stamps), *in 1987 was $5,112, or $98.30 a week—56 percent of the official poverty level.*[31]

The severity of poverty for blacks in the bottom quintile, has contributed to the growing perception that to be poor is to be black, a perception that offsets black gains in the middle class, and which functions to reinforce racial stereotypes held by whites. The conservative assault on means-tested programs and affirmative action has capitalized on white stereotypes about black poverty, and on white resentment of perceived black dependence on welfare and on racial preferences. The use of themes ranging from law and order to Willie Horton to the ACLU has sought to take political advantage of the linkage of blacks to crime. Regardless of the legitimacy of the issues of black poverty and crime as subjects for public policy debate, their political function has been to polarize the electorate in a manner beneficial to the development of a majority conservative coalition.

Just at the time that the continuing rise of the suburbs is lessening pressure on Republican strategists to accentuate these divisive issues in order to maintain the conservative coalition, a second major demographic development, the expansion of the underclass, is spontaneously functioning to contribute to and aggravate this polarization. The most damaging *political* consequence of the underclass, and of the dysfunctional social behavior associated with it, is that it fuels the core of racial conflict—even without additional prodding from conservative interests.

––––––––––

Racial and other kinds of biases have been described as characterized by a "screening" phenomenon: the underlying stereotype held by one group about another race, class, gender, or ethnic type acts as a screen, tending to allow into conscious recognition evidence that sustains the stereotype, and blocking or rejecting from consciousness information that defies that stereotype.[32]

TABLE 11.3

## Average Family Income, for Each Quintile of White and Black Families, 1973, 1978, and 1987

(All dollar figures are in 1988 dollars to adjust for inflation. The bottom panel describes black income as a percent of white income from the bottom, middle, and top quintiles for the same time period.)

| | 1973 | 1979 | 1987 | Percentage Change 1973–1987 |
|---|---|---|---|---|
| *White Families* | | | | |
| Bottom quintile | $ 8,495 | $ 8,495 | $ 7,866 | −7.4 |
| Second | 16,912 | 17,934 | 18,092 | 7.0 |
| Middle | 23,677 | 25,643 | 27,216 | 15.0 |
| Fourth | 32,251 | 35,318 | 38,779 | 20.2 |
| Top | 55,534 | 59,703 | 69,142 | 24.5 |
| Ratio of top to bottom | 6.5–1 | 7.0–1 | 8.8–1 | |
| *Black Families* | | | | |
| Bottom | $ 4,012 | $ 3,933 | $ 3,304 | −17.6 |
| Second | 8,259 | 8,810 | 8,731 | 5.7 |
| Middle | 13,259 | 14,867 | 16,123 | 21.3 |
| Fourth | 20,373 | 23,283 | 26,115 | 28.2 |
| Top | 38,307 | 42,398 | 51,050 | 33.3 |
| Ratio of top to bottom | 9.5–1 | 10.8–1 | 15.5–1 | |

## Black Income as a Percent of White Income for Each Quintile, 1973, 1979, and 1987

| | 1973 | 1979 | 1987 | Gain (+) or Loss (−) 1973–1987 |
|---|---|---|---|---|
| Bottom quintile | 47.2% | 46.3% | 42.0% | −5.2 |
| Second | 48.8% | 49.1% | 48.3% | −0.5 |
| Middle quintile | 56.1% | 58.0% | 59.2% | +3.1 |

TABLE 11.3 (Cont.)

| | 1973 | 1979 | 1987 | Gain (+) or Loss (−) 1973–1987 |
|---|---|---|---|---|
| Fourth | 63.2% | 65.9% | 67.3% | +4.1 |
| Top quintile | 69.0% | 71.0% | 73.8% | +4.8 |

SOURCE: Based on House Ways and Means Committee. *The 1990 Green Book* (Washington, D.C., June 5, 1990), pp. 1106–7, Table 45. The average family size in Table 11.3 is calculated on the basis of the 1988 figure of 2.41 people, with a 1987 poverty level for a family of this size set at $7,886. The dollar amounts in Table 11.3 differ somewhat from those in Tables 11.1 and 11.2, because the data in Table 11.3 is based on census surveys of income, which provide reported differences by race, while the data in Tables 11.1 and 11.2 is based on actual income tax reports which do not provide racial breakdowns.

The steady entry of a majority of black Americans into the solidly working and middle classes—after centuries of slavery and legal segregation—has worked to break up racial stereotypes and to penetrate the "screen" of race prejudice. In all major metropolitan areas, the workplace is now integrated, and white Americans are earning their livings increasingly in circumstances in which persons of other races hold positions of approximate, equal, or, increasingly, of higher stature.

In the years before the outbreak of World War II, 73 percent of all black college graduates became ministers or teachers, almost all serving exclusively black constituencies. In 1940, only 187,520 blacks held white-collar jobs, and 135,340 were clergymen, teachers, or owners of generally small, ghetto-based retail stores producing marginal incomes.[33] By 1989, 1.86 million blacks held managerial and professional-level jobs in all public and private sectors. From 1950 to 1989, the black population doubled, but the number of blacks holding white-collar jobs increased by 522 percent.[34]

Race prejudice has been attacked through an increasing degree of daily job integration and black achievement at the most elite and competitive levels of American society, assaulting racial preconceptions. Exclusive white sovereignty no longer exists in the nation's universities and professional schools, in hospitals and law firms, in the most influential industries and corporations, or in America's political literary, musical, or artistic establishments.

In political terms, the power of evidence that *contradicts* racial stereotypes is, in effect, at war with the consequences of the growing underclass, as the underclass becomes a symbol and representation of the disproportionate share of social dysfunction in the poor black community.[35]

The debate over what factors created and sustain the underclass, and over proposed solutions, runs a left-to-right gamut, with attribution ranging from the historic consequences of racism (traditionally an argument of the left) to a "culture of poverty" argument (appropriated in recent years by the right); from the departure of manufacturing jobs from the city, to the power of criminals to disrupt daily life in poor neighborhoods; from the acute vulnerability of the most disadvantaged to the consequences of national trends in divorce and illegitimacy, to the negative incentives to work and marriage created by the welfare system and by Great Society programs.[36]

While this debate continues, a debate that exists in far greater sophistication and detail than the foregoing summary suggests, one clear fact remains: that the underclass and the larger problem of the black poor remain the Achilles heel of the liberal movement to achieve racial equality, and that the underclass has, in addition, become the Achilles heel of the Democratic party.

In political and social terms, the underclass serves to reinforce the most damaging racial preconceptions about black America. Major studies of prejudice have found that the most effective way to break the hold of negative racial, religious, or ethnic stereotypes is for members of alienated or adversarial groups to work cooperatively toward a shared goal under circumstances that permit those who hold stereotyped views to repeatedly see evidence that conflicts with those views. "Prejudice may be reduced by equal status contact between majority and minority groups in the pursuit of common goals. The effect is greatly enhanced if sanctioned by institutional supports, (i.e., by law, custom, or local atmosphere), and provided it is of the sort that leads to the perception of common interests and common humanity between members of the two groups," Gordon W. Allport wrote in his classic work, *The Nature of Prejudice.*

"Attitude change favorable to a disliked group will result from equal status contact with stereotype-disconfirming persons from that group, provided that the contact is cooperative and of such a nature as to reveal the individual characteristics of the person contacted and that it takes place in a situation characterized by social norms favoring equality and equalitarian association among the participating groups," wrote Stuart Wellford Cook, former chairman of the psychology departments at New York University and the University of Colorado, who studied prejudice for over twenty-five years.[37]

It has been in the nature of the contact of whites with the black underclass that this contact has routinely violated every standard necessary for the breakdown of racial stereotypes. Most white contact with the underclass is either through personal experience of crime and urban squalor, or through such experience reported by friends and family, or through the almost daily reports about crime, drugs, and violence on local and national television news and in newspapers. To a lesser extent, news coverage involves periodic reports on illegitimacy, welfare dependency, drug-related AIDS, crack babies, and inner-city worklessness, including, for example, television programs such as Bill Moyers's CBS series, "The Vanishing Family: Crisis in Black America." It is precisely the degree to which such media coverage not only amplifies bad news, but in fact accurately reflects a situation that exists across the country, that these reports create such a damaging impact: "The stereotype is not a stereotype any more. The behavior pattern [in the underclass] is not stereotypical in the pejorative sense, but it is a statement of fact," says Kenneth S. Tollett, a black professor of education at Howard University's Graduate School of Arts and Sciences. "A stereotype is an overgeneralization. 'This is the way people are' and then we say all are like that. The behavior of black males [in the underclass] is now beginning to look like the black stereotype. The statements we have called stereotypes in the past have become true."[38]

Crime, in this context, becomes a volatile ingredient in the politics of race. From 1979 to 1988, victimization surveys conducted by the Department of Justice found that an annual average 44.3 out of every 1,000 blacks were victims of a violent crime, with much higher rates in very poor areas, compared to 34.5 out of every 1,000 whites who were violent-crime victims.[39] At the same time, however, a far higher percentage of the crimes committed by blacks is interracial than of the crimes committed by whites. In 1986 and 1987, whites commiting crimes of violence—robbery, rape and assault—chose white victims 97.6 percent of the time and black victims in 2.4 percent in those incidents, when the victim could identify the race of the offender. Blacks commiting violent crimes chose white victims 53.8 percent of the time and black victims 46.2 percent.[40] For the specific crime of robbery, the figures are even more striking. In 1986–87, of those robberies in which the race of the offenders was identified by the victims, 95.8 percent of robberies committed by whites had white victims and 4.8 percent had black victims; 59.9 percent of robberies committed by blacks had white victims and 40.1 percent had white victims.[41]

For many white voters living in major cities, no issue is more divisive than crime, and no issue more undermines the prospects for lessening the racial stereotyping that forms the basis for prejudice. In October 1988, as the presidential campaign reached its height, white residents of Chicago's

Garfield Ridge neighborhood, angry over reports of three rapes and increasing incidents of robbery and vandalism, formed an organization called People Against Crime. At the group's first meeting in the Nathan Hale Elementary School, Peggy Angelair, the newly elected president, told the applauding, all-white crowd that filled the auditorium: "I guess our federal government decided it was going to take the minorities and put them with us, and our goodness would rub off on them. But unfortunately, it's turned around the other way. And we have to stay together on this issue."[42] On November 8, 1988, the Democratic precincts of the Twenty-third ward of Chicago, which contains Garfield Park, voted for George Bush by a margin of 59–41.

Among urban blacks, who suffer the consequences of crime more than whites, the view of the underclass and attendant problems diverges markedly from the view held by Peggy Angelair. Focus groups held separately under Democratic and Republican party auspices reveal a view held widely among blacks: that the white power structure has permitted, if not actually encouraged, the flow of crack cocaine into black neighborhoods. "In every focus group we held [among blacks] someone would raise the idea of drugs as a white conspiracy, every group. [A conspiracy] to keep blacks down, 'just as we were making progress.' Now whites are supplying blacks with machine guns to kill each other," said Frederick Steeper, of the GOP firm Market Strategies. Ed Reilly, the Democratic pollster, said his firm's recent work in the black community found among northern, urban blacks "a sense of being in an ongoing conflict with the white establishment, that there is an organized approach to keep them [blacks] isolated from mainstream America, that the government system is rigged to keep them in poverty. . . . Most blacks believe that while drugs may not be brought in by whites, [the drug problem] is being treated differently by white law enforcement than if it were causing the same ravages in white communities."[46]

Bernard Boxill, a black scholar at the University of North Carolina, has argued that that the growing problems of the underclass may be used by the white community as "an excuse to undo the legal, social, and economic advances made by the black middle class, plunge the country into a race war, and worst of all, be a pretext for genocide."[44] In other words, the causes and consequences of the underclass are seen from very different perspectives by substantial numbers of whites and blacks, and these differing visions of what has become the most pressing and daunting domestic issue before the nation have the effect of mutually reinforcing separate racial worldviews and, thus, of intensifying divisions between blacks and whites.

Louis Farrakhan, Leader of the Nation of Islam, took the issue a step farther, arguing that the black underclass and all the attendant problems are the creation of a white society now seeking to discard a growing and politically threatening black population:

> The black man and woman in America is of no further use to the children of our former slavemasters and when a thing loses its use or utility, it loses its value. If your shoes wear out, you don't keep them around, if an old dress become old, you don't keep it around. Once it loses utility, you move to get rid of it. . . . We cannot accept the fact that they think black people have become a permanent underclass. . . . If we have become useless in a racist society, then you must know that, not public policy, but a covert policy is being already formulated to get rid of that which is useless since the economy is going down, and the world is going down. Follow me brothers and sisters. According to demographers, if the plummeting birth rate of white people in America continues, in a few years, it will reach zero population growth. As for blacks, Hispanics and native Americans, if their present birth rate continues, by the year 2080, demographers say, blacks, Hispanics and native Americans will conceivably be 50 percent or more of the United States population. . . . If things continue just birthwise, we could control the Congress, we could control the Supreme Court, we could control state legislatures and then "Run, Jesse, run," or "Run, Jesse Junior, run," or "Run, Jesse the Third, run."[45]

Underlying the strikingly different views of the underclass, and of possible future relations between the races, are some developments suggesting an even deeper divergence of perspective between many whites and blacks, a divergence which threatens to undermine the workings of essential institutions in some of the country's major cities. In the Bronx, black and Hispanic juries in the 1980s produced verdicts that reflected a clear lack of belief in police and prosecutorial testimony in cases involving black defendants, including not-guilty verdicts in two separate murder and attempted murder trials of alleged drug dealer Larry Davis. The verdict exonerating Davis of charges of attempted murder in the shooting of nine police officers who were arresting him surprised even the defense attorneys.[46] "When I started in this office 20 years ago, the strongest case you could have as an assistant district attorney was when all your witnesses were police officers," Bronx District Attorney Paul T. Gentile said. "Now, sadly, it is the weakest." The verdict in the Davis case, because it involved the shooting of nine officers, produced a vehement reaction among police. "Police officers feel that open season has been declared on them," said Phil Caruso, president of the Patrolmen's Benevolent Association. In the South Bronx's Forty-fourth Precinct station, officers hung a banner reading: "Need Help? Call Larry Davis."[47]

On the opposite side of the fence, significant numbers of blacks, both middle-class and those in poor neighborhoods hit heavily by the drug epidemic and by crime, view the failure to contain narcotics as extending far beyond the culpability of individual lawbreakers. "It's almost an accepted fact," said Andrew Cooper, publisher of the black weekly Brooklyn newspaper, the *City Sun,* in an analysis of the situation often heard on black radio talk shows and in other all-black forums. "It's a deep-seated suspicion. I believe it. I can't open my desk drawer and say 'Here it [the evidence] is.' But there is just too much money in narcotics. People really believe they are being victimized by The Man. If the government wanted to stop it, it could stop it."[48]

In a broader vision of white conspiracy, Dr. Frances Welsing, a black psychiatrist, was loudly applauded when she argued at a predominately black "town meeting" organized and televised by ABC-TV and Ted Koppel in 1989:

> Racism is a behavior system that is organized because white people are a minority on the planet. . . . If we understand the white fear of genetic annihilation, which is why Willie Horton could be used as a very profound symbol by the Republican Party to win this election, then we will understand what is happening to the black male in this society. The black male is a threat to white genetic annihilation. And so he is profoundly attacked in this society. And if we begin to understand that, we understand what happens to the black family if you remove the father, then the son is wandering around confused, doesn't know what to do, will get together with a gang, and ends up being depressed, getting on drugs, and going to prison."[49]

While these views are extreme, they are by no means uncommon; there is a significant gulf between the view of the police and court systems by blacks and whites in public opinion surveys. On the basic question of whether judges and courts treat whites and blacks fairly, 56 percent of white New Yorkers believe that the system is fair and 27 percent say the system favors one race over another, with that 27 percent evenly split between those who see black favoritism and those who see white favoritism. Among black New Yorkers, only 30 percent see the system as fair, and 49 percent see it as unfair, with the overwhelming majority of those who perceive unfairness seeing a bias in favor of whites.[50]

Such highly controversial cases as the 1987 allegations by Tawana Brawley that she was raped and assaulted by a group of white men, and the 1985 shooting by "subway vigilante" Bernhard Goetz of four black teenagers he believed were about to rob him, provoke sharply divergent views among blacks and whites. After a grand jury determined that Brawley had fabricated her story, 73 percent of white New Yorkers said she lied, while only 33 percent of blacks were prepared to make that judgement (18 percent said she told the truth, 14 percent said she didn't know what happened to her, and 35 percent were unwilling to make an assessment). In the case of Goetz, the ratio of whites describing themselves as supportive of his action, against those who were critical, was 50–37, compared to a reverse 23–59 ratio among blacks. Whites felt that Goetz was innocent of attempted murder by a margin of 47–18 (with the rest undecided), while blacks said that Goetz was guilty by a margin of 42–19. (Hispanics sided more with whites than blacks, with the margin favoring innocence over guilt at 41–23.)[51]

---

The divergence of opinion between blacks and whites on such matters is a surface reflection of a much deeper economic division between poor blacks and the rest of the nation, a division driven to an important degree by the economics of the central cities. Propelled in part by the shift from manufacturing to services, and in part by the reluctance of corporate America to remain in or to relocate to centers of high crime where the work force has inadequate education and training, the market economy has effectively discarded the poorly educated black male.

One of the most detailed analyses of the urban job market has been performed by John D. Kasarda, chairman of the Sociology Department at the University of North Carolina. Kasarda found that during the decade 1970 to 1980, the number of jobs that did not require high school degrees fell by 1.05 million in the center city areas of Boston, Chicago, Cleveland, Detroit, New York, and Philadelphia alone, and the number of jobs requiring only a high school education fell by 398,500. At the same time, the number of jobs requiring at least some college rose by 464,500, and those requiring a college degree rose by 530,890.[52]

These trends have produced a major mismatch between undereducated black men and the jobs available in big cities. In Baltimore, for example, only 29.6 percent of the jobs in 1980 did not require a high school education, but 54.4 percent of the black men in the city did not have high school degrees, and 67.5 percent of those black men who were not working did not have high school degrees. In New York, the figures were comparable: 22 percent of the jobs in the city did not require high school graduation, 39.3 percent of black men did not have high school diplomas, and 52.5 percent of black men who did not have high school diplomas were out of work; in Philadelphia, the figures were: 23.2 percent of the jobs in the city did not require a high school education, 46 percent of all black men did not have a high school degree, and 60.1 percent of black men without a high school degree were not working.[53]

The widening disparity between the availability of jobs with low education requirements and blacks with a minimal education contributed in turn to the *growth* in every one of the studied cities, from 1970 to 1980, in the percentage of black men without high school degrees who were not working: growth from, for example, 23.7 percent to 45 percent in Baltimore; from 26.7 percent to 50.6 percent in Philadelphia; from 28.2 percent to 43.9 percent in New York.[54]

For young black men with high school educations or less, if the the 1970s were a hard decade, then the 1980s were disastrous. From October 1973 to October 1986, the labor force participation rate for white and Hispanic high school dropouts fell by 7 and 8 percentage points respectively, but for black dropouts, it fell by 25 percentage points.[55] This sharp decline cannot be attributed to Reagan administration policy or to the 1981–82 recession: the single worst year for 16- to 24-year-old black dropouts was from 1979 to 1980, Carter's last year in office, when labor force participation fell by over 15 percentage points. Nor did the economic recovery beginning in 1983 in the first Reagan term do much for black dropouts. From 1974 to 1986, sharp racial disparities began to emerge in the work experience of both dropouts and high school graduates: the growth in the percentage of young black men between the ages of 20 and 24 who did not work at *all* during the year far outpaced that of their white and Hispanic counterparts, with the percentage for black high school graduates who did not work at all rising by 1986 to 15.7 percent, and for dropouts rising to a staggering 39.7 percent.

The 1982 recession was a severe setback to black dropouts, and the recovery produced almost no improvement for them by 1986, in sharp contrast to white and Hispanic dropouts. Among 20 to 24-year-old high school dropouts who do work, there has been another sharply negative trend: from 1979 to 1986, the percentage of employed black dropouts working for the full year (50 to 52 weeks) fell from 37.7 to 28.1 percent, while the percentage working half a year (26 weeks) or less rose from 31.2 percent to 54.5 percent. These trends contrasted with those among white and Hispanic dropouts, for whom the percentages working full time increased from 47.2 to 53.3 for whites, and from 47.2 to 58.9 for Hispanics.[56]

Among female high school dropouts without children, the labor force participation rate among whites and Hispanics between the ages of 16 and 24 in 1987 was much higher, 62.4 percent and 58 percent respectively, than for black women dropouts, 40.6 percent. White and black female dropouts with children had almost identical labor force participation rates, 35.5 and 36.3 percent respectively, while Hispanic women with children had the

TABLE 11.4

Percentages of 20- to 24-Year-Old Male High School Graduates and Dropouts Who Had *No* Work Experience (Not Even One Week on a Job), in 1974, 1979, 1982 (a Recession Year), and 1986

|  | Total | White | Black | Hispanic |
|---|---|---|---|---|
| *High School Graduates* | | | | |
| 1974 | 5.3% | 4.6% | 9.0% | 9.2% |
| 1979 | 5.4% | 3.7% | 15.2% | 8.7% |
| 1982 | 9.6% | 7.2% | 22.9% | 9.5% |
| 1986 | 6.7% | 4.8% | 15.7% | 8.9% |
| *Dropouts* | | | | |
| 1974 | 10.4% | 9.1% | 15.1% | 8.8% |
| 1979 | 12.4% | 9.3% | 22.9% | 9.4% |
| 1982 | 19.6% | 14.9% | 40.1% | 14.3% |
| 1986 | 16.8% | 11.8% | 39.7% | 9.6% |

SOURCE: James P. Markey, "The Labor Market Problems of Today's High School Dropouts," *Monthly Labor Review* 3, no. 6 (June 1988), 41.

lowest, 21.2 percent. But of the female dropouts with children in the 16 to 24-year-old age group in 1987, 61.1 percent of the whites and 56.9 percent of the Hispanics were married, while only 10.5 percent of the black women were married. Marriage for women with children, in turn, is one way to avoid welfare dependency and poverty. Among the white female dropouts with children, 34 percent received some from of government assistance, generally AFDC or foodstamps, while 74 percent of the black women dropouts with children did so.[57]

At the same time, the steady decline in two-parent families continued among all racial and ethnic groups, but with the deterioration of the black nuclear family far outpacing the decline among either whites or Hispanics. Among all families with children, the percentage functioning with just one parent present rose from 12.9 percent in 1970, to 21.5 percent in 1980, to 27.3 percent in 1988, while the percentage of black families functioning with just one parent had by 1988 risen to 59 percent. The following Table 11.5 shows the pattern for white, black, and Hispanic families over the same period.

The political consequences of these trends in employment, work force participation, crime, single parenthood, and welfare dependency is to fur-

TABLE 11.5

Percentage Distribution of One and Two-Parent Families with
Children for Whites, Blacks, and Hispanics for 1970, 1980, and 1988

|  | 1970 | 1980 | 1988 |
|---|---|---|---|
| *White* | | | |
| Two-Parent | 89.9% | 82.9% | 78.3% |
| One-Parent | 10.1% | 17.1% | 21.7% |
| *Black* | | | |
| Two-Parent | 64.3% | 48.1% | 40.6% |
| One-Parent | 35.7% | 51.9% | 59.4% |
| *Hispanic* | | | |
| Two-Parent | (NA) | 74.1% | 66.4% |
| One-Parent | (NA) | 25.9% | 33.6% |

SOURCE: Bureau of the Census, *Studies in Marriage and the Family*, ser. P-23, no. 162, (Washington, D.C., June 1989), Table B, p. 14.

ther isolate and separate the black poor from the rest of society. The geographic isolation fostered by the growth of a predominately white suburbia is being compounded, at the lower levels of the income distribution, by the creation of economic and behavioral boundaries separating the races.

Together, these developments further incorporate race as a pervasive factor in the public perception of the country's social and economic structure. That incorporation, in turn, establishes race as pervasive in political and public policy decisions. Long-term poverty, and all the problems associated with it, becomes identified as a black condition, increasingly separable from the mainstream of society, and, for many whites, separable from governmental and public obligation. If entrenched poverty is seen more as a condition of race than of class, and if the problems linked to such poverty—illegitimacy, joblessness, drug abuse, criminality—have all worsened *after* enactment of anti-discrimination laws, after affirmative action programs in the public and private sectors, and after a substantial expansion of government investment in programs geared to the poor, then public commitment to maintain, let alone to increase, this support declines.

It is in all of these ways that the underclass and the acuteness of the

problems of black poverty function to help sustain a right-of-center conservative coalition: through the reinforcement of racial stereotypes;
through the creation of entire neighborhoods where reproductive patterns, lifestyles, and work patterns are alien to, and disapproved of by,
much of the rest of the population; and through the development of racially conflicting views on the causes of poverty, crime, and black disadvantage. Insofar as the underclass is made visible through all of these
phenomena—visible through the rippling out of crime beyond urban
ghettos into downtown business districts and into suburbs, and magnified
by television and newspaper coverage—the underclass has become a powerful factor in sustaining a presidential coalition dominated by the affluent.

For a beseiged national Democratic party, the consequences are debilitating. On one side of the racial equation, white Democratic voters have
begun "to take issue with the Democratic rhetoric of representing the
'middle class and the poor.' These [voters] perceive themselves to be neither rich nor poor, and they do not like to be referred to in the same breath
with 'the poor.' They describe themselves as 'working people,' " according to a voter study conducted by KRC Research and Consulting for
Democrats for the 90s, a private organization affiliated with the Democratic party. Black urban Democratic voters, conversely, "feel that the
country and the Democratic party are increasingly racist and that the
party cares little for their needs and interests."[58]

———

The concentration among the black poor of single motherhood, crime
and withdrawal from the labor market—combined with an intensified
geographic isolation—has made it possible to partially segregate this segment of the population from the political, social, and economic mainstream. Poor black urban neighborhoods—covering extensive areas of
most large cities—are avoided by whites and increasingly abandoned by
middle-class blacks; the engines of the local economy in such neighborhoods are disproportionately government welfare payments and criminally generated income. Perhaps most important, the emergence of the
underclass and of an expanding body of the black urban poor has created a
growing perception of a society in which the poor are no longer linked to
the larger social network; for many Americans, the bottom rung on a
ladder no longer leads up—to middle-class well-being, status, or security.
The black urban poor have increasingly come to constitute a divergent
and threatening segment of society from which ties to the mainstream
through work, neighborhood, and shared communal values have been
severed.

If the steady, slow progress toward racial parity in the upper working and middle classes has been functioning since the mid-1960s to counter racial stereotypes, even this progress is now threatened by fundamental changes in the nation's economy, and by a divergence in black and white patterns of education. Starting in the mid and late-1970s, two basic education-related trends began to emerge:

• The job market began to place an increasingly higher value on education. The average pay of entry-level workers with college and more advanced degrees rose from 132 percent of the pay of workers with only a high school degree in 1975, to 180 percent in 1988, constituting a sharply rising *college wage premium*. This represented a sharp reversal of pay trends in the preceeding twelve-year period, from 1963 to 1975, the years of greatest gains for blacks. During that period, the college wage premium for entry-level workers had fallen from the range of 142-147 percent of high school graduates, down to 132 percent.[59]

• Not only did this trend work to the relative disadvantage of blacks— in 1988, 13.2 percent of blacks between the ages of 25 and 34 had college degrees compared to 24.5 percent of whites[60]—but just as the value of a college education began to skyrocket, the percentage of blacks between the ages of 18 and 24 going on to college and getting a degree began to fall. From 1976 to 1988, the percentage of black 18 to 24 year olds enrolled in college fell from 22.6 to 21.1 percent, while the percentage of whites rose from 27.1 to 31.3 percent.[61] At the same time, while the number of blacks in this age group grew by 8.7 percent from 1976 to 1987, the number of college degrees awarded annually to blacks fell by 4.3 percent. Conversely, the number of whites in this age group fell by 8 percent, while the number of college degrees going to whites rose by 3.7 percent. These trends of the late 1970s and the 1980s are a contrast to the surge in black college attendance in the 1960s and early 1970s. From 1967 to 1976, the percentage of black 18 to 24 year olds enrolled in college shot up from 13 to 22.6 percent[62]—a trend that, had it continued, would have produced virtual parity in college attendance between the young of both races by 1983.

The effect of these two trends—in college enrollment and in the college wage premium—has been to undermine what had been, through the 1960s and into the mid-1970s, a powerful drive toward economic and educational equality between the working and middle classes of the two races. In the ten years immediately following passage of the 1964 Civil Rights Act, the economy pushed the wages of both blacks and whites *who were in the work force* steadily upwards. As income for workers at all levels rose, the federal government passed legislation barring employment discrimination and establishing non–quota-based affirmative action goals for the public and private sectors under the jurisdiction of Title VII of the Civil Rights Act.

The result was a strong convergence of shared prosperity and growing racial equality. From 1963 to 1973, average weekly earnings for everyone grew from $175.17 to $198.35 (in 1977 inflation-adjusted dollars). As wages rose for whites and blacks, blacks made substantial gains in reducing white and black income differentials: in 1963, white wages were 45 percent higher than black wages; in 1973, they were 35 percent higher. There were even sharper drops in racial wage differentials for younger, well-educated workers for whom the gap had almost disappeared by the mid-1970s.[63]

In the mid-1970s, the economy began to stagnate, and weekly wages fell to $183.41 in 1979,[64] but black and white wages continued to converge, with the differential falling to 30 percent by 1979.[65] When comparisons were made between blacks and whites with the same education and experience in similar regions of the country, the wage differential for younger workers fell to the 14 to 18 percent range by the late 1970s.[66] Much of the inequality between the races was due to differences between the earnings of black and white men; black women, by many measures, achieved full or near wage parity with white women by the end of the 1970s.[67]

Starting in the second half of the 1970s and continuing into the early 1980s, however, the situation began to change radically. In effect, the blade of the economic plow was lifted so that increasing numbers of workers holding low and middle status jobs no longer gained as much from periods of economic growth. While the income of college graduates continued to rise, the income of high school graduates began to fall, and black college attendance, both in absolute terms and relative to whites, began to decline.

Just as the college wage premium rose, the wage levels for job categories that employed disproportionately larger percentages of whites—professionals, managers, and sales personnel—grew substantially faster than wage levels for those categories employing disproportionate numbers of blacks—operatives, and clerical, service, and household workers.[68]

The result has been a striking shift in racial wage patterns. The convergence between the income of working blacks and whites—a convergence that had the potential in the long run to enlarge the economic common ground between the races—came to a halt, starting at the end of the 1970s. From 1963 to 1977–78, the differences between black and white wages dropped from the 45 percent range down to the 30 percent range, a drop of about 1 percentage point a year. In the late 1970s, black wages abruptly stopped catching up to white wages, with the differential stagnating at roughly 30 percent.[69]

For a Democratic party seeking to build a majority coalition aligning the interests of blacks and whites, the abrupt halt of racial wage convergence in the late 1970s was a grave blow. The failure to continue the trend toward wage equality encourages conflicting black and white worldviews in which black gains are seen as a cost to whites, and in which white advantages are seen as a reflection of racism. Few developments could serve better than the stagnation of racial wage convergance to sustain a top-down conservative coalition fed by divisions between economic competitors in the bottom half of the income distribution.

Not only has the wage premium for college graduates slowed the movement toward racial wage parity, but it has also infused the debate over federal college tuition assistance with new conflict, creating what amounts to a zero-sum competition between blacks and whites over an increasingly vital resource: the money to finance post-secondary education. This debate, in turn, is a reflection in miniature of how race has become integral to the formulation of broad social and economic policy; race in this case pervading the seemingly race-neutral issue of whether to provide tuition assistance through loans or grants.

As the cost of going to college shot up in the 1970s, the federal government in 1975 shifted student aid from grants—scholarships, gifts, and other direct benefits which do not have to be paid back—to loans, which must be repaid. The switch from grants to loans permitted many more members of the working and middle class, who faced increasingly prohibitive tuition costs, to get some form of federal help. There is, however, strong evidence that while the switch to loans may have helped significant numbers of whites to go to college, the decrease in grants contributed to the reduction of college entry among blacks, who, on average, were not only individually far poorer than whites, but had poorer extended families, and were less well situated to take on long-term debt. The following Figures 11.1 and 11.2 show how the rise in black college entry (as a proportion of white entry) closely paralleled the growth of the availability of grants and gifts through the mid-1970s, and how the subsequent decline in black college entry parallels the replacement of grants with loans.

What these charts suggest is that there is a genuine racial conflict of interest in federal tuition assistance policy. In a study of the effect of federal assistance on the college entry of students from poor and low-income backgrounds, assistance which closely correlates with black and Hispanic college entry, the American College Testing Program found that "between 1966 and the late 1970s, when grant assistance was greatly

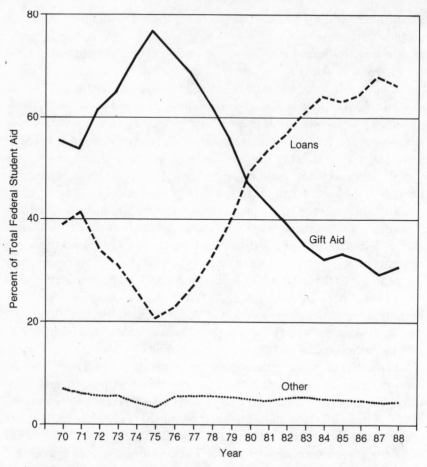

FIGURE 11.1 The Percentage Distribution of Federal Student Aid by Program Type, 1970 to 1988

SOURCE: Thomas G. Mortenson, *The Impact of Increased Loan Utilization among Low Family Income Students* (Iowa City, Iowa: American College Testing Program, 1990), page 4.

expanded, the participation of individuals from lower income groups [which are heavily black and Hispanic] also greatly increased. Between 1980 and the present, when loans have become the dominant form of federal student financial aid, between 40 and 50 percent of the participation gains made by students from the bottom quartile of the family income distribution between the mid-1960s and the mid-1970s have been lost. . . . There are risks and financing costs [to loans as opposed to grants], both of which have extraordinary impact on the poor."[70]

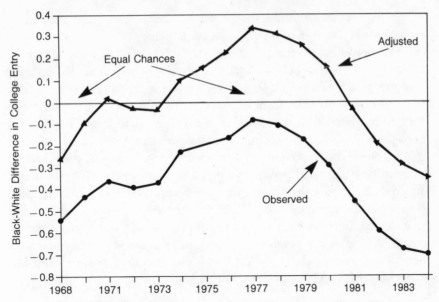

FIGURE 11.2  Proportion of black high school graduates entering college as a ratio of white high school graduates entering college. The chart is based on three-year rolling averages.

SOURCE: Robert M. Hauser, *The Decline in College Entry among African Americans* Department of Sociology, University of Wisconsin, (March 19, 1990), Figure 13.

While there are other factors involved, including the variable intensity of affirmative action drives and the attractiveness of the armed services as an alternative to college, as well as a willingness on the part of students and their families to make long-term financial sacrifices, the choice between grants and loans appears to have had strong consequences in determining black and white college entry. These policies have become particularly important as the value of a college education has escalated tremendously during the 1980s, while the wage prospects for a high school graduate have declined.

The racial conflict of interest does not end, however, with federal tuition-assistance policies. The resulting decline in black and Hispanic college attendance produced increased efforts on the part of colleges to boost *private* financial aid and support services for minority groups in order to meet affirmative action goals. Richard Rosser, president of the National Association of Independent Colleges and Universities, has pointed out that between 1980 and 1990, financial aid at private institutions has doubled. In addition, from 1975 to 1985, the number of non-academic support staff at public and private colleges—including financial-aid counsellors, specialists handling the problems of minorities and the handicapped, and others—have grown by over 61 percent.[71]

The net effect of the private efforts by colleges to boost grants to minority students has been to force sharper tuition hikes, completing what amounts to a vicious circle. Tuition costs, which grew 42 percent faster than the rate of inflation from 1976 to 1987,[72] pressured the government to shift from grants to loans in order to provide aid to larger numbers of hard-pressed middle class, largely white parents. With the cut-back on grants, black and Hispanic enrollment dropped. Colleges, disturbed by these trends, increased private grant and support services for minorities, and did so, in part, by again raising tuitions. The raised tuitions then completed the circle by intensifying pressure on the federal government to continue the shift from grant to loan programs in order to accommodate middle-class voters who have much more political leverage on members of Congress and on the White House than do far poorer and less numerous blacks, Hispanics, and low-income whites.

---

Economic forces underlie the growing wage premium for college graduates, the halting of black and white wage convergence, and the growing intensity of competition for college tuition aid. At the same time, the combination of deregulation, intensified international competition, the deterioration of unions, the shift from manufacturing to services, and the growth of computer technology have interacted together to place a much higher market value on advanced skills, training, and education. This interaction has worked to the detriment of blacks and Hispanics— who are the least trained and educated groups in American society—just it would have worked to the disadvantage of the Irish, Italians, or Poles during earlier waves of immigration.

The intensification of competition from domestic deregulation and from international challenge is, furthermore, providing economic leverage to the conservative assault on affirmative action. Just as globalization has weakened the strength of American labor, creating a job market in which unionization is seen by many as contributing to economic inefficiency, intensified international competition is placing a severe strain on the premise that the achievement of racial equity in the work force justifies the use of measures that create a degree of short-term inefficiency—a basic premise behind much traditional affirmative action regulation.

Until 1989, the core of this premise was embodied in the 1971 Supreme Court decision, *Griggs v. Duke Power Co.*, written by Chief Justice Warren Burger. Until the Civil Rights Act took effect on July 1, 1965, the Duke

Power Company of North Carolina had discriminated against blacks by limiting their employment to the labor department, where the highest level of pay was lower than starting levels in all other departments. On July 2, 1965, in the wake of the act, Duke Power set up new rules for hiring and advancement. For new hires into all departments other than the labor department, and for upward transfers to better paying jobs in all departments, the company would henceforth require applicants to take the Wonderlic and Otis aptitude tests. In addition, a requirement that persons seeking promotion have a high school diploma was expanded to include upper-level positions in the labor department. The EEOC in an *amicus* brief filed with the Supreme Court provided evidence that when requirements for the aptitude tests were set at certain specified levels, 58 percent of whites had passed, but only 6 percent of blacks passed. In the case of the high school diploma requirement, 34 percent of all whites in North Carolina in 1960 had diplomas, while only 12 percent of blacks did.[73]

*Griggs v. Duke Power* was written during the final years of America's post-war boom, an era of steadily rising prosperity and a period characterized by relatively broad support for efforts to promote black equality. In *Griggs,* writing for a unanimous Court, Burger came down firmly on the side of racial equity. The Court found that while the requirement of a high school degree and of aptitude test scores may not have been intended to discriminate against blacks, these requirements operated "to disqualify Negroes at a substantially higher rate"—having an "adverse impact," the issue of intent aside. In order to justify such practices, the Court ruled that the employer must prove that the practice is driven by "business necessity," a rigorous legal standard, and one that places "on the employer the burden of showing that any given requirement must have a manifest relationship to the employment in question."[74]

The effect of *Griggs,* and of subsequent rulings, along with the parallel adoption of stringent regulations by the EEOC, was to severely restrict the use of ability tests for employment, unless scores were adjusted for differences between whites, blacks, Hispanics, and other groups (a scoring process termed "within group scoring," "within group adjustment," or "race-norming"). The importance of restricted ability testing for the employment prospects of blacks and Hispanics has been documented in two book-length studies, *Ability Testing* (1982), and *Fairness in Employment Testing* (1989), by the National Academy of Sciences.[75] On almost all ability tests studied, the National Academy found, blacks scored substantially below whites, and Hispanics scored somewhere between the two groups.[76] The National Academy found, for example, that on average, if hiring were done strictly on the basis of ability test scores, by rank order, an employer selecting from a pool of 100 whites and 100 blacks would chose only three blacks after picking twenty whites, or six blacks after thirty whites. These differences in test score results are reduced, but remain substantial, for blacks and whites of similar income and education.[77]

To meet the legal standards set by *Griggs,* employers using ability tests that produce an adverse impact on blacks or on other minorities have faced, since 1971, basically four alternatives: 1) to abandon test use; 2) to abandon strict top-down hiring on the basis of test scores and to establish a racially and ethnically mixed pool of applicants by ranking applicants within their race or ethnic group ("within group adjustment" or "race norming"); 3) to set a *minimum* test level score to qualify for employment, and to then hire with an eye to making sure that there is rough proportionality by race and ethnic group; or 4) to conduct extensive studies to legally demonstrate both the validity of the test for each specific job and the "business necessity" for the use of such tests for each job category.[78]

---

In the years since *Griggs,* a substantial assault has been mounted, based both on ideology and on economic claims, challenging the legitimacy of the primacy granted to the goal of racial equality—an assault mounted mainly, but not exclusively, by conservatives. The ideological attack—led in the 1980s by such Reagan appointees as William Bradford Reynolds and Edwin Meese (and a staple of Bush administration rhetoric in 1990 and 1991)—has focused on the charge that the consequence of *Griggs* and of the legally hard-to-prove "business necessity" standard has been to institutionalize reverse discrimination against whites. According to this view, employers become fearful of discrimination lawsuits and, in consequence, disregard merit and job qualification, hiring instead by quotas—by race and by ethnic group in direct proportion to the make-up of the local population. The hiring practices developed under *Griggs,* this argument goes, ignores "the whole issue of individual rights and individual fairness . . . there is no provision for the constitutional rights, the civil rights of whites"—an argument formulated in this instance by Linda S. Gottfredson of the University of Delaware, a frequently published critic of affirmative action, of race-norming, and of other practises evolving out of court and regulatory rulings.[79]

The issue of "fairness to whites" is an effective mobilizing device for the proponents of a conservative coalition, although liberals have countered with considerable success in the federal courts that the consequences of past *group* discrimination against blacks requires redistributional group-oriented remedies. Far more threatening to contemporary advocates of race-based affirmative action, however, are arguments that attempt to shift the issue to economic terrain.

With the active support of the U.S. Office of Personnel Management (OPM) during the Reagan years, a number of consultants and academics started to aggressively press two closely related, controversial arguments. The first argument was that contrary to the position favored by some minority advocates (that general aptitude tests are poor measures of individual performance), such tests do in fact have broad applicability and correlate, in varying degrees, with worker performance; this is referred to as the issue of "validity generalization"—that is, whether ability tests provide valid predictions—whether one can generalize accurately about job performance from test results. The National Academy of Sciences, attempting to serve as a neutral arbiter in the policy debate over ability testing, has disputed the scope of the claims of proponents of test validity, but has concluded that there is basic merit to the theory: "The general thesis of the theory of validity generalization, that validities established for some jobs are generalizable to some unexamined jobs, is accepted by the [Academy] committee . . ."; and "[T]here is evidence in the economics and industrial/organizational psychology research literature that people who score higher on ability tests tend to produce more and make fewer errors, as well as to complete training somewhat faster and stay on the job longer."[80]

Conservative critics of the *Griggs* decision have been quick to argue that validity generalization provides the legitimate basis for justifying the use of tests and of other mechanisms with adverse or disparate impact on blacks and Hispanics; justifying such use on the grounds that ability testing has legitimate benefits in terms of improved efficiency and productivity: "If adverse impact based on *Griggs* is the general presumption of employment discrimination, validity generalization becomes the general rebuttal. . . . In the long run, no matter how well intended, the trashing of objective employment standards in the pursuit of equal employment results—without any attention to the development of alternative solutions—may well have contributed to this nation's productivity decline. Given the implications that use of objective standards (such as measures of cognitive ability) have for improving both organizational as well as national workforce productivity, this issue is of considerably more importance than a mere philosophical debate," argued James C. Sharf, of the U.S. Office of Personnel Management (OPM), in 1988.[81]

While the ability testing/validity generalization debate may seem arcane, it in fact has the potential for enormous impact on future black and Hispanic hiring. If American hiring were to proceed strictly on the basis of current test score results, there would be very small numbers of blacks employed, for example, by the Birmingham police and fire departments. On a broader scale, strict top-down hiring on the basis of current test scores would nullify large-scale government-directed efforts to move substantial numbers of blacks, Hispanics, and other minorities up the income ladder—a movement often effected earlier in American history through patronage hiring, when municipal jobs and contracting were controlled by political machines and distributed to Irish, Italian, Polish, Jewish, and other immigrants and their families. Basing contemporary hiring on the current generation of ability tests (without race norming) would diminish the possibility of long-range, inter-generational advances in test scoring— insofar as test scores are tied to socioeconomic status—for the children and grandchildren of minority parents who might find secure, well-paying employment with the help of affirmative action.

At the same time, heightened economic pressures on American corporations created by intensified global competition and by domestic deregulation have made the inefficiencies of race-conscious remedies, even if "slight" as described by the National Academy, vulnerable to attack. In a 1986 memorandum to the NAACP Legal Defense Fund, the Lawyers' Committee for Civil Rights Under Law, and other civil rights groups, anticipating dangers in the ability testing debate, Marc Bendick, Jr., a labor economist who has served as a consultant to those organizations and to individual plaintiffs in discrimination cases, warned that the civil rights community could well be blindsided by developments in employment testing:

> These developments are occuring in a national political environment in which great emphasis is being placed on economic growth and U.S. international competitiveness. If proponents of this type of testing were to argue before congressional committees that validity generalization is an ingenious, innovative use of 21st Century information technology and that it is essential to the efficient management of the American labor force, they would receive a very sympathetic reception. Persons concerned with methodological limitations of the approach or with its potential inequitable impact on individuals or minority groups would find themselves out of touch with the realities of the modern economy.[82]

The globalization of economic competition amounts to a direct assault on liberal Democratic policies seeking to protect and enhance the status of minorities and organized labor. The situation has the ingredients necessary for a "confrontation between the civil rights community [which is] concerned about equity issues and the business community concerned about productivity issues," Bendick said in 1990.[83]

While Bendick's 1986 memorandum pointed to the possibility of congressional action, the issue is in fact being forced by the post-1988 conservative majority on the Supreme Court. The stringent "business necessity" standard set in 1971 in *Griggs,* the standard that severely restricted corporate use of ability tests, was radically revised in 1989 in *Wards Cove Packing Co. v. Atonio.* The 5–4 *Wards Cove* decision not only shifted much of the burden of proof in cases alleging effects-based employment discrimination from employer to employee, but, perhaps more importantly, it significantly modified the *Griggs* requirement that an employment practice resulting in disparate impact on minorities meet a legal standard of "business necessity." Instead, the Court in *Wards Cove* determined that hiring practices must now meet a much lower legal threshhold standard of "business justification"—subject only to "reasoned review"; finding that "there is no requirement that the challenged practice be 'essential' or 'indispensable' to the employer's business."[84]

*Wards Cove* together with *City of Richmond v. J.A. Croson Co.*—a 1989 decision imposing stringent requirements on cities and states setting up minority contracting set-aside programs—represent major policy shifts in direction by the Supreme Court in terms of the application of civil rights remedies. The combination of two forces—1) a conservative ideology justifying opposition to redistributional civil rights remedies with arguments built around 'reverse discrimination'; and 2) conservative, market-oriented economic theory buttressed by the intensifying demands of global competition—have together helped to create a climate that has led to the transformation of the Supreme Court into an adversary of the traditional civil rights community. In contrast to the Burger and Warren courts, the Supreme Court as reshaped by Reagan has, under the leadership of Chief Justice Rehnquist, moved away from its earlier position of sympathy with minority litigants—minority litigants who allege that hiring, promotion, and contracting decisions favoring whites have never in reality been uniformly made on objective standards of merit, and have always involved a sizable component of favoritism and privilege.[85] The post-Reagan Court, resistant to this position and finding little justification in government protection of minorities from competition, has moved decisively toward the side of increased efficiency in the ongoing struggle in American democracy between efficiency and equity.

# 12

# The Stakes

O VER the past generation, race has fueled the ascendancy of the presidential wing of the Republican party and has blunted Democratic efforts to revive a majority coalition. While there are some indications, at the start of the 1990s, of efforts to counteract the virulence of race as an issue in domestic politics, race remains a powerful force structuring the political debate, the two parties, and the values separating liberalism from conservatism.

With considerable success George Bush, during his first two years in office, eliminated the marked anti-black tenor that had characterized the Reagan administration. During the same period, abandoning his "no new taxes" pledge, Bush defused some of the polarizing strength of the issue of taxes—the issue that, when linked to race, had created deep divisions between taxpayers and tax recipients; divisions critical to the sustaining of a conservative presidential majority.

On the Democratic side of the aisle, Douglas Wilder of Virginia, in November 1989, established that a black man could win the governorship of a southern state—a state where twenty-five years before, segregation had operated under the sanction of law. In 1989, Ronald Brown became the first black chairman of the Democratic National Committee, and black Democrats won mayoral contests in five majority-white cities: New York, Cleveland, New Haven, Seattle, and Durham, North Carolina. In 1990, Harvey Gantt, a black former mayor of Charlotte, North Carolina, won 47.5 percent of the vote in a Senate race against Jesse Helms. The 1990 congressional budget deliberations, Bush's insistent advocacy of reductions in the capital gains tax, and the 1990 midterm elections provided the Democratic party with the opportunity to revive issues of tax fairness, and to reinforce the image of the GOP as the party of the rich.

These trends represent only cracks in a dam, however, that has for over twenty years blocked prospects for a constructive engagement of the political parties on the issues of race, poverty, bifurcating incomes, employment policy, and educational reform. There is, at this writing, the tentative outline of a shift in the partisan debate—a shift towards productive rather than destructive competition for solutions to the dilemmas of race—but the pressures on both sides to maintain an inflexible, unyielding conflict are intense. In every 1990 election in which Republicans made race a major factor, through the issue of quotas or through campaign advertising linking the Democratic candidate to Jesse Jackson, the Republican won: in the Helms-Gantt Senate contest; in the Feinstein-Wilson California gubernatorial race; in the Hubbard-Hunt Alabama gubernatorial race, and in the Hightower-Perry election for Texas Secretary of Agriculture. These successes reinforce the attractiveness of such tactics.

A shift to a more constructive political competition would require a wrenching alteration of habit, strategy, and worldview by all the participants, at the same time that dominant pressures are working against such progress. These dominant pressures, many of which have been addressed in earlier chapters, fall into a number of categories which include:

• *Demographic and economic forces.* These are forces that work to encourage the maintenance of two racially separate universes—or, at the least, that function to encourage a lack of common ground. The most important demographic force is the continuing suburbanization of the nation, which, for an overwhelmingly white majority of the electorate, is securing a separate governmental base from which to provide carefully targeted public services—a base that is isolated from heavily poor, black, and Hispanic central cities.

Among the most important economic forces functioning to the disadvantage of blacks is the college wage premium (the generally higher wages paid to college graduates), which works, in tandem with declining black college entry and completion, to slow, if not to halt, what had been a steady trend since 1965 toward black-white wage equality.

An additional force deriving from both economic and demographic factors is the crisis in urban education, as preponderantly black and Hispanic school systems are qualitatively less good than those in suburbia. Not only is the spread between student test scores stark, but the teaching of fundamental skills in the two systems is carried out according to vastly different standards.

• *Ideological and substantive conflict.* As measured by public opinion surveys, there is a substantial ideological divide between whites and blacks on the role and responsibility of government. This divide, in turn, is based to a degree on real differences in the economic structures of the white and black communities. In terms of developing biracial coalitions, these differences in point of view present significant roadblocks.

A decisive majority (64–36 percent) of blacks believe that it is the responsibility of the federal government to guarantee a job and a good standard of living,[1] while an even stronger majority (66–34 percent) of whites believe that government should let individuals get ahead on their own. Through most of the 1980s, whites were evenly split on whether government should increase spending for improved services, while blacks were decisively in favor by margins as high as 77–23 percent.[2] These differences of opinion reflect substantive differences in the white and black relationship to government; differences that remain strong even when whites and blacks of the same income and education are compared. Not only are blacks far more dependent on government programs serving the poor, but those blacks who have made it into professional and managerial ranks are twice as likely as their white counterparts to work for the city, state, or federal government. Both as a source of jobs and as a powerful engine for social change, government for blacks has been an agent of transformation, development, and advancement. Finally, differences of opinion between the races on the role of activist government reach an extreme on the issue of racial preferences in hiring, minority set-asides, and in college scholarship awards and admissions policies.

• *The underclass and the values debate.* First, the expansion of the underclass stands as testimony to the failure of larger political and economic processes, and as painful testimony to the shortcomings of liberal initiatives. Second, the underclass is functioning to reinforce racial stereotypes and to justify those who would stall or roll back integration. Third, and perhaps most important, the underclass has come to epitomize one side of the values debate that now shapes much of the country's political competition.

In part because of the underclass, the endorsement of so-called traditional values has taken on a racial cast. In rough terms, the current values debate can be described as a conflict between 1) "traditional" values oriented towards commitments and responsibilities that override individual rights; and 2) a competing set of values oriented toward the protection of often previously unrecognized individual and/or minority rights.

On a level essentially ignored by liberal elites—but a level, nonetheless, of stark reality to key voters—the values debate has become conflated with racial politics. Among Democrats and liberals, the stigmatization—

that is, the discrediting—of racism in the 1960s had the unintended, detrimental, and paradoxical consequence of stigmatizing the allegiance of many voters to a whole range of fundamental moral values. In the late 1960s and early 1970s, the raising of the "traditional values" banner over such issues as law and order, the family, sexual conduct, joblessness, welfare fraud, and patriotism was seen by liberals, and by blacks—with some accuracy—as an appeal to racist, narrow-minded, or xenophobic instincts, an appeal designed to marshal support for reactionary social policies. The conflation by the political right of values issues with attempts to resist racial integration, with attempts to exclude women from public life, and with attempts to discredit the expansion of constitutional rights to disadvantaged minorities, fueled an often bitter resistance by the left and by blacks to the whole package of traditional values.

The result was that liberal Democrats often barred from consideration what are in fact legitimate issues for political discourse; issues of fundamental social and moral concern that must be forthrightly addressed by any national candidate or party. This stigmatization as "racist" or as "in bad faith" of open discussion of value-charged matters—ranging from crime to sexual responsibility to welfare dependency to drug abuse to non-participation in the labor force to standards of social obligation—has for more than two decades created a *values barrier* between Democratic liberals and much of the electorate at large.

Even as factions within the Democratic party struggle to address perceived gaps in earlier social welfare legislation (for example, through the Civil Rights Act of 1990, vetoed by Bush in the fall of 1990 and revived again in 1991), the weak public credibility of the national party on values issues remains a major political liability, with the public far more prepared to entrust such matters to Republicans. Republicans, who have only token support from blacks, and relatively little support from other groups suffering from discrimination, are unencumbered by fear of contamination by the label of "racism" and need not restrict their advocacy of issues and ideas oriented toward traditional values.

• *The South.* Throughout the past decade, the South has been on the cutting edge of national politics, and in the South, race has increasingly become the defining characteristic of partisanship. While the South has produced more examples of biracial coalition than any other region, the general thrust in the South is a steady movement toward a politics of black and white. The Republican party, especially for the younger voters of the region, is becoming the political party of the white South. In some of the deep southern states, in turn, blacks are steadily moving toward majority status in Democratic primaries, and very few whites are prepared to be part of a coalition in which they are a minority. ABC election-day exit polls in 1988 showed that young, ages 18–29, white voters lined up with the Republican party over the Democratic party by a margin of 56 to 30 percent, with the remaining 14 percent describing themselves as independents. Blacks, young and old, describe themselves as Democratic by a margin of 88 to 6 percent. Looked at another way, among young Mississippi Democrats between the ages of 18 and 29, 62 percent were black and 38 percent were white. Vitually all Republicans in Mississippi were white.[3] These kinds of divisions are an open invitation to those seeking to build a political majority on the basis of racial polarization.

• *The power of race to rupture an economically based populism.* The continued success of those using race to build top-down coalitions dominated by the affluent—a success that dates back to the late nineteenth century in the South—has created a compelling incentive to maintain race as a divisive issue in national politics. In South Carolina, the home of Lee Atwater and of Strom Thurmond—and the state that kept the flame of conservatism alive for Barry Goldwater—race historically served as the anchor for the planter, banking, and textile elite. "When the going gets rough, when a glimmer of informed political self-interest begins to well up from the masses, the issue of white supremacy may be raised to whip them back into line," wrote V.O. Key in 1949.[4] On a national scale, race has served as such a powerful tool to divide an economically liberal coalition that it is very unlikely that the political right will give it up.

———

While such forces as those listed above work to keep race alive as a wedge issue, there are factors pushing in the other direction. The post-1982 economic recovery, the success of the conservative movement in stemming the rights revolution and in slowing the growth of welfare expenditures, and the troubling extremes over the past decade of affluence and poverty for both whites and blacks have substantially changed the political dynamic. The strategies and tactics of "conservative egalitarianism"—that doctrine concerned primarily with the "unfairness" to whites of remedial government action targeted to blacks—are no longer adequate to guarantee secure voting majorities.

Suburban voters, among others, are experiencing a revived sense of moral disquiet over economic, racial, and social inequities, inequities marring the distinctively American commitment to equality. This disquiet is reflected in polls showing increased support for such domestic initiatives as child care, catastrophic health care, and maternity-leave legislation. Median family income by 1989 had climbed back to the earlier high levels of 1972 and 1973,[5] liberating some of the social humanitarianism which had been crushed by the erosion of family income in the late 1970s and early 1980s.

Nowhere have these trends been better understood than in the offices of top-drawer Republican operatives—party strategists who are aware of both the threat and the opportunity inherent in the changing outlook of the electorate. This recognition was reflected in the stress by the 1988 Bush campaign on "a kinder and gentler" America, in the Republican call for a renewed volunteerism, in the GOP support for federal child care, education, and environmentalism, in renewed relations between the Bush administration and civil rights leaders, in the invitations to officers of gay and lesbian organizations to join in White House bill-signing ceremonies, in Bush's strong endorsement of the Americans with Disabilities Act (1990) (greatly expanding legal protections for the disabled), and in the efforts of the Republican National Committee to build GOP support among middle-class blacks.

The recognition of the new dynamic of domestic politics was most articulately expressed by Republican Representative Vin Weber of Minnesota, one of the architects of contemporary conservatism:

> Our political problem [in failing to achieve a full-scale realignment] is not just in appealing to poor voters. We're also hurt because this country has a political conscience. Americans of all income levels think government should address the problems of the poor. The country now thinks that the government will be indifferent, if not hostile, to the problems of the poor if conservatives are given control. . . . Our major mistake has been to focus only on *wedge* issues against the Democrats, without also creating *magnet* issues that would attract the public.[6]

Insofar as the tactical "leftward" or accommodationist shifts of the GOP represent a substantial long-term commitment to compete for the support of traditionally Democratic black, Hispanic, or other minority voters, nothing could be better for the nation's social and political health.

If such a contest offers the GOP the potential to further debilitate a weakened Democratic party, the competition could force Democratic ideological and intellectual growth. Such a Republican challenge could lead as well to the purging of a corrupting dependency among Democrats on incumbency and on guaranteed block voting support, two of the factors that have contributed to the development within the Democratic party of a monopolistic, complacent mentality.

———

The national Democratic party enters the fray tired, buckling at the knees after five defeats in six rounds; its defenses down, gasping for a second wind. The preponderance of evidence suggests that twenty-five years after passage of major civil rights legislation—legislation crowning a movement of such simple justice and revolutionay moral coherence that by 1964 it had brought new life to the oldest political party in the world— the Democratic party *as it is now constituted* is in danger of losing its stature as a major competitor in national politics.

The Democratic party faces a demographic hurdle, a vitality hurdle, and the values hurdle. Each of these hurdles appears tougher to surmount than the barriers facing the GOP: barriers such as the remnants of an entrenched racism, ideological and financial constituencies hostile to inclusive strategies, and the strong—and perhaps decisive—incentives to maintain the strategic status quo.

At stake in what may seem to be a largely irrelevant battle between two increasingly irrelevant political parties is in fact a contest to establish two very different governing majorities for the country. The Democrats remain a bottom-heavy coalition, and the Republicans a top-heavy coalition. Because of the strong consensus underlying American politics, because of the relatively confined ideological range—socialists and pure-market libertarians falling outside the realm of working politics—the coalitional structure of the governing majority determines direction and thrust—the tilt—of government policy.

The Republican coalition, when in control of the agenda, inherently tilts government largess, favor, and incentive toward those in the top half of the income distribution; the Democratic coalition, *when effective,* tilts the same set of government rewards and benefits towards those in the bottom half. While this tilting is a matter of degree, not of extremes, the range of outcomes for individuals and for entire classes can have extraordinary impact. Witness the decline in the poverty rate from 18.1 percent to 9.7 percent in the Democratic 1960s,[7] and witness the huge increase (from $213,675 in 1980 to $399,697 in 1990, both in 1990 dollars)[8] in family income for those in the top 1 percent of the distribution in the Republican 1980s. Forces other than domestic politics contributed to these changes, but the political system in each of these periods actively encouraged and nurtured these very different economic outcomes.

In the high-stakes struggle by the two parties to establish governing majorities, both Republicans and Democrats face sizable obstacles, some internally caused, others developing externally. For the national Democrats, it is the "values barrier" that has proven to be most insurmountable.

This barrier evolved, in complex and ironic ways, from one of the grand struggles of the twentieth century; a struggle between so-called traditional values and a competing set of insurgent values. "Traditional" values have generally been seen as revolving around committments to a larger (if exclusive) community—to the family, to parental responsibility, to country, to the work ethic, to sexual restraint, to self-control, to rules, duty, authority, and to a stable social order. A competing or insurgent set of values—values that have been the focus of the rights revolution and of the civil rights movement—has been largely concerned with freedom from confinement, from hierarchy, from authority, from stricture, from repression, from rigid rulemaking, and *from* the status quo. Insofar as the post-war Democratic party has been geared towards the liberation of disenfranchised minorities, and towards an assault on hierarchy, on embedded privilege, and on the power of the strong over the weak—the party has allied itself with insurgent rather than with traditional values.

It is a central tragedy of liberalism that its commitment to oppose racism, prejudice, and oppression—and its commitment to challenge the power of the few to impose economic injustice on the many—has carried within it some of the seeds of its own debilitation. As the goal of liberalism became to secure rights for minorities—often through redistributive mechanisms—the losers, and those who felt themselves likely to lose, began to outnumber the winners. Furthermore, those who saw themselves as losers in this redistributive struggle included a disproportionate percentage of just those voters whose participation is most necessary to a liberal *economic* coalition.

As proponents of the new liberal agenda became defensive, and as the goals of liberalism came to be seen as reallocating old, rather than generating new, resources, the liberal agenda itself became integral to the larger values conflict.

The values problem, standing between the national Democratic party and many of its own former constituents, has helped to force the Democratic party to increased dependence on special interests for the maintenance of its congressional majority. Insofar as key voters feel that their cherished beliefs and practices have been routed, the values barrier has been a major factor contributing to the fracturing of once deeply felt loyalty to a liberal economic agenda.

Without the resource of plurality voter loyalty, Democratic members of the House of Representatives, the seemingly unshakable bastion of Democratic power in Washington, have been forced to turn increasingly to an essentially corrupt system of campaign finance, to excessive reliance on the perquisites of incumbency, and to the gerrymandering of districts in order to thwart continuing demographic and ideological shifts favoring their opponents.

The excessive Democratic reliance for political control on special interests in fact extends beyond Congress to a second party stronghold, the nation's major cities. Public direction of essential services—most importantly, the public school system—has been lost in varying degrees to institutionalized bureaucracies. Within urban school systems faced with declining tax bases and lessened federal support, associations and unions representing teachers, janitors, principals, administrators, clerical staff, and security guards have become politically influential in protecting their own tenure, while carefully restricting their responsibility to the larger goal—of producing well-educated students.

Democratic vulnerability on this terrain is perhaps no better reflected than in the election in recent years of a black Republican school board president and a black Republican city councilman in Detroit—possibly the most Democratic city in the nation, and a city with one of the worst school systems and the worst delivery of public services. Both Republicans were elected on platforms promising to break through bureaucratic ossification and to revive competitive market forces—through parental choice in school assignment, through private alternatives to public services, and through the transfer of power and responsibility from administrators downtown to principals and teachers in the trenches.

————

Under seige, the national Democratic party has, to a large degree, lost its creative strength. Alienated from the general electorate by racial polarization and by a values barrier, and deeply enmeshed in a network of special interests, the national party has faltered repeatedly over the past twenty-five years in its efforts to develop strategies and policies successful in winning back majority support.

In decline, the party has become the forum for internal contests between a range of factions losing national power—principally trade unions, blacks, and reform liberals—rather than becoming the arena for the mobilization of a general election majority. The party has been forced to abandon mid-term "issue" conventions as these gatherings became war zones for interest groups instead of forums for successful political innovation or for the generation of politically marketable ideas. The core "issues" of Democratic conventions are no longer issues at all, but battles over rules. These rules fights are essentially factional struggles—competitions to use the timing and the delegate selection rules of primaries and caucuses in order to gain advantage in the presidential nomination process; at their core, these fights in 1984 and in 1988 were being waged over how much leverage a black candidate, Jesse Jackson, would carry into the convention.

Attempts to develop moderate-to-liberal policy positions and strategies have emanated from organizations such as the Democratic Leadership Council (DLC), Common Cause, and from environmental organizations, all of which have repeatedly operated as adversarial critics of the party, rather than as partners with it. In contrast, Republican gatherings, from the biannual meetings of the Republican National Comittee, to sessions of the Southern Republican Leadership Conference, to seminars conducted by GOPAC (a conservative Republican party group), consistently include attempts to formulate politically salable policy: policy voters will buy, policy voters can be persuaded of, or policy voters can be led towards. Such Republican-leaning groups as the Heritage Foundation and the Free Congress Foundation work in constant alliance and consultation with party strategists and with congressional Republican leaders.

The danger for the Democratic party is that its obligations to institutionalized special interests at the national level, and to institutionalized bureaucracies at the local level, have locked the party into an alliance with the forces of reaction—with interests and bureaucracies conducting largely futile efforts to resist, among other things, the consequences of international economic change. Already numb from assault on their right in presidential elections, the Democratic party could be outflanked by a nascent conservative reform movement seeking to subsume the issues of the left.

While the Bush administration has worked to further undermine Democratic liberalism through accommodation, the more ideologically committed leaders of the political right have been developing policy strategies designed, in effect, to encircle and choke off Democratic liberalism. It is not at all clear that the Republican party and the conservative movement are equipped to conduct such a high-wire ideological maneuver. The GOP does, however, retain the combative and strategic vigor lacking to a wounded Democratic party, a consciousness of the necessity to at least attempt to move past an anti-government ethic towards a political philosophy that the public will entrust with control of the central mechanisms of federal, state, and local government.

———

There is within conservatism a compelling drive to achieve what amounts to a *forced realignment*. After chipping away at the margins of the Democratic coalition, the central thrust of this drive is to go after the heart of the Democratic party: its claim to be the party of reform, its claim to be the party of the working man, of Joe Six-Pack, of the average family, of the middle-of-the-road, middle-income wage earner; and its claim to be the party of those down on their luck, the downtrodden, the urban poor, and the discriminated-against.

The conservative Republican strategy for a forced realignment is threefold. The first aspect is to restore for the GOP the reform credibility that was lost in Watergate, to attack (via congressional "ethics" probes such as those targeted against Jim Wright or Barney Frank) the diminishing Democratic advantage as the party of clean government and of official probity, an advantage won during the calamitous Nixon years.

The second aspect of GOP strategy is to chop away at the Democratic advantage as the party effective in addressing the problems of minorities and of the poor. The goal is to restore at least partial credibility to the GOP as a party of humanitarian concern—a Republican credibility that, while always provisional for most middle and lower-income voters, was eroded substantially during the Reagan years.

The third aspect of the GOP strategy is itself double-pronged. GOP strategists hope to drive home to the public a portrayal of the Democratic party as a party of losers, a party doing active (if unintended) harm to its own constituents by encouraging spurious values and by adhering to outmoded paradigms and obsolete economic models. This is an attempt to portray the Democratic party as committed to outdated notions of class antagonism on the one hand (the reactionary "politics of envy"), and as overly "permissive" towards aberrant and counter-productive behavior, on the other. Republican strategists intend in addition (the second prong) to paint the Democratic party as lacking a firm grip on the kinds of hard-nosed military, economic, and political expertise that will be necessary to a future of increased productivity and of technological innovation—productivity without which America's continued leadership in a competitive high-stakes global economy will surely be doomed.

The cumulative Republican goal, in sum, is to portray the Democratic party as the institution insulating from challenge those parts of society that are not performing up to high standards; to portray Democrats as sheltering, not only a backsliding "bottom of the ladder," but as protecting a moribund Washington order dominated by lobbyists and PACs, focused on diverting government revenues towards self-serving and unproductive ends. Conservative Republican strategists are attempting to cast the Democratic party as protecting from public judgement an array of slipshod workers and obstructionist unions; as allowing basic services like public education to be dominated by alliances of incompetent teachers and lazy bureaucrats feeding at the public trough. GOP strategists hope to craft an image of their entrenched Democratic rivals as embroiled in an unholy alliance of insider lobbyists, functionaries, laggards, and losers inextricably wedded to the stifling of initiative, to expanding welfare benefits, to undermining traditional morality, to subverting the family, to weakening the military, and to fatally inflating an already overgrown centralized and omniverous state.

The Republican party and the conservative movement are seeking, in effect, to abruptly reverse field on the Democrats' issues. Increasingly secure in its suburban base, interested in expanding beyond an agenda of race, rights, and taxes, the GOP is demonstrating a growing willingness to attack on what have been the most reliable Democratic issues: the problems of economic justice and poverty, and, more narrowly, the topic of congressional reform.

The political right may have considerable difficulty in establishing its credibility among voters on these issues, but there is no question of Democratic vulnerability to serious challenge.[9]

As recently as the mid-1970s, the Democratic party was able to portray itself as the party of political reform, battling a GOP dominated by monied interests. Now, Democrats in the House of Representatives are more dependent on institutionalized special interest groups than their Republican adversaries. In 1988, the majority, 51.5 percent, of the campaign contributions received by Democratic incumbent House members running for re-election was from political action committees (PACs), while the percentage of support from individual donors steadily declined, from 44.8 percent in 1984 to 39.5 percent in 1988. Republican House incumbents, in contrast, received 52.5 percent of their financial support from individuals in 1988, and 39.6 percent from PACs, in a pattern the mirror image of the Democrats'.[10] In addition, not only did labor PACs follow tradition by giving far more to House Democratic incumbents ($16.7 million) than to Republican incumbents ($1.9 million), but corporate PACs—the 1988 version of "monied interests"—gave more money to Democratic House incumbents in 1988, $15.8 million, than to their GOP counterparts, $13.5 million.[11] While helpful to incumbents in the short term, this kind of contribution pattern weakens any claim the Democratic party may make of providing popular representation.

The resignations under duress in 1989 of Democratic House Speaker Jim Wright of Texas and Democratic House majority whip Tony Coelho of California—both of whom were principals in negotiations in behalf of special interests, particularly savings and loan interests—demonstrated the vulnerability of a party dependent on fundamentally anti-democratic manipulations of the system in order to survive, a party with a severely damaged public mandate.

On the terrain of Congressional reform, House Democrats have, furthermore, been at every juncture fused to a system of incumbency protection that is coming under increasing attack from a bipartisan lineup of political observers and organizations—from David Broder in the *Washington Post* to Common Cause. These experts argue that, with an incumbent return rate in excess of 98 percent, democratic competition in congressional elections has been dangerously attenuated.

The system of incumbency protection under attack stems, to a large degree, from developments that unfolded in the first half of the 1970s, a time during which the presidential wing of the Democratic party (having nominated George McGovern in 1972) was under assault from the right. Democratic House members set out in response to protect and to insulate themselves—under the aegis of reform—from national trends.

The structure of the House was subsequently in many respects transformed into a network of miniature political machines, as a significant share of House power, held by 22 standing committee chairmen, was transferred to a proliferation of 151 subcommittees. These subcommittees, in turn, became Democratic fundraising bases, targeting very specific, and highly compliant, segments of the private sector. Subcommittee titles, in many cases, defined their fundraising constituencies: the Subcommittee on Cotton, Rice and Sugar; the Subcommittee on Financial Institutions Supervision, Regulation and Insurance; Subcommittee on Surface Transportation, etc.

Throughout the 1970s, the Democratic Congress steadily insulated itself from challenge: In 1974, under the rubric of reform, Congress passed legislation sanctioning the formation of PACs by the private sector, so that a whole system of special interest campaign financing was legalized and institutionalized. From 1967 to 1979, the number of staffers serving House members was increased from 4,055 to 7,067; and from 1970 to 1977, the number of staffers assigned to congressional district offices doubled, from 1,035 to 2,058. The number of House committee staffers shot up from 702 in 1970, to 1,844 in 1978. Mail costs for the House and Senate rose from $11.2 million in 1971, to $48.9 million in 1978.[12]

A clear danger of this House-constructed edifice of incumbent protection is that it inherently places Democrats in a defensive position in any reform debate. The party has lost possession of the moral high ground. Republican members of the House, who were once the major defenders of the PAC system—on the assumption, quickly proven false, that business and trade association PACs would prove to be key allies in a GOP foray— are now increasingly free to assume the role of a reform vanguard.

"We can be, if you will excuse me, a little bit hypocritical. What do I mean by that? I mean: take some positions that I think are really good government positions, which, if they came about, would probably make a better place to live. And [we can] require the Democrats to defend [the opposite] position. . . . Wrap yourself in the flag. Let's talk about doing some things that may appear radical, but don't have a chance to pass given the Democrats control anyway, but let them justify why we are doing it," Republican Representative Bill Thomas of California told his GOP colleagues in early 1989. "It's an absolute golden opportunity for Republicans to advocate any number of campaign reforms. . . . You want to get rid of PACs? Great. . . . If newsletters are such a good thing, there are more Democrats, they send out more. . . . Let's get rid of them."[13]

The degree to which basic reforms can now come home to haunt the Democratic party is reflected in the current impact of one of the earliest reforms to make it through the mill of the 101st Congress (1989): a provision prohibiting retiring members of the House from converting money in their campaign chests to personal use, after Janurary, 1993. The elimination of this special exemption creates a strong incentive for members of the House with large campaign treasuries to retire. There were 83 members who qualified and who had at least $200,000 at the start of 1990. Of this group, 60, or 72 percent, are Democrats. Encouraging these members to retire before the 1992 election meshes perfectly with Republican goals for two reasons: not only are a majority of those who are eligible Democrats, but also, many of these older Democrats represent conservative districts that could well turn Republican once they open up.

———

While Republican members of the House are free to adopt aggressive, if sometimes hypocritical, stands on congressional reform, the GOP is in a position to whipsaw the Democratic party by pressing for the most rigorous possible enforcement of another Democratic-initiated reform: the Voting Rights Act of 1965. This measure had, by 1990, become a key political weapon for the Republican party, offering not only the possibility of larger numbers of secure Republican districts, but also the chance to split white and black Democrats into warring camps.

A major piece of civil rights legislation originally intended to guarantee voting rights to blacks, the Voting Rights Act was expanded by congressional amendment and by court ruling to become a powerful tool for guaranteeing minority representation wherever possible. Under amendments to the act passed in 1982, as interpreted by the Supreme Court in 1986 *(Thornburgh v. Gingles)*, blacks and other minorities bringing suit against districting plans governing elections from school boards to congressional seats in communities where there is racial bloc voting, do not need to prove discriminatory intent on the part of those who drew up such districts. Instead, those bringing suit need to prove only that it is possible to create a majority black or Hispanic district and that officials failed to do so.[14]

The Republican party, which has itself been one of the major beneficiaries of racial bloc voting in the South and elsewhere—and which as recently as 1986 sought to improve GOP chances by forcing the purging of black voter rolls in Louisiana and in other states—by 1990 was seeking to become the de facto ally of black and Hispanic plaintiffs in voting rights suits in connection with legislative and congressional redistricting. This is a strategy clearly designed to force creation of as many majority black and majority Hispanic districts as possible, and, as a corollary, as many solidly white—and consequently Republican—districts at the same time.

The Republican National Committee in late 1989 set up a tax-exempt foundation called Fairness For The 90s to finance the transfer of technical expertise to black and Hispanic organizations. The foundation raised money from a network of individuals and organizations whose interests before 1990 had been in channeling cash to the conservative movement, not to black voter enfranchisement. The Lynde and Harry Bradley Foundation—which in 1989 donated $256,000 to the Heritage Foundation and $90,000 to the research work of Charles Murray, author of *Losing Ground*—gave $100,000 in 1990 to finance the transfer of Voting Rights Act computer software to black and Hispanic organizations. Similarly, the Fred L. Lennon Foundation—which in 1989 gave $46,000 to Phyllis Schlafly's Eagle Forum, and $15,000 to the anti-union National Right to Work Legal Defense Fund—in 1990 gave $25,000 to Fairness For The 90s. By 1990, the GOP saw the Voting Rights Act as a key tool to segregate black and Hispanic voters into separate districts, increasing the likelihood that Republicans would win elections in adjoining and nearby white districts.

The Republican Voting Rights Act strategy to divide white from black Democrats coincides with a larger and continuing problem facing the Democratic party. In heavily black states like Mississippi, Alabama, Georgia, and South Carolina, blacks have recently been moving steadily toward majority status among those who identify themselves as Democrats. In Mississippi, a decisive majority of all voters under the age of 45 identifying themselves as Democrats are black. Older Democrats in the South remain majority white by margins of 69–31 percent among those 45 to 59 years old, and by 76–24 percent among those Democrats over 60—the very voters who are dying off.[15]

These trends present a continuing dilemma for Democrats, as struggles for party control become increasingly defined in terms of race. "For a long time now, Democrats generally in the South have been walking a fairly narrow line between using black support as an advantage and letting blacks take over and the Democratic Party becoming a black party. Blacks, if they control the Democratic Party, will make it lose its viability. It will not be a viable party," Donald Fowler, former chairman of the South Carolina Democratic party said in an interview in 1985, describing the party's difficulties. "Blacks understandably are restless in the Democratic Party because they look at their level of loyalty and say 'Damn, if anybody deserves anything, we do.' And in normal political terms, that's true. But the other side of it is that if we gave them everything they wanted, it would be a black party."[16] In 1990, the hemorrhaging of whites from the South Carolina Democratic party resulted in the Democratic guber-natorial nomination of maverick black state senator Theo Mitchell, who proceded to lose the general election to Republican governor Carroll Campbell by the landslide margin of 29 to 71 percent.

In Alabama in 1989, just the kind of battle anticipated by Fowler, took place when Joe Reed, chairman of the predominately black Alabama Democratic Conference, brought suit in federal court demanding 50 per-cent black control of the Alabama Democratic party. "Blacks are 50 per-cent of the party in Alabama," Reed argued, citing the pattern of racial voting in presidential elections: "Blacks didn't leave Jimmy Carter, they didn't leave McGovern, they didn't leave Dukakis. It was so-called white Democrats who left."[17]

———

Voting rights suits and assaults by the GOP on the Democrats under cover of congressional reform dovetail with a potentially serious—if at present marginal—challenge to liberalism. This is the nascent attempt of one faction within the Republican party to use conservative anti-poverty doctrines in order to pursue a Republican realignment; this "realignment-oriented" faction of the GOP seeks to discredit Democratic efforts to fight for social equality, and to convince voters instead of the superiority of market-based strategems for waging war on poverty and for creating eco-nomic justice. Such an attempt is designed not only to attack the problems of poverty, but perhaps more immediately to give a dimension of justice and "fairness" to a conservative party seeking to attract middle-class vot-ers. Among those leading this charge are hard-core members of the Re-publican right such as Department of Housing and Urban Development (HUD) secretary Jack Kemp, House minority whip Newt Gingrich, Congressman Vin Weber, White House Policy Planning aide James Pinkerton, and Free Congress Foundation president Paul Weyrich.[18]

The core strategy of this wing of the GOP is to replace the sustained assault on government that has characterized the right with a conservative reform movement that seeks to apply principles of market competition and public choice to social programs in general and to the problems of the poor specifically.

The clearest example of this brand of Republican thinking is the movement to force competition into the system of public education, a movement with varying degrees of bipartisan support, and an innovative if highly risky effort to break the record of poor performance in an essential public service. Other examples of social intervention espoused by Republicans include a major expansion of the earned income tax credit; the raising of the standard tax deduction to reward the working poor; child-care tax credits as opposed to expansion of government-run child-care programs; tenant management and control of public housing; the sale of public-housing units to tenants; the replacement of housing subsides with rent vouchers, negotiable in city or suburb; a substantial expansion of tax incentives for businesses locating in poor neighborhoods; and the privatization of such public services as garbage collection, automobile inspection, park maintenance, and prisons.

None of these proposals is inherently conservative, and some such proposals have in fact been initiated by Democrats in Congress and by local Democratic officials—with a willingness to commit large sums, in the case of tax breaks and rent vouchers, for example. Such proposals all assume, in addition, a strong *liberal* role for government in shaping and steering market forces, and in manipulating the tax code in order to direct incentives toward those on the bottom rungs—just as the 1981 tax bill directed incentives to those in the upper brackets. Insofar as factions within the GOP are willing to engage these issues, such engagement is part of a long range process of political *accommodation* that seeks to move the GOP away from its earlier, rigid opposition to government intervention, an opposition that has historically created invaluable openings for liberalism and for the Democratic party. Insofar as the right can accommodate to social pressures from the left, this faction of the GOP argues that it broadens its own opportunities to undermine the legitimacy of its liberal, activist opposition.

What the realignment-oriented wing of the conservative movement is attempting to do in its struggle to achieve a new electoral majority is to construct an ideologically coherent set of initiatives to demonstrate the applicability of conservative principles to large areas of public life. Ideological coherence is sought based on the conservative goal of introducing market forces into the public sector. These forces include the creation of competition in public services (through privatization and choice), and the conversion of the poor from passive recipients of government largess into consumers acting in their own self-interest, empowered by tax credits (for those who work), by rent vouchers (negotiable in all housing markets), and, taking a page from the FHA Democrats, vested in mainstream American values through homeownership.

In theory the goal is to encourage the introduction of legal markets to poor areas where there are now virtually none, and to provide the residents of such areas with a degree of leverage to influence, if not to control, their earnings, their consumption, and their lives.

In political terms, the new-found conservative compassion for the poor has the following goals:

• To establish that the Republican party and conservatism are not inherently adverse to government intervention in behalf of those in the bottom half of the income distribution; and that governments can activate market forces to work to the advantage of all income groups—to establish, in other words, that the GOP is not a party dedicated exclusively to the rich. "Helping those left behind and left out is not only a moral imperative for our nation, I am convinced it is also a winning—indeed decisive— political strategy for bringing impoverished communities and low income people and minorities into the ranks of the party of Lincoln," Jack Kemp argued to a gathering at the Heritage Foundation on June 6, 1990.[19]

• To force public attention toward the inadequacy of existing public services under Democratic governance, especially those services provided in major cities. Advocacy of school choice in this context is designed to demonstrate to voters of all income groups the qualitative difference between public schools and private and parochial schools, and to place the blame for those differences on the public-sector bureaucracies and unions now allied with the Democratic party.

• In this context, privatized garbage collection and prison operation become mechanisms through which to demonstrate to taxpayers the superior efficiencies and cost savings of market-oriented alternatives to government services. The goal is to force "confrontations between the poor and the welfare state that serves them so badly. These confrontations will help conservatives to build the coalitions needed to tip the political balance in favor of their proposals," according to Stuart Butler, director of Domestic Politics Studies at the Heritage Foundation.[20]

• To brand the Democratic party and its leaders as the defenders of government bureaucracies and as the adversaries of genuine help for the disadvantaged. Insofar as the low quality of government services can be driven home to voters, and insofar as Democratic officials are forced to defend those services, the goal is to establish a polarization very similar to the tax-payer versus tax-recipient polarization conservatives have already posited. The new polarization aims to pit the heavily Democratic providers of government services against the citizen-recipients of those services. This division turns, in theory, those seeking to preserve the status quo—city, state, and federal workers, teachers, administrators, public housing managers, social workers, welfare workers, and their unions—into the enemies of increasingly empowered urban voters who will demand the same level and quality of services provided in the suburbs.

• The ultimate goal of this conservative campaign is to persuade Americans that Democratic politicians behind an inefficient, recalcitrant bureaucratic state should be treated in the same way that consumers would treat the proprietors of a badly run business: "If any private business in America treated you [the voter] the way you routinely get treated by government, you would put them out of business," Newt Gingrich told GOP strategists on March 30, 1990.[21]

• To maintain the assault on a liberal, left-leaning elite establishment—in the right-populist tradition of Wallace and Reagan. In a 1990s version of themes developed by the Alabama governor in 1968 and in 1972, James Pinkerton, Bush's policy planning assistant, has argued that: "The Great Society has been a continuing, if well-intentioned, failure because it falsely assumes that experts, wise bureaucrats in league with university professors and politicians, can somehow administer supply and demand, prosperity and equality, from an office building far away."[22]

This conservative strategy is clearly not without substantial weaknesses. Just as with Pinkerton's liberal "experts, wise bureaucrats in league with university professors and politicians", almost all the Republican social service strategizing is done in "office building[s] far away" from the precincts of poverty. The reality is that the Republican party has virtually no one, nor any party structure, on the ground in the nation's major cities to mount a recruitment drive for a new "populist capitalism."

Except for Kemp and a tiny band of Republicans willing to occasionally cross the tracks into the nation's ghettos, the new Republican advocates of a conservative anti-poverty strategy are far more comfortable trading theories with each other over cocktails at conservative think-tank seminars or in tactical sessions at Washington's University Club. Doctrinaire conservatives in the decade since Reagan's inauguration have become as much a Washington elite as their liberal adversaries, if not more so. The anti-poverty rhetoric of many conservatives has a tinny, self-serving ring that will be hard to mute without a record of tangible achievement.

The credibility of conservative born-again concern for those in poverty is likely to be viewed with a degree of suspicion by significant numbers of voters, particularly if economic developments should expand the ranks of the poor and the jobless. Not only have conservatives traditionally used race to split and weaken the bottom half of the income distribution, and to promote the interests of the affluent, but the track record of conservatism in behalf of the poor over the past decade has been particularly weak. From 1980 to 1990, average family after-tax income grew by 15.7 percent, but for those in the bottom 30 percent of the income distribution—the poor—it fell. For the very poor—those in the bottom tenth of the income distribution—over the past ten years of Republican rule average income has fallen by 10.4 percent, from $4,791 to $4,295, in 1990 dollars.[23]

In terms of pursuing race-conscious, polarizing tactics, on the one hand, or a broad-based partisan realignment based on a "kinder, gentler" form of Republicanism, on the other, the 1990 election results did not resolve strategic issues for the GOP, providing instead contradictory information. Republican success in the North Carolina Senate race (Jesse Helms), and in the California and Alabama (Pete Wilson and Guy Hunt) gubernatorial contests, all suggest the effectiveness of campaign tactics that capitalize on racial polarization. Helms, Hunt, and Wilson all used race-freighted imagery and issues, including "quotas," Jesse Jackson, and busing. Conversely, two newly elected midwestern GOP governors, Illinois' James Edgar and Ohio's George Voinovich, specifically sought out black voters, and made careful efforts to accentuate their support of the 1990 civil rights bill (despite Bush's veto). Edgar and Voinovich demonstrated that, with some effort, a Republican can collect more than 20 percent of the black vote, enough, in a close contest, to mean victory.

———

The substantial shortcomings of the conservative record on fighting poverty—and the mixed record of the "realignment-oriented" wing of the GOP—do not preclude recognition of an issue that manifests itself at an entirely different level of American politics. Conservatives have grasped a central truth in the on-going struggle to address the issues of race and poverty that liberals have been reluctant to grapple with: that the enforced exclusion of the discriminated-against from markets accessible to other citizens in itself creates economic dysfunction. At the core of slavery and of legal segregation was the denial of both political rights and marketplace rights. Legal exclusion from market participation suppresses—and is designed to suppress—initiative, entrepreneurship, and competitive zeal in order to create a subjugated class.

While refusing to struggle with the considerable shortcomings and dangers of market-oriented ideologies, conservative thinkers have in fact grasped an important concept frequently brushed aside by liberals: the extent to which any welfare system—based on entitlement by failure—paradoxically rewards failure. For minorities, the welfare system replicates some of the most powerfully crippling effects of legal segregation. The dilemma for any public assistance program is that even as it relieves suffering, such a system unintentionally constructs pervasive disincentives to economic initiative, discouraging hard work, creative imagination, and productive enterprise.

Liberal thinkers—focused on the brutality of unbuffered markets and committed to sheltering the vulnerable from the penalties of competitive failure—have gone on to shortchange ideas propounded more or less exclusively over the past twenty-five years by conservatives. These ideas include the argument that protectionist systems, including the system of public welfare, have the unwanted consequence of excluding many of their potentially able beneficiaries from a learning process—from the feedback inherent in failing or succeeding in competition—and from the possibilities for improved skills, for more effective participation, and for greater economic well-being that such learning can encourage. A small number of Democratic candidates have recently attempted to attack traditional party positions favoring welfare spending—just as some Democrats in Congress have begun to support some form of work requirement in conjunction with public assistance grants—but for key voters, the link of the Democratic party to "welfarism" severely weakens the party's overall credibility.

In modern economies, exclusion from the marketplace carries an increasingly heavy price. For liberals, the paradox has been that the welfare state not only serves and protects, but may help to create, reinforce, and expand an economically disadvantaged population, locking key sectors of the poor into virtually permanent under-employment or unemployment. The welfare system, even while defending its impoverished clientele, deprives some of those recipients of a flow of information about activities likely to produce negative economic and social consequences, on the one hand, or desired rewards, on the other. Insofar as liberals and civil rights activists have recently accepted workfare-type provisions as an element of welfare policy—and insofar as Democratic candidates (such as John Silber in Massachusetts in 1990) have begun to campaign against traditional forms of social service spending—conservatives have already gained ground in forcing some factions of the Democratic party to their point of view.[24]

Current conservative anti-poverty dogma—while neglecting the crucial issues of volatile markets, of widespread mental and physical illnesses and disabilities among the poor, of structural unemployment, of low wage scales, and of conservative opposition to publicly-funded contraception and abortion—parallels much earlier left-wing attacks on the welfare state. Newt Gingrich's polemics against a government welfare "bureaucracy that destroys people" echoes strikingly a radical critical tradition that includes such figures as Stokely Carmichael and Charles Hamilton, who wrote in 1967, in *Black Power: The Politics of Liberation in America*: "Many of the social welfare agencies—public and private—frequently pretend to offer 'uplift' services; in reality, they end up creating a system which dehumanizes the individual and perpetuates his dependency."[25]

------

In many respects, a central strength of American conservatism over the past two decades derives from its ability to reveal—and to deliberately exploit—the gulf between two contradictory currents of modern political life. This contradiction has been between the protectionist impulse within the liberal ethos—that aspect of liberalism committed to shielding the weak from suffering and misfortune—and the prized emphasis in the American tradition on self-reliance, entrepreneurial individualism, and hard work.

Conservatives benefit politically to the extent that they are able to divert public attention from the danger and instability of market forces (a diversion possible only in times of relative economic calm), and focus public attention instead on the circumstances under which the protectionist shield of liberalism becomes a system of retreat, providing asylum from the demands of competition and social adaptation—harboring those who fail or who are unable to commit themselves to the "traditional" virtues of responsibility, diligence, foresight, thrift, and self-restraint. A failure to pay sufficient attention to the tension between liberal protectionism and to the strong indigenous American emphasis on work and self-reliance touches voters as few other issues do, and has profound political consequences for liberalism and for the national Democratic party.

Some of these consequences have been partially captured in another context: in the responses to two seemingly similar questions in surveys conducted by the University of Michigan's National Election Studies (NES) just before, and again at the height of, the civil rights revolution. Although little attention was paid at the time, these poll results indicate the difficulties that face a liberal agenda that mixes race, rights, entitlements, and taxes.

In 1960, the NES asked respondents whether they agreed with the statement: "The government in Washington ought to see to it that everyone *who wants to work* can find a job." Four years later, in 1964, the wording of the statement was altered to read: "In general, some people feel that the government in Washington should see to it that *every person has a job and a good standard of living.* Others think the government should let each person get ahead on his own. Have you been interested enough in this to favor one side or the other?" [Emphasis added.]

The differences in the answers to the two versions of the question were striking, and provided an early clue to some of the political difficulties that would face Democratic liberalism as it evolved in the years following 1965. The following Table 12.1 shows the sharp difference in the response to the two phrasings of the question.

Clearly, a program or agenda using government to provide job opportunities to those seen as "wanting to work," that is to say, to those seen as abiding by the work ethic, had strong consensual backing among large numbers of Americans. The degree of support among respondents varied by income, status, employment, race, and partisanship; but if policy initiatives had been kept within the framework of the 1960 question—that is, if social welfare policy had been more clearly, publicly, and unmistakably aligned with *wanting* to work, Democratic liberalism would have remained far more competitive in the contest for voter approval, despite the considerable movement in public opinion over the past generation to the right.

Conversely, when policies and programs are defined in terms of the right of passive constituents to a government-provided "job and a good standard of living"—a phrase that in this context connotes to many respondents government help on demand—consensual political support evaporates. By 1986, an agenda involving government obligation to provide a job and a good standard of living no longer had majority support even among Democrats.

———

The debate on social policy over the past two decades has in large part been framed, by proponents, critics, and by the courts, as a yes-or-no, acceptance or rejection of programs and policies granting rights and entitlements. There has been little consistent public emphasis on accompanying responsibilities or on standards of reciprocal obligation. In political terms, such a fundamental omission from the social policy debate by liber-

TABLE 12.1.*

| | 1960 Version: Washington Ought to See to It That Everybody Who Wants to Work Can Find a Job. | 1964 Version: Washington Should See to It That Every Person Has a Job and a Good Standard of Living. | |
|---|---|---|---|
| | 1960 | 1964 | 1986 |
| All | +34 | −12 | −23 |
| Poor | +61 | +15 | +1 |
| Working class | +45 | −3 | −16 |
| Middle Class | +39 | −11 | −24 |
| Upper Middle | +18 | −30 | −37 |
| Rich | +14 | −42 | −51 |
| White | +30 | −21 | −32 |
| Black | +84 | +64 | +28 |
| Professional | +13 | −35 | −43 |
| White Collar | +21 | −32 | −28 |
| Blue Collar | +45 | +4 | −14 |
| Unskilled | +57 | +3 | +17 |
| Housewives | +41 | −10 | −9 |
| Democrats | +47 | +3 | −8 |
| Republicans | +10 | −40 | −48 |

*The figures are the *net* percentage of the group in favor (+) or opposed (−) to the policy, excluding those without an opinion.

SOURCE: Miller and Traugott, *American National Election Studies*, 179–80.

als has opened the door for conservatives to profit by focusing public attention on morality-laden "values" issues—issues running the gamut from the lack of labor-force participation in the ghetto, to sexual promiscuity, to drug abuse, to teen pregnancy,[26] to crime, and so on.

The polarization of voters around "those who work" versus "those who do not"—or in the terms of an earlier era, around the "deserving" versus the "undeserving" poor[27]—is a powerful *political* tool, even as it raises questions that have been slighted by the left. In conservative hands, such a polarization can work to the advantage of those seeking to discredit the claims of all the poor, including the low skilled working poor, and the disabled, and to the advantage of those seeking to create a top-down political coalition—a coalition encouraging and facilitating an upward redistribution of income to the already well-to-do, and operating against the interests of the least well-off members of the coalition.

The divisiveness of this political construct is recognized not only by conservatives, but also by blacks. Ron Walters, a black political scientist at Howard University, argues that the fundamental issue in the politics of race is: "Who is responsible for our condition? Once you draw the line on that, you draw the line on a lot of other race-value issues. Whites see blacks as generally responsible for their own situation, which means that whites refuse to take responsibility. Blacks see it differently. They believe there ought to be a continuing assumption of responsibility for their condition by the government. And therein lies a lot of the difference."[28] Walters's characterization of the sharply divergant views of whites and blacks finds substantial support in poll data.[29]

This racially-loaded confrontation over the issue of responsibility, both historic and contemporary, is perhaps best illustrated by representative quotes from two well-known political analysts, Roger Wilkins and Patrick Buchanan. Wilkins, a black professor of history at George Mason University, an assistant attorney general in the Johnson administration, a well-known commentator, and a former editorial writer for the *New York Times* and the *Washington Post*, argues:

> The issue isn't guilt. It's responsibility. Any fair reading of history will find that since the mid-seventeenth century, whites have opposed some blacks so completely as to disfigure their humanity. Too many whites point to the debased state of black culture and institutions as proof of the inferiority of the blacks they have mangled. [The logical implication] is simple: black people simply need to pull up their socks. That idea is wrong and must be resisted. . . . Like it or not, slavery, the damage from legalized oppression during the century that followed emancipation, and the racism that still infects the entire nation follow a direct line to ghetto life today.[30]

On the other side, Buchanan, an Irish Catholic, a ranking conservative strategist for both the Nixon and the Reagan administrations, and a widely followed political columnist and television commentator of the hard right, argues:

> Why did liberalism fail black America? Because it was built on a myth, the myth of the Kerner Commission, that the last great impediment to equality in America was 'white racism.' That myth was rooted in one of the oldest of self-delusions: It is because you are rich that I am poor. My problems are your

fault. You owe me! There was a time when white racism did indeed block black progress in America; but by the time of the Kerner Commission, ours was a nation committed to racial justice. The real root causes of the crisis in the underclass are twofold. First, the old character-forming, conscience-forming institutions, family, church and school, have collapsed under relentless secular assault; second, as the internal constraints on behavior were lost among the black poor, the external barriers—police, prosecutors, and courts—were systematically undermined. . . . What the black poor need more than anything today is a dose of the truth. Slums are the products of the people who live there. Dignity and respect are not handed out like food stamps; they are earned and won. . . . The first step to progress, for any group, lies in the admission that its failures are, by and large, its own fault, that success can come only through its own efforts, that, while the well-intentioned outsider may help, he or she is no substitute for personal sacrifice.[31]

When these are the lines that are drawn, reconciliation is extremely difficult. Whites are not going to take collective responsibility for the wrongs of past generations to the degree implicit in Wilkins's "fair reading of history." Nor are blacks going to submit to the moral hectoring of an arch-conservative political strategist for the Nixon and Reagan administrations.

———

Race will remain an exceptionally divisive force in politics as long as the debate is couched in covert language and in coded symbols—and as long as major participants fail to be explicit about their goals. Proponents of the civil rights revolution initially portrayed their movement as relatively cost-free, as one that would provide equality of opportunity for all Americans. In fact, to impose equality inevitably requires a redistribution of resources—from money to jobs to authority to status. The failure of elected Democratic members of the House and Senate to anticipate and to deal with both the necessity and inevitability of this redistribution had the effect of shifting to the federal courts the responsibility for fleshing out and giving specificity to the Civil Rights Act of 1964 and the Voting Rights Act of 1965. Working politicians absented themselves from the task of responsively and innovatively crafting, marketing, and shaping the enlarging civil rights agenda. House Democrats may well have made the tacit calculation that avoidance of these issues was essential to the maintenance of a Democratic congressional majority.[32]

The federal courts, in turn—still bearing the ideological imprint of the New Deal, influenced by earlier American success in absorbing wave after wave of immigrants, and often morally committed to protecting the rights of an historically discriminated-against black minority—showed little regard for the partisan consequences of the remedies chosen to address discrimination. Nor had they any political stake in the fact that the most controversial of those remedies—busing and the imposition of racial preferences in hiring, scholarships, school admissions, and government contracting—would fall most heavily on an angry and resentful Democratic constituency, the white working and lower-middle classes. The Democratic party, once it was committed to the long-range goal of black equality, had no alternative but to participate in imposing burdens and costs; the central failure of the party was its refusal to acknowledge those burdens and costs and, consequently, its refusal to make adequate efforts to minimize those costs and to distribute them more equitably.

Going further, the Democratic party failed to understand the *political* need to couple newly granted rights and preferences with a persuasive and visible message of reciprocal obligation. In a purely strategic sense, furthermore, Democrats failed to pass along as many of the costs as possible to Republican constituencies. In this regard, the problem facing Democrats has been that at an elite, policy-making level, it has been difficult to shift burdens onto Republicans: an attempt by Democrats to place costs on GOP interests means placing burdens on Democratic elites as well—because Democratic elites are often indistinguishable from Republican elites in their affluence, in the schools their children attend, and in the location of their homes. Finally, the refusal on the part of many Democratic interests to acknowledge the costs of racial equality made cost-oriented calculations impossible.

Explicit discussion and assessment of the costs and rewards of efforts to achieve racial equality have been further censored in the course of another, otherwise positive development of the civil rights revolution: the encompassing discrediting—that is, the stigmatization—of racism over the past twenty-five years. To raise for public consideration not only the costs of equality, but a host of other potentially racially-tinged subjects—from street violence to illegitimacy to welfare dependency to joblessness—has come to risk, among Democrats and liberals (both white and black), accusations of racism. *The resulting failure to place squarely on the table before the essential participants in a "bottom-up" coalition some of the most conflict-ridden issues guarantees that these conflicts will remain unresolved.* Such failure helps to guarantee that the "top-down" conservative coalition will remain dominant in presidential politics. Democrats and liberals have allowed the debate to become toxic and thus highly destructive to the interests of both the Democratic party and of liberalism.

The failure of liberalism to explore the most difficult issues involving values and resource competition has helped to sustain strongly ambivalent racial attitudes among whites, attitudes that have proven fatal to the Democratic party in presidential elections. The percentage of whites who ascribe the social and economic differences between blacks and whites to a belief in inherent or genetic differences in ability has declined steadily. But survey data indicate that a strong plurality of whites who believe that blacks lack the motivation and willpower to compete with whites has remained constant.[33]

Such white voters, who fall predominantly into the lower-middle and middle classes, and who are thus essential targets for Democrats seeking to revive their party, reject policies providing special benefits to blacks and other minorities because they view the economic disadvantages suffered by blacks as caused by individual failures of motivation and of effort, not by systemic or structural factors, such as discrimination, alone.[34] Such white voters are not prepared to join in a biracial presidential coalition as it has been presented in recent years by the national Democratic party. Until the national Democratic party can develop politically sustainable ways of addressing and dealing with problems of values and the concomitant problems of crime, illegitimacy, welfare dependency, drug abuse, workless-ness, etc.—or until economic factors come to supercede such matters—significant numbers of white voters are likely to continue to move, or to be pushed, to the right.

Although the anxieties of middle and lower-income white voters have unquestionably been manipulated and exploited by Republican political strategists, this exploitation is only possible because these voters hold strong opinions independent of organized politics. There are many citizens who share the ambivalence about government programs expressed by white Illinois voter Beryl Fredell: "I'm thankful that my mother has Social Security. She had to have both knees replaced and public aid picked up everything. She's entitled to food stamps but won't take them. . . . She's too proud." A few moments later, Mrs. Fredell added, "There are too many people on the rolls, too many multiple babies. The first time is a mistake. The second is their fault. If they are able to work, some kind of job should be found for them. Let them keep their medical cards [for a while]. When they reach a certain level, they should be on their own."[35] Mrs. Fredell speaks for millions of once-loyal Democrats who have a clear sense in their own minds of the legitimacy of government help under certain circumstances, but who just as clearly rebel at government programs they feel are overly generous and contribute to, rather than resolve, social problems.

Mrs. Fredell and voters like her are essential to a biracial political coalition with the muscle to channel economic rewards toward those in the bottom half of the income distribution. The abdication of such voters from the Democratic presidential coalition has gravely weakened the political leverage of the "have nots." The politics of mutual recrimination—a politics captured eloquently in the remarks of Roger Wilkins and Pat Buchanan—functions to preclude genuine consideration of the complex causes of poverty and the multiple disadvantages of the poor: the deficits in social and economic capital common to the poor of all races, and those deficits that are specific to the poor of this country.

———

To an extraordinary degree, the distribution not only of economic reward but also of social recognition and regard is determined by political power. The political power of those on the bottom rungs of the ladder has, for the past two decades, been fractured by the dynamic interaction of race, the rights revolution, the rise of a Demcoratic middle-class reform elite, and the intensifying battle over taxes.[36]

This fracturing has permitted the moral, social, and economic ascendance of the affluent in a nation with a strong egalitarian tradition, and has permitted a diminution of economic reward and social regard for those who simply work for a living, black and white. In spite of American success in eliminating legally protected racial subjugation, race remains a powerful wedge issue, and for as long as that is the case, the incentive to capitalize on racial conflict will tend to supersede pressures to address the economic bifurcation that increasingly plagues the country.

The real tragedy is that liberalism—which helped to produce a strong labor movement, which used the Fourteenth Amendment to extend basic rights to all citizens, and which nurtured free political and artistic expression—has lost the capacity to mobilize a majority of the electorate. Liberalism is no longer seen as a powerful agent of constructive change; instead, liberal values, policies, and allegiances have become the source of bitter conflict between groups that were once mutual beneficiaries of the progressive state. Liberalism has come to be identified with redistributive policies intended to create greater racial equality, but which—in part, because of their redistributive nature—now fail to gather majority support.

Racially preferential policies are claimed as a "right" by one side and denounced as a fundamental violation of democratic principle by the other. Conflicts over such policies have created an intractable dilemma that overrides shared interests.

Racial divisions have become ingrained in partisan politics in the deep

South and, increasingly, across the urban and suburban wards of all major metropolitan areas. At a time when nearly 50 percent of the American people live in the twenty largest metropolitan areas,[37] the liabilities of urban racial conflict—and of urban squalor, danger, deviance, and decay—are increasingly resented and disapproved of by white city dwellers and by white suburbanites, and, as such, gravely endanger the Democratic coalition. There has come to be a deep gulf between the views of many whites and blacks on the most basic questions of government and of individual responsibility, as well as a troubling degree of callousness towards each other among Americans of both races.

The conflict between blacks and whites was reflected at the extreme in the series of weekend demonstrations over the murder of a black youth by a group of white men in the Italian Bensonhurst section of Brooklyn in 1990; in the strikingly different assessments by blacks and by whites of the Goetz and Brawley cases in New York in the 1980s; and in the polarized responses of blacks and whites in the summer of 1990 to the rape in Central Park of a white woman jogger by a gang of black and Hispanic teenagers.

Racial animosity can be found in community meetings, courtrooms, American Legion bars, political rallies, softball clubs, PTA sessions, public parks, and private gatherings across America. In Peoria, Illinois, once known as the heartland of America, neighborhood meetings in racially changing areas produce angry denunciations by whites of deteriorating conditions, noise, and crowding in the wake of black migration. "We've got to be more aggressive setting the standards in our neighborhoods and not letting them set the standards. . . . If we don't, they've got control of the neighborhood, not us," warns David Koehler, a liberal white city councilman, meeting with a group of Peoria neighborhood organizations. Koehler struggles to portray neighborhood conflict as economic and not racial, but the voters he talks to discuss these issues in terms of black and white.[38] On a daily level, a substantial number of whites view blacks as dangerous and as antagonistic to basic American values; these whites do not distinguish between blacks of different social and economic classes. A significant number of blacks, in turn—the most middle-class and successful among them—view whites as not only attempting to evade responsibility for the continuing consequences of slavery and discrimination, but as the entrenched wielders of power in a lopsided whites-only system.

Liberalism and the Democratic party have not been able to contain or to resolve these conflicts. Such a failure means that the party that guided the nation through the Great Depression, the party that produced a coalition committed to protecting the interests of the working man and woman, and the party that, twenty-five years ago, set the nation on a course towards racial equality—with often successful results—no longer has the capacity to establish a reliable national voting majority.

———

"Nothing is irredeemable until it is past," Gunnar Myrdal wrote in *An American Dilemma* over forty-five years ago.[39] The dilemma posed for liberalism today is that its proponents may well have made choices that are in fact irredeemable—choices that render problematic, at least for the foreseeable future, the restoration of a nationally competitive coalition representing the interests of those in the bottom half of the income distribution. Instead of struggling to resolve the conflict between the drive towards a racial equality on the one hand and the need to create a cooperative voting majority on the other, Democratic liberals—intellectually fearful, reluctant to engage in the values debate, debilitated by a reformist agenda that has effectively disenfranchised core constituents, driven less by principle than by a desperate need to protect past gains—Democratic liberals have lost much of the capacity to learn, and thus to adjust, protect, enlarge, and fight for what is really valuable.

The failures of Democratic liberalism pose a larger dilemma for the nation. With the decline of liberal hegemony, conservatism has gained control over national elections and, to a significant degree, over the national agenda. No matter what its claims, conservatism has served for much of the twentieth century as the political and philosophical arm of the affluent. Entrusting the economic interests of the poor and of the working class to such a philosophy risks serious damage to both groups.

That conservatism represents the interests of the well-to-do is to be expected—and even respected—as part of the system of representation in American democracy. A far more threatening development is that as liberalism fails to provide effective challenge, even effective minority challenge, to the interests of the powerful and the rich, the country will lack the dynamism that can be provided only by a sustained and vibrant insurgency of those on the lower rungs. A healthy insurgency, sustained by recognizably legitimate claims for an equal opportunity to participate and to compete, is critical, not only to the politics and the economics of the nation, but also to the dynamism of its broader culture.

———

The national Democratic party has successfully avoided bearing the full brunt of its losses in the political marketplace, but until it does, and learns what is behind voter rejection, it will lack the capacity to fully compete in the public forum, or to live up to the obligation to represent the economic interests and the shared values of its own core constituents. Liberalism and the Democratic party are headed for a wrenching period as the political process—particularly the incentive to win the presidency— forces explicit public consideration of race and rights. As the nexus of liberal policies, values associations, ideological rigidities, and economic hardships continues to create electoral liabilities, Democratic politicians enmeshed in party dogma will be subject to attack from every side—by Republicans, as well as by competing Democrats.

As the awareness of electoral liability grows within the Democratic party, as public funds grow increasingly scarce, and as the competition for such funds becomes more and more bitter, the incentive to assault liberal orthodoxies—many strongly tied to race—will intensify. Such a process is likely to be ugly, clouded by real and imagined racism and bias, as political competition forces to the surface issues of crime, illegitimacy, family structure, racial disparities in standardized test scores, the scope of government welfare spending, school performance, immigration, and a host of other deeply felt matters.[40] As this conflict develops, it is likely to produce two distinct outcomes: on the one hand, the municipal unions, the civil rights community, civil liberties organizations, teachers groups, feminists, gay rights activists, and all those interests that have been targeted for attack by conservatives are likely to become more ideologically unyielding; on the other hand, these interests will be forced to engage in increasingly bloody competition with each other. Such conflict is likely to lead, for a time, to a form of civil war within Democratic ranks, and the right is likely to continue to profit.

Political strife will be fueled by an intellectual debate with many new participants—a debate that must have, as its ultimate goal, breaking the claim of a monopoly on truth by ideologues of the right or left, as well as by the vast and powerful array of interests that have become entrenched in government.

This debate is likely to become harsher as global competition intensifies—competition providing little or no room for traditional liberal Democratic policies sheltering the disadvantaged. Intensified international competition will exert increasingly brutal pressure on America's economic and political systems, and on policies offering special protection, preference, or subsidy to groups within the population—whether they be ethnic or racial minorities, unskilled workers, prisoners, elected officials, the elderly, the disabled, AIDs victims, or single mothers.

At stake in all this is something far more important than partisan victory. First, stagnation at the bottom of the income distribution, together with the poverty, disappointment, and rage of America's disadvantaged

288 · *Chain Reaction*

minority populations, threatens our social order. Secondly, at stake is our sense of ourselves as inhabiting an intelligible moral universe, committed to a form of social and economic organization that offers at least rough justice to its citizens in exchange for their participation. And thirdly, at stake is the American experiment itself, endangered by a rising tide of political cynicism and alienation, and by basic uncertainties as to whether or not we are capable of transmitting a sense of inclusion and shared citizenship across an immense and diverse population—whether or not we can uphold our traditional commitment to the possibilities for justice and equality expressed in our founding documents and embedded in our most valued democratic institutions.

# Notes

## 1 Building a Top-Down Coalition

1. Dan Donohue, interview with author, September 1988, at campaign headquarters of State Senator Robert Raica (R) in Chicago.

2. "Research Report: Democrats for the 90's," a report on the views of various voter groups by KRC Research and Consulting, of New York, November 1989; "Report on Democratic Defection," a study of working-class white voters in Detroit suburbs, by The Analysis Group, New Haven and Washington, April 15, 1985; and "Strengthening the Democratic Party through Strategic Marketing: Voters and Donors," a 1985 report for the Democratic National Committee, by CRG Research Institute, Washington.

3. Howard Schuman, Charlotte Steeh, and Lawrence Bobo, *Racial Attitudes In America* (Cambridge, MA: Harvard University Press, 1985) 71–138.

4. "Crime and the Administration of Criminal Justice," in *A Common Destiny: Blacks and American Society,* ed. Gerald David Jaynes and Robin M. Williams, Jr. (Washington, D.C.: National Academy Press, 1989), 451–507; and the victimization reports issued by the Department of Justice, Washington, D.C.

5. Bureau of the Census, *Studies in Marriage and the Family,* ser. P-23, no. 162 (Washington, D.C., June 1989); and Department of Labor, Bureau of Labor Statistics, *American Families, 75 Years of Change* (Washington, D.C., March 1990). Cf. additional material cited in Chapters Five and Eight.

6. James P. Smith and Finis R. Welch, *Closing the Gap: Forty Years of Economic Progress for Blacks* (Washington, D.C.: The Rand Corporation, 1986), 12, 13.

7. There were in 1986 (the most recent year for which racial breakdowns of prison populations are available) eleven times as many state prisoners as there were federal prisoners, according to the Bureau of Justice Statistics, U.S. Department of Justice. State prisoners in 1986 were 45.3 percent black; 39.5 percent white; 12.6 percent Hispanic; and 2.5 percent other races. Federal prisoners in 1986 were 65.7 percent white; 31.8 percent black; and 3.5 percent other. (Federal prison statistics include Hispanics as either white or black.) There were, in 1986, 485,951 state prison inmates, and 36,531 federal prison inmates. Therefore, combining the numbers of state and federal prison inmates, there were more black than white prison inmates. The proportion of minority inmates, according to the Bureau of Justice Statistics, is growing.

Figures are from unpublished data from the Survey of Inmates of State Correctional Facilities, 1986, supplied by the Bureau of Justice Statistics, Department of Justice, by telephone October 1, 1990; and from the Federal Bureau of Prisons, U.S. Department of Justice, supplied by telephone October 1, 1990.

8. In 1988, 39.8 percent of all Aid to Families with Dependent Children (AFDC) recipients were black, 38.8 percent were white, 15.7 percent were Hispanic, and the remaining 5.7 percent were of other races, according to "Characteristics and Financial Circumstances of

AFDC Recipients," an annual publication issued by the U.S. Department of Health and Human Services.

9. Bureau of the Census, *Studies in Marriage and the Family*, ser. P-23, no. 162 (Washington, D.C., June 1989), 15.

10. National Center for Health Statistics, *Monthly Vital Statistics Report* (Washington, D.C., September 1990), 32. (The percentage of white children born out of wedlock in 1988 was 17.7 percent. The percentage of Hispanic children born out of wedlock was 34 percent in 1988.)

11. Department of Justice, Bureau of Justice Statistics, *Criminal Victimizations in the United States, 1987* (Washington, D.C., June 1989), Table 43, p. 49, and Table 48, p. 52.

12. Among Democratic groups recently attempting to counter the competition from the right is the Democratic Leadership Council and its think-tank offshoot, the Progressive Policy Institute. See for example, the PPI paper released on September 27, 1990: *Putting Children First: A Progressive Family Policy for the 1990s*, by Elaine C. Kamarck and William A. Galston.

The Kamarck-Galston report reads in part:

> The path to [a family] policy has been obstructed by the polarized political reaction to the revolution in the American family. Most liberals talk about the economic pressures on families and neglect family values; most conservatives talk about the values and neglect the economics. Liberals tend to reach for bureaucratic solutions even when they are counterproductive; conservatives tend to reject government responses even when they would work. Both are wrong. Traditional conservatives' support for families is largely rhetorical; their disregard for new economic realities engenders a policy of unresponsive neglect—expressed for example, in President Bush's misguided veto of the Family Leave Act. Conversely, traditional liberals' unwillingness to acknowledge that intact two-parent families are the most effective units for raising children has led them into a series of policy cul-de-sacs. (p. 1)

13. Selim Jones, employment analyst for the Bureau of the Census, telephone interview with author, September 1989. Among whites holding jobs classified as professional or managerial, 71.5 percent are in the private sector and 28.5 percent are in the public sector. For blacks with similar level jobs, 46.5 percent are in the private sector and 53.5 percent are in the public sector.

In addition, the armed services employ disproportionate numbers of non-civilian blacks: by 1980, more than 22 percent of all active-duty recruits were black, according to "Social Representation in the U.S. Military", Congressional Budget Office, October, 1989.

14. Smith and Welch, *Closing the Gap*, 85–100. The EEOC requires that all companies with over one hundred employees and all contractors doing $50,000 or more a year worth of business with the federal government file annual reports on the racial makeup of their work force.

15. Congressional Budget Office, *The Economic and Budget Outlook: Fiscal Years 1990–1994*, part I, (Washington, D.C., 1989), 135.

16. These five cases—*Wards Cove Packing Co., Inc. v. Atonio; City of Richmond v. J. A. Croson Co.; Martin v. Wilks; Patterson v. McLean Credit Union;* and *Lorance v. AT & T Technologies*—are discussed in Chapter Nine and Chapter Eleven.

17. House Ways and Means Committee, *Overview of Entitlement Programs: The 1990 Green Book*, 101st Cong., 1st sess., June 5, 1990, 1,183.

18. The major exception to Democratic success in protecting the trade union movement was the passage in 1947 of the Taft-Hartley Labor Act by a Republican-controlled Congress over the veto of Harry S. Truman. The legislation prohibited secondary boycotts by unions and allowed states to enact laws barring union shops.

19. Among the most recent polls, at this writing, is "The People, the Press, & Politics 1990," released September 19, 1990, by the Times Mirror Company: "Republicans have a 41%–25% margin as better able to make 'America competitive in the world economy.' And 40% see Republicans as better able to generate economic growth, compared with only 29% who see that description as better characterizing the Democrats," the poll found (p. 54).

20. For a fuller discussion of focus-group findings of anti-black affect among Michigan voters, see Chapter Seven.

21. Bureau of the Census, *Statistical Abstract of the United States, 1987,* (Washington, D.C., 1988), chart 34, "Metropolitan Statistical Areas," p. 28.

## 2   A Pivotal Year

1. Elder Witt, ed., *Guide to the U.S. Supreme Court* (Washington, D.C.: Congressional Quarterly, 1979), 595.

2. Gavin Wright, *Old South, New South,* (New York: Basic Books, 1986), p. 201. Michael Barone, *Our Country* (New York: The Free Press, 1990), 273.

3. V. O. Key, Jr., *Southern Politics in State and Nation* (New York: Vintage Books, 1949), 335.

4. National Election Studies data supplied by Martin Wattenberg, professor of political science at the University of California, Irvine, by telephone, January 10, 1990.

5. Edward G. Carmines and James A. Stimson, *Issue Evolution: Race and the Transformation of American Politics* (Princeton, N.J.: Princeton University Press, 1989), 165–66; further data supplied by Carmines by telephone, January 4, 1990. [For a fuller discussion of the influence of racial issues on partisan identification, see Chapter Three and Chapter Seven.]

6. James L. Sundquist, *Dynamics of the Party System* (Washington, D.C., The Brookings Institution, 1983), 388.

7. Johnson's remark to Bill Moyers quoted in a story by Michael Oreskes, *The New York Times,* 2 July 1989, sec. 1 p. 16.

8. Robert Novak, *The Agony of the GOP 1964* (New York: Macmillan, 1965), 61.

9. Ibid., 63–64.

10. Barry Goldwater, *The Conscience of a Conservative* (Shepherdsville, Ky.: Victor Publishing, 1960), 33, 34, and 37.

11. Richard Scammon, *America Votes 16* (Washington, D.C.: Congressional Quarterly, 1985), 29.

12. Sundquist, *Dynamics of the Party System,* 360–61.

13. Norman H. Nie, Sidney Verba and John R. Petrocik, *The Changing American Voter* (Cambridge, MA: Harvard University Press, 1976), 243–69.

14. Ibid.

15. William A. Rusher, *The Rise of the Right* (New York: Morrow, 1984), 109–10.

16. Ibid., 177, 201.

17. Jack Craddock, interview with author, in his East Memphis insurance office, March 1986.

18. Wirt A. Yerger, Jr., "Two-Party System Established," *The Rebel Magazine,* 27 March 1964, two; published by the Mississippi Republican Party from the John Davis Williams Library, Department of Archives and Special Collections, University of Mississippi, Oxford.

19. Wirt A. Yerger, Jr., *Memorandum To Key Leadership,* March 11, 1964, Department of Archives and Special Collections, University of Mississippi, Oxford.

20. Harry S. Dent, *The Prodigal South Returns to Power* (New York: Wiley & Sons, 1978), 67–70.

21. Rusher, *The Rise of the Right,* 179.

## 3   After 1964: The Fraying Consensus

1. James L. Sundquist, *Politics and Policy* (Washington, D.C.: The Brookings Institution, 1968), 496.

2. Sundquist, *Politics and Policy,* 275.

3. Ibid., 139.

4. David J. Garrow, *Bearing the Cross: Martin Luther King, Jr., and the Southern Christian*

*Leadership Conference* (New York: William Morrow, 1986), 439–40; Allen J. Matusow, *The Unraveling of America: A History of Liberalism in the 1960s* (New York: Harper and Row, 1984), 360–61.

5. *The Kerner Report: The 1968 Report of the National Advisory Commission on Civil Disorders* (New York: Pantheon, 1988), 133–34.

6. Ibid., 38–40.

7. Ibid., 112–13.

8. Ibid., 56–69 and 84–108.

9. James W. Button, *Black Violence: Political Impact of the 1960s Riots* (Princeton, N.J.: Princeton University Press, 1978), 10.

10. Gary Orfield, "Race and the Liberal Agenda: The Loss of the Integrationist Dream, 1965 to 1974," in *The Politics of Social Policy in the United States,* ed. Margaret Weir, Ann Shola Orloff, and Theda Skocpol (Princeton, NJ: Princeton University Press, 1988), 313–55.

11. Sundquist, *Politics and Policy,* 286.

12. Sundquist, *Politics and Policy,* 281.

13. Elder Witt, ed., *Congress and the Nation, Volume II* (Washington, D.C.: Congressional Quarterly, 1969), 310–11; and *Volume III, 1969–1972,* 256–57.

14. Jaynes and Williams, *A Common Destiny,* 459.

15. *Statistical Abstract of the United States, 1987,* Table 86, p. 61.

16. Lee Rainwater and William L. Yancey, *The Moynihan Report and the Politics of Controversy,* (Cambridge, MA: M.I.T. Press, 1967), 126.

17. Orlando Patterson, "Toward a Study of Black America," *Dissent* (Fall 1989): 476.

18. William Julius Wilson, *The Truly Disadvantaged: The Inner City, the Underclass, and Public Policy* (Chicago: University of Chicago Press, 1987).

19. *Congress and the Nation,* Vol. 2, 389–91.

20. Rainwater and Yancy, *The Moynihan Report,* 410.

21. Ibid., 458, 464.

22. Wilson, *The Truly Disadvantaged,* 149–50.

23. Gerald M. Pomper, "Toward A More Responsible Two-Party System. What, Again?" *Journal of Politics* 33 (1971): 932.

24. John R. Petrocik, *Party Coalitions* (Chicago: University of Chicago Press, 1981), Figures 9.5, 9.6, and 9.7 on pp. 135, 137, and 138.

25. Ibid., pp. 136, 148–49.

26. Paul Kleppner, *Chicago Divided: The Making of a Black Mayor,* (DeKalb, IL: Northern Illinois University Press, 1985), 46–47.

27. *Congress and the Nation, Vol. II,* 402–6.

28. *Congress and the Nation, Vol. II,* 406; Gary Orfield, *Must We Bus?* (Washington, D.C.: The Brookings Institution, 1978), 320.

29. David J. Garrow, *Bearing The Cross,* 489–92, and Matusow, *The Unraveling of America,* 205–6.

30. Petrocik, *Party Coalitions,* 136–39.

31. Ibid., Figure 9.1 on pp. 124–25. Petrocik's data show that from the 1950s to the 1970s there was a sharp class bias in terms of which groups became more liberal on race issues and which groups became more conservative. Upscale WASPS, for example, became more liberal, while low-status WASPs became more conservative. White union members and lower status Catholics, both key Democratic constituencies, became more conservative on race.

32. Matusow, *The Unraveling of America,* 353–55.

33. Ibid., 367–73.

34. Sundquist, *Politics and Policy,* 498–99.

35. *Congressional Quarterly Almanac, 1966* (Washington, D.C.: Congressional Quarterly, 1967), 1,398.

36. The ward boundaries were changed between 1960 and 1966 but every effort was made to insure that the voting patterns of similar areas were compared for these findings.

37. *Congress and the Nation, Vol. II,* 183.

38. *Congress and the Nation, Vol. II,* 198–99.

39. Edward G. Carmines and James A. Stimson, *Issue Evolution* (Princeton, NJ: Princeton University Press, 1989), 63.

40. Ibid., 64–65.

41. *The Kerner Report,* 55, 56.

42. *Congress and the Nation, Vol. II,* 376.

43. *Congressional Quarterly Almanac, 1967* (Washington, D.C.: Congressional Quarterly, 1968), 446–47; and Richard L. Lyons, *Washington Post,* July 21, 1967, page A1.

44. Andrew J. Glass, *Washington Post,* 8 August 1967, page A1, and George Lardner, Jr., *Washington Post,* 17 August 1967, page A1.

45. Matusow, *The Unraveling of America,* 249.

46. Ibid., 248.

47. Richard A. Cloward and Frances Fox Piven, "A Strategy To End Poverty," *The Nation,* 2 May 1966, 510–17.

48. Nick Kotz and Mary Lynn Kotz, *A Passion for Equality: George Wiley and the Movement,* (New York: Norton, 1977), 260.

49. Irwin Unger and Debi Unger, *Turning Point: 1968* (New York: Scribners, 1988), 44.

50. Kotz and Kotz, *A Passion for Equality,* 233.

51. Linda Greenhouse, "New Look at an 'Obscure' Ruling, 20 Years Later," *New York Times,* 11 May 1990, B7

52. Kotz and Kotz, *A Passion for Equality,* 286.

53. See, for example, Richard G. Niemi, John Mueller, and Tom W. Smith, *Trends in Public Opinion: A Compendium of Survey Data* (New York: Greenwood Press, 1989), 89.

54. Richard A. Cloward and Frances Fox Piven, "Finessing The Poor," *The Nation,* 7 October 1968, 332–33.

55. This series of Supreme Court cases is discussed in Chapter Two.

56. *Congress and the Nation, Vol. II,* 25a.

57. Ibid., 35a.

58. Ibid., 34a.

59. Sundquist, *Dynamics of the Party System,* 382.

60. Ibid., 383.

61. Ibid., 383–84.

62. *Congress and the Nation, Vol. II,* 20a, 36a; and Matusow, *The Unraveling of America,* 214.

63. Norman Mailer, *Miami and the Siege of Chicago* (New York: Signet, 1968), 51 and 53.

## 4 The Nixon Years

1. Garry Wills, *Nixon Agonistes* (Boston: Houghton Mifflin, 1970), 272–75.

2. Harry S. Dent, *The Prodigal South Returns to Power* (New York: Wiley, 1978), 73–117.

3. Stephen E. Ambrose, *Nixon: The Triumph of a Politician, 1962–1972,* Vol. 2 (New York: Simon and Schuster, 1989), 187.

4. Schuman, Steeh, and Bobo, *Racial Attitudes in America,* 71–138.

5. Jody Carlson, *George C. Wallace and the Politics of Powerlessness* (New Brunswick, N.J.: Transaction Books, 1981), 6.

6. George Lardner, Jr., *Washington Post,* 13 September 1968, A1.

7. Carlson, *George C. Wallace,* 129.

8. Lardner, op. cit.

9. Laurence Stern, *Washington Post,* 20 October 1968, H1.

10. Theodore H. White, *The Making of the President, 1968* (New York: Atheneum Publishers, 1969), 346–47.

11. White, *The Making of the President, 1968,* 349.

12. Kevin P. Phillips, *The Emerging Republican Majority* (New York: Doubleday, 1970), 287.

13. Ibid., 37.

14. Orfield, *Must We Bus?* 286–87.

15. Rowland Evans, Jr., and Robert D. Novak, *Nixon in the White House,* (New York: Random House, 1971), 156.

16. Ambrose, *Nixon,* 316–17.

17. Evans and Novak, *Nixon in the White House,* 170–71.

18. *Congress and the Nation, Vol. III,* 494–99.

19. *Washington Post,* April 12, 1968, page A1.

20. Sundquist, *Dynamics of the Party System,* 387.

21. Ibid., 386–87.

22. Mark Eddy, *Federal Programs for Minority and Women-Owned Businesses,* Congressional Research Service, May 1, 1989.

23. Hugh Davis Graham, *The Civil Rights Era: Origins and Development of National Policy* (New York: Oxford University Press, 1990), 327. Graham's book provides an excellent description of the development of the Philadelphia Plan in two separate chapters, pp. 278–97 and 322–45.

24. David L. Rose, "Twenty-Five Years Later: Where Do We Stand on Equal Employment Opportunity Law Enforcement?" *Vanderbilt Law Review* (May 1989): 1141–43.

25. Graham, *The Civil Rights Era,* 325 (quoting John Ehrlichman, *Witness to Power,* 1982).

26. *Congress and the Nation, Vol. III,* 512–17.

27. Peter Milius, *Washington Post,* 4 August 1971, p. A1.

28. Orfield, *Must We Bus?* 332.

29. Ambrose, *Nixon,* 460.

30. Orfield, *Must We Bus?* 103–4.

31. Ibid., 338–39.

32. In late 1971, the Gallup poll showed the nation opposed to busing by a margin of 76 to 18, with 6 percent holding no opinion. Even blacks were divided, 47 percent opposed and 45 percent in favor. *Washington Post,* November 1, 1971.

33. Gary Orfield, *Must We Bus?* 255–56.

34. *Congressional Quarterly Almanac, 1972,* (Washington, D.C.: Congressional Quarterly Inc., 1973), 72H–73H.

35. Byron E. Shafer, *Quiet Revolution: The Struggle for the Democratic Party and the Shaping of Post Reform Politics* (New York: Russell Sage Foundation, 1983), 30.

36. Ibid., 34.

37. Byron E. Shafer, *Bifurcated Politics* (Cambridge, MA: Harvard University Press, 1988), 90.

38. Shafer, *Quiet Revolution,* 530.

39. Shafer, *Bifurcated Politics,* 100–107.

40. Theodore H. White, *The Making of the President, 1972,* (New York: Bantam, 1973), 218.

41. Ibid., 219.

42. Ibid., 218–19.

43. White, *The Making of the President, 1972,* 237.

44. Scammon, *America Votes 14,* 25.

45. Donald Bruce Johnson, ed., *National Party Platforms,* Volume II, 1960–1976, (Champaign, IL: University of Illinois Press, 1978), 789–95.

46. *Economic Report of the President, 1979,* (Washington, D.C., 1979), Table B-25, p. 212.

47. Johnson, *National Party Platforms,* Vol. II, 790.

48. Ibid., 792.

49. Ibid., 809.

50. Ambrose, *Nixon,* 636–37.

51. Ibid., 637.

52. Ibid., 637.

## 5   The Conservative Ascendance

1. Peter E. Quint, "The Separation of Powers Under Nixon: Reflections on Constitutional Liberties and the Rule of Law," *Duke Law Journal,* 1981, no. 1.

2. J. Anthony Lukas, *Nightmare: The Underside of the Nixon Years* (New York: Bantam, 1977), 732.

3. Jonathan Schell, *The Time of Illusion* (New York: Knopf, 1976), 293–94.

4. Samuel Walker, *In Defense of American Liberties: A History of the ACLU* (New York: Oxford University Press, 1990) 287–95.

5. Patrick H. Caddell, "Initial Working Paper on Political Strategy," a memorandum dated December 10, 1976, provided by a Carter administration source.

6. Everett Carll Ladd, Jr., *Transformations of the American Party System* (New York: Norton, 1978), 258–59.

7. *Economic Report of the President, 1987* (Washington, D.C.: U.S. Government Printing Office), 292.

8. Ibid., 278.

9. Robert Kuttner, *The Revolt of the Haves* (New York: Simon and Schuster, 1980), 211–12. Ladd, *Transformations,* 220.

10. Eugene Steuerle and Michael Hartzmark, *Individual Income Taxation, 1947–1979,* Office of Tax Analysis, Department of the Treasury, Supplied in 1981 by Steuerle to the author.

11. *Statistical Abstract of the United States, 1987,* Table 586, p. 348.

12. Dept. of Health and Human Services, *Social Security Bulletin,* Annual Statistical Supplement, 1986, (Washington, D.C.: GPO, 1986) Table 204, p. 282.

13. Henry Owen and Charles L. Schultze, ed., *Setting National Priorities: The Next Ten Years,* (Washington, D.C.: The Brookings Institution, 1976), 340.

14. *Statistical Abstract of the United States, 1987,* 61.

15. Walker, *In Defense of American Liberties,* 300.

16. Data supplied by the American Petroleum Institute, by phone, July 18, 1990.

17. *Statistical Abstract, 1987,* 382.

18. Department of Health and Human Services, National Center for Health Statistics, *Advance Report on Final Divorces, 1986* (Washington, D.C., 6 June 1989), 4.

19. Department of Health and Human Services, National Center for Health Statistics, *Children of Divorce* (Washington, D.C., January 1989), ser. 21, no. 46, p. 14.

20. Anne Koedt, "The Myth of the Vaginal Orgasm," as quoted in Irwin Unger and Debi Unger, *Turning Point: 1968* (New York: Scribner's, 1988), 441.

21. *Statistical Abstract of the United States, 1987,* 67.

22. Bureau of the Census, *Statistical Abstract of the United States, 1989,* (Washington, D.C., 1989), 64.

23. Tim LaHaye, *The Battle for the Mind* (Old Tappan, N.J.: Fleming H. Revell, 1980). Material quoted from the interior cover of the book.

24. Joyce Vialet, *A Brief History of U.S. Immigration Policy,* (Washington, D.C.: Congressional Research Service, Library of Congress, November 25, 1988), pages 34–36. Overall figures on size of Asian and Hispanic populations supplied by the Bureau of the Census by telephone, March 3, 1991.

25. Arthur S. Leonard, *Gay & Lesbian Rights and Protections in the U.S.* (Washington, D.C.: National Gay and Lesbian Task Force).

26. Walker, *In Defense of American Liberties,* 309.

27. Leonard Rubenstein, director of the Mental Health Law Project, Washington, D.C., interview with author, 17 February 1990.

28. *Congress and the Nation Vol. III,* 255–56.

29. Ibid., 13.

30. Ibid., 311.

31. Witt, *Guide to the Supreme Court,* 576–78.

32. Niemi, Mueller, and Smith, *Trends in Public Opinion,* 136.

33. Ibid., 138.

34. Department of Justice, *Sourcebook of Criminal Justice Statistics 1988* (Washington, D.C., 1989), 225.

35. Department of Justice, *Report to the Nation on Crime and Justice,* 2nd ed. (Washington, D.C., March 1988), 90.

36. Ibid., 104; and *New York Times,* 8 October 1990, p. A8.

37. There is an large body of data and literature on the subject of racial disparities in crime rates. The Department of Justice annually releases a survey, "Criminal Victimization in the United States," based on large polls of 40,000 or more households. The FBI issued in June 1988, a report called "Age-Specific Arrest Rates and Race-Specific Arrest Rates for Selected Offenses 1965–1986," and provides on request data for more recent years. A summary of various findings is provided in a chapter called "Crime and the Administration of Criminal Justice," in Jaynes and Williams, *A Common Destiny* (Washington, D.C.: National Academy of Sciences): 451–508. The Academy report concluded:

> Blacks have much higher arrest rates, convictions, and imprisonment rates than whites for criminal offenses. Some part of the differences may be due to bias and the resulting differential treatment, but systematic evidence of discrimination against blacks is not evident. . . . Two conclusions seem unavoidable. First, as long as great disparities in the socioeconomic status of blacks and whites remain, blacks' relative deprivation will continue to involve them disproportionately in the criminal justice system as victims and offenders. Second, because of this status difference, the degree to which this overrepresentation can be associated with differential treatment by race cannot be precisely determined. (page 498)

Among the other significant contributions to this debate are two articles by Michael J. Hingelang, "Variations in Sex-Race-Age-Specific Incidence Rates of Offending," and "Race and Involvement in Common Law Personal Crimes," both in the *American Sociological Review,* August 1981 and February 1978, respectively. Very useful analysis and material were supplied by Alfred Blumstein and Jacqueline Cohen of Carnegie-Mellon University, including Blumstein's "On the Racial Disproportionality of the United States' Prison Populations," *The Journal of Criminal Law and Criminology* 73, no., 3 (1982); and Blumstein, Cohen and Harold D. Miller, "Demographically Disaggregated Projections of Prison Populations," in *Research in Public Policy Analysis* (Greenwhich, CT: Jai Press, 1981).

38. Jaynes and Williams, *A Common Destiny,* 461, and cf. footnote 7, Chapter One.

39. The black percentage of the U.S. population has grown from 9.9 percent in 1950, to 11.1 percent in 1970, to 12.2 percent in 1987. *Statistical Abstract of the United States, 1987* Table 18, p. 16.

40. Hingelang, "Race and Involvement," 100.

41. Charles Murray, "The British Underclass," *The Public Interest* (Spring 1990): 4–28.

42. Herbert J. Gans, "Deconstructing the Underclass: The Term's Danger as a Planning Concept," *American Planning Association Journal* (Summer 1990): 271–77.

## 6 The Tax Revolt

1. Richard Freeman, *Black Elite,* as quoted in Martin Kilson, "Black Social Classes and Intergenerational Poverty," *The Public Interest* (Summer 1981) no. 64.

2. Deborah J. Carter and Reginald Wilson, *Minorities in Higher Education*, (Washington, D.C.: American Council on Education, December 1989), 20.

3. Kilson, "Black Social Classes and Intergenerational Poverty," 65.

4. Jaynes and Wilson, *A Common Destiny*, 170.

5. James P. Smith and Finis Welch, "Affirmative Action and Labor Markets," *Journal of Labor Economics* 2, no. 2 (April 1984): 273.

6. Hanes Walton, Jr., *When the Marching Stopped: The Politics of Civil Rights Regulatory Agencies*, (Albany: State University of New York Press, 1988), 32.

7. Jaynes and Wilson, *A Common Destiny*, 492–95.

8. James P. Smith, "Poverty and the Family," in *Divided Opportunities*, ed. Gary D. Sandefur and Marta Tienda (New York: Plemum, 1988), Table 6, p. 160.

9. *Statistical Abstract of the United States 1989*, Table 60, p. 46.

10. James P. Smith and Finish Welch, "Race and Poverty: a Forty-Year Record," *The American Economic Review* (May 1987), 156.

11. William Julius Wilson, *The Declining Significance of Race* (Chicago: University of Chicago Press, 1980), 182 and 22.

12. Quoted in Kilson, "Black Social Classes and Intergenerational Poverty," 60.

13. Resolution quoted in Alphonso Pinkney, *The Myth of Black Progress* (New York: Cambridge University Press, 1984), 15.

14. Ibid., 17.

15. Charles V. Willie, *Caste and Class Controversy on Race and Poverty* (Dix Hills, N.Y.: General Hall, Inc., 1989), 175–76.

16. Charles Murray, "Have the Poor Been 'Losing Ground'?" *Political Science Quarterly* (Fall 1985): 443–44.

17. *Congress and the Nation, Vol. II*, 397.

18. David L. Rose, "Twenty-five years later: Where Do We Stand on Equal Employment Opportunity Law Enforcement," *Vanderbilt Law Review* (May 1989); and telephone interviews on February 6 and 12, 1990 with Rose who was the chief of the section of the Justice Department Civil Rights Division responsible for enforcement of Title VII of the Civil Rights Act of 1964 from 1969 to 1987. Rose estimated that roughly half the early Justice Department employment cases were initiated against unions.

19. Rose, "Twenty-five Years Later," 1,138.

20. Elder, *Guide to the U.S. Supreme Court*, 621.

21. Based on material supplied by the Employment Litigation Section of the Department of Justice, January 18, 1990.

22. Stuart Taylor, Jr., "Second Class Citizens," *The American Lawyer* (September 1989), 44.

23. Barbara A. Perry and Julia A. McDonough, "Affirmative Action in Higher Education: *Bakke* to the Future" (Paper delivered at the American Political Science Association, Atlanta, 31 August–3 September, 1989), 13–14.

24. Ibid., 14.

25. Smith and Welch, *Closing the Gap*, 88–100; and telephone interviews with Smith in January and February 1990.

26. Smith and Welch, *Closing the Gap*, 88–100.

27. Jonathan S. Leonard, "What Was Affirmative Action?" *The American Economic Review* (May 1986): 359.

28. James P. Smith and Finis Welsh, "Affirmative Action and Labor Markets," *Journal of Labor Economics* (April 1984): 274.

29. "EEOC Announces Record-Breaking First Quarter in Enforcement of Equal Employment Opportunity Statutes" An EEOC press release, January 29, 1986.

30. House Ways and Means Committee, *Tax-Exempt Status of Private Schools: Part II of Hearings before the Subcommittee on Oversight*, Ways and Means 1979, 594–95.

31. David O. Sears and Jack Citrin, *Tax Revolt: Something for Nothing in California*, (Cambridge, MA: Harvard University Press, 1982), 47–64, 98, 153.

32. Kuttner, *The Revolt of the Haves,* 70; and David D. Schmidt, *Citizen Lawmakers* (Philadelphia: Temple University Press, 1989), 132.

33. Patrick B. McGuigan, *The Politics of Direct Democracy* (Washington, D.C.: The Institute for Government and Politics, 1985), 4–8.

34. Phillips, *The Emerging Republican Majority,* 89, 470.

35. These racial divisions will be explored in more detail in the next chapter.

36. Jerome Kurtz, telephone interviews with author, 17, 18 January 1990.

37. Richard Viguerie, telephone interview with author, 17 January 1990.

38. Kurtz interview.

39. Michael Kirst, professor of Education at Stanford University, interview with author, 16 February 1990.

40. A. James Reichley, *Religion in American Public Life* (Washington, D.C.: The Brookings Institution, 1985), 321.

41. Robert Billings, Sr., phone interview with author January 18, 1990.

42. Robert Billings, Sr. *Conservative Digest,* (August 1979): 14.

43. *1980 Congressional Quarterly Almanac* (Washington, D.C.: Congressional Quarterly, 1981), p. 63-B.

44. Reichley, *Religion in American Public Life,* 323; and information from the National Election Studies survey, 1980, supplied by phone by Arthur Miller, of the University of Iowa, January 18, 1990.

45. *Economic Report of the President,* (Washington, D.C.: GPO, January 1987), 244–368.

46. *Washington Post,* January 2, 1980.

47. Frederick Steeper, telephone interview, 9 January 1990, with author. (Steeper left Market Opinion Research in August 1989, and helped to found another polling firm, Market Strategies, in Southfield, Michigan.)

## 7  Race, Rights, and Party Choice

1. Conservatives, like Reagan, who oppose government intrusion in general often see no inconsistency in advocating government regulation of abortion.

2. *A Time for Choosing: The Speeches of Ronald Reagan 1961–1982* (Chicago: Regnery Gateway, 1983), 52.

3. In March 1981, a *Washington Post* poll found that 51 percent of blacks said Reagan would do less for them than Carter, and only four percent said more. By the time that two-thirds of Reagan's term in office had elapsed, more than half of all blacks surveyed, 56 percent, described Reagan as "racist."

4. Lou Cannon, *Reagan* (New York: Perigee Books, 1984), 111.

5. Ibid., pages 102–4. Cannon in his biography of Reagan describes how Holmes P. Tuttle, "a soft-spoken and highly successful entrepreneur whose Ford Motor Company dealerships were the base of a highly profitable complex of businesses," A. C. (Cy) Rubel, chairman of the board of Union Oil Company, and Henry Salvatori, founder of the Western Geophysical Company, meeting in the wake of Goldwater's defeat decided to run Reagan for governor in 1966. "They made their decision two months after Goldwater's defeat in a conference of millionaires at Tuttle's home." Tuttle then went to Reagan who appeared interested and agreed to think it over. Tuttle hired Stuart Spencer, of the political consulting firm Spencer-Roberts, to run the campaign. "In no other populous state of the nation at this time could a handful of millionaires and a political consultant so easily have decided on their own to run an aging actor for governor without consulting with party leaders. But in California, such consultation wasn't necessary. Statewide campaigns in California have a partyless peculiarity" that grew out of early reformers in the state, particularly former governor Hiram Walker. See Cannon, pp. 98–118 for full description of this process.

6. Speech to the American Conservative Union banquet, February 6, 1977, in Washington, included in *A Time for Choosing,* 184–89.

7. Ibid.

8. Schuman, Steeh, and Bobo, *Racial Attitudes in America,* 74–75.

9. Warren Miller and Santa A. Traugott, *American National Election Studies Data Sourcebook* (Cambridge, MA: Harvard University Press, 1989), 195.

10. Donald R. Kinder and Lynn M. Saunders, "Pluralistic Foundations of American Opinions on Race" (Paper delivered at the American Political Science Association meeting in Chicago, Sept. 3–6, 1987), 8.

11. *1980 Congressional Quarterly Almanac* (Washington, D.C.: Congressional Quarterly, 1981), 62-B.

12. Lee Atwater, interview with author on December 11, 1984, at the Alexandria, Va., offices of Black, Manafort and Stone.

13. *New York Times,* February 15, 1976.

14. *Washington Post,* January 28, 1976, page A2.

15. National Election Studies (NES) data supplied by Arthur Miller, of the University of Iowa, by telephone, January 17 and 19, 1990.

16. Ibid.

17. Carmines and Stimson, *Issue Evolution,* 131–37.

18. Petrocik, *Party Coalitions,* 149.

19. Carmines and Stimson, *Issue Evolution,* 150.

20. Richard G. Niemi, John Mueller, and Tom W. Smith, *Trends in Public Opinion: A Compendium of Survey Data* (New York: Greenwood Press, 1989), 33, 35 and 76.

21. Ibid., 79, 80, 82, 83, 84, and 87.

22. Ibid., 85 and 87.

23. Miller and Traugott, *American National Elections Studies Data Sourcebook,* 163.

24. Frederick Steeper, formerly of Market Opinion Research, now with Market Strategies, Inc., telephone interview with author, January 9, 1990.

25. Miller and Traugott, *American National Election Studies* 181. This calculation includes only those who take a side on the question, and leaves out those who either take the middle ground, or say they don't know.

26. Ibid., 327.

27. Ibid., 324.

## 8   A Conservative Policy Majority

1. Jonathan Rieder, *Canarsie: The Jews and Italians of Brooklyn against Liberalism* Cambridge, MA: (Harvard University Press, 1985), 57, 62–64, 68, 102.

2. Alphonso Pinkney, *The Myth of Black Progress* (New York: Cambridge University Press, 1984), 2.

3. Manning Marable, *Black American Politics: From The Washington Marches to Jesse Jackson* (London: Verso-New Left Books, 1985), 2.

4. Ambrose, *Nixon,* 580.

5. Testimony of Robert D. Reischauer, director of the Congressional Budget Office, before the House Ways and Means Committee, April 19, 1989, and average income tables for different quintiles supplied by the Congressional Budget Office, January 30, 1990.

6. Bureau of the Census, "Household After-Tax Income: 1985," *Current Population Reports,* ser. P-23, no. 151 (Washington, D.C., 1985), Table 1, pp. 7 and 8.

7. These charts are based on the following calculations: In 1980, 86.5 million people voted. For the top income quintile, however, turnout is much higher, 78 percent, than for the bottom quintile, 54 percent, according to data supplied by the American National Election Study, 1980, conducted by the Center for Political Studies at the University of Michigan. Using the turnout rates, the top income quintile produced 20.14 million votes and the bottom quintile 13.94 million. In terms of ethnic and racial breakdown, the top quintile is 93 percent white, 5 percent black and 2 percent Hispanic; the bottom quintile is 75 percent

white, 19 percent black and 6 percent Hispanic, according to the Bureau of the Census report, "After-Tax Money Income Estimates of Households: 1981," ser. P-23, no. 132 (Washington, D.C., February 1984). In the bottom quintile, the division of white votes between Reagan and Carter was 49–51, and in the top quintile, 68–32, according to NES. Blacks voted for Carter over Reagan by a margin of 94–6, and Hispanics favored Carter over Reagan by a margin of 60–40. The votes for John Anderson were not included in these calculations.

8. Department of Agriculture, *Characteristics of Food Stamp Households, Winter 1988,* (Washington, D.C., 1990), 72.

9. Department of Health and Human Services, *Characteristics and Financial Circumstances of AFDC Recipients,* (Washington, D.C., 1989).

10. Ibid.

11. Data from the National Election Studies supplied by the Center for Political Studies, the University of Michigan, by letter, September 9, 1983.

12. Current Population Survey, U.S. Department of Labor, Bureau of Labor Statistics, material supplied by phone by John Stimson of the Bureau of Labor Statistics, and Selim Jones, of the Bureau of the Census.

For a discussion of public sector employment for blacks, see Steven P. Erie, "Two Faces of Ethnic Power: Comparing the Irish and Black Experiences," *The Journal of the Northeastern Political Science Association* (Winter 1980): 260–84; Steven P. Erie, "Public Policy and Black Economic Polarization," *Policy Analysis* (Summer 1980): 304–17; and Michael K. Brown and Steven P. Erie, "Blacks and the Legacy of the Great Society: The Economic and Political Impact of Federal Social Policy," *Public Policy* (Summer 1981): 299–330.

13. Equal Employment Opportunity Commission, *Annual Report on the Employment of Minorities, Women, and People with Disabilities in the Federal Government Fiscal Year 1988* (Washington, D.C., 1989), Table 1-8, pp. 28-37.

14. Claudia H. Deutsch, *New York Times,* January 4, 1987, page 1, section 3.

15. Ibid.

16. Sundquist, *Dynamics of the Party System,* 422–23.

17. David Vogel, *Fluctuating Fortunes: The Political Power of Business in America* (New York: Basic, 1989), 59, 100, and 108.

18. Palmer and Sawhill, *The Reagan Record,* op. cit., pages 148 and 306.

19. Ibid., 155.

20. Kevin Phillips, *The Politics of Rich and Poor: Wealth and the American Electorate in the Reagan Aftermath* (New York: Random, 1990), 92.

21. Theodore J. Eismeier and Philip H. Pollock, III, *Business, Money, and the Rise of Corporate PACs in American Elections* (New York: Quorum Books, 1988), 50.

22. Thomas Byrne Edsall, *The New Politics of Inequality* (New York: Norton, 1984), 117–20.

23. For a detailed analysis of this process, see Ibid., Chapter Three: "The Politicization of the Business Community," pp. 107–40; and Vogel, *Fluctuating Fortunes.*

24. Press Release, Federal Election Commission, "FEC Releases Final PAC Report for the 1979-89 Election Cycle," February 21, 1982.

25. Eismeier and Pollock, *Business Money,* 47–57; and Edsall, *The New Politics,* 98–104.

26. Joint Committee on Taxation, *General Explanation of the Economic Recovery Tax Act of 1981,* December 29, 1981; and *The Changing Distribution of Federal Taxes: 1975–1990,* Congressional Budget Office, October, 1987.

27. Niemi, Mueller, and Smith, *Trends in Public Opinion,* tables, pp. 33, 35, 76, 80, 85, 87.

28. The Republican Senate candidates won fewer votes, but the votes they did win were far better targeted than the Democrats, who carried such mega-states as California, Ohio, and Illinois by huge margins, while losing by razor-thin margins contests in such states as New York, North Carolina, Idaho, and Wisconsin.

29. *Public Opinion,* (American Enterprise Institute), (April 1987) 34.

30. Tony Coelho interview with author, November 22, 1986.

31. Eismeier and Pollock, *Business Money,* 47.

## 9 The Reagan Attack on Race Liberalism

1. Richard M. Scammon and Alice V. McGillivray, *America at the Polls 2*, (Washington, D.C.: Congressional Quarterly, 1988), 3 and 29.

2. CBS News/New York Times exit poll data as developed by James L. Sundquist, "The 1984 Election: How Much Realignment," *The Brookings Review* (Winter 1985): 10.

3. Robert Beckel [Democratic consultant], interview with author, February 5, 1990.

4. From an interview with Richard Wirthlin by Bill Moyers, broadcast on "The Public Mind," a public affairs television program.

5. Remarks accepting the presidential nomination at the Republican National Convention in Dallas, Texas, August 23, 1984, in the official papers, *Administration of Ronald Reagan, 1984*, page 1,174.

6. Frederick T. Steeper and John R. Petrocik, "New Coalitions in 1988," (Paper supplied by the authors June 1987), Figure 4.

7. Miller and Traugott, *American National Election Studies*, 325.

8. Stanley B. Greenberg, *Report on Democratic Defection*, (Washington, D.C.: The Analysis Group April 15, 1985), 13–18, 28.

9. Milton Kotler and Nelson Rosenbaum, "Strengthening the Democratic Party through Strategic Marketing: Voters and Donors" (A confidential report for the Democratic National Committee) (Washington, D.C.: CRG Research Institute, 1985).

10. Miller and Traugott, *American National Election Studies*, 181.

11. Ibid., 183.

12. Kotler and Rosenbaum, "Strengthening the Democratic Party"; Greenberg, "Report on Democratic Defection," 24-25.

13. *1980 Congressional Quarterly Almanac* (Washington, D.C.: Congressional Quarterly Inc., 1981), 91-B.

14. *1983 Congressional Quarterly Almanac* (Washington, D.C.: Congressional Quarterly Inc., 1985), 89-B.

15. See Chapter 11 for further details on these cases.

16. Miller and Traugott, *American National Election Studies*, 199.

17. Data is from the 1986 NES survey, as reported by Susan E. Howell of the University of New Orleans in a paper, "Racial Attitudes Survey," March 1980.

18. William Bradford Reynolds, "The Reagan Administration and Civil Rights: Winning the War Against Discrimination," *University of Illinois Law Review*, 1986, Issue 4, page 1,014.

19. John L. Palmer and Isabel V. Sawhill, eds., *The Reagan Record* (Washington, D.C.: The Urban Institute, 1984), 201–205.

20. Reynolds quoted in Joel L. Selig, "The Reagan Justice Department and Civil Rights: What Went Wrong," *University of Illinois Law Review*, 1985, no. 4: 823.

21. Quoted in Drew S. Days, III, "Turning Back the Clock: The Reagan Administration and Civil Rights," *Harvard Civil Rights-Civil Liberties Law Review*, 19 (1984): 1,984.

22. While not unbiased, one of the most comprehensive summaries of the civil rights policies of the Reagan administration can be found in report issued by The Citizens' Commission on Civil Rights, *One Nation, Indivisible: The Civil Rights Challenge for the 1990s* (Washington, D.C., 1989).

23. *The Legal Services Record*, a bulletin regularly issued by the Legal Services Corporation, Washington, D.C., Fall, 1989, page 4.

24. Days, "Turning Back the Clock," 312.

25. Ibid., 342, and n. 169, p. 343.

26. Ibid., 824.

27. Interview in *U.S. News and World Report*, August 27, 1982.

28. Ernest Holsendolph, *New York Times*, July 3, 1982.

29. White House press release, "Civil Rights Nominees", issued July 7, 1983.

30. Palmer and Sawhill, *The Reagan Record*, 185–192.

31. Ibid., 185.

32. Figures based on Congressional Budget Office estimates to be published by the Ways and Means Committee, "Appendix I: Poverty, Income and Tax Burden Distributions, Wealth and Homeless Statistics," *Background Material and Data on Programs within the Jurisdiction of the Committee on Ways and Means* (Washington, D.C., 1990), 146, 147.

33. Ibid., Table 81, pp. 151–52.

34. Peter T. Kilborn, *New York Times,* March 13, 1990, page A24.

35. Jonathan Tasini, *New York Times,* October 30, 1988, page 4, Business Section.

36. Data supplied by telephone by the Bureau of Labor Statistics, Department of Labor, January. 1990.

37. Data supplied by telephone by the Bureau of Labor Statistics, Department of Labor, May 15, 1990.

38. *Economic Report of the President 1990,* Table C-44, p. 344.

39. Lou Cannon and Juan Williams, *Washington Post,* June 29, 1983, page A1.

40. Palmer and Sawhill, *The Reagan Record,* 305.

41. Phillips, *The Politics of Rich and Poor,* 173.

42. Ibid., 169, 178, 179.

43. Ways and Means Committee, *Background Material and Data 1990,* 146–47.

44. Joint Committee on Taxation, *General Explanation of the Economic Recovery Tax Act of 1981* 227–30. (Washington, D.C.: 1981)

45. Ibid., 6.

## 10    Coded Language: "Groups," "Taxes," "Big Government," and "Special Interests"

1. Figures based on computer-run of month-by-month employment data, supplied by the Bureau of Labor Statistics, the Department of Labor, April 1990.

2. Lawrence Quinn, "Workers See Future as Bleak," *The Vindicator* (Youngstown, Ohio), (September 20, 1977), p. 1.

3. Rose, "Twenty-Five Years Later," 1,145.

4. Witt, *Guide to the U.S. Supreme Court,* 605.

5. Figures based on computer-run of month-by-month employment data, supplied by the Bureau of Labor Statistics, the Department of Labor, April, 1990.

6. John J. Sheehan, legislative director, United Steelworkers of America, interview with author, February, 1990.

7. Carl Martilla, of the UAW in Detroit, supplied information to the author, on February 7, 1990.

8. Testimony to the Subcommittee on Employment Opportunities of the House Committee on Education and Labor, March 6, 1984.

9. Compensation figure from the Department of Labor, as reported by the *New York Times,* November 28, 1982, p. F-17.

10. See, for example, an interview with Lewis W. Foy, chairman of the Bethlehem Steel Corporation *U.S. News and World Report,* November 21, 1977, p. 90. Foy is quoted: "I told the government, 'If we're going to reopen that plant [in Johnstown, Pa.] and spend 35 or 40 million dollars just to clean it up, we've got to have some leeway on environmental expenditures there. Otherwise, we'll shut it down.' "

11. Peter F. Drucker, "Low Wages No Longer Give Competitive Edge," *Wall Street Journal,* March 16, 1988, p. 30.

12. Peter F. Drucker, *Wall Street Journal,* April 22, 1987, p. 32.

13. "The End of Corporate Loyalty?" *Business Week,* August 4, 1986, pp. 42–49; and "Middle Managers: Are They an Endangered Species?" *Business Week,* September 12, 1988, pp. 80–86.

14. *Economic Report of the President, 1986* (Washington, D.C.: GPO), 277.

15. Jack W. Germond and Jules Witcover, *Wake Us When It's Over; President Politics of 1984* (New York: Macmillan, 1985), 46–47.

16. Reuters News Service, February 12, 1984.

17. Germond and Witcover, *Wake Us When It's Over,* 376–77.

18. *Congressional Quarterly Almanac, 1984,* (Washington, D.C.: Congressional Quarterly, 1985), 64-B and 92-B.

19. *Congressional Quarterly Almanac, 1984,* 297.

20. Greenberg, *Report on Democratic Defectors,* 23.

21. Explanatory documents released by the Mondale campaign in 1984.

22. From Reagan's 1984 acceptance speech, Dallas, Texas, August 23, and again in the papers of the president, *Administration of Ronald Reagan, 1984* (Washington, D.C.: GPO, 1984), p. 1,179.

23. Germond and Witcover, *Wake Us When It's Over,* 266–77.

24. Speech to the Democratic National Convention, July 17, 1984, taken from: Rev. Jesse L. Jackson, *Straight from the Heart* (Philadelphia: Fortress Press, 1987), 3 and 5.

25. Arthur H. Miller, Anne Hildreth, Kevin M. Leyden and Christopher Wlezien, "Judging by the Company Candidates Keep: What's a Democrat to Do?" *Public Opinion* (July/August, 1988): 15.

26. *New York Times,* November 24, 1985, page 1.

27. Jonathan Moore, ed. *Campaign for President: The Managers Look at '84* (Dover, MA: Auburn House, 1986), 203.

28. The following account of the mobilization of fundamentalist Christians is based on interviews by the author during the 1984 campaign with Dr. Tim LaHaye, Gary Jarmin, Joe Rogers, Ronald Godwin, and on examination of tax and Federal Election Commission records available during the election.

29. Documents supplied by the Louisiana Commissioner of Elections for the periods ending March 31, 1984, and December 31, 1985.

30. Registration data supplied by the North Carolina State Board of Elections as of April 9, 1984 and as of October 8, 1984.

31. Lee Atwater, telephone interview with author, January 20, 1990.

32. This is based on estimates given to the author in interviews with present and former DNC officials.

33. Based on monthly RNC reports to the Federal Election Commission (FEC).

34. Based on reports of the Republican National, Congressional and Senatorial Committees to the FEC, available for inspection at the FEC, Washington, D.C.

35. Peter Hart, telephone interview with author, May 17, 1990.

36. Data on the percentage share of union membership made up of blacks and of government workers supplied by the Bureau of Labor Statistics, December 1989.

## 11  White Suburbs and a Divided Black Community

1. Sheldon Goldman, "Reagan's Judicial Legacy: Completing the Puzzle and Summing Up," *Judicature* (April-May 1989): 319–20.

2. David L. Rose, "Twenty-Five Years Later: Where Do We Stand on Equal Employment Opportunity Law Enforcement?" *Vanderbilt Law Review* (May 1989): 1121–82.

3. Department of Health and Human Services, data supplied by telephone, December 1989.

4. Department of Justice, "Criminal Victimization 1988," (October 1989), *Bureau of Justice Statistics Bulletin,* Table 4, p. 4.

5. Congressional Budget Office, "The Economic and Budget Outlook: Fiscal Years 1990–1994," *1989 Annual Report* (Washington, D.C., 1990) Table F, p. 133.

6. Lee Atwater, interview with author, in the Alexandria, Virginia, offices of Black, Manafort and Stone, December 11, 1984.

7. Ibid.

8. Lee Atwater, "The South In 1984," an unpublished analysis of Southern politics prepared for the Reagan-Bush campaign.

9. Thomas Byrne Edsall, *Washington Post*, January 20, 1989, A1.

10. Johnson, *National Party Platforms*, 809.

11. The account of the Horton case is well summarized in Robert James Bidinotto, "Getting Away with Murder," *The Reader's Digest* (July 1988): 57–63.

12. Ibid.

13. Dukakis was a strong supporter of the furlough program which was begun in 1972 during the administration of a liberal Republican governor, Frank Sargent.

14. Bidinotto, "Getting Away with Murder."

15. From a tape recording of Atwater's remarks to the GOP gathering in Atlanta, July 1988.

16. For an excellent summary of these arguments, see Richard Morin, *Washington Post*, February 12, 1989, K1.

17. "The People, The Press, & Politics, Survey VII, November Post-Election Typology Survey," conducted for Times Mirror by the Gallup Organization, Inc., released November 15, 1988, pages 4 and 8.

18. Ibid., 79 and 80.

19. Ed Reilly, telephone interview with author, April 19, 1990. Reilly conducted voter studies and focus groups for KRC Research and Consulting, of New York, Democrats For the '90s, a Democratic organization chaired by Pamela Harriman.

20. Michael Caccitolo, interview with author, October 1988, at campaign headquarters of State Senator Robert Raica (R) in Chicago.

21. John Morgan, demographic specialist for the Republican National Committee, telephone interview with author December 1988.

22. Population shifts favoring the suburbs in part grew out of policies initiated by the Democratic party, including construction of the interstate highway system, subsidized FHA mortgages, and veterans housing assistance.

23. Bureau of the Census, *Patterns of Metropolitan Area and County Population Growth: 1980 to 1987*, ser. P-25, no. 1039, p. 19.

24. *Statistical Abstract of the United States 1989*, 33–35.

25. I am indebted to Carl Pinkele of Ohio Wesleyan University for his knowledge of suburban politics in Ohio.

26. David Hurt, public affairs director of Gwinnett County, telephone interview with author, January 23, 1990.

27. Gary Orfield, "Racial Change and Desegregation in Large School Districts," Report to the National School Boards Association (June 1988), p. 7.

28. Caccitolo interview.

29. Data supplied by telephone by Jerry Jennings of the voting division of the Bureau of the Census, May 1, 1990.

30. Richard Scammon and Alice V. McGillivray, *America Votes 18* (Washington, D.C.: Congressional Quarterly, 1988); Scammon and McGillivray, *America at the Polls 2*, tables on each of these elections.

31. House Ways and Means Committee, *The 1990 Green Book*, 1108–9.

32. A large number of experiments have been performed to support this theory of prejudice. For a variety of analyses of this and other closely related issues, along with extensive listing of sources, see *The Journal of Social Issues*, Vol. 41, no. 3 (1985) on "Intergroup Contact," edited by Walter G. Stephan and John C. Brigham. I am also indebted to Myron Rothbart of the University of Oregon and Oliver P. John of the University of California, Berkeley, who generously shared their knowledge on this subject.

33. Jaynes and Williams, *A Common Destiny*, 165.

34. 1989 job data supplied by telephone by the Current Population Survey, Bureau of Labor Statistics on March 12, 1990; *Statistical Abstract of the United States 1989*, 16.

35. For summaries of some of the major work on the underclass see: *The Annals of the American Academy of Political and Social Sciences,* January 1989, with articles by Loic J.D. Vacquant, William Julius Wilson, John D. Kasarda, Mercer L. Sullivan, Marta Tienda, Robert D. Reischauer, Jennifer L. Hochschild, Lawrence M. Mead, Richard P. Nathan; *Focus,* a publication of the University of Wisconsin-Madison Institute for Research on Poverty, Spring and Summer 1989, with articles by Sheldon Danziger, David T. Ellwood, Christopher Jencks, Martha Van Haitsma, and Erol Ricketts; the Summer 1989 issue of *The Public Interest,* with articles by Isabel V. Sawhill, Daniel Patrick Moynihan, and John J. DiIulio Jr.; *The Public Interest,* Fall 1987, with articles by George Gilder, Michael Novak, and Leslie Lenkowsky; *Political Science Quarterly,* Fall, 1985, with articles by Charles Murray and Sar Levitan.

36. The articles cited in note 35 explore these issues.

37. Both the Allport and Cook quotes are taken from a summary of studies of group relationships, Stephan and Brigham, "Intergroup Contact," 1.

38. Kenneth Tollet, telephone interview with author, April 25, 1990.

39. Summary of a Justice Department Press release, "Black Victims," released by the Bureau of Justice Statistics, April 22, 1990.

40. From *Criminal Victimization in the United States,* 1986 and 1987.

41. Ibid. The overall offender-victim figures by race for violent crime and robbery specifically in 1986–87 are:

Offender-Victim Figures for Robbery, Rape and Assault, 1986–87

| Victims | White Offenders | | Black Offenders | |
|---|---|---|---|---|
| White | 6,757,991 | 97.6% | 1,549,896 | 53.8% |
| Black | 167,842 | 2.4% | 1,330,538 | 46.2% |
| Total | 6,925,833 | 100% | 2,880,434 | 100% |

Offender-Victim Figures for Robbery Alone in 1986–87

| Victims | White Offenders | | Black Offenders | |
|---|---|---|---|---|
| White | 737,621 | 95.8% | 568,275 | 59.9% |
| Black | 32,132 | 4.8% | 379,943 | 40.1% |
| Total | 769,753 | 100% | 948,218 | 00% |

42. Tape recorded by author at the October meeting of Parents against Crime in Chicago.

43. Ed Reilly, telephone interview with author, April 1990.

44. Bernard R. Boxill, "Is Further Civil Rights Legislation Irrelevant to Black Progress?" in Wilson A. Van Horne and Thomas V. Tonnesen, *Race: Twentieth Century Dilemmas—Twenty-first Century Prognoses* (Milwaukee: University of Wisconsin System, Institute on Race and Ethnicity, 1989).

45. From a speech given by Farrakhan in New Orleans at the African American Summit '89, April 23, 1989.

46. William G. Blair, *New York Times,* November 21, 1988, p. 1; *Newsweek,* December 5, 1988, p. 94.

47. John Kifner, *New York Times,* December 5, 1988, p. B1.

48. Howard Kurtz, *Washington Post,* December 29, 1989, p. A1.

49. Welsing quoted by Leon Wieseltier, "Scar Tissue," *New Republic,* June 5, 1989, p. 19.

50. WCBS-TV News/The New York Times poll, taken June 21–25, 1988. Generally similar findings were produced in polls taken in January 1987, and January 1988.

51. WCBS-TV News/The New York Times polls taken June 21–25, 1988, in the case of the Brawley data; and April 27–May 3, 1985, in the case of the Goetz data.

52. John D. Kasarda, "Urban Industrial Transition and the Underclass," *The Annals of the American Academy of Political and Social Science* (January 1989), 29 and 31.

53. Ibid., 34.

54. Ibid., 37.

55. James P. Markey, "The Labor Market Problems of Today's High School Dropouts," *Monthly Labor Review* 3, no. 6 (June 1988), 41 and 42.

56. Ibid., Table 5, p. 41.

57. Ibid., p. 39.

58. "Research Report," by KRC Research and Consulting, of New York, for "Democrats For the '90s," November 1989, pages 3 and 4.

59. Kevin Murphy and Finis Welch, "Wage Differentials in the 1980s: The Role of International Trade," page 8a; and Chinhui Juhn, Kevin M. Murphy and Brooks Pierce, "Accounting for the Slowdown in Black-White Wage Convergence." Both papers were delivered at an American Enterprise Institute conference, Washington, D.C., November 3, 1989.

60. Bureau of the Census, *The Black Population of the United States: March 1988*, ser. P-20, no. 442 (Washington, D.C.: 1989), 7.

61. Deborah J. Carter and Reginald Wilson, "Minorities in Higher Education." A report published by the American Council on Education (December, 1989), 20.

62. Department of Education, *Digest of Education Statistics 1989*, (Washington, D.C.: December 1989), Table 182, p. 199.

63. Juhn, Murphy and Pierce, "Accounting for the Slowdown." John Bound and Richard B. Freeman had similar findings in "What Went Wrong? The Erosion of the Relative Earnings and Employment of Young Black Men in the 1980s," preliminary draft made available by Freeman in May 1990.

64. *Economic Report of the President, 1990*, 344.

65. Juhn, Murphy and Pierce, "Accounting for the Slowdown," 4.

66. Ibid., 6.

67. See, for example, Reynolds Farley and Walter R. Allen, *The Color Line and the Quality of Life in America* (New York: Russell Sage Foundation, 1987), which found black women between the ages of 35–44 and 45–54 making 107 and 101 percent of white women's income in 1984, while their black male counterparts were making 60 and 63 percent of white male income. Murphy and Welch, "Wage Differentials in the 1980s," found that by 1980, black male weekly wages had reached 80 percent of white male wages, while the wages of black women were equal to those of white women.

68. Juhn, Murphy and Pierce, "Accounting for the Slowdown," Tables 7 and 8, p. 33.

69. Ibid., figure 1a, p. 4.

70. From Thomas G. Mortenson, *The Impact of Increased Loan Utilization Among Low Family Income Students* (Iowa City, Iowa: American College Testing Program, 1990.)

71. Fred M. Hechinger, "About Education," and Edward B. Fiske, "Lessons," *New York Times*, April 25, 1990.

72. Computed from *Economic Report of the President, 1990*, 359 and *Digest of Education Statistics 1989*, 281.

73. For extensive discussion of the *Griggs* case and of subsequent decisions see Hugh Davis Graham, *The Civil Rights Era* (New York, Oxford University Press, 1990), 383–92; Charles V. Dale, "Federal Civil Rights Decisions of the Supreme Court during the 1988–89 Term." A report issued by Congressional Research Service, July 28, 1989; and Alexandra K. Wigdor and Wendell R. Garner, eds., *Ability Testing: Uses, Consequences, and Controversies Part I and II* (Washington, D.C.: National Academy Press, 1982).

74. Dale, "Federal Civil Rights Decisions," 3 and 4.

75. Wigdor and Garner, eds., *Ability Testing Part I and Part II;* John A. Hartigan and Alexandra K. Wigdor, eds., *Fairness in Employment Testing* (Washington, D.C.: National Academy Press, 1989).

76. Wigdor and Garner in *Ability Testing* found that studies showed that "on tests of verbal and non-verbal ability, reading comprehension, mathematics achievement, and general information" the "largest differences in group averages usually existed between blacks and whites on all five tests and at all grade levels. In terms of the distribution of scores for whites, the average score for blacks was roughly one standard deviation below the average for whites." (Part 1, p. 72) That is, "a rule [or test result] that would select 20 percent of the group with the higher average would select only 3 percent of the group with the lower average." (Part 1, p. 72)

The academy considered the charge that the ability tests studied failed to predict accurately academic and job performance for blacks, and found that: "The results do not support the notion that the traditional use of test scores in a prediction equation yields predictions for blacks that systematically underestimate their actual performance. If anything, there is some indication of the converse, with actual criterion performance being more often lower than would be indicated by test scores of blacks. Thus, in the technically precise meaning of the term, ability tests have not been proved to be biased against blacks: that is, they predict criterion performance as well for blacks as for whites." (Part 1, p. 77)

Studies cited by the academy in addition found that: "Though generally not quite as large as the black-white average differences, [study authors] Coleman et al. found differences large enough to result in considerable adverse impact for Mexican Americans, Puerto Ricans, and Indian Americans when compared to whites." (Part 1, p. 73)

77. Wigdor and Garner, *Ability Testing, Part I,* 71–73.

78. For a more detailed description of these practices see Hartigan and Wigdor, *Fairness in Employment Testing;* the December 1986 and December 1988 issues of the *Journal of Vocational Behavior* (Academic Press, San Diego); and the March/April 1990 issue of *Society* (on the topic of race norming), published by Rutgers University, New Brunswick, N.J.

79. Linda S. Gottfredson, interview with author, April 27, 1990. Gottfredson has written in *Public Interest, Society,* and in numerous journals on the subject of ability testing.

80. Hartigan and Wigdor, *Fairness in Employment Testing,* 132 and 247. This study by the National Academy of Sciences provides an extensive discussion of all the issues surrounding validity generalization, and provides detailed references to related work.

81. James C. Sharf, "Litigating Personnel Measurement Policy," *Journal of Vocational Behavior* (December 1988): 254 and 239.

82. Memorandum from Marc Bendick Jr. to NAACP Legal Defense Fund, the Ford Foundation, the Mexican American Legal Defense Fund, and five other organizations and individuals, November 17, 1986.

83. Marc Bendick, Jr., telephone interview with author, May 26, 1990.

84. Dale, "Federal Civil Right Decisions," 5 and 6.

85. Raymond Tatalovich and Byron W. Daynes, eds., *Social Regulatory Policy* (Boulder, CO: Westview Press, 1988), 176.

## 12   The Stakes

1. Cf. Table 12.1, p. 279, for alternative wordings of this question.

2. Miller and Traugott, *American National Election Studies,* 179–84.

3. Data from ABC exit polls compiled by Merle Black, of the Political Science Department of Emory University, supplied to author by phone, May 22, 1990.

4. V.O. Key, Jr., *Southern Politics in State and Nation* (New York: Vintage, 1949), 131.

5. *Economic Report of the President, 1990,* 328.

6. Interview with Vin Weber by Adam Meyerson in *Policy Review,* (Heritage Foundation), (Spring 1990): 38 and 42.

7. *Economic Report of the President, 1987,* 278.

8. House Ways and Means Committee, *The 1990 Green Book,* 1,189.

9. Various scholars and political analysts have pointed out that one reason for continued Democratic party strength in the House lies in the difficulty of the GOP in recruiting strong candidates. See Gary C. Jacobson, "The Persistence of Democratic House Majorities: Structure or Politics?" (Paper presented at the American Political Science Association meeting, San Francisco, August 30–September 2, 1990.

10. Federal Election Commission (FEC), *$458 Million Spent by 1988 Congressional Campaigns* (Washington, D.C., February 24, 1989), 6.

11. Federal Election Commission (FEC), *FEC Finds Slower Growth of PAC Activity During 1988 Election Cycle* (Washington, D.C., April 9, 1989), 4.

12. All the data on committees and mail costs is from Norman J. Ornstein, Thomas E. Mann and Michael J. Malbin, eds., *Vital Statistics on Congress, 1987–88* (Washington, D.C.: Congressional Quarterly, 1987), 123–57.

13. Transcript from a GOPAC conference in Washington, January 1989, provided by the organization.

14. Abigail M. Thernstrom, *Whose Votes Count?* (Cambridge, MA: Harvard University Press, 1987), p. 192–231.

15. Data from ABC exit polls compiled by Merle Black, of the Political Science Department of Emory University, supplied to author by phone, May 22, 1990.

16. Don Fowler, interview with author, in Fowler's offices in Columbia, SC, 1985.

17. Joe Reed, telephone interview with author, May 1989.

18. See, for examples, James Pinkerton, "The New Paradigm." (A speech to the Reason Foundation in Los Angeles, April 23, 1990); Paul Weyrich, "Memorandum—Our New Conservative Agenda," dated April 18, 1990 (Washington, D.C.: The Free Congress Foundation); Jack Kemp, "An Inquiry into the Nature and Causes of Poverty in America and How to Combat It," (A speech given at the Heritage Foundation, June 6, 1990); Jack Kemp, "Tackling Poverty: Market-Based Policies to Empower the Poor," *Policy Review,* (Heritage Foundation), (Winter 1990); also an untitled speech by Newt Gingrich to the Southern Republican Leadership Conference in Raleigh, NC, March 30, 1990.

The status of the "realignment-oriented" faction within the GOP is far from dominant. White House policy makers in 1990 rejected proposals of an executive branch anti-poverty task force as too expensive and too controversial. (Robert Pear, *New York Times,* July 6, 1990, page A1.) In November 1990, in an additional indication of schisms within the Republican party surrounding such issues, Richard Darman, head of the Office of Management and Budget, went out of his way to publicly ridicule the work of conservative anti-poverty strategist aide James Pinkerton. Darman said about Pinkerton's "New Paradigm" theory: "The effete might debate whether the new paradigm is, perhaps, enigmatically paradigmatic. . . . At the same time, in the real world, others might simply dismiss it by picking up the refrain, 'Hey brother, can you paradigm?' . . ." (David Rosenbaum, *New York Times,* November 17, 1990, p. 12.)

19. Kemp, "An Inquiry into the Nature and Causes of Poverty," p. 2.

20. Stuart Butler, "Razing the Liberal Plantation: A Conservative War on Poverty," *National Review,* November 10, 1989, p. 28.

21. Gingrich, speech at the Southern Republican Leadership Conference, p. 7.

22. Pinkerton, "The New Paradigm," p. 2.

23. *House Ways and Means Committee, 1990 Green Book,* 1,189.

24. Lawrence M. Mead, "The Changing Agenda of Welfare Reform in the United States, 1967–1988", chapter from the forthcoming book, *The New Dependency Politics* (a paper presented at the American Political Science Association meetings, San Francisco, August 30–September 2, 1990).

25. Stokely Carmichael and Charles V. Hamilton, *Black Power: The Politics of Liberation in America* (New York: Vintage Books, 1967), 18.

26. The political power of teen pregnancy, for example, is reflected in the enormous and

growing cost to taxpayers of such pregnancies. In 1989, the U.S. government paid $21.55 *billion* in Food Stamps, A.F.D.C., and Medicaid benefits for families in which the first child was born when the mother was a teenager, according to a report issued on September 23, 1990 by the Center for Population Options, Washington, D.C.

The costs of teen pregnancy are increasing, according to Child Trends, a Washington, D.C. non-profit research institute: For whites, the proportion of teen pregnancies to unmarried females (most likely to require government help) went from 18 percent in 1970, to 33 percent in 1980, to 54 percent in 1988. For blacks, the proportion went from 64 percent in 1970, to 86 percent in 1980, to 91 percent in 1988.

27. See Gertrude Himmelfarb, *The Idea of Poverty: England in the Early Industrial Age* (New York: Vintage Books, 1983), 523–34.

28. Ronald Walters, telephone interview with author, April 1, 1990.

29. In 1986, for example, 74 percent of blacks said federal spending on programs to assist blacks should be increased and 26 percent said it should be kept the same or decreased, while only 17 percent of whites said spending should be increased, and 83 percent said it should be kept the same or decreased. Asked whether spaces should be reserved on a quota basis at colleges for blacks, 78 percent of blacks said yes, 22 percent said no, while for whites 74 percent said no, and 26 percent said yes. See Donald R. Kinder and Lynn M. Sanders, "Pluralistic Foundations of American Opinion on Race," (A paper presented at the Annual Meeting of the American Political Science Association, Chicago, September 3–7, 1987).

30. Roger Wilkins, "Harping on Racism," *Mother Jones* (December 1989).

31. Patrick J. Buchanan, *The Arizona Republic* (May 24, 1990): A17.

32. R. Douglas Arnold, in his book *The Logic of Congressional Action* (New Haven CT: Yale University Press, 1990), argues that "the most persuasive explanation for why policy issues do not play a larger role in congressional elections is that legislators constantly adjust their decisions in Washington to satisfy their constituents back home." His argument indirectly suggests that avoidance of difficult racial issues may well be a strategy of accommodation to conflicting and ambivalent constituent views.

33. James R. Kluegel, "Trends in Whites' Explanations of the Black-White Gap in Socioeconomic Status, 1977–1989," *American Sociological Review* (August 1990): 512–25. Kleugel employs data from five years of the General Social Survey (GSS): 1977, 1985, 1986, 1988, and 1989. The following question was asked in each of the five survey years: "On the average blacks have worse jobs, income, and housing than white people. Do you think these differences are:

A. mainly due to *discrimination.*

B. because most blacks have less *in-born ability* to learn.

C. because most blacks don't have the *chance for education* that it takes to rise out of poverty.

D. because most blacks don't have the *motivation* or will power to pull themselves out of poverty."

34. Ibid., 512: "Individualist and structuralist explanations of the black-white economic gap are not necessarily seen by whites as mutually exclusive. Indeed, a number of scholars have proposed that ambivalence or inconsistency is an important hallmark of contemporary racial attitudes among whites. . . .

'Apparently blacks are seen as both disadvantaged (by the system) and deviant (in the sense of having qualities that go counter to the main society's values and norms).' (Katz, Wackenhut, and Hass, "Racial Ambivalence, Value Duality, and Behavior," in John Dovidio and Samuel Gaertner. *Prejudice, Discrimination, and Racism.* Orlando: Academic Press, 1986, p. 42)."

35. Beryl Fredell, interview with author, in front of the Fredell home in the East Bluff section of Peoria, September 6, 1990.

36. The future for social spending looks grim. In the 1990 midterm elections, citizen anger over rising taxes transcended partisan boundaries, with anti-tax sentiment knocking

off incumbent governors Mike Hayden (R) in Kansas, Kay Orr (R) in Nebraska, Bob Martinez (R) in Florida, and James Blanchard (D) in Michigan. Intense voter discontent in New Jersey in the wake of tax increases and downwardly-redistributive legislation pushed through by Democratic governor Jim Florio produced the near defeat of once-invincible senator Bill Bradley (D).

37. *Statistical Abstract of the United States, 1987,* Table 34, p. 28.

38. David Koehler tape-recorded by author at a meeting of the Averyville Community Association, September 6, 1990, in Peoria.

39. Gunnar Myrdal, *An American Dilemma* vol. 2 (New York: Pantheon Books, 1972), 997.

40. For example, intraparty controversy reared its head in September 1990, when the Progressive Policy Institute issued a report, "Putting Children First", by Elaine Kamarck and William Galston—a report which breached liberal orthodoxy (cf. Chapter One, note 12).

At another level, an example of a bitter appropriations battle—likely to be seen more often in the future—was reported by Dan Morgan in *The Washington Post* on September 25, 1990: "The stage is set in the Senate Appropriations Committee for 'the battle of the needy.' It pits lobbyists for AIDS patients and big cities hardest hit by the AIDS epidemic against advocates for other sick, poor, and disadvantaged groups in a Dickensian scramble for scarce federal dollars."

# Bibliography

Abramson, Paul R., John H. Aldrich, and David W. Rohde. *Change and Continuity in the 1984 Elections.* rev. ed. Washington, D.C.: Congressional Quarterly, 1987.

Amaker, Norman C. *Civil Rights and the Reagan Administration.* Washington, D.C.: Urban Institute Press, 1988.

Ambrose, Stephen E. *Nixon: The Triumph of a Politician 1962–1972.* Vol. 2. New York: Simon and Schuster, 1989.

*The Annals of the American Academy of Political and Social Sciences.* January 1989, with articles by Loic J.D. Vacquant, William Julius Wilson, John D. Kasarda, Mercer L. Sullivan, Marta Tienda, Robert D. Reischauer, Jennifer L. Hochschild, Lawrence M. Mead, Richard P. Nathan.

Arnold, Douglas. *The Logic of Congressional Action.* New Haven: Yale University Press, 1990.

Atwater, Lee. "The South In 1984." Unpublished analysis of southern politics prepared for the Reagan-Bush campaign.

Ashmore, Harry S. *Hearts and Minds: A Personal Chronicle of Race in America.* Cabin John, MD: Seven Locks Press, 1988.

Auletta, Ken. *The Underclass.* New York: Vintage, 1982.

Barone, Michael. *Our Country.* New York: Free Press, 1990.

Barone, Michael, Ujifusa Grant, and Douglas Mathews. *The Almanac of American Politics 1972.* Gambit, 1972.

Barone, Michael, Ujifusa Grant, and Douglas Mathews. *The Almanac of American Politics 1978.* New York: Sunrise Book, Dutton, 1977.

Barone, Michael, Ujifusa Grant, and Mathews, Douglas. *The Almanac of American Politics 1980.* E.P. Dutton, New York, 1979.

Barone, Michael, and Ujifusa, Grant. *The Almanac of American Politics 1982.* Washington, D.C.: Barone & Company, 1981.

Barone, Michael, and Ujifusa, Grant. *The Almanac of American Politics 1984.* Washington, D.C.: National Journal, 1983.

Barone, Michael, and Ujifusa Grant. *The Almanac of American Politics 1988.* Washington, D.C.: National Journal, 1987.

Barone, Michael, and Ujifusa Grant. *The Almanac of American Politics 1990.* Washington, D.C.: National Journal, 1989.

Barrett, Laurence I. *Gambling with History: Reagan in the White House.* New York: Penguin, 1984.

Bell, Derrick. *And We Are Not Saved: The Elusive Quest for Racial Justice.* New York: Basic Books, 1979.

Bellah, Robert N., Richard Madsen, William M. Sullivan, Ann Swidler, and Steven M. Tipton. *Habits of the Heart: Individualism and Commitment in American Life.* Berkeley: University of California Press, 1985.

Bendick, Marc, Jr. Memorandum to NAACP Legal Defense Fund, the Ford Foundation, the Mexican American Legal Defense Fund, and five other organizations and individuals. November 17, 1986.

Bennett, David H. *The Party of Fear: From Nativist Movements to the New Right in American History.* Chapel Hill: University of North Carolina Press, 1988.

Berger, Raoul. *Government by Judiciary: The Transformation of the Fourteenth Amendment.* Cambridge: Harvard University Press, 1977.

Berman, Larry, ed. *Looking Back on the Reagan Presidency.* Baltimore: John Hopkins University, 1990.

Bidinotto, Robert James. "Getting Away with Murder." *The Reader's Digest,* July 1988.

Birnbaum, Norman. *The Radical Renewal: The Politics of Ideas in Modern America.* New York: Pantheon Books. 1988.

Black, Earl. *Southern Governors and Civil Rights.* Cambridge: Harvard University Press. 1976.

Black, Earl, and Merle Black. "The 1988 Presidential Election and the Future of Southern Politics", Paper presented at the Southern Political Science Association. Memphis, Tenn. Nov. 2–4, 1989.

———. *Politics and Society in the South.* Cambridge: Harvard University Press, 1987.

Blackburn, McKinley L., David E. Bloom, and Richard B. Freeman. "The Declining Economic Position of Less-Skilled American Males." *Working Paper Series.* no. 3186, National Bureau of Economic Research, November 1989.

Blasi, Vincent. *The Burger Court: The Counter Revolution That Wasn't.* New Haven: Yale University, 1983.

Blauner, Bob. *Black Lives, White Lives: Three Decades of Race Relations in America.* Berkeley: University of California Press, 1989.

Blits, Jan H., and Linda S. Gottfredson. "Employment Testing and Job Performance." *The Public Interest,* no. 98 (Winter 1990).

Blumenthal, Sidney. *Pledging Allegiance: The Last Campaign of the Cold War.* New York: HarperCollins. 1990.

———. *The Rise of the Counter-Establishment: From Conservative Ideology to Political Power.* New York: Times Books. 1986.

Blumstein, Alfred, and Jacqueline Cohen. "On the Racial Disproportionality of the United States' Prison Populations." *The Journal of Criminal Law and Criminology* 73, no. 3 (1982).

Blumstein, Alfred, Jacqueline Cohen, and Harold D. Miller. "Demographically Disaggregated Projections of Prison Populations." *Research in Public Policy Analysis.* (JAI Press) 1 (1981).

Bobo, Lawrence. "Group Conflict, Prejudice, and the Paradox of Contemporary Racial Attitudes." In *Eliminating Racism: Profiles in Controversy.* edited by Phyllis A. Katz and Dalmas A. Taylor. New York: Plenum Press, 1988.

———. "Whites' Opposition to Busing: Symbolic Racism or Realistic Group Conflict?" *Journal of Personality and Social Psychology* 43. no. 6 (1983).

Bodnar, John. *The Transplanted: A History of Immigrants in Urban America.* Bloomington, IN: Indiana University Press. 1985.

Borjas, George J. *Friends and Strangers: The Impact of Immigrants on the U.S. Economy.* New York: Basic, 1990.

Boskin, Michael J. *Reagan and the Economy.* San Francisco: Institute for Contemporary Studies Press, 1987.

Bound, John, and Richard B. Freeman. "What Went Wrong? The Erosion of the Relative Earnings and Employment of Young Black Men in the 1980s." Preliminary draft made available by Freeman. May 1990.

Braddock, Jomills Henry, II. "School Desegregation and Black Assimilation," *Journal of Social Issues* 41, no. 3 (1985).

Brady, David W. *Critical Elections and Congressional Policy Making.* Stanford, CA: Stanford University Press, 1988.

Brady, David W., and Bernard Grofman. "The Decline in Electoral Competition and the Swing Ratio in the U.S. House Elections: 1850–1980." (Paper provided by David Brady.)

Brady, David W., and Patricia A. Hurley. "The Prospects for Contemporary Partisan Realignment." *PS.* 18, no. 1 (Winter 1985).

Branch, Taylor. *Parting the Waters: America in the King Years, 1954–1963.* New York: Simon and Schuster, 1988.

Broder, David S. *The Party's Over: The Failure of Politics in America.* New York: Harper and Row, 1971.

Broder, David, Lou Cannon, Haynes Johnson, Martin Schram, and Richard Harwood. *The Pursuit of the Presidency 1980.* New York, Berkley Books, 1980.

Brown, Michael K., and Steven P. Erie. "Blacks and the Legacy of the Great Society: The Economic and Political Impact of Federal Social Policy." *Public Policy* (Summer 1981).

Brown, Thad A. *Migration and Politics: The Impact of Population Mobility on American Voting Behavior.* Chapel Hill: University of North Carolina Press. 1988.

Browning, Rufus P., Dale Rogers Marshall, and David H. Tabb. *Protest Is Not Enough.* Berkeley: University of California Press, 1984.

Bullock, Charles S., III, and Charles M. Lamb. *Implementation of Civil Rights Policy.* Monterey, CA: Brooks/Cole, 1984.

Bullock, Paul, ed. *Watts: The Aftermath by the People of Watts.* New York: Grove Press, 1969.

Burnham, Walter Dean. "Voting Specialists: Permanent Campaigns and the Prospects for Critical Realignment." (Paper provided by the author.)

Butler, Stuart. "Razing the Liberal Plantation: A Conservative War on Poverty." *National Review,* November 10, 1989.

Button, James W. *Black Violence: Political Impact of the 1960s Riots.* Princeton, NJ: Princeton University Press, 1978.

Button, James W. *Blacks and Social Change.* Princeton, NJ: Princeton University Press, 1989.

Caddell, Patrick H. "Initial Working Paper on Political Strategy." Memorandum dated December 10, 1976.

Cannon, Lou. *Reagan.* New York: Perigee Books, 1984.

Carlson, Jody. *George C. Wallace and the Politics of Powerlessness.* New Brunswick, NJ: Transaction Books, 1981.

Carmichael, Stokely, and Charles V. Hamilton. *Black Power: The Politics of Liberation in America.* New York: Vintage Books, 1967.

Carmines, Edward G., and James A. Stimson. "Issue Evolution, Population Replacement, and Normal Partisan Change." *The American Political Science Review* 75 (March 1981).

———. *Issue Evolution: Race and the Transformation of American Politics.* Princeton, NJ: Princeton University Press. 1989.

———. "On the Structure and Sequence of Issue Evolution". *The American Political Science Review* 80 (September 1986).

———. "Racial Issues and the Structure of Mass Belief Systems." *The Journal of Politics* 44 (1982).

Carter, Deborah J., and Reginald Wilson. "Minorities in Higher Education." Report to the American Council on Education, December 1989.

Carter, Stephen L. "The Best Black and Other Tales." *Reconstruction* 1, no. 1 (Winter 1990).

Chubb, John E., and Terry M. Moe. *Politics, Markets and America's Schools.* Washington, D.C.: Brookings Institution, 1990.

Citizens' Commission on Civil Rights. *One Nation, Indivisible: The Civil Rights Challenge for the 1990s.* Washington, D.C., 1989.

Cloward, Richard A., and Frances Fox Piven. "Finessing The Poor." *The Nation,* October 7, 1968.

———. "A Strategy To End Poverty." *The Nation,* May 2, 1966.

*Congress and the Nation.* Vol. II, 1965–1968. Washington, D.C.: Congressional Quarterly, 1969.

*Congress and the Nation.* Vol. III, 1969–1972. Washington, D.C.: Congressional Quarterly, 1973.

*Congress and the Nation.* Vol. IV, 1973–1976. Washington, D.C.: Congressional Quarterly, 1977.

*Congress and the Nation.* Vol. V, 1977–1980. Washington, D.C.: Congressional Quarterly, 1981.

*Congress and the Nation.* Vol. VI, 1981–1984. Washington, D.C.: Congressional Quarterly, 1985.

Congressional Budget Office. "Appendix I: Poverty, Income and Tax Burden Distributions, Wealth and Homeless Statistics." Data compiled for the Ways and Means Committee. Washington, D.C., 1990.

Congressional Budget Office. "The Changing Distribution of Federal Taxes: 1975–1990." Washington, D.C., October 1987.

Congressional Budget Office. "The Economic and Budget Outlook: Fiscal Years 1990–1994." Part I. Washington, D.C., 1989.

*Congressional Quarterly Almanac 1966.* Washington, D.C.: Congressional Quarterly Inc., 1967.

*Congressional Quarterly Almanac 1967.* Washington, D.C.: Congressional Quarterly Inc., 1968.

*Congressional Quarterly Almanac 1972.* Washington, D.C.: Congressional Quarterly Inc., 1973.

*Congressional Quarterly Almanac 1980.* Washington, D.C.: Congressional Quarterly Inc., 1981.

*Congressional Quarterly Almanac 1984.* Washington, D.C.: Congressional Quarterly Inc., 1985.

*Congressional Quarterly Almanac 1990.* Washington, D.C.: Congressional Quarterly Inc., 1991.

Cottingham, Phoebe H., and David T. Ellwood, eds. *Welfare Policy for the 1990's.* Cambridge: Harvard University Press, 1989.

CRG Research Institute. "Strengthening the Democratic Party through Strategic Marketing: Voters and Donors." Report for the Democratic National Committee, 1985.

Cuddihy, John Murray. *The Ordeal of Civility.* New York: Dell, 1974.

Dale, Charles V. "Federal Civil Rights Decisions of the Supreme Court During the 1988–89 Term." Report issued by Congressional Research Service, July 28, 1989.

Days, Drew S., III. "Turning Back the Clock: The Reagan Administration and Civil Rights." *Harvard Civil Rights-Civil Liberties Law Review* 19 (1984).

DeNardo, James. *Power in Numbers: The Political Strategy of Protest and Rebellion.* Princeton, NJ: Princeton University Press, 1985.

Dent, Harry S. *The Prodigal South Returns to Power.* New York: Wiley, 1978.

Diamond, Edwin, and Stephen Bates. *The Spot.* Cambridge: MIT Press, 1988.

Domhoff, William. *The Powers That Be.* New York: Random House/Vintage, 1979.

*Economic Report of the President,* Washington, D.C.: GPO 1990.

*Economic Report of the President.* Washington, D.C.: GPO, 1987.

*Economic Report of the President.* Washington, D.C.: GPO, 1986.

*Economic Report of the President.* Washington, D.C.: GPO, 1979.

Eddy, Mark. "Federal Programs for Minority and Women-Owned Businesses." Congressional Research Service. May 1, 1989.

Edsall, Nicholas C. *The Anti-Poor Law Movement: 1834–1844.* Manchester, England: Manchester University Press, 1971.

Edsall, Thomas Byrne. *The New Politics of Inequality.* New York: Norton, 1984.

Eismeier, Theodore J., and Philip H. Pollock, III. *Business Money and the Rise of Corporate PACs in American Elections.* New York: Quorum Books, 1988.

*Business Week,* "The End of Corporate Loyalty?" August 4, 1986.

Equal Employment Opportunity Commission. "Annual Report on the Employment of Minorities, Women, and People with Disabilities in the Federal Government Fiscal Year 1988." Washington, D.C.: GPO, 1982.

Equal Employment Opportunity Commission. "EEOC Announces Record-Breaking First Quarter in Enforcement of Equal Employment Opportunity Statutes." January 29, 1986.

Erie, Steven P. "Public Policy and Black Economic Polarization." *Policy Analysis* (Summer 1980).

———. *Rainbow's End.* Berkeley: University of California Press, 1988.

———. "Two Faces of Ethnic Power: Comparing the Irish and Black Experiences." *The Journal of the Northeastern Political Science Association* (Winter 1980).

Evans, Rowland, Jr., and Robert D. Novak. *Nixon in the White House.* New York: Random House, 1971.

Evans, Sara. *Personal Politics.* New York: Random House, 1980.

Ewen, Stuart. *All Consuming Images.* New York: Basic Books, 1988.

Farley, Reynolds. *Blacks and Whites: Narrowing the Gap?* Cambridge: Harvard University Press, 1984.

Farley, Reynolds, and Walter R. Allen. *The Color Line and the Quality of Life in America.* New York: Russell Sage Foundation, 1987.

Federal Election Commission. "$458 Million Spent by 1988 Congressional Campaigns." February 24, 1989.

Federal Election Commission. "FEC Finds Slower Growth of PAC Activity during 1988 Election Cycle." April 9, 1989.

Federal Election Commission. "FEC Releases Final PAC Report for the 1979–89 Election Cycle." February 21, 1982.

Ferguson, Thomas, and Rogers, Joel. *Right Turn.* New York: Hill and Wang. 1986.

Feulner, Edwin J., Jr., *Conservatives Stalk the House: The Story of The Republican Study Committee.* Ottawa, IL: Green Hill Publishers, Inc., 1983.

*Focus.* A publication of the University of Wisconsin-Madison Institute for Research on Poverty, (Spring/Summer, 1989). See articles by Sheldon Danziger, David T. Ellwood, Christopher Jencks, Martha Van Haitsma, and Erol Ricketts.

Forster, Arnold, and Benjamin R. Epstein. *Danger on the Right.* New York: Random House, 1964.

Foy, Lewis W. Interviewed in *U.S. News and World Report.* November 21, 1977.

Fraser, Steve, and Gary Gerstle. *The Rise and Fall of the New Deal Order.* Princeton, NJ: Princeton University Press, 1989.

Freeman, Richard B. *Black Elite: The New Market for Highly Educated Black Americans.* New York: McGraw-Hill, 1976.

Fremon, David K. *Chicago Politics Ward by Ward.* Bloomington, IN: Indiana University Press, 1988.

Fuchs, Lawrence H. *The American Kaleidoscope: Race, Ethnicity, and the Civic Culture.* Hanover, NH, and London. University Press of New England, 1990.

Galderisi, Peter F., Michael S. Lyons, Randy T. Simmons, and John G. Francis, ed. *The Politics of Realignment: Party Change in the Mountain West.* Boulder, CO: Westview Press, 1987.

Galston, William A. "Liberal Virtues." *The American Political Science Review* 82, (December 1988).

Gans, Herbert J. "Deconstructing the Underclass: The Term's Danger as a Planning Concept." *The American Planning Association Journal* (Summer 1990).

Garrow, David J. *Bearing the Cross: Martin Luther King, Jr., and the Southern Christian Leadership Conference.* New York: Morrow, 1986.

Gates, Henry Louis, Jr. "What's in a Name?" *Dissent* (Fall 1989).

Germond, Jack W., and Jules Witcover. *Wake Us When It's Over; President Politics of 1984.* New York: Macmillan, 1985.

———. *Whose Broad Stripes and Bright Stars?* New York: Warner Books, 1989.

Gingrich, Newt. *Window of Opportunity: A Blueprint for the Future.* New York: Tom Doherty Associates, 1984.

Ginsberg, Benjamin. *The Captive Public: How Mass Opinion Promotes State Power.* New York: Basic Books, 1986.

Ginsberg, Benjamin, and Martin Shefter. *Politics By Other Means: The Declining Importance of Elections in America.* New York: Basic Books, 1990.

Gitlin, Todd. *The Sixties.* New York: Bantam, 1987.

Glazer, Nathan. "The Affirmative Action Stalemate," *The Public Interest.* no. 90 (Winter 1988).

———. *The Limits of Social Policy.* Cambridge: Harvard University Press, 1988.

Goldberg, David Theo. *Anatomy of Racism.* Minneapolis: University of Minnesota Press, 1990.

Goldman, Sheldon. "Reagan's Judicial Legacy: Completing the Puzzle and Summing Up." *Judicature* (April-May 1989).

Goldwater, Barry. *The Conscience of a Conservative.* Shepherdsville, KY: Victor Publishing, 1960.

Gosnell, Harold F. *Negro Politicians: The Rise of Negro Politics in Chicago.* Chicago: University of Chicago, 1967.

Gottfredson, Linda S., ed. "The 'g' Factor in Employment." *Journal of Vocational Behavior* 29, no. 3, (December 1986).

Gottfredson, Linda S., and James C. Sharf, eds. "Fairness in Employment Testing," *Journal of Vocational Behavior* 33, no. 3 (December 1988).

Gottfredson, Michael R. and Travis Hirschi. *A General Theory Of Crime.* Stanford, CA: Stanford University Press, 1990.

Gould, Stephen Jay. *The Mismeasure of Man.* New York: Norton, 1981.

Graham, Hugh Davis. *The Civil Rights Era: Origins and Development of National Policy 1960–1972.* New York: Oxford University Press, 1990.

Greenberg, Stanley B. *Report on Democratic Defection.* Washington, D.C.: The Analysis Group, April 15, 1985.

Grossman, James R. *Land of Hope: Chicago, Black Southerners, and the Great Migration.* Chicago: University of Chicago Press, 1989.

Hacker, Andrew. "Affirmative Action: The New Look." *The New York Review of Books,* October 12, 1989.

———. "Black Crime, White Racism." *The New York Review of Books,* March 3, 1988.

Hacker, Andrew, and Lorrie Millman, eds. *U/S: A Statistical Portrait of the American People.* New York: Viking/Penguin, 1983.

Hamill, Pete. "Breaking the Silence: A Letter to a Black Friend." *Esquire,* March 1988.

Hampton, Henry, and Steve Fayer. *Voices of Freedom.* New York: Bantam Books, 1990.

Harrington, Mona. *The Dream of Deliverance in American Politics.* New York: Knopf, 1986.

Harris, Fred R., and Tom Wicker, eds. *The Kerner Report: The 1968 Report of the National Advisory Commission on Civil Disorders.* New York: Pantheon, 1988.

Harris, Fred R., and Roger W. Wilkins, eds. *Quiet Riots: Race and Poverty in the United States.* New York: Pantheon Books, 1988.

Hartigan, John A., and Alexandra K. Wigdor, eds. *Fairness in Employment Testing.* Washington, D.C.: National Academy Press, 1989.

Hauser, Robert M. "The Decline in College Entry Among African Americans." (Paper). Department of Sociology, University of Wisconsin. March 19, 1990.

Hertzberg, Hendrik. "Wounds of Race." *The New Republic*, July 10, 1989.

Haveman, Robert. *Starting Even: An Equal Opportunity Program to Combat the Nation's New Poverty*. New York: Simon and Schuster, 1988.

Hess, Stephen, and David S. Broder. *The Republican Establishment: The Present and Future of the G.O.P.* New York: Harper and Row, 1967.

Hibbs, Douglas A., Jr. *The American Political Economy*. Cambridge: Harvard University Press, 1987.

Hickman, Harrison, and Paul Maslin. *Report on Electoral College Strategy*. Washington, D.C.: Hickman-Maslin Research Incorporated, June 22, 1988.

Higgs, Robert. *Competition and Coercion: Blacks in the American Economy, 1865–1914*. Chicago: University of Chicago, 1977.

Hill, Norman. "Blacks and the Unions," *Dissent* (Fall 1989).

Himmelfarb, Gertrude. *The Idea of Poverty: England in the Early Industrial Age*. New York: Vintage Books, 1985.

Himmelstein, Jerome L. *To the Right: The Transformation of American Conservatism*. Berkeley: University of California Press, 1990.

Hingelang, Michael J. "Race and Involvement in Common Law Personal Crimes." *American Sociological Review* (February 1978).

———. "Variations in Sex-Race-Age-Specific Incidence Rates of Offending." *American Sociological Review* (August 1981).

Hirsch, Arnold R. *Making the Second Ghetto: Race and Housing in Chicago 1940–1960*. Cambridge: Cambridge University Press, 1983.

Hochschild, Jennifer L. "Equal Opportunity and the Estranged Poor." *The Annals of the American Academy of Political and Social Science* 501 (January 1989).

Hochschild, Jennifer L., and Monica Herk. " 'Yes, but . . .': Principles and Caveats in American Racial Attitudes." Paper provided by Jennifer Hochschild.

Hoffman, Mark S., ed. *The World Almanac and Book of Facts 1989*. New York: World Almanac, 1989.

Hofstadter, Richard. *Anti-intellectualism in American Life*. New York: Knopf, 1963.

———. *The Paranoid Style in American Politics*. Chicago: University of Chicago Press, 1979.

Honomichl, Jack J. *Honomichl on Marketing Research*. Lincolnwood, IL: National Textbook Company, 1986.

Howell, Susan E. "Racial Attitudes Survey." University of New Orleans, March 1980. (Unpublished paper supplied by author.)

Huckfeldt, Robert, and Carol Weitzel Kohfeld. *Race and the Decline of Class in American Politics*. Urbana, IL: University of Illinois Press, 1989.

Huntington, Samuel P. *American Politics: The Promise of Disharmony*. Cambridge: Belknap/Harvard University Press, 1981.

Jackson, Brooks. *Honest Graft*. New York: Knopf, 1988.

Jackson, Jesse L., *Straight from the Heart*. Philadelphia: Fortress Press, 1987.

Jacobson, Gary C. "The Persistence of Democratic House Majorities: Structure or Politics?" Paper presented at the American Political Science Association, San Francisco, August 30–September 2, 1990.

———. "Strategic Politicians and the Dynamics of U.S. House Elections, 1946–86," *The American Political Science Review* 83 (September 1989).

Jamieson, Kathleen Hall. *Packaging the Presidency: A History and Criticism of Presidential Campaign Advertising*. New York: Oxford University Press, 1984.

Jaynes, Gerald David, and Robin M. Williams, Jr. *A Common Destiny: Blacks and American Society*. Washington, D.C.: National Academy Press, 1989.

*Jigsaw Politics: Shaping the House After the 1990 Census*. Washington, D.C.: Congressional Quarterly Inc., 1990.

Johnson, Donald Bruce, ed. *National Party Platforms,* Vol. II, 1960–1976. Urbana, IL: University of Illinois Press, 1978.

Johnson, Haynes. *In The Absence of Power: Governing America.* New York: Viking, 1980.

Juhn, Chinhui, Kevin M. Murphy, and Brooks Pierce. "Accounting for the Slowdown in Black-White Wage Convergence." Paper presented at the annual American Enterprise Institute Conference, Washington, D.C., November 3, 1989.

Judis, John. *William F. Buckley, Jr.* New York: Simon and Schuster, 1988.

Kamarck, Elaine C., and William A. Galston. *Putting Children First: A Progressive Family Policy for the 1990s.* Washington, D.C.: Progressive Policy Institute, September 1990.

Kasarda, John D. "Urban Industrial Transition and the Underclass." *The Annals of the American Academy of Political and Social Science* 501 (January 1989).

Katz, Jack. *Seductions of Crimes: Moral and Sensual Attractions in Doing Evil.* New York: Basic Books, 1988.

Kaufman, Jonathan. *Broken Alliance: The Turbulant Times Between Blacks and Jews in America,* New York: Scribner, 1988.

———. "The Color Line." *The Boston Globe Magazine.* Parts I and II. June 18 and 25, 1989.

Kaus, Mickey. "The Work Ethic State: The Only Cure for the Culture of Poverty." *The New Republic,* July 7, 1986.

Kemp, Jack. "Tackling Poverty: Market-Based Policies to Empower the Poor." *Policy Review* (The Heritage Foundation) (Winter 1990).

Kennedy, Randall L. "Racial Critiques of Legal Academia." *Harvard Law Review* 102:1745 (1989).

Key, V. O., Jr. *Public Opinion and American Democracy.* New York: Knopf, 1961.

———. *Southern Politics in State and Nation.* New York: Vintage Books, 1949.

Kilson, Martin. "Black Social Classes and Intergenerational Poverty." *The Public Interest,* No. 64 (Summer 1981).

———. "Problems of Black Politics." *Dissent* (Fall 1989).

Kimball, Roger. *Tenured Radicals: How Politics Has Corrupted Our Higher Education.* New York: Harper and Row, 1990.

Kinder, Donald R. "The Continuing American Dilemma: White Resistence to Racial Change Forty Years after Myrdal." *Journal of Social Issues* 42 (summer 1986).

Kinder, Donald R., and Lynn M. Saunders. "Pluralistic Foundations of American Opinion on Race." Paper presented at the American Political Science Association, Chicago, September 3–6, 1987.

Kinder, Donald R., and David O. Sears. "Prejudice and Politics: Symbolic Racism Versus Racial Threats to the Good Life." *Journal of Personality and Social Psychology* 40, no. 3 (1981).

King, Anthony. *The New American Polticial System.* Washington, D.C.: American Enterprise Institute, 1978.

King, Martin Luther, Jr. *Why We Can't Wait.* New York: Signet, 1963.

Kleppner, Paul. *Chicago Divided: The Making of a Black Mayor.* DeKalb, IL: Northern Illinois University Press, 1985.

Klein, Joe. "Race: The Issue." *New York,* May 1989.

Kluegel, James R. "Trends in Whites' Explanations of the Black-White Gap in Socioeconomic Status, 1977–1989." *American Sociological Review* (August 1990).

Kotler, Milton, and Nelson Rosenbaum. "Strengthening the Democratic Party through Strategic Marketing: Voters and Donors." A confidential report for the Democratic National Committee by the CRG Research Institute, Washington, D.C., 1985.

Kotz, Nick, and Mary Lynn Kotz. *A Passion for Equality: George Wiley and the Movement.* New York: Norton, 1977.

KRC Research and Consulting. *Research Report: Democrats for the 90's.* New York. November 1989.

Kuttner, Robert. *The Economic Illusion.* Boston: Houghton Mifflin, 1984.

———. *The Life of the Party.* New York: Viking, 1987.

——. *The Revolt of the Haves.* New York: Simon and Schuster, 1980.

Ladd, Everett Carll, Jr. "The Prejudices of a Tolerant Society." *Public Opinion* (July/August 1987).

Ladd, Everett Carll, Jr., with Charles D. Hadley. *Transformations of the American Party System.* New York: Norton, 1978.

LaHaye, Tim. *The Battle for the Mind.* Old Tappan, NJ: Fleming H. Revell Company, 1980.

Lamis, Alexander P. *The Two-Party South.* New York: Oxford University Press, 1984.

Landry, Bart. *The New Black Middle Class.* Berkeley: University of California Press, 1987.

Lanoue, David J. *From Camelot to the Teflon President.* New York: Greenwood Press, 1988.

Lasch, Christopher. "Reagan's Victims." *The New York Review of Books,* July 21, 1988.

Legal Services Corporation. *The Legal Services Record.* (Washington, D.C.), (Fall 1989).

Lemann, Nicholas. "The Origins of the Underclass," (Parts 1 and 2) *The Atlantic.* June 1986 and July 1986.

——. "The Unfinished War." (Parts 1 and 2) *The Atlantic.* December 1988 and January 1989.

Leonard, Jonathan S. "What Was Affirmative Action?" *The American Economic Review* (May 1986).

Levitan, Sar. "Government Programs and the Poor." *Political Science Quarterly* (Fall 1985).

Levy, Frank. *Dollars and Dreams.* New York: Norton, 1988.

Lewontin, R. C., Steven Rose, and Leon J. Kamin. *Not in Our Genes: Biology, Ideology, and Human Nature.* New York: Pantheon, 1984.

Lieberson, Stanley. *A Piece of the Pie: Blacks and White Immigrants Since 1880.* Berkeley: University of California Press, 1980.

Lipset, Seymour Martin. "Blacks and Jews: How Much Bias?" *Public Opinion* (July/August, 1987).

Lipset, Seymour Martin, and William Schneider. *The Confidence Gap: Business, Labor, and Government in the Public Mind.* New York: Free Press, 1983.

Lisio, Donald J. *Hoover, Blacks, and Lily-Whites: A Study of Southern Strategies.* Chapel Hill: University of North Carolina Press, 1985.

Lodge, Milton, Karen Callaghan, and John Wahlke. "The 'L' Word: Is Liberal a Code Word for Black?" Paper presented at the American Political Science Association. Atlanta, Georgia, August 1989.

Loury, Glenn C. "Beyond Civil Rights." *The New Republic,* October 7, 1985.

——. "The Moral Quandry of the Black Community." *The Public Interest,* no. 79 (Spring 1985).

——. "Why Should We Care About Group Inequality?" *Social Philosophy and Policy* 5, no. 1 (Autumn 1987).

Lowi, Theodore. *The End of Liberalism.* New York: Norton, 1979.

Lukas, Anthony. *Common Ground.* New York: Knopf, 1985.

——. *Nightmare: The Underside of the Nixon Years.* New York: Bantam Books, 1977.

McAll, Christopher. *Class, Ethnicity, and Social Inequality.* Montreal and Kingston: McGill-Queen's University Press, 1990.

McClosky, Herbert, and John Zaller. *The American Ethos: Public Attitudes Toward Capitalism and Democracy.* Cambridge: Harvard University Press, 1984.

McFate, Katherine, ed. *The Metropolitan Area Fact Book.* Washington, D.C.: Joint Center for Political Studies, 1988.

McGinniss, Joe. *The Selling of the President 1968.* New York: Trident Press, 1969.

McGuigan, Patrick B. *The Politics of Direct Democracy in the 1980's.* Washington, D.C.: The Institute for Government and Politics, 1985.

Magaziner, Ira C., and Robert B. Reich. *Minding America's Business: The Decline and Rise of the American Economy.* New York: Harcourt Brace Jovanovich, 1982.

Magleby, David B., and Candice J. Nelson. *The Money Chase: Congressional Campaign Finance Reform.* Washington, D.C.: The Brookings Institution, 1990.

Mailer, Norman. *Miami and the Siege of Chicago.* New York: Signet, 1968.

———. *Some Honorable Men: Political Conventions, 1960–1972.* 2d ed. Boston: Little, Brown, 1976.

Marable, Manning. *Black American Politics: From the Washington Marches to Jesse Jackson.* London: Verso-New Left Books, 1985.

Marciniak, Ed. *Reclaiming the Inner City.* Washington, D.C.: National Center for Urban Ethnic Affairs, 1986.

Markey, James P. "The Labor Market Problems of Today's High School Dropouts." *Monthly Labor Review* (U.S. Dept. of Labor, Washington, D.C.) 3, no. 6, (June 1988).

Matusow, Allen J. *The Unraveling of America: A History of Liberalism in the 1960s.* New York: Harper and Row, 1984.

Mayhew, David R. *Congress: The Electoral Connection.* New Haven: Yale University Press, 1974.

Mead, Lawrence M. "The Changing Agenda of Welfare Reform in the United States, 1967–1988," chapter from *The New Dependency Politics* (forthcoming). Paper presented at the annual meeting of the American Political Science Association, San Francisco, August 30–September 2, 1990.

———. "The Logic of Workfare: The Underclass and Work Policy," *The Annals of the American Academy of Political and Social Science* 501 (January 1989).

Meyerson, Adam. "Interview with Vin Weber," *Policy Review* (The Heritage Foundation) (Spring 1990).

"Middle Managers: Are They an Endangered Species?" *Business Week,* September 12, 1988.

Miller, Arthur, and Christopher Wlezien. "The Social Group Dynamics of Political Evaluations." Paper presented at the annual meeting of the American Political Science Association, Atlanta, Georgia, August 31–September 3, 1989.

Miller, Arthur H., Anne Hildreth, Kevin M. Leyden, and Christopher Wlezien. "Judging by the Company Candidates Keep: What's a Democrat to Do?" *Public Opinion* (July/August 1988).

Miller, Norman, Marilynn B. Brewer, and Keith Edwards. "Cooperative Interaction in Desegregated Settings: A Laboratory." *Journal of Social Issues* 41, no. 3 (1985).

Miller, Warren E. "Policy Direction and Performance Evaluation: Complementary Explanations of the Reagan Elections." Paper presented at the annual meeting of the American Political Science Association, New Orleans, August 29–September 1, 1985.

Miller, Warren E., and M. Kent Jennings. *Parties in Transition: A Longitudinal Study of Parties and Party Supporters.* New York: Russell Sage Foundation, 1986.

Miller, Warren E., and Santa A. Traugott. *American National Elections Studies Data Sourcebook.* Cambridge: Harvard University Press, 1989.

Mladenka, Kenneth R. "Blacks and Hispanics in Urban Politics," *American Political Science Review* 83 (March 1989).

"Mobilizing the Moral Majority." *Conservative Digest*

Moore, Jonathan, ed. *Campaign for President: The Managers Look at '84.* Dover, MA: Auburn House, 1986.

Morris, Aldon D. *The Origins of the Civil Rights Movement: Black Communities Organizing for Change.* New York: Free Press, 1984.

Mortenson, Thomas G. *The Impact of Increased Loan Utilization Among Low Family Income Students.* Iowa City, Iowa: The American College Testing Program, 1990.

Murphy, Kevin, and Finis Welch. "Wage Differentials in the 1980s: The Role of International Trade," Paper presented at the American Enterprise Institute Conference, November 3, 1989.

Murphy, Reg, and Hal Gulliver. *The Southern Strategy.* New York: Scribner, 1971.

Murray, Charles. "The British Underclass." *The Public Interest,* no. 99 (Spring 1990).

———. "Have the Poor Been 'Losing Ground'?" *Political Science Quarterly* (Fall 1985).

———. "Government Programs and the Poor." *Political Science Quarterly* (Fall 1985).

———. *Losing Ground: American Social Policy, 1950–1980.* New York: Basic Books, 1984.

Myrdal, Gunnar. *An American Dilemma.* Vols. 1 and 2. New York: Pantheon Books, 1972.

Nash, George H. *The Conservative Intellectual Movement in America.* New York: Basic Books, 1976.

Nathan, Richard P. "Institutional Change and the Challenge of the Underclass," *The Annals of the American Academy of Political and Social Science* 501, (January 1989).

National Gay and Lesbian Task Force. *Gay & Lesbian Rights and Protections in the U.S.* Washington, D.C.: National Gay and Lesbian Task Force, 1985.

Nie, Norman H., Sidney Verba, and John R. Petrocik. *The Changing American Voter.* Cambridge: Harvard University Press, 1976.

Niemi, Richard G., John Mueller, and Tom W. Smith. *Trends in Public Opinion: A Compendium of Survey Data.* New York: Greenwood Press, 1989.

Novak, Robert. *The Agony of the GOP 1964.* New York: Macmillan, 1965.

O'Neill, June. *Work and Welfare in Massachusetts: An Evaluation of the ET Program.* Boston: Pioneer Institute for Public Policy Research, 1990.

Orfield, Gary. *Must We Bus?* Washington, D.C.: The Brookings Institution, 1978.

———. "Race and the Liberal Agenda: The Loss of the Integrationist Dream, 1965 to 1974." In *The Politics of Social Policy in the United States,* edited by Margaret Weir, Ann Shola Orloff, and Theda Skocpol. Princeton, NJ: Princeton University Press, 1988.

———. "Racial Change and Desegregation in Large School Districts." Report to the National School Boards Association, June 1988.

Ornstein, Norman J., Thomas E. Mann, and Michael J. Malbin, eds. *Vital Statistics on Congress, 1987–1988.* Washington, D.C.: Congressional Quarterly, 1987.

———. *Vital Statistics on Congress 1989–1990.* Washington, D.C.: Congressional Quarterly, 1990.

Palmer, John L., and Isabel V. Sawhill, eds. *The Reagan Experiment.* Washington, D.C.: The Urban Institute, 1982.

———. *The Reagan Record.* Washington, D.C.: The Urban Institute, 1984.

Palmer, John L., Timothy Smeeding, and Barbara Boyle Torrey, eds. *The Vulnerable.* Washington, D.C.: The Urban Institute, 1988.

Parker, Frank R. *Black Votes Count: Political Empowerment in Mississippi after 1965.* Chapel Hill: University of North Carolina Press, 1990.

Patterson, James T. *America's Struggle Against Poverty 1900–1980.* Cambridge: Harvard University Press, 1981.

Patterson, Orlando. "Toward a Study of Black America." *Dissent* (Fall 1989).

Pechman, Joseph A. *Federal Tax Policy.* Washington, D.C.: Brookings Institution, 1987.

Peele, Gillian. *Revival and Reaction: The Right in Contemporary America.* New York: Oxford University Press, 1986.

Perlmann, Joel. *Ethnic Differences.* New York: Cambridge University Press, 1988.

Perry, Barbara A., and Julia A. McDonough. "Affirmative Action in Higher Education: *Bakke* to the Future." Paper presented at the annual meeting of the American Political Science Association, Atlanta, Georgia, August 31–September 3, 1989.

Pertschuk, Michael, and Wendy Schaetzel. *The People Rising: The Campaign Against the Bork Nomination.* New York: Thunder's Mouth Press, 1989.

Petrocik, John R. "Issues and Agendas: Electoral Coalitions in the 1988 Election." Paper presented at the annual meeting of the American Political Science Association, Atlanta, Georgia, August 31–September 2, 1989.

———. *Party Coalitions: Realignments and the Decline of the New Deal Party System.* Chicago: University of Chicago Press, 1981.

———. "Thinking About 1984: Reagan's Prospects Against the Background of 1980–82." (Paper supplied by author.)

Petrocik, John R., and Frederick T. Steeper. "Realignment and 1984: New Coalitions and New Majorities?" *Election Politics* (Winter 1984–1985).

———. "Wedges and Magnets: Issues and the Republican Coalition in 1988." (Paper prepared for Market Opinion Research, provided by John Petrocik.)

Phillips, Kevin P. *The Emerging Republican Majority.* New York: Doubleday/Anchor, 1970.

————. *The Politics of Rich and Poor: Wealth and the American Electorate in the Reagan Aftermath.* New York: Random House, 1990.

————. *Post-Conservative America.* New York: Random House, 1978.

Pinkney, Alphonso. *The Myth of Black Progress.* New York: Cambridge University Press, 1984.

Piven, Frances Fox, and Richard A. Cloward. *Regulating the Poor: The Functions of Public Welfare.* New York: Random House, 1971.

Polsby, Nelson W. *Consequences of Party Reform.* New York: Oxford University Press, 1983.

Polsby, Nelson W., and Aaron Wildavsky. *Presidential Elections: Strategies of American Electoral Politics.* 6th ed. New York: Scribner, 1984.

Pomper, Gerald M. *The Election of 1980: Reports and Interpretations.* Chatham, NJ: Chatham House, 1981.

————. *The Election of 1984: Reports and Interpretations.* Chatham, NJ: Chatham House, 1985.

————. *The Election of 1988: Reports and Interpretations.* Chatham, NJ: Chatham House, 1988.

————. "From Confusion to Clarity: Issues and American Voters, 1956–1968." *American Political Science Review* 66 (June 1972).————. "Toward A More Responsible Two-Party System"? What, Again?" *Journal of Politics* Vol 33 (August 1971).

————. *Voters' Choice: Varieties of American Electoral Behavior* New York: Dodd, Mead, 1975.

Preston, Michael B., Lenneal J. Henderson, Jr., and Paul L. Puryear. *The New Black Politics: The Search for Political Power.* New York: Longman, 1987.

*The Public Interest.* no. 96 (Summer 1989). See articles by Isabel V. Sawhill, Daniel Patrick Moynihan, and John J. DiIulio Jr.

*The Public Interest.* no. 89 (Fall 1987). See articles by George Gilder, Michael Novak, and Leslie Lenkowsky.

Quinn, Lawrence. "Workers See Future As Bleak," *The Vindicator* (Youngstown, Ohio), September 20, 1977.

Quint, Peter E. "The Separation of Powers Under Nixon: Reflections on Constitutional Liberties and the Rule of Law," *Duke Law Journal* 1 (1981).

Raines, Howell. *My Soul is Rested.* New York: Penguin, 1977.

Rainwater, Lee and William L. Yancey. *The Moynihan Report and the Politics of Controversy.* Cambridge: M. I. T. Press, 1967.

Rawls, John. *A Theory of Justice.* Cambridge: Belknap Press of Harvard University Press, 1971.

Reagan, Ronald. *A Time for Choosing: The Speeches of Ronald Reagan 1961–1982.* Chicago: Regnery Gateway.

Reed, Adolph L., Jr. *The Jesse Jackson Phenomenon.* New Haven: Yale University Press, 1986.

Reichley, A. James. *Conservatives in an Age of Change: The Nixon and Ford Administrations.* Washington, D.C.: The Brookings Institution, 1981.

————. *Religion in American Public Life.* Washington, D.C.: The Brookings Institution, 1985.

Reider, Jonathan. *Canarsie: The Jews and Italians of Brooklyn Against Liberalism.* Cambridge: Harvard University Press, 1985.

Reischauer, Robert D. "Immigration and the Underclass." *The Annals of the American Academy of Political and Social Science* 501 (January 1989).

Reynolds, William Bradford. "The Reagan Administration and Civil Rights: Winning the War Against Discrimination." *University of Illinois Law Review* 4 (1986).

Rich, Wilbur C. *Coleman Young and Detroit Politics.* Detroit: Wayne State University Press, 1989.

Ricketts, Erol R., and Isabel V. Sawhill. "Defining and Measuring the Underclass." Paper presented at the American Economic Association, New Orleans, December 28, 1986.

Rodriguez, Clara E. *Puerto Ricans: Born in the U.S.A.* Boston: Unwin Hyman, 1989.

Rose, David L., "Twenty-Five Years Later: Where Do We Stand on Equal Employment Opportunity Law Enforcement?" *Vanderbilt Law Review* (May 1989).

Rossell, Christine H., Diane Ravitch, and David J. Armor. "Busing and 'White Flight.' " *The Public Interest.* no. 53 (Fall 1978).

Rossi, Peter H., and James D. Wright. "The Urban Homeless: A Portrait of Urban Disloca-tion," *The Annals of the American Academy of Political and Social Science* 501 (January 1989).

Rossiter, Clinton. *Conservatism in America.* Cambridge: Harvard University Press, 1982.

Rothenberg, Stuart. "The Second Generation of Black Leaders." *Public Opinion* (July/August 1987).

Rothbart, Myron, and Oliver P. John. "Social Categorization and Behavioral Episodes: A Cognitive Analysis of Intergroup Contact." *Journal of Social Issues* 41, no. 3 (1985).

Rusher, William A. *The Rise of the Right.* New York: William Morrow, 1984.

Sabato, Larry. *PAC Power.* New York: Norton, 1984.

———. *The Party's Just Begun.* Glenview, IL: Scott, Foresman, 1988.

Saloma, John S., III. *Ominous Politics: The New Conservative Labyrinth.* New York: Hill and Wang, 1984.

Sawhill, Isabel V. "Poverty in the U.S.: Why Is It So Persistent?" *Journal of Economic Literature* 26 (September 1988).

Scammon, Richard. *America Votes 14.* Washington, D.C.: Congressional Quarterly, 1981.

Scammon, Richard, and Alice P. McGillivray. *America Votes 16.* Washington, D.C.: Con-gressional Quarterly, 1985.

———. *America Votes 18.* Washington, D.C.: Congressional Quarterly, 1988.

———. *America at the Polls 2.* Washington, D.C.: Congressional Quarterly, 1981.

Scammon, Richard, and Benjamin J. Wattenberg. *The Real Majority.* Coward-McCann, 1970.

Schell, Jonathan. *The Time of Illusion.* New York: Knopf, 1976.

Schiller, Herbert I. *Culture Inc.: The Corporate Takeover of Public Expression.* New York: Oxford University Press, 1989.

Schmidt, David D. *Citizen Lawmakers.* Philadelphia: Temple University Press, 1989.

Schneider, William. "A Consumer's Guide to the Democrats in '88." *The Atlantic.* April 1987.

———. "The New Shape of American Politics." *The Atlantic,* January 1987.

Schuman, Howard, and Lawrence Bobo. "Survey-based Experiments on White Racial Attitudes Toward Residential Integration." *American Journal of Sociology* 94, no. 2 (September 1988).

Schuman, Howard, Charlotte Steeh, and Lawrence Bobo. *Racial Attitudes In America.* Cambridge: Harvard University Press, 1985.

Schwartz, Bernard. *The Ascent of Pragmatism: The Burger Court in Action.* Reading, MA: Addison-Wesley, 1990.

Sears, David O. "Symbolic Racism." in *Eliminating Racism: Profiles in Controversy,* edited by Phyllis A. Katz and Dalmas A. Taylor. New York: Plenum Press, 1988.

Sears, David O., and Jack Citrin. *Tax Revolt: Something for Nothing in California.* Cam-bridge: Harvard University Press, 1982.

Sears, David O., Jack Citrin, and Rick Kosterman. "Jesse Jackson and the Southern White Electorate in 1984." In *Blacks in Southern Politics.* L.W. Moreland, R.P. Steed, and T.A. Baker. New York: Praeger, 1987.

Selig, Joel L. "The Reagan Justice Department and Civil Rights: What Went Wrong," *The University of Illinois Law Review* 4 (1985).

Shafer, Byron E. *Bifurcated Politics: Evolution and Reform in the National Party Convention.* Cambridge: Harvard University Press, 1988.

———. "The Notion of an Electoral Order: The Structure of Electoral Politics at the Accession of George Bush." (Paper provided by the author.)

———. *Quiet Revolution: The Struggle for the Democratic Party and the Shaping of Post Reform Politics.* New York: Russell Sage Foundation, 1983.

Sharf, James C. "Litigating Personnel Measurement Policy," *Journal of Vocational Behavior* (December 1988).

Shulman, Steven, and William Darity, Jr., eds. *The Question of Discrimination: Racial Inequality in the U.S. Labor Market.* Middletown, CT: Wesleyan University Press, 1989.

Siegel, Frederick F. *Troubled Journey: From Pearl Harbor to Ronald Reagan.* New York: Hill and Wang, 1984.

———. "What Liberals Haven't Learned and Why." *Commonweal,* January 13, 1989.

Slavin, Robert E. "Cooperative Learning: Applying Contact Theory in Desegregated Schools." *Journal of Social Issues* 41, no. 3 (1985).

Sleeper, Jim. *The Closest of Strangers: Liberalism and the Politics of Race in New York.* New York: Norton, 1990.

Smith, James P. "Poverty and the Family," In *Divided Opportunities,* edited by Gary Sandefur and Marta Tienda. New York: Plenum, 1988.

Smith, James P., and Finis R. Welch. "Affirmative Action and Labor Markets." *Journal of Labor Economic* 2, no. 2 (April 1984).

———. *Closing the Gap: Forty Years of Economic Progress for Blacks.* Washington, D.C.: Rand Corporation, 1986.

———. "Race and Poverty: a Forty-Year Record." *The American Economic Review.* May 1987.

Sniderman, Paul M., and Michael Gray Hagen. *Race and Inequality: A Study in American Values.* Chatham, NJ: Chatham House, 1985.

Sniderman, Paul M., Thomas Piazza, Phillip E. Tetlock, and Amy Kendrick. "The New Racism." (Paper provided by Paul Sniderman, 1990.)

Snyderman, Mark, and Stanley Rothman. *The IQ Controversy: The Media and Public Policy.* New Brunswick, NJ: Transaction, 1990.

Sowell, Thomas. *The Economics and Politics of Race.* New York: Morrow, 1983.

———. *Ethnic America: A History.* New York: Basic, 1981.

———. *Markets and Minorities.* New York: Basic, 1981.

Stanley, Harold W. "The 1984 Presidential Election in the South: Race and Realignment." *The 1984 Presidential Election in the South* edited by Robert P. Steed, Lawrence W. Moreland, and Tod A. Baker, New York: Praeger Special Studies, 1985.

———. *Voter Mobilization and the Politics of Race.* New York: Praeger, 1987.

Stanley, Harold W., William T. Blanco, and Richard G. Niemi. "Partisanship and Group Support Over Time: A Multivariate Analysis." *American Political Science Review* 80 (September, 1986).

Steele, Shelby. *The Content of Our Character.* New York: St. Martin's Press, 1990.

Steeper, Frederick T., and John R. Petrocik. "New Coalitions in 1988." (Paper provided by John Petrocik, 1989).

Steinberg, Stephen. *The Ethnic Myth: Race, Ethnicity, and Class in America.* New York: Beacon, 1989.

Stephan, Walter G., and John C. Brigham, eds. "Intergroup Contact: Introduction," *Journal of Social Issues* 41, no. 3 (1985).

Steuerle, Eugene, and Michael Hartzmark. "Individual Income Taxation, 1947–1979." Office of Tax Analysis, Department of the Treasury, Washington, D.C.

Stone, Clarence N. *Regime Politics: Governing Atlanta 1946–1988.* University Press of Kansas, 1989.

Sundquist, James L. *The Decline and Resurgence of Congress.* Brookings Institution, Washington, D.C. 1981.

———. *Dynamics of the Party System: Alignment and Realignment of Political Parties in the United States.* Washington, D.C.: The Brookings Institution, 1983.

————. "The 1984 Election: How Much Realignment?" *The Brookings Review.* (Winter 1985).

————. *Politics and Policy.* The Brookings Institution, Washington, D.C., 1968.

Sweet, James A., and Larry L. Bumpass. *American Families and Households.* New York: Russell Sage Foundation, 1987.

Tatalovich, Raymond, and Byron W. Daynes, eds. *Social Regulatory Policy: Moral Controversies in American Politics.* Boulder, CO, and London, Westview Press, 1988.

Taylor, Stuart, Jr. "Second Class Citizens." *The American Lawyer* (September 1989).

Thernstrom, Abigail M. *Whose Votes Count: Affirmative Action and Minority Voting Rights.* Cambridge: Harvard University Press, 1987.

Tufte, Edward R. *Political Control of the Economy.* Princeton, NJ: Princeton University Press, 1978.

Unger, Irwin and Debi. *Turning Point: 1968.* New York: Scribner, 1988.

U.S. Bureau of the Census. The Black Population in the United States: March 1988. *Current Population Reports,* ser. P-20, no. 442. Washington, D.C., 1988.

U.S. Bureau of the Census. Household After-Tax Income: 1985. *Current Population Reports,* ser. P-23, no. 151. Washington, D.C.: GPO, June 1987.

U.S. Bureau of the Census. Patterns of Metropolitan Area and County Population Growth: 1980 to 1987. *Current Population Reports,* ser. P-25, no. 1039. Washington, D.C.: GPO, 1987.

U.S. Bureau of the Census. *Statistical Abstract of the United States 1987,* Washington, D.C., 1987.

U.S. Bureau of the Census. *Statistical Abstract of the United States 1989.* Washington, D.C., 1989.

U.S. Congress. Joint Committee on Taxation. *General Explanation of the Economic Recovery Tax Act of 1981. H.R. 4242. Public Law 97–34.* 97th Congress, December 29, 1981.

U.S. Congress. Joint Economic Committee. "The Growth in Poverty: 1979–1985." 99th Congress, December, 1986.

U.S. Congress. House. Committee on Education and Labor. *A Report on Equal Employment Opportunity and Affirmative Action in the Southern California Aerospace Industry.* Serial 100-Y. 100th Congress, June 1988.

U.S. Congress. House. Committee on Education and Labor. Subcommittee on Employment Opportunities. *Equal Employment Opportunity Commission Policies Regarding Goals and Timetables in Litigation Remedies.* Serial 99–97, 99th Congress, March 11 and 13, 1986.

————. *Oversight Hearing on the Equal Employment Opportunity Commission's Enforcement Policies.* Serial 99–27, 99th Congress July 18, 1985.

————. *Oversight Hearing on Office of Federal Contract Compliance Programs.* Serial 100-38, 100th Congress, June 3 and 4, 1987.

————. *Oversight Hearings on Equal Employment Opportunity in the Southern California Aerospace Industry.* Serial 100-60, 100th Congress, October, 23 and 24, 1987.

U.S. Congress. House. Committee on the Judiciary. Subcommittee on Civil and Constitutional Rights. *Authorization Request for the Civil Rights Division of the Department of Justice, Fiscal Year 1988.* Serial 114, 100th Congress, February 26, 1987.

U.S. Congress. House. Ways and Means Committee. *Overview of Entitlement Programs: The 1990 Green Book.* Report. June 5, 1990.

————. *Tax Progressivity and Income Distribution.* Report. 101 Congress, March 26, 1990.

U.S. Congress. House. Ways and Means Committee. Subcommittee on Oversight. *Tax-Exempt Status of Private Schools.* Part II, Report. 96th Congress, 1979.

U.S. Department of Agriculture. "Characteristics of Food Stamp Households, Winter 1988." Washington, GPO: 1990.

U.S. Department of Education. *Digest of Education Statistics 1989.* Washington, D.C.: GPO, December 1989.

U.S. Department of Health and Human Services. "Advance Report on Final Divorces. 1986." Washington, D.C.: National Center for Health Statistics, June 6, 1989.

———. "Characteristics and Financial Circumstances of AFDC Recipients." Washington, D.C., GPO: 1989.

———. "Children of Divorce." Ser. 21, no. 46. Washington, D.C.: National Center for Health Statistics, January 1989.

———. "Monthly Vital Statistics Report" Washington, D.C.: National Center for Health Statistics, September, 1990.

———. *Social Security Bulletin.* Annual Statistical Supplement. Washington, D.C.: GPO, 1986.

U.S. Department of Justice. Bureau of Justice Statistics. "Black Victims." Washington, D.C.: GPO, April 22, 1990.

———. "Criminal Victimization in the United States." Annual reports for 1986, 1987, 1989. Washington, D.C.: GPO.

———. *Report to the Nation on Crime and Justice.* 2nd ed. Washington, D.C.: GPO, 1989.

———. *Sourcebook of Criminal Justice Statistics, 1988.* Washington, D.C.: GPO, 1989.

———. Federal Bureau of Investigation. "Age-Specific Arrest Rates abd Race-Specific Arrest Rates for Selected Offenses, 1965–1986." Washington, D.C.: GPO, June 1988.

———. "Crime Index Rate. United States, 1960–1988." Washington, D.C.: GPO, annual.

———. "Index of Crime, United States, 1960–1988." Washington, D.C.: GPO, annual.

U.S. Department of Labor. Bureau of Labor Statistics. *American Families. Seveny-Five Years of Change.* Washington, D.C.: GPO, March 1990.

———. *Population Survey, 1989.* Washington, D.C.: GPO, March 12, 1990.

Van Horne, Winston A., and Thomas V. Tonnesen, eds. *Race: Twentieth Century Dilemmas—Twenty-First Century Prognoses.* Madison, WI: University of Wisconsin Press, 1989.

Verba, Sidney, Steven Kelman, Gary R. Orren, Ichiro Miyake, Joji Watanuki, Ikuo Kabashima, and G. Donald Ferree, Jr. *Elites and the Idea of Equality.* Cambridge: Harvard University Press, 1987.

Verba, Sidney, and Gary R. Orren. *Equality in America: The View from the Top.* Cambridge: Harvard University Press, 1985.

Vialet, Joyce. *A Brief History of U.S. Immigration Policy.* A Congressional Research Service report. Library of Congress, November 25, 1988.

Viguerie, Richard A. *The Establishment vs. The People.* Chicago: Regnery Gateway, 1983.

———. *The New Right: We're Ready to Lead.* Falls Church, VA: Viguerie Company, 1980.

Villarreal, Roberto E., Norma G. Hernandez, and Howard D. Neighbor *Latino Empowerment: Progress, Problems, and Prospects.* New York: Greenwood Press, 1988.

Viorst, Milton. *Fall from Grace.* New York: New American Library, 1968.

Vogel, David. *Fluctuating Fortunes: The Political Power of Business in America.* New York: Basic, 1989.

Wacquant, Loic J. D. "The Ghetto, the State, and the New Capitalist Economy." *Dissent* (Fall 1989).

Wacquant, Loic J. D., and William Julius Wilson. "The Cost of Racial and Class Exclusion in the Inner City," *The Annals of the American Academy of Political and Social Science* 501 (January 1989).

Walker, Samuel. *In Defense of American Liberties: A History of the ACLU.* New York: Oxford University Press, 1990.

Walters, Ronald W. *Black Presidential Politics in America: A Strategic Approach.* Albany: State University of New York Press, 1988.

Walton, Hanes, Jr. *When the Marching Stopped: The Politics of Civil Rights Regulatory Agencies.* Albany: State University of New York Press, 1988.

Wanniski, Jude. *The Way the World Works.* New York: Simon and Schuster, 1978.

Wattenberg, Martin P. "The Building of a Republican Regional Base in the South: The Elephant Crosses the Mason-Dixon Line." (Paper provided by the author, 1988.)

————. *The Decline of American Political Parties 1952–1980*. Cambridge: Harvard University Press, 1984.

Watts, Jerry G. "Dilemmas of Black Intellectuals." *Dissent* (Fall 1989)

Weicher, John C., ed. *Maintaining the Safety Net*. Washington, D.C.: American Enterprise Institute, 1984.

Weigel, Russell H., and Paul W. Howes. "Conceptions of Racial Prejudice: Symbolic Racism Reconsidered." *Journal of Social Issues* 41, no. 3 (1985).

Weyrich, Paul. "Memorandum—Our New Conservative Agenda." April 18, 1990 (Supplied by author.)

Whitaker, Robert W., ed. *The New Right Papers*. New York: St. Martin's Press, 1982.

White, F. Clinton, and William J. Gill. *Why Reagan Won: The Conservative Movement 1964–1981*. Chicago: Regnery Gateway, 1981.

White, John Kenneth. *The New Politics of Old Values*. University Press of New England, Hanover, 1988.

White, Theodore H. *The Making of the President 1960*. New York: Bantam, 1961.

————. *The Making of the President 1964*. New York: Atheneum, 1965.

————. *The Making of the President 1968*. New York: Atheneum, 1969.

————. *The Making of the President 1972*. New York: Bantam, 1973.

Wieseltier, Leon. "Scar Tissue." *The New Republic*, June 5, 1989.

Wigdor, Alexandra K., and Wendell R. Garner. eds. *Ability Testing: Uses, Consequences, and Controversies*. 1982. Part I and Part II. National Academy Press, National Academy of Sciences, Washington, D.C., 1982.

Wildavsky, Aaron. "Oh, Bring Back My Party to Me!" *The Public Interest*. no. 57 (Fall 1979).

Wilkins, Roger. "Harping on Racism." *Mother Jones* (December 1989).

————. *A Man's Life: An Autobiography*. New York: Simon and Schuster, 1982.

Williams, Juan. *Eyes on the Prize: America's Civil Rights Years 1954–1965*. New York: Viking, 1987.

Willie, Charles V. *Caste and Class Controversy on Race and Poverty: Round Two of the Willie/Wilson Debate*. Dix Hills, New York: General Hall, 1989.

Wills, Garry. *Nixon Agonistes*. Boston: Houghton Mifflin, 1970.

————. *Reagan's America: Innocents at Home*. New York: Doubleday, 1987.

Wilson, James Q. *Negro Politics: The Search for Leadership*. Free Press/Collier-Macmillian Limited, New York/London, 1960.

————. *Political Organizations*. New York: Basic, 1973.

Wilson, James Q., and Richard J. Herrnstein. *Crime & Human Nature*. New York: Simon & Schuster, 1985.

Wilson, William Julius. *The Declining Significance of Race*. Chicago: University of Chicago, 1980.

————. "Social Theory and Public Agenda Research: The Challenge of Studying Inner-City Social Dislocations," Presidential Address. Annual Meeting of the American Sociological Association, August 12, 1990.

————. *The Truly Disadvantaged: The Inner City, the Underclass, and Public Policy*. Chicago: University of Chicago Press, 1987.

————. "The Underclass: Issues, Perspectives, and Public Policy." *The Annals of the American Academy of Political and Social Science* 501 (January 1989).

Witt, Elder, ed. *Guide to the U.S. Supreme Court*. Washington, D.C.: Congressional Quarterly, 1979.

Wolfe, Alan. "The Day-Care Dilemma: A Scandinavian Perspective," *The Public Interest*. 95 (Spring 1989).

Wolfe, Tom. *Radical Chic & Mau-Mauing the Flak Catchers*. New York: Bantam, 1971.

Woodward, C. Vann. *The Burden of Southern History*. New York: Vintage, 1961.

————. *Reunion and Reaction*. New York: Little, Brown. 1966.

————. *The Strange Career of Jim Crow*. New York: Oxford, 1966.

Wright, Gavin. *Old South, New South*. New York: Basic Books, 1986.

X, Malcolm, and Alex Haley. *The Autobiography of Malcom X.* New York: Ballantine, 1965.

Yerger, Wirt A. "Memorandum to Key Leadership." Department of Archives and Special Collections, University of Mississippi, March 11, 1964.

———. "Two-Party System Established," *The Rebel Magazine* (The Mississippi Republican Party), March 27, 1964.

# Index